# Inquiry Graphics in Higher Education

Nataša Lacković

# Inquiry Graphics in Higher Education

New Approaches to Knowledge,
Learning and Methods with Images

palgrave
macmillan

Nataša Lacković
Department of Educational Research
Lancaster University
Lancaster, UK

ISBN 978-3-030-39386-1     ISBN 978-3-030-39387-8   (eBook)
https://doi.org/10.1007/978-3-030-39387-8

This Palgrave Macmillan imprint is published by the registered company Springer Nature Switzerland AG.
The registered company address is: Gewerbestrasse 11, 6330 Cham, Switzerland

# Acknowledgements

I would like to thank with all my heart many people who provided help, time, support and inspiration to write this monograph. I wish to thank my beloved parents, Nebojša and Katica Lacković, for the gift of life, dedication, and the home where all my dreams were conceived. Special thanks go to my dearest and loving sister, Maja Mraković, for always being the one I can count on, share all my experiences, and the one who would remind me of all the times we had as children, and thankfully, are still having, and thank you for my Mateja and Nina. My deep gratitude goes to Charles Crook and Roger Murphy, for their guidance and friendship. The support and kindness they provided during my research scholarship at the Learning Sciences Research Institute (LSRI) of the University of Nottingham is worth all my praise. I am especially indebted to Charles Crook for his time, and for all the thought-provoking and challenging conversations. Importantly, I wish to express my gratitude to all the PhD and MA students who were my empirical studies participants. Special thanks to the anonymous book reviewers and the reviewer who provided thorough recommendations on the draft. I thank many dear people who enriched my life during the research presented in this book and the writing of it. Thank you so much Andi Setiawan for making the illustrations for the book. Thank you, Edward Fisher, for reading my draft, your witty and creative company, sharing music and laughter. Thank you, Claudia Cialone, for all those chats, cups of tea, enthusiasm, the wisdom we gained and the music and art we made. Thank you, Michael Pearson, for the kindness, help, consistency, laughs, joint music and the sound of your piano. Huge thank you to all doctoral research students at Lancaster University who have been developing, tweaking and applying inquiry graphics) in a variety of contexts in their own ways: Wilma Teviotdale, Zoe Hurley, Nim Yan Sun, Denise MacGiolla, Geraldine McDermott, Biliana Popova, Cliona Flood, Naoimh O'Reilly, Naïm Asbaa and Errol Luders, and thank you in advance to all of you joining us in the future. Thank you to all my PhD and MA students on the doctoral HEREE (Higher Education Research, Evaluation and Enhancement) and MA Education and Social Justice programs at Lancaster University at the department of Educational Research, who engaged on my modules and grappled with inquiry graphics. I have learnt so much from all of you. Thank you to the academic and doctoral staff I interacted with at the Athlone Institute of Technology (Ireland), the Department of Semiotics at the University of Tartu (Estonia) and the International Semiotics Institute at the Kaunas University of Technology (Lithuania). Thank you to all friends and/or scholars who have enriched my life, provided inspiration, support and kindness: Miriam Sturdee, Alin Olteanu, Carey Jewitt, Niall Winters, Yishay Mor, Kathrin Otrel-Cass, Lone Dirckinck-Holmfeld, Petar Jandrić, Jayne White, Michael Peters, Tina Besley, Aleksandar Pavlović, Nick Sousanis, Dario Martinelli, Sarah Hayes, Siân Bayne and the Digital Education team (@Edinburgh), Vivien Hodgson, Aleksandra Acker, Susana Correira, Helena T. Valentim, Luísa Magalhães, Andrew Tate, Emma Gittens, Dane Lukić, Corina Balaban, Hayley Alter, Joel Bennet, Johnny Unger, Kristina Spionjak, Jung In Jung, Maja Obradović, Usha, Vitus Vestergaard, Àgata Alcañiz, Liam Rogers, Stefan M.E. and Lee Thomas, Natasha He, Bridgette Redder, Snjezana Čiča, David Guille; thank you, Brett Bligh and Nicola Ingram, for the interesting conversations and support. Thank you Michael Sharples and Shaaron Ainsworth for all the support and time at the LSRI. Thank you, Steve Dempster and Shane Banks, you passed away, but I'll cherish the memory of you as lovely people and dedicated teachers. Thank you for your friendship and constant support Kika Pavlović, Ana Todorović-Radetić, Marija Huber and Nataša Pantić: you have all made a great impact on my life and its trajectory. Thank you goes to the lovely Nottingham "crew"' of that time: Madeline Hallewell, Mathew McFall, Jitti Niramitranon, Paul Dempster, Terry Willmer, Ian Pearshouse, Andrew Manches, Rafael M. de Albuquerque, Dimitrios Panagiotopoulous, Jessica Mason, Ulises Xolocotzin, Theodosia Albanti, Earl Kehoe and Steven Watson. Thank you, Palgrave Editors Eleanor Christie and Rebecca Wyde, and the book production lead Sudha Soundarrajan for all the support, wonderful patience and understanding, and all Palgrave professionals who helped with proofreading. Thank you to the University of Nottingham's LSRI – The Visual Learning Lab scholarship that allowed me to do the empirical research presented in this book, and thank you my dearest MA cohort for our time at the Institute of Education in London – we were and always will be family; that is when and where my academic journey of images, education and multimodality started. Thank you to the department of Educational Research and Lancaster University for the sabbatical that allowed me to prepare this book for publication, and all departmental colleagues, academic and administrative staff who support me and believe in me and the quality of my work. In the end, I would like to remember my deceased grandparents and uncle – Sreten and Jelena Lacković, Sevdalina, Života and Budimir Pešić. The time I spent with them filled my childhood with adventures, dreams and many flavors. My grandmother's brother-in-law Jovan gave me an interesting compound nickname, an 'engineer-writer', claiming that, as I always explored, inquired and wrote in my notebooks, I was destined to become some-thing in between a scientist and writer when I "grew up." I suppose if I add the "engineered" compound image-concept IG sign, here is this book that I hope you'll enjoy, dear reader.

**Parts of these following publications by the author have been incorporated in this book:**

Lackovic, N. (2020). Social Media and Social (In)Justice in Higher Education: Twitter and Social Media as critical media pedagogy "tools". In J. McArthur & P. Ashwin (Eds.) *Locating Social Justice in Higher Education Research*, Bloomsbury.

Lacković, N. (2020). Thinking with Digital Images in the Post-Truth Era: A Method in Critical Media Literacy. *Postdigital Science and Education*, 2, 442–462 .

Lacković, N. (2018). Analysing videos in educational research: an "Inquiry Graphics" approach for multimodal, Peircean semiotic coding of video data. *Video Journal of Education and Pedagogy*, 3(1), 1–23.

Lackovic, N. (2010, November). Creating and reading images: towards a communication framework for Higher Education learning. In *Seminar. net* (Vol. 6, No. 1).

# About the book

Global universities, everyday digital technology and urban life abound with graphics. **Graphics** is the term used for external representations that leave a *trace* on a surface or screen. These can range from graffiti and words to digital and social media photographs and hybrid pictures. Simply put, this book is about inquiry graphics in higher education. **Inquiry graphics (IG)** are graphics integrated within concepts or thematic units across educational domains, thus forming integral signs of knowledge development. They promote **relational approaches** to educational theory and practice at international universities. Such approaches bridge common dualisms, such as image–concept, mind–matter, society–materiality, abstract–concrete, and internal–external.

The book contributes to higher education knowledge and concept theorization and practice. It advances an emerging but growing field of **edusemiotics**, brought together with related approaches to **images, criticality** and **learning sciences** (such as sociocultural constructivist approaches). Edusemiotics, also conceptualized as the semiotic theory of learning, tackles how signs make meaning in relation to knowledge, foregrounding Charles Sanders Peirce's semiotics and philosophy as its key approach. It is an encompassing and interdisciplinary domain. Whereas publications in edusemiotics and semiotics of learning have set the foundations for adopting a semiotic approach to education, there is a scarcity of studies that have applied and explored it in situ at university level. This book addresses the gap. Its design-based and action research projects focus on micro-practices and robust, fine-grain empirical analyses of learning and thinking processes, acts and designs with pictorial graphics that mediate student reflection and dialogue.

This book is also about higher education communities as interpreters of communication messages. Central to the book is moving beyond knowledge or conceptual development and learning as perceived in opposition to images and senses, in strongly logocentric and glottocentric terms, and as a deterministic acquisition of definitional concepts and rules. In contrast, this book argues that knowledge, teaching and learning are types of semiotic engagement, via learners' creative work and growth. It views concepts as open, non-dualist entities. They are relational, processual, pluralistic, and multimodal. As such, they include diverse modes of communication (e.g., graphics). The graphics types that are explored in the empirical studies are **digital photographs**. The pedagogic principles of an inquiry graphics method proposed are: **externalization** and **sharing**. This means *externalizing students' thinking to integrate students' experiences, opinions, beliefs and prior knowledge into their shared (as well as individual) knowledge building processes*. It is a student-oriented practice.

The main tenets of inquiry graphics signs, artefacts and practices are:

1) **dynamic relationality** between external materiality, here represented via external graphics, and knowledge and concept development, as an open-ended process linked by situated sociocultural and sociomaterial environmental contexts, conditions, prior knowledge and historicity; and

2) **shared pluralism/ multiplicity** and complexity of such relational approach to knowledge and concepts, focusing on the plurality of interpretations via IG signs, arguing for interpretation externalization and sharing in diverse learner communities.

The book consists of two parts and the parts jointly consist of nine chapters. **Part I** of the book contributes to educational theory by theorizing IG. It focuses on the questions of *why* one develops and applies inquiry graphics and *what* perspectives it integrates, consisting of six chapters. It provides a rationale as to why to tackle images as constituents of IG in higher education, building on a range of interrelated and complementary approaches to signs, images, concepts and learning. **Chapter 1** provides examples of the power and role of images in society, mainly by considering digital media communication as linked to students' lives and their digital media engagement, arguing for taking images seriously as part of critical and transformative practices in higher education. It includes an inquiry into leading higher education journals, showing that semiotics, photographs and multimodality are peripheral concerns in higher education studies, although many tackle visually salient technology and social media. **Chapter 2** addresses the context of digital higher education that marginalizes innovation, semiotics and photographs by mapping the current non-relational neoliberal policies and initiatives that are operating where the main concerns of the book are situated, highlighting how this context poses challenges for practice innovation and relational culture, suggesting possibilities for IGs as humble contributors toward change. **Chapter 3** focuses on semiotics in and of education. It tackles selected, focused aspects of Peirce's semiotics and its diagrammatic tripartite sign as the core inspiration model for inquiry graphics signs, merging conceptual and pictorial signs into one IG sign for learning purposes. It considers inquiry graphics as edusemiotic thinking signs and artefacts. **Chapter 4** turns to images to consider a selection of relevant perspectives to image integration in and for learning, moving from expository to creative approaches to images in education, all of which inquiry graphics signs and practices incorporate, challenge and expand on. **Chapter 5** tackles the notion of concept in relation to how it is conceived in this book, as a creative, multiple, mindful, dialogic, open-ended and non-dualistic unit in education, as an image–concept multimodal artefact that can act as an inquiry graphic. **Chapter 6** expands these considerations to discuss knowledge development as mediated by inquiry graphics artifacts and modes of learning inquiry.

　　**Part II** proceeds to put Part I into practice by showing the complexities of visual and multimodal learning at a micro-level exploration of image–concept thinking, tackling the questions of *how* the relationality between the image and the concept in and of inquiry graphics works for learning, in what ways and via which acts, and *what* this means for learning designs, as well as approaches to knowledge and research in higher education. It presents robust, fine-grain empirical analyses of learning processes, image-concept coupling, via students' multimodal IG narrative work and ways of thinking with/from/through/into images. These studies and analyses explore inquiry graphics as a reflection method and a part of a pedagogical design within PhD studies and an MA program in education in the UK, focusing on the applications of digital photographs as specific types of graphics. It provides selected examples of two in-depth studies, and one brief iterative design example that links to the second study in **Chaps.** 7 and **8**, to show an iterative development in the spirit of design-based and action research that framed the studies. In summary, these chapters explore the mechanisms of learners' thinking and acts realized at the intersection of image and concept narrative, an IG artefact (IGA). **Chapter 9** closes the book with reflections and discussion related to the empirical findings, practical and theoretical contributions, and the development and future potential of inquiry graphics. Also addressed are the potential of and further work for interdisciplinary, relational, post-digital, and sociomaterial educational futures.

# Contents

# List of Figures

# List of Tables

# Part I

## Why and What

# 1

# Introduction: Why Inquiring Images in Higher Education?

*We are searching for an ideal image of our own world: we go in quest of a planet, a civilization superior to our own but developed on the basis of a prototype of our primeval past.*
(S. Lem, *Solaris*, translated by J. Kilmartin and S. Cox. C 6 'The Little Apocrypha', p. 72, 1970)

The epigraph from Polish science fiction writer Stanislaw Lem suggests that humans are searching for an ideal image of our world in outer space. This image, including the search itself and the very concept of "superiority" (or inferiority), is imbued with human sociocultural heritage and histories. It is underpinned by a presumption or perhaps a hope that a putative alien community or individual entity would share some features with our own civilization, for example our interpretative organs and the sense of time and space. The quote reminded me of the Pioneer plaque picture, the image designed to communicate key information about humans and Earth pictorially to tentative intelligent extraterrestrials, sent into and now beyond outer solar system space on NASA Pioneer 10 and 11 spacecraft, in 1972 and 1973. Figure 1.1 shows a drawing of the

© The Author(s) 2020
N. Lacković, *Inquiry Graphics in Higher Education*,
https://doi.org/10.1007/978-3-030-39387-8_1

plaque, originally devised by Carl Sagan, Frank Drake and Linda Salzman Sagan.

The team who created the plaque tried to represent humans and the world in the way that seemed to them to be most effective and representative. This was and would always be a hard task. Those who worked on it deserve our appreciation for trying to do it and then producing it. As the intention behind the Pioneer plaque is broadly to communicate key facts about humans and human positioning in the solar system via *only one image/ illustration*, it is no wonder that its interpretations have raised controversies. Some of the issues included the represented nudity and what is suggested as a subservient and passive position of the woman in the image, as opposed to the man who is waving. Inquiring the Pioneer picture and its depicted elements do not stop with these examples. NASA's web site[1] provides these explanations of the image: "The key to translating the plaque lies in understanding the breakdown of the most common element in the universe— hydrogen (…) Anyone from a scientifically educated civilization having enough knowledge of hydrogen would be able to translate the message." Yet, how many people on Earth at this very moment are familiar with the drawn hydrogen symbol at the top left corner and cosmic pulsars spreading centrally on the left part of the plaque (see Fig. 1.1)? A good part of educated humanity, let alone the putative alien life, may not have the implied knowledge required for intended interpretation.

The reference to the Pioneer plaque is important as it points at a common presumption by a human message creator that others would make meaning of the message as its creator intended, or in similar ways. While we only have our human nature as the basis for creating messages for aliens hoping they could decode it somehow, we do have an opportunity to tackle the question of interpretation in the context of the university. If higher education involves a message exchange between teachers and learners, we may also agree that it still provides much more space and time for the production and dissemination of resources and teachers' messages to learners, rather than the opportunities for learners to externalize their own interpretations (of these messages and resources) in order

[1] https://www.nasa.gov/centers/ames/missions/archive/pioneer.html

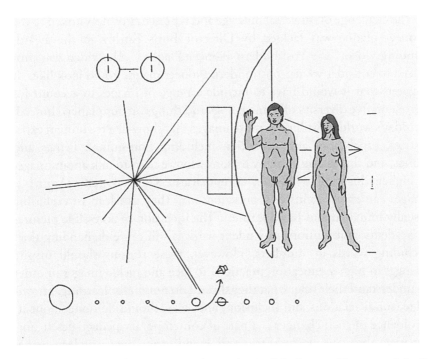

Fig. 1.1 A drawing of the Pioneer plaque, by Andi Setiawan. (Courtesy of Andi Setiawan © Andi Setiawan 2019, all rights reserved)

to exchange meanings in a more equal manner. What the plaque exemplifies is something very human, perhaps the very thing that makes us human: humans (1) interpret the world from their own experiences and point of view, from their unique biological, cultural, epistemological and ontological stance; and humans (2) create things and content that act as signs-for-interpretations from their own experiences and point of view, from their unique biological, cultural, epistemological and ontological stance. A simple truth about the central importance of interpretation, artifact creation and meaning-making processes in human life (Worth & Gross, 1974), still marginally explored and acknowledged in higher education studies. This book accounts for the externalization of learners' interpretation and meaning-making, focusing on image and concept pluralism as mediators of such an externalization.

The challenge of universal message and representativeness linked to the Pioneer plaque was tackled by Director Boris Kozlov in the award-winning video "The Postmodern Pioneer Plaque."[2] The video was produced to consider what a postmodern Pioneer plaque could look like.[3] It suggests that it would have to include a range of images to account for representative diversity of living beings and things on our planet). Indeed, in today's world we still need more images that show diverse human experiences, capabilities and identities, including non-human beings and things, and that is one of many reasons why we need to talk about images in higher education, while they saturate learners' digital media. Arguably, images can show exclusive representations. They can lead to excluding visually impaired and blind learners. The inclusion of accessible pictures in academic publications or student work is still more demanding than including words or numbers. However, these reasons should inspire changes in higher education practices, to face and tackle images in order to understand their role, what they do and do not do for learning, knowledge, social relations and inclusion, and what should be done about it. Avoidance of such changes is a part of contemporary pedagogies at universities; they are glottocentric and logocentric; they privilege verbal communication, reasoning and theory, marginalizing other senses (Cobley, 2016). In that way, these pedagogies are exclusive. The arguments in this book are linked to images, but the relational approach argued in the book encapsulates a general inclusion of diverse senses and emotions as integral in learning and knowledge.[4]

---

[2] https://www.youtube.com/watch?v=8gfDffpkQI0; http://postmodernpioneerplaque.com/?page_id=4504

[3] Disclaimer (by Boris Kozlov, provided on postmodernpioneerplaque.com): "Please don't get offended by this video! I do not intend to make fun of any individual nor any particular group of people."

[4] Visually impaired and blind people would be highly attuned to other modes that inform their understanding of the environment and meanings in it, such as sound, touch, smell, air, space-time, and different sensation of light. Edusemiotic relationality principles (e.g., as stated in the Glossary) and multimodal perspective to learning would include a variety of communicative modes, such as sound and touch, not just graphics. This could take different focal perspectives, such as inquiry dance, inquiry haptics, and so on. It could also be referred to as a "multimodal inquiry" approach.

## 1.1. The Underexplored Dimensions of Higher Education Studies

Exploring how images and other signs in communication make meaning, which can inform learning and knowledge, is an aspect of the discipline of semiotics.[5] This discipline, broadly speaking, studies signs and how they mediate meaning-making and action by humans and diverse organisms in diverse environments. The Pioneer plaque image can be defined as an illustration, a pictorial external image, a type of graphic, and a semiotic sign. Signs mediate interpretations. One of sign's definitions, according to Peirce's triadic sign diagram, is "(a) sign, or representamen, is something which stands to somebody for something in some respect or capacity" (CP 2.218).[6] It emphasizes that three things are necessary for sign meaning-making: some sensation or sign form/ vehicle; the mind that interprets it; and the physically or virtually existent object that the sign vehicle expresses, and the minds interpret. Translated into a photographic sign, this would be photographic content that embodies an object in the external world (existing although possibly invented and/or digitally fabricated), interpreted by someone (some mind). If we accept that thinking and conceptual development in higher education are mediated by semiotic signs of various kinds, the perspectives of semiotics are highly relevant to higher education, although studies in higher education

---

[5] Semiotics may still have the reputation of being a linguistic and immaterial discipline as a consequence of de Saussure's semiotics associated with the linguistic turn and logocentric and glottocentric approaches. However, the field of semiotics has several sub-fields, and the developments made in semiotics went beyond the linguistic with the work of Peirce in the nineteenth century, further developed and evident in ecosemiotics, zoosemiotics, biosemiotics and recently edusemiotics and the semiotic theory of learning, which have all made connections with the world's matter, non-human signification, and diverse signs beyond language, incorporating various communication modes.

[6] CP = Peirce, C. S. (1931–1935, 1958). *The collected papers of Charles Sanders Peirce (digital version)*. Cambridge, MA: Belknap. (In-text references are to CP, followed by paragraph number); EP = Peirce, C. S. (1893–1913). *The essential Peirce* (Vol. 2). Bloomington, IN: Indiana University Press. (In-text references are to EP, followed by page number); MS = Peirce, C.S. (1967, 1971). *Manuscripts in the Houghton Library of Harvard University, as identified by Richard Robin, "Annotated Catalogue of the Papers of Charles S. Peirce,"* Amherst, MA: University of Massachusetts Press (1967), and in "The Peirce Papers: A supplementary catalogue," *Transactions of the C. S. Peirce Society*, Volume 7 (1971): 37–57. In-text references are to MS, followed, when available, by page number.

rarely adopt semiotic approaches, as will be shown in the next section. As Quay (2017, p. 79) argues, "much more research needs to be done to connect education and semiotics as regards teaching and learning." Inquiry graphics do this in the present work.

The Pioneer plaque, as well as the imagery discussed in this chapter, belongs to the group of objects termed graphics (from Greek γραφικός, *graphikos*, "belonging to drawing"), broadly referring to shapes, images or designs that leave a material or digital trace on a surface (e.g., on a wall, digital screen, paper), including photographs, murals, drawings but also numbers, graphs, diagrams and data visualizations. This book considers pictorial (depictive) images as distinct types of graphics or graphic signs, such as illustrations and photographs, with the focus on digital photographs.

Although Pioneer 10 signal loss occurred in 2003, we can say with certainty that at least two graphics were launched in outer space, further away from the Earth than any human being has reached so far, forever representing humanity. In contrast to the lonely floating Pioneer plaques, of course, it is fair to say that graphics abound on planet Earth, all around us in urban environments. Imagine yourself in the street of a city. Imagine walking around guided by your senses, one of them being vision. If I consider the act of seeing, I cannot help but be aware of a myriad of pictures, posters, artifacts, graffiti, murals, designs and advertisements, of people's gaze fixed on their cellphones. The whole environment is swarming with icons and symbols promoting and reinforcing notions of what the world is like, how it should be and how it can be, creating a phantasmagoric landscape of desires, dreams, biases and ideologies (Ewen & Ewen, 1992, 2006). Higher education is a part of this visual and multimodal existence. Students and educators are deeply embedded within it. In the contemporary world of an unprecedented pixilation around humans and on social media, higher education studies and research are still echoing the concerns raised by David Sless (1981, p. 180) back in the 1980s:

> the overall culture in our societies is increasingly dominated by hybrid forms that use many visual forms of communication which our education system either ignores or simply takes for granted. If our general education does not, in the formative years, develop and enlarge the expectations stu-

dents have of visual materials, we lose a potential method of understanding which higher education cannot fully take advantage of without engaging in the remedial activity.

Despite the proliferation of visual media in students' lives, it can be said that postgraduate programs in higher education still do not consider photographs in the media as a potential "higher level" learning or analytical resource, apart from the programs, subjects and schools that are traditionally labeled as image-friendly or "visual." However, this approach is needed in order to address the current state of human–media interaction in a world "of hyper-visuality, in a world of remediation and cross-mediation in which experience of content both appears in multiple forms and migrates from one form to another" (Peters, Besley, Jandrić, & Bajić, 2016, p. 2). Visual technologies, such as virtual reality platforms, gears and drones, develop at high speed, promoting rapid changes in scopic regimes and social dynamics. Such intense hypervisuality operates in a post-digital bubble where promoted media content seamlessly infiltrates and influences online and offline behaviors. It stirs media users to seek instant, affective and comforting solutions to difficult and complex problems, tapping into the public fear of insecurity, conflict and uncertainty. In such a society of post-truth and spectacle (Debord, 1994), materiality-through-visuality is present everywhere in our daily life, from the things that we eat, wear, watch, drink, purchase, to the things that we possess, dwell in, or crave for.

Images can show the material character of the life on Earth that is sensed through corporeality, which rarely gets considered in the body of theoretical knowledge in and of higher education (Olteanu, 2017). Digital photographs are carriers of visual and material cultures that mediate social practices. They embody the world's materiality and can help understand how abstract concepts manifest in the physical world and how the two are intrinsically linked (Elleström, 2014; Lackovic, 2020). As such, they can bring in the lacking but needed dimension of exploring the world's materiality (Barad, 2003) in learning and knowledge (Fenwick, 2010; Fenwick & Edwards, 2013). Matter is indispensable for the functioning of the world (Barad, 2003, 2007, 2011). All the seas, land, animals and plants, all the oil reserves, fossil fuels, and other exhaustable natural resources, all the plastic, wood, and metal, tangible artifacts, all the bodies, houses and clothes, the matter seamlessly entangled with the ecosystem and sociocultural actions and life, all of this matters. They matter as these types of matter are fundamental for the maintenance of life on Earth and they mediate everyday production and consumption.

For education to support a generation that will be at the forefront of changes for the benefit of the planet in its totality and for a more just world, more relational approaches in education are needed, such as the ones that acknowledge material–immaterial, mind-body, individual-collective relations. Pictorial digital images can act as a catalyst for deep reflection on the material world they embody and as triggers for creative insight that can lead to new problem solutions. This could have significant implications by emphasizing the relational coexistence of various types of animate and inanimate matter intersecting with societal (individual and collective) mind, production and other types of action and events. The point is that higher education across disciplines would benefit from a serious engagement with visual media meaning-making, to cultivate an awareness of materiality in the world and its various effects (Lackovic, 2020).

As photographs are commonly used in media and social media communication, they can act as powerful emotional and persuasion vehicles (Apple, 2004). Thinking about images or any other sign involves and influences emotions (Burkitt, 2014). Images are not passive but action-signs that elicit action accompanied or preceded by an emotional reaction such as offence, pride, disgust, anger, insecurity, indifference, desire, awe, excitement or longing. Many scholars identify suggestive properties of images which may shape and are shaped by the values, beliefs and norms of communities (e.g., relating to advertisements (Williamson, 1978; Amouzadeh & Tavangar, 2004), art (Fulkova & Tipton, 2008), personal memories (Devereux, 2010)). While one image such as the Pioneer plaque cannot represent worldwide diversity, diverse images of worldwide struggles and suffering are flooding the media. Seeing an image that violates human rights (Adelman, 2012) or shows an ecological destruction can reinforce a spectrum of emotions, such as shock, disorientation and helplessness, disillusion, despondency, indifference, horror, outrage and/or anger. On the one hand, constant repetition of disturbing images could numb feelings and make suffering in the world a common place. On the other hand, the feelings of guilt, sympathy and outrage have been identified as prosocial emotions that can motivate action for social change among the advantaged groups (Thomas, McGarty, & Mavor, 2009).

Although we do not automatically accept or believe that images are truth, seeing an image accompanied with a verbal message many times, "plants" that image (and the message) into our subconscious, whether we want this or not (Ewen & Ewen, 2006).[7] Via problematic communication practices, news and social media can mix images with suggestive narratives to reinforce the cultural fear of "otherness" and negative stereotypes, that is, to reinforce

> the notion of a deviant "other"—feared, loathed, or both—as the means to maintaining an idealized self. An understanding of "otherness" helps to explain why identities are often characterized by polarization and by the discursive marking of inclusion and exclusion within oppositional classificatory systems: "insiders" and "outsiders," "us" and "them," men and women, black and white, "normal" and "deviant." (Greer & Jewkes, 2005, p. 20)

If we adhere to the idea that universities should, among other goals, fulfill their duties to civil society, we can relate to Olteanu's (2019) reflection. The author questions what we as academics, having the university as our professional home, are doing or have done in our lives and our teaching to act upon divisive populist media discourses and the current crises of humanity, as well as the non-relational and non-pluralist concept of culture and identity. Such a non-relational concept widely practiced in national curricula imagery (Lackovic, 2010b) attempts to bind people to exclusive singular identities (Olteanu, 2019). It plays with individual need for belonging, love, and acknowledgment, by promoting monolithic, better or superior notions of identity and being in the world. Photographs can both reinforce and challenge such non-relational and non-pluralist stereotypes. It depends how and where they are presented and used. Problematically, they can show only one aspect of any idea or

---

[7] Stereotypical image associations contrary to participant's conscious beliefs, studied in Chap. 7, confirm this.

concept, one version of what worldly things and concepts look like. However, this does not mean that we should avoid tackling photographs in higher education, or that they are "evil." On the contrary, this is exactly the reason why they can not only help critically examine the effects of the media, but can help us explore the plurality of meanings, deeply reflect on how represented materiality affect life and confront identity and other stereotypes (Lackovic, 2010b; Olteanu, 2019). They can support an awareness of interconnectedness and relationality between abstract concepts and concrete world, body and mind, emotions and intellect (Burkitt, 2014).

As images flood the media and students' lives on daily basis, they are consumed fast, and students rarely have the opportunity to use images to mediate deep thinking and conceptual advancement (Lackovic, 2010a, 2016, 2020). The same photograph can often be used in social media to reinforce an idea—problematically, ideas that may not have been checked. This is a symptom of post-truth viral images that aim to reinforce particular ideas and can spread lies at previously unimagined speed (Lackovic, 2020). Common examples include the appropriation and labeling of photographs aiming to support some ideology, which may rely on key visual codes rather than evidence as a point of reference. Yet they are readily accepted on the internet, shared and go viral. Such is the life-history of a photograph taken in the late 1980s at Emory University in Atlanta, Georgia, depicting a performance by a local "guerrilla theatre" group, yet circulated on the internet far and wide claiming to show the Argentinian Cuban revolutionary Che Guevara executing two women, merely based on the visual cue that the man, whose face is not visible, is wearing a military uniform and a beret, a key feature of the iconic (stereotypical) image of Guevara. That photograph is still frequently shared across a wide variety of websites and online media as a meme with the caption "This is the image of Che Guevara that should be seen on t-shirts," as Che t-shirts commonly show him wearing a beret.[8]

---

[8] For information and reflection about the photograph, see: https://factcheck.afp.com/no-not-photo-argentine-revolutionary-che-guevara

Therefore, to reiterate, images as signs are not passive, but they are signs-in-action, and the acts of signs— semioses—have an influence on human affect (Tateo, 2018) and action (Strand, 2013). Such characteristics of signs and images recommend them for educational integration and exploration. If higher education (and education in general) does not integrate a serious relationship with images, educational institutions will continue to fail to educate students about nuances and characteristics of material and visual culture, and related semioses that affect human action (Lackovic, 2020; Strand, 2013). Graphics such as photographs should be subject to inquiry, not just because they can be persuasive or manipulative triggers for emotions, actions and beliefs, but because they are and can play an important part in teaching–learning designs and acts of learning and thinking (Lackovic, 2010a, 2016, 2020). They can support the development of minds that inquire and ask questions of great importance to global social and educational futures. We can integrate and explore various images in our educational work as imaginative and/or practical material instantiations of theoretical/ scientific as well as political ideas (Leonardi, 2010).

## 1.2.  The Presence of Photographs and Semiotics in Higher Education Studies

This chapter proceeds by zooming in on the field of higher education studies and higher education scholarship to provide relevant figures on the scarce inclusion of semiotics, photographs and multimodality in higher education studies, as key concepts embedded within inquiry graphics signs. The questions that led that inquiry were:

* To what extent are the terms *photograph, semiotic* and *multimodal* present (as key search words) in leading HE journals addressing practice and research, between January 2009 and December 2019?
* How does that compare and relate to the references to *technology* and *social media* in the same journals, for the same period of time?

Nine leading higher education journals were investigated, building on Tight (2012, 2013), leaving out *RHI Review of Higher Education*, and adding *Active Learning in Higher Education*. The journals selected were prominent publications in the field of higher education, edited and/or published in Australasia, Europe and North America: Assessment and *Evaluation in Higher Education, Higher Education, Higher Education Quarterly, Higher Education Research & Development, Innovative Higher Education, Research in Higher Education, Review of Higher Education, Studies in Higher Education, Teaching in Higher Education* and *Active Learning in Higher Education*. Table 1.1 shows the outcomes for six search words: photographs, technology, social media, multimodal, semiotic, visual.

It is obvious that a photograph is sporadically considered or present in articles, conceptualizations or methods in the majority of leading higher education journals examined, within the time span of 10 years. This is notable if compared to the high number of articles tackling social media, most of those media photograph-saturated, in the same higher education journals. Words such as "image" and "picture" were excluded from the search as too broad and often not used to refer to actual material or an

**Table 1.1** The number of articles in nine leading higher education journals over the period 2009–2019 with search words relevant to the book content

| Journals | Photograph | Technology | Social media | Multimodal | Semiotic | Visual |
|---|---|---|---|---|---|---|
| *AEHE* | 25 | 428 | 193 | 12 | 4 | 107 |
| *HE* | 14 | 664 | 1074 | 6 | 15 | 73 |
| *HEQ* | 7 | 201 | 115 | 3 | 1 | 16 |
| *HERD* | 28 | 513 | 279 | 11 | 22 | 119 |
| *IHE* | 11 | 231 | 291 | 0 | 1 | 45 |
| *RHE* | 3 | 174 | 368 | 0 | 0 | 51 |
| *SHE* | 36 | 770 | 487 | 12 | 18 | 139 |
| *THE* | 36 | 367 | 237 | 13 | 25 | 99 |
| *ALHE* | 6 | 173 | 120 | 0 | 0 | 40 |
| **Total** | **166** | **3521** | **3164** | **57** | **86** | **689** |

*AEHE* Assessment and Evaluation in Higher Education, HE Higher Education, *HEQ* Higher Education Quarterly, *HERD* Higher Education Research & Development, *IHE* Innovative Higher Education, *RHE* Research in Higher Education, *RHI* Review of Higher Education, *SHE* Studies in Higher Education, *THE* Teaching in Higher Education, *ALHE* Active Learning in Higher Education

external image or picture, yielding too many false positives, evidencing an ocularcentric linguistic paradigm (Kavanagh, 2004).[9]

Both technology and social media research in the examined journals have been tackled from perspectives that rarely acknowledge photographs as parts of technology or social media, and rarely consider any semiotic and multimodal characteristics of them (Table 1.1). This means that semiotic meaning-making, the role of interpretation and different modes of communication (e.g. photographs) are marginalized areas and interest in the specialist higher education field and in its leading publication outlets. Human understanding of what images do for "higher" education knowledge and learning remains underdeveloped, especially empirically, maintaining a strict line between the more linear, conceptual, abstract and symbolic sciences-oriented vertical communication and what is deemed to be a more social, fuzzy, distributed communication of horizontal discourses such as in the arts and humanities (Bernstein, 2006).

The consideration of pictorial images in this book is situated in the arena of education studies, such as international postgraduate education studies (e.g., MA, EdD or PhD), and more specifically studies in higher education and educational research. This may include any discipline that currently does not actively and comprehensively practice multimodal or image inquiry in the curriculum, at a program, module, teaching–learning assessment or organizational level.

## 1.3. Key Themes, Messages and General Content of the Book

The section 'About the Book' in the preliminary pages provides a brief summary of the book and each chapter. This section discusses the book content in general, and elaborates on the summary. As the narrative thread has signified so far, a central concern is the matter of interpretation, the

---

[9] Phrases such as: a holistic picture, a general picture, a new picture, an accurate picture, a coherent picture and similar uses, referring to a mental idea of a "picture."

way that meaning is mediated and how it can be explored *with digital photographs, acting as creative semiotic scaffolding for deep reflection.* The book centers on a novel mix of perspectives to concept and knowledge development, looking toward future development of Edusemiotic Relationality (ER) or a relational theory of education. It argues for new relational perspectives to learning, teaching and research in higher education (see Burkitt (2008, 2014) for sociological perspectives on relationality[10]) that integrates non-verbal signs such as images and graphics into higher education practices. This book makes a case for viewing teaching–learning and knowledge as relational and multimodal developments where both verbal and non-verbal modes of communicating are indispensable for deep understanding and learners' growth. The book does not reject or deny the value of language or logocentric approaches to knowledge. It aims to go *beyond* them by adding the corporeality of knowing via concrete representations and other forms of sensing to what is popularly deemed "higher knowledge" and "higher education" in all disciplines. The book challenges dualisms in higher education studies that separate body and mind, image and concept. That is why it offers new approaches not only to method and analysis in higher education, but to knowledge and learning conceptualization and theorization.

The term *inquiry graphics* can be understood as a response to the rise and widespread use of *infographics* (*information graphics*). Whereas *infographics* are used to summarize information visually for fast impactful presentation and consumption of often large-scale data, *inquiry graphics* turns graphics into inquiry artifacts to slow down unreflective image consumption (that in most cases cannot be avoided in today's pixelated frenzy).

An inquiry graphics approach foregrounds *slow*, analytical and semiotic unpacking of visual information, and engagement via image–concept inquiry graphics (IG) artifact creation. As such, it also represents a

---

[10] The model of Edusemiotic Relationality is included in the Glossary and introduced at the end of the book to embed the image-concept relational character of inquiry graphics developed in the book in a relational theory of education, for example by considering the perspectives of relational sociology that foregrounds social relations and a relational approach to body and emotions (Burkitt, 2008, 2014), material artifacts and digital technology, material engagement theory and edusemiotics.

version of a counter-acceleration movement that stemmed around the notions of *dromology* (Bartram, 2004). Dromology is conceptualized as the unprecedented speed of visual information and telecommunication that blurs the line between online and offline, real and imaginary, taking over and controlling many vital aspects of social life, and building new scopic regimes such as seamless surveillance (e.g., via military technology, drones, satellites, social media data) (Bartram, 2004; Kellner, 1999). A dromology-aware inquiry graphics practice encourages slowing-down for reflection, aware of visual technologies and their unprecedented speed. This is done without falling into technophobia, or any one-sided vilification of technology and technological representation and visualization, but recognizing its emancipatory and other beneficial aspects (Kellner, 1999). There are many wonderful and progressive aspects of visual technological advancement, and they should be celebrated. Yet, the present times are also riddled with ecological, geopolitical and socio-cultural crises, a destabilizing era of digital reason, digital manipulation, control and uncertainties surrounding technological unemployment and precarity (Jandrić, 2017; Lackovic, 2019; Peters, Jandrić, & Means, 2019). With these tensions and challenges in mind, developing an education that can inspire possible ways of tackling those crises should be a key educational preoccupation. Inquiry graphics is one approach that can help develop such an education, as it invites exponents to seek connections and relations in seemingly unrelated objects and ideas. Such thinking can lead to moments of unexpected, sudden insight into new solutions and ways of understanding and living.

Integrating inquiry graphics into education is intended to support learners to adopt the role of *futurologists*, namely, to be interpreters, explorers and developers of possible future worlds (Bruner, 2009), imagining what a future world would be and what it would mean, starting from present-day resources. This kind of thinking will help learners to think of various scenarios and free them from the trap of "dead-end" thinking and a singular solution. Dead-end thinking is characterized by finding only limited number of solutions to problems, mainly seeing a singular or narrow definition-driven purpose and meaning of everyday experiences, concepts, events and phenomena, as if there were no alternative ways of existing or resolving a problematic situation. I am referring to everyday problems linked to emotions, values, people, work and finances to distinguish them from the gravest possible, life-threatening circumstances. If there is a multiplicity of meanings, there must always be a multiplicity of solutions. If one concept can be represented in as many ways as there are representing beings, then practicing and sharing this conceptual plurality and creative insight has merits. The world is always pregnant with possibilities. Relevant to the development of inquiry graphics in education is Paulo Freire's powerful quote that starts Cassie Earl's book about spaces of political pedagogy:

> There is no tomorrow without a project, without a dream, without utopia, without hope, without creative work, and work towards the development of possibilities, which can make the concretization of that tomorrow viable. (Freire, 2007, p. 26, quoted in Earl, 2018, p. 1)

Inquiry graphics can act as springboards for imagining possibilities, and as concretizations of abstract idea and concepts to address the past, present and future. The overarching approach I propose here is an educational one which can feed into remedial activity for building better, more sustainable and just education. This approach is expanded into a dynamic multimodal Edusemiotic Relationality (ER) metamodel, introduced at the end of the book to incorporate its key arguments. This metamodel, the inquiry graphics approach and related designs and methods contribute to the edusemiotic theory of learning (Stables & Semetsky, 2014; Semetsky & Stables, 2014; Olteanu & Campbell, 2018; Stables, Nöth, Olteanu, Pesce, & Pikkarainen, 2018) and an edusemiotic turn to theorizing and practice of HE teaching-learning and conceptual development. The perspective followed here builds on selected aspects of Peirce's semiotics, mainly focusing on the tripartite sign discussed in depth in Chap. 3. This is to account for the central role of meanings and interpretations at the nexus of society, culture, nature and materiality. Such an approach to education is an interdisciplinary exploration that views signs of the world as signs developing in relational evolution, and as a step toward desired relational education futures.

In an article co-written with Alin Olteanu (Lacković & Olteanu, forthcoming), we develop an argument for inquiry graphics as we observe knowledge and concepts to include both symbolic abstract conceptualizations and iconic images, either external or internal images. The argument is positioned within our criticism of theory and philosophy of education that considers the vehicle of knowledge to be the analytical concept understood in opposition to image (Dearden, Hirst, & Peters, 1972, p. 3). This conceptualist view still influences the design and application of educational curricula and methods internationally in the field of higher education studies, by foregrounding abstract verbal conceptualizations as higher knowledge and learning. Yet such view was contested by Dewey and Bentley (1960) some time ago, arguing against educational reliance on "concepts" as distinct mental entities that exclude other modes. In the present book, concept and knowledge development are embodied, distributed, multimodal and multisensory, represented in an inquiry graphics sign model and method.

With this book I also seek to act in response to the crisis of the arts and humanities (Martinelli, 2016), and as a general reaction to the contemporary global challenges amidst the proliferation of digital and hybrid images and multimodal artifacts in society and media. As Martinelli (2016, p. 1) argues,

> Humanities—it has been underlined by many sources—are currently facing a multilayered type of crisis that involves, at the same time (and in organic fashion), their impact on, and role within, society; their popularity among students and scholars; and ultimately their identity as producers and promoters of knowledge.

There are complex reasons behind this crisis, especially with regards to profit and impact-driven priorities across governments worldwide as well as higher education institutions, rooted in capitalist and neoliberal logic. Higher education as marketplace is almost a hostile environment to creative, innovative pedagogies and relational approaches to knowledge and practice, as will be discussed in Chap. 2. Inquiry graphics pedagogy and research adopt graphics and pictorial signs as not just an important part of the arts and humanity domains, such as media studies and communication and visual arts, but an important rather than minor or marginal part of thinking and scientific inquiry. This inquiry is here exemplified via empirical studies with concepts in educational psychology and doctoral training in education, which are social science fields. As an interdisciplinary approach that integrates graphics in knowledge development, inquiry graphics can be also understood as an "art–science" relational approach, applicable across disciplinary domains and programs. This counteracts the belittling of the arts and humanities as "useless" and "dispensable" (Martinelli, 2016). Inquiry graphics design explored in the present work brings together semiotics, the arts and humanities (via visual arts, media, graphics, historical and cultural aspects of interpretation) and other sciences (e.g., learning sciences and psychology) to argue and exemplify their inter-connectedness.

The knowledge development approach adopted here is governed by an overarching theme of *image–concept–knowledge relationality and multiplicity*. Under this overarching focus, I weave the threads of a variety of related approaches. Therefore, my own conceptual and writing style can be observed as an eclectic assemblage of vignettes around the leading theme, to conceptualize edusemiotic learning and knowledge development with pictorial signs. This could be related to a type of bricolage writing (Bone, 2009), as it is layered and multiple in its perspectives. Yet, it is firmly focused on the key principles of *relationality* and *multiplicity* in conceptual, semiotic, and knowledge-development sense via inquiry graphics. Such an assemblage orientation (Winters, 2010) is chosen as educational practices are also complex, multifaceted, fluid and hybrid. In my opinion, the same hybrid approach mimics the character of educational practices. Through IG, I want to build a bridge connecting the highly intellectualized and abstracted type of educational knowledge that over-privileges verbalized theory and abstract concepts to sensed and graphic modes of being, thinking and inquiry. The central stage is given to *externalization* for subsequent sharing of learners' interpretations, prior experience, their imagination and representations of life in constant processes of becoming, with digital photographs as vehicles of this externalization.

This chapter provided reflections and examples that show how pictorial images are important for interpreting, understanding and acting in the world and, therefore, provided introductory reasons to integrate them in higher education contexts and practices. Further arguments as to why applying images and inquiry graphics, and in relation to what theoretical and philosophical underpinnings will be provided in the remainder of Part I in Chaps. 2, 3, 4, 5 and 6; how this can be done in practice will be presented via empirical examples in Part II, Chaps. 7 and 8. Conceptual and empirical implications and a summary are provided in Chap. 9. The book proceeds to consider the context where inquiry graphics are situated: neoliberal academia.

# References

Adelman, R. A. (2012). Tangled complicities: Extracting knowledge from images of Abu Ghraib. In *Knowledge and pain* (pp. 353–379). New York: Brill/Rodopi.

Amouzadeh, M., & Tavangar, M. (2004). Decoding pictorial metaphor: Ideologies in Persian commercial advertising. *International Journal of Cultural Studies, 7*(2), 147–174.

Apple, M. W. (2004). *Ideology and curriculum* (3rd ed.). London: Routledge.

Barad, K. (2003). Posthumanist performativity: Toward an understanding of how matter comes to matter. *Signs: Journal of Women in Culture and Society, 28*(3), 801–831.

Barad, K. (2007). *Meeting the universe halfway: Quantum physics and the entanglement of matter and meaning.* Durham, NC: Duke University Press.

Barad, K. (2011). Erasers and erasures: Pinch's unfortunate 'uncertainty principle'. *Social Studies of Science, 41*(3), 443–454.

Bartram, R. (2004). Visuality, dromology and time compression: Paul Virilio's new ocularcentrism. *Time & Society, 13*(2–3), 285–300.

Bernstein, B. (2006). Vertical and horizontal discourse: An essay. In *Education and society* (pp. 53–73). London: Routledge.

Bone, J. (2009). Writing research: Narrative, bricolage and everyday spirituality. *New Zealand Research in Early Childhood Education, 12*, 143.

Bruner, J. S. (2009). *Actual minds, possible worlds.* Cambridge, MA: Harvard University Press.

Burkitt, I. (2008). *Social selves: Theories of self and society.* London: Sage.

Burkitt, I. (2014). *Emotions and social relations.* London: Sage.

Cobley, P. (2016). *Cultural implications of biosemiotics.* Dordrecht, Netherlands: Springer.

Dearden, R. F., Hirst, P., & Peters, R. S. (Eds.). (1972). *Education and the development of reason*. London: Routledge & Kegan Paul.

Debord, G. (1994). *The society of the spectacle* (Donald Nicholson Smith, Trans.). Brooklyn/New York: Zone Books.

Devereux, L. (2010). From Congo: Newspaper photographs, public images and personal memories. *Visual Studies, 25*(2), 124–134.

Dewey, J., & Bentley, A. F. (1960). *Knowing and the known* (No. 111). Boston: Beacon Press.

Earl, C. (2018). *Spaces of political pedagogy: Occupy! And other radical experiments in adult learning*. London: Routledge.

Elleström, L. (2014). Material and mental representation: Peirce adapted to the study of media and arts. *The American Journal of Semiotics, 30*(1/2), 83–138. https://doi.org/10.5840/ajs2014301/24.

Fenwick, T. (2010). Re-thinking the "thing" sociomaterial approaches to understanding and researching learning in work. *Journal of Workplace Learning, 22*(1/2), 104–116.

Fenwick, T., & Edwards, R. (2013). Performative ontologies. Sociomaterial approaches to researching adult education and lifelong learning. *European journal for Research on the Education and Learning of Adults, 4*(1), 49–63.

Freire, P. (2007). *Daring to Dream: Toward a Pedagogy of the Unfinished*. Boulder: Paradigm Publishers.

Fulkova, M., & Tipton, T. (2008). A (con)text for new discourse as semiotic praxis. *The International Journal of Art and Design Education, 27*(1), 27–42.

Greer, C., & Jewkes, Y. (2005). Towards "them", the people that are not like "us". Extremes of otherness: Media images of social exclusion. *Social Justice, 32*(1(99)), 20–31.

Jandrić, P. (2017). *Learning in the age of digital reason*. New York: Springer.

Kavanagh, D. (2004). Ocularcentrism and its others: A framework for metatheoretical analysis. *Organization Studies, 25*(3), 445–464.

Kellner, D. (1999). Virilio, war and technology: Some critical reflections. *Theory, Culture & Society, 16*(5–6), 103–125.

Lackovic, N. (2010a). Creating and reading images: Towards a communication framework for higher education learning. In *Seminar. Net: Media, technology & life-long learning* (pp. 121–135).

Lackovic, N. (2010b). Beyond the surface: Image affordances in language textbooks that affect National Identity Formation (NIF). In M. Raesch (Ed.), *Mapping minds* (pp. 53–65, 13 p.) Inter-disciplinary Press.

Lackovic, N. (2016). MultiMAP: Exploring multimodal artefact pedagogy in digital higher education. *Proceedings*, 148–162.

Lackovic, N. (2019). Graduate employability (GE) paradigm shift: Towards greater socio-emotional and eco-technological relationalities of graduates' futures. In M. Peters, P. Jandrić, & A. Means (Eds.), *Education and technological unemployment* (pp. 193–212). Singapore: Springer.

Lackovic, N. (2020). Thinking with digital images in the post-truth era: A method in critical media literacy. In *Postdigtial science and education*. Springer.

Lacković, N., & Olteanu, A. (forthcoming). Learning in times of visual technologies: A relational approach to educational theory and practice that integrates external and internal images. *Educational Philosophy and Theory*.

Leonardi, P. M. (2010). Digital materiality? How artifacts without matter, matter. *First Monday, 15*(6).

Martinelli, D. (2016). *Arts and humanities in progress: A manifesto of numanities*. Cham, Switzerland: Springer.

Olteanu, A. (2017). Reading history: Education, semiotics, and edusemiotics. In *Edusemiotics – A handbook* (pp. 193–205). Singapore: Springer.

Olteanu, A. (2019). *Multiculturalism as multimodal communication*. Cham, Switzerland: Springer.

Olteanu, A., & Campbell, C. (2018). A short introduction to edusemiotics. *Chinese Semiotic Studies, 14*(2), 245–260.

[CP =] Peirce, C. S. (1931–1935, 1958). *The collected papers of Charles Sanders Peirce*. Cambridge, MA: Belknap. [In-text references are to CP, followed by paragraph number].

[EP =] Peirce, C. S. (1893–1913). *The essential Peirce* (Vol. 2). Bloomington, IN: Indiana University Press. [In-text references are to EP2, followed by page].

[MS =] Peirce, C. S. (1967, 1971). *Manuscripts in the Houghton Library of Harvard University, as identified by Richard Robin, "Annotated catalogue of the papers of Charles S. Peirce"*. Amherst, MA: University of Massachusetts Press (1967), and in The Peirce Papers: A supplementary catalogue. *Transactions of the C. S. Peirce Society, 7*(1971), 37–57. [In-text references are to MS number, followed, when available, by page number].

Peters, M. A., Besley, T., Jandrić, P., & Bajic, M. (2016, January). Educational research and visual cultures: The case of video publishing. In *American Educational Research Association Annual Meeting*.

Peters, M. A., Jandrić, P., & Means, A. (2019). *Education and technological unemployment*. Singapore: Springer.

Quay, J. (2017). Education and reasoning: Advancing a Peircean semiotic. In I. Simietsky (Ed.), *Semiotics – A handbook* (pp. 79–91). Berlin, Germany: Springer Nature.

Semetsky, I., & Stables, A. (Eds.). (2014). *Pedagogy and edusemiotics: Theoretical challenges/practical opportunities* (Vol. 62). Springer.

Sless, D. (1981). *Learning and visual communication*. Halsted Press.

Stables, A., Nöth, W., Olteanu, A., Pesce, S., & Pikkarainen, E. (2018). *Semiotic theory of learning: New perspectives in the philosophy of education*. Routledge.

Stables, A., & Semetsky, I. (2014). *Edusemiotics: Semiotic philosophy as educational foundation*. Routledge.

Strand, T. (2013). Peirce's rhetorical turn: Conceptualizing education as semiosis. *Educational Philosophy and Theory, 45*(7), 789–803.

Tateo, L. (2018). Affective semiosis and affective logic. *New Ideas in Psychology, 48*, 1–11.

Thomas, E. F., McGarty, C., & Mavor, K. I. (2009). Transforming "apathy into movement": The role of prosocial emotions in motivating action for social change. *Personality and Social Psychology Review, 13*(4), 310–333.

Tight, M. (2012). Higher education research 2000–2010: Changing journal publication patterns. *Higher Education Research & Development, 31*(5), 723–740.

Tight, M. (2013). Discipline and methodology in higher education research. *Higher Education Research and Development, 32*(1), 136–151.

Williamson, J. (1978). *Decoding advertisements: Ideology and meaning in advertising*. New York: Marion Boyars.

Winters, K. L. (2010). Quilts of authorship: A literature review of multimodal assemblage in the field of literacy education. *Canadian Journal for New Scholars in Education/Revue canadienne des jeunes chercheures et chercheurs en éducation, 3*(1), 1–12.

Worth, S., & Gross, L. (1974). Symbolic strategies. *Journal of Communication, 24*, 27–39.

# 2

# Neoliberal Higher Education: Digital, Innovative, Relational, Pictorial?

This chapter maps a larger higher education landscape where the proposed new approaches are located by considering the ongoing state of governance and policy, and the ways in which this contemporary neoliberal profile of universities is a reliable indicator of the practice of suppressing relational teaching–learning innovation, being and change. It addresses two important questions: What is the broader context of contemporary higher education system and policies that inquiry graphics and related empirical studies are positioned within? How are images related to this situation, how could they be related? It must be said that the considered context is mainly the Western one (the UK), the so-called research-intense universities. However, global universities could arguably relate to the commented challenges, as they are a part of globalization and internationalization forces applying to most higher education institutions, albeit in varied ways and to various extent.

© The Author(s) 2020
N. Lacković, *Inquiry Graphics in Higher Education*,
https://doi.org/10.1007/978-3-030-39387-8_2

# Digital Technology Implementation: Less Innovative Pedagogy, More Data Management

We live in interesting times for academia. Electronic media have become pillars of the information age (Fuchs, 2008) of digital reason (Jandrić, 2017), and the so-called "network society" (Castells, 1996) of digital acceleration. Unsurprisingly, universities have been quick to embrace the promise of electronic instruction and adopt digital technologies, such as VLEs (virtual learning environments). Although university staff are encouraged to use resources available through VLEs, the communication and interaction affordances of VLEs for teaching do not seem to be used to their full potential (Blin & Munro, 2008). Furthermore, VLEs often marginalize or treat pictorial modes of communication as add-ons rather than integrated parts of dialogic forms of communication (White, 2014) and learning (Lackovic, 2010a). Thus, the VLE medium and other technologies (e.g., lecture capture mechanism) are controversial in terms of their role in higher education pedagogic creativity and innovation. What I mean by pedagogic innovation is using technology in new ways that go beyond assimilation, reproduction and management to re-shape what teaching, learning and knowledge are via a wide range of digital modes of communication, including visual modes. The introduction and development of ubiquitous technology, along with internationalization and other competitive agendas, seem only rarely to have initiated fresh interest in, and subsequent evolution of, university teaching and learning methods that integrate that technology in novel, inclusive and transformational ways. Rather, old hierarchies are reproduced that are structured according to linguistic, analytical and hierarchical linearity (Bayne, 2008), undermining visual or spatial granularity. For example, the forum discussion is still linear in most common VLEs, with discussion threads nested one after another (ibid.), which does not allow a discussion around, or a reply via, an image or a video (as is the case for example with Thinglink or Voice Thread digital platforms).

VLEs risk becoming a crude delivery mechanism, readily encouraging a transmission discourse of educational practice, acting in this dynamic as resource "silos" and process management systems. Indeed, Gabriel, Campbell, Wiebe, MacDonald, & McAuley (2012) used surveys and focus groups with a large sample of first-year students to investigate university instructional practices with digital technologies. They found that these practices were largely oriented toward individual knowledge transmission, hence they recommended

> uses of digital technologies that go beyond information transmission, the need for extended pedagogical discussions to harness the learning potentials of digital technologies, and for pedagogies that embrace the social construction of knowledge … (Gabriel et al., 2012, p. 1)

The use of multimodal features of technology offers promise to integrate various modalities of expression in knowledge development (Hallewell & Lackovic, 2017; Breuer & Archer, 2016). However, the multimodality of technology is still under-utilized in the programs that tackle higher education teaching and research. One obstacle is the difficulty of embedding non-verbal modalities to make websites and digital learning environments accessible. The lack of advanced technologies to verbalize digital images for screen readers indicates that access to verbal communication holds primacy in terms of communication technologies for access, which effectively obstructs blind and visually impaired learners' access to visual culture. Why would we not equally develop technologies for image description? Why would visual culture not be accessible to the blind, when the written language is also visual? There is a necessity for teachers at all levels of education to be supported further in order to develop inclusive digital pedagogy (Cranmer, 2019). Recently, Facebook and Instagram introduced automatic alt text for images, which is a welcome development, with more investment needed toward the advancement of image-reading AI. Academic publishing practices still have a long way to go to tackle the issue of image inclusion; progress is made at a slow pace, with some recent openings for visual and comics-based abstracts. Although widely used to underpin teaching and communication practices, technology seems to be taken as some sort of marginal or hidden institutional artefact when it comes to the way that global universities (Lackovic & Popova, forthcoming) and UK schools (Crook & Lackovic, 2017) choose to represent themselves and their practices on their websites.

The promise and potential of the versatility of web 2.0 and open access in higher education still lingers in some limbo, failing to empower students to participate in "knowledge creation and sharing" (Scardamalia and Bereiter 2006; Henderson, Finger, & Selwyn, 2016), or to mobilize technology to be integrated more into creative and reflective (rather than management) practices. As Henderson and colleagues (2016) remark with regard to the survey of the use of technology by 253 postgraduate students across two universities in Australia,

> postgraduate students' academic uses of technologies could be seen to follow the largely restrictive expectations that continue to pervade higher education with regard to knowledge, the development of what constitutes knowledge and understanding, and what counts as postgraduate learning, study and scholarship. (Henderson, Finger, & Selwyn, 2016; see Selwyn, 2014)

Furthermore, in their survey of 1658 students, Henderson and colleagues (2015) show how students highlight mostly practical uses of technology as spectators, managers and consumers, marginalising any creative production with it (Henderson, Selwyn, Finger, & Aston, 2015). Such restricted uses of technology in teaching and learning (in most cases) are unsurprising:

> the lack of more active, participatory or creative uses of technology within our survey data suggests that only certain forms of digital practice are being legitimized through wider institutional regimes and systems of configuration. As we have discussed, these appear to be the digital practices, applications and artefacts that "best" allow students to "make sense of institutional work, while, at the same time, establishing and maintaining institutionally embedded routines." (Palmer, Simmons, & Hall, 2013, p. 488)

These routines are mirrored in students' uses of technology primarily for management, organization and efficiency, and highlight the traditional orientation of lectures and the primacy given to verbal expression

(Lackovic & Popova, forthcoming). These limited digital practices are positioned in a university landscape characterized by clear encouragement for wide use of digital resources on university premises (e.g. "Higher education in a Web 2.0 World" report (JISC, 2009); "NMC Horizon Report: 2013 Higher Education Edition" (Johnson et al., 2013)). Universities (particularly in the UK) have experienced an influx of private companies to support university digitalization and the outsourcing of university provisions (e.g. services brought from the outside, such as Box for filing, Panopto for video recording, and VLEs as digital learning systems, among many other services). This phenomenon has been conceptualized as university unbundling (Robertson & Komljenovic, 2016), a neoliberal restructuring and unbundling of services in the spirit of platform capitalism (Srnicek, 2017). It is also critically theorized as the case of complex, entangled and fluid assemblages of actors, agencies and factors, beyond the unbundling perspective, encouraging critical scholars to reflect on what their own role in the critiqued system is (Bacevic, 2019). We all need to be honest and accept our own contribution to the current system unless we are investing efforts to change the status quo.

Digital data access and production have become an established part of contemporary market sector. Although digital data has become more central in communication and education, the development of cutting edge pedagogies to grapple with it continue to lag significantly (Selwyn, 2011). Little time is dedicated to developing and reinventing pedagogy, since this takes time, is risky, and does not seem to bring any direct financial benefits to universities. In many cases, as mentioned earlier, the same pedagogical practices are imported into VLEs, which mainly support linear exposition and expression (Bayne, 2008) in a world in which modularity and granularity of digital media designs and hypervisuality permeate students' lives. Staff time dedicated to discussion and engagement with teaching–learning methods and activities are scarce at research-intense universities. Such discussion about pedagogic innovation might be readily dismissed as potentially demotivating and an unnecessary impingement upon academic freedom (of how to teach) rather than being seen as collective professional development. However, other aspects of teaching such as digital supervision monitoring, filing and evaluation mechanisms might not be so readily classed as an impingement upon academic freedom.

Although the teaching–research nexus is celebrated and promoted, it is fair to say that "it needs nurturing locally" (Tight, 2016). This can be related to a common recognition of the need for research to be innovative and break new ground whereas an interest in teaching *methods* innovation lags behind. This pedagogical lagging behind happens while technology develops at high speed, offering new modes of learning experiences (Themelis & Sime, 2020) and new constructs of digital engagement, such as digital agency (DA) (Passey et al., 2018).

# The Teaching Challenge and Non-relational Practices

An imperative in promoting and developing innovative teaching and learning in universities today is commonly placed within the notion of neoliberal "human capital," focusing on human productivity and provision of services that makes HE yet another marketplace commodity (Parker, 2011). Ambition for university excellence and competitive advantage is unsurprising. Yet, under these conditions, innovative, and ground breaking interdisciplinary teaching and learning can suffer. In the current HE climate, academics are torn between two demands: 1) economic values—obtaining research funding, enhancing their research, publication and social media profile, following a policy agenda, securing satisfactory student feedback and employability, ticking boxes, answering e-mails, meeting deadlines and following rules; and 2) personal or collective teaching and learning values (Abbas & McLean, 2003),— co-teaching, developing innovation for new frontiers in pedagogy. Such developments can often be challenging, time-consuming and unpleasant for learners, as they take learners outside their comfort zone. Innovative teaching–learning practice is both messy and risky, it requires intense teaching support, and it may not result in what is conceptualized as desirable student satisfaction and feedback. It takes staff time that is often not valued or recognized as supporting career progress, thus sending implicit messages about what is valued and what to focus on instead. Therefore, teaching–learning and research methods in general seem not to be the priority for universities, and gaining substantial funding for merely developing or applying new methods seems to be nearly impossible. Given the increase in workloads over the last decade, especially for early-career academics, faculty feel the pressure to economize on teaching time, yet still meet all measures of efficiency targets, assessment and interactions. Attwood (2009) reports the findings on promotion policies of 104 UK universities:

> (u)niversities stand accused of hypocrisy ... over their claims to value teaching, after a major study of promotions policy and practice found that many are still failing to reward academics for leadership in pedagogy.

Attwood remarks that "one academic, speaking anonymously, said that while teaching and learning criteria were included in their university's promotion policies, they were not aware of anyone promoted on that basis." Many years after Attwood's (2009) commentary, the situation has hardly changed. Pedagogical leadership is a type of leadership that should be acknowledged as it contributes to the social good. It is certainly not easier than any other leadership, but it is much less valued than managerial or research leadership and profit in the contemporary university landscape. This is interesting in the context of British universities which are formally charities to serve the social good and act as not-for-profit organizations. These concerns can be further related to the HE "audit culture" issue (Shore, 2008). If universities become preoccupied with audit, then they start to worry about creating auditable "trails" (of teaching–learning). To satisfy the requirement of leaving such teaching–learning trails, there is no need for any notable innovation in teaching methods and resources or teaching–learning designs that take students on transformational journeys. Such transformational journeys are often liminal as they require grappling with new, subaltern approaches, concepts and theories that often shake up students' epistemologies and ontologies. Of course, academic teachers can and do innovate but, in many places, innovation in pedagogy or public engagement is placed at a lesser value than managerial or mentorship capacity. In such an environment, the need for accountability and targets per se is not critiqued; rather, the inflexible, and possibly unfair and oppressive practices and cultures that it may foster, such as toxic cultures or power, control, status, favoritism and competitive advantage tend to thrive. In such cultures, hegemonic types of managerialist and market practices, and words and phrases like professionalism, deadlines, proving oneself and one's worth dominate the struggle over the set targets, easily available and used to undermine unruly academics who disobey or underperform, perhaps owing to a different belief, competency or system of practice, or to personal struggles they encounter (Grey, 2013; Tett & Hamilton, 2019). As Blunden (2012, p. 9) argues

> the market is probably the most powerful and most characteristic institution of our times, but we also live in exceptionally bureaucratic times. Our lives are dominated by bureaucratic procedures which oblige us to endlessly tick boxes (…) This leads to the dominance of *formalism*.

And he continues: "Formalism has long been the dominant mode of thought, but the ubiquity of bureaucratism in our lives has made the 'art of handling concepts' a lost art" (ibid.). In the university context, this means that satisfying a stipulated learning efficiency target and deadline, becomes more important than maintaining a caring, relational and protective environment and interactions that can lead to transformative experiences and change for both students and staff.

While neoliberal efficiency is critiqued by many commentators in higher education, the very efficiency of publication and management activities as well as winning research grants, on the other hand, are the recognized and most valued prerequisites for moving up the career ladder (Gornall & Salisbury, 2012). Academic staff's mental health struggles are acknowledged to be situated in such an accelerated target-driven environment (Guthrie et al., 2018). Academia is becoming a space that celebrates and fosters a hyperproductive academic manager and researcher (Gornall & Salisbury, 2012), even applying meritocracy practices (Lawless & Chen, 2017). In such a climate, cherishing supportive and nurturing relationships and culture is stalled, although interpersonal relationships have a powerful impact that fluctuates between stimulating and demotivating for staff in educational environments (Schlichte, Yssel, & Merbier, 2005). When academic or administrative staff are not supported and appreciated for the merits of their work, and when they do not openly communicate when issues arise, they can become alienated and isolated from the working environment and each other (ibid.; Hill, 2017). Their work and well-being inevitably suffers. Such unsupportive working environments are essentially non-relational.

Administrative staff at universities should be applauded and valued for tackling ever-larger volumes of work in managing the ever-increasing demands of the university system and its regulations. It is hard work to make sure that the organization runs smoothly, and these professionals are important in acting as the spine of any departmental, faculty or organizational unit. What is problematic at the level of organizational or departmental culture is the lack of space for dialogue to build and cherish a supportive, relational and protective culture between administrative and academic staff, as well as between "senior" and "junior" staff, rather than maintain fragmented and differential relations (Kuo, 2009). Diversity and inclusion of students and staff are the legal and moral duty of universities, yet the need and right for a supportive environment is rarely acknowledged, nor is the need for diversity in communication, culture, working style and a safe-space dialogue. Each university staff member has unique strengths. Only the nurturing of collegial culture of recognition and support underpins healthy organizational relationships (Kuo, 2009), where all staff protect and celebrate each other by recognizing and building on individual unique strengths and roles to support the collective culture of "we" rather than "I." Unless we recognise we have all done something that someone else disagrees to and can complain about, we will not allow for a culture of care, compassion, dialogue and forgiveness, the culture that prevents gaslighting and silent treatment that many academics experience, especially women, racial and ethnic minorities (Cooke, 2019).

Further university changes include a maintenance of and an increase in fierce competition among universities via various policy strategies such as internationalization (Gao, 2015) and graduate employability (Lackovic, 2019). A strong rhetoric of university internationalization (Ryan, 2012; Speight, Lackovic, & Cooker, 2013) in many cases promotes overseas expansion and international student income rather than sociocultural, humanistic/ post-humanistic, and multicultural interactions or diversification of the curriculum (including diversification of methods) (Teichler, 2004; Ryan, 2011). HE institutions should help students develop and transform themselves by supporting the development of their relationship with knowledge (Ashwin, Abbas, & McLean, 2014), as socially, technologically and ecologically mindful human beings (Lackovic, 2019) prepared for informed action—rather than strongly driving them toward achieving prescribed results within universities as consumer-oriented corporate networks (Lynch, 2006; Molesworth, Nixon, & Scullion, 2009). This is especially relevant in the times of unstable economies and higher education systems that charge student fees.

Graduate employability is indisputably important. It would be hypocritical to claim otherwise from the comfortable position of a permanently employed academic, having obtained a doctoral degree, and having possessed something which was deemed a "competitive advantage" to gain my current employment position. However, most graduate employability conceptualizations to date have been concerned with the employment of individuals in relation to their individual gain, situated within a strong rhetoric and value system of an individualist marketplace. The issue with the current approaches and strategies toward graduate employability is that they observe graduate employment from the position of individualist separation between a closed-bubble employment market led by employers' needs (the work bubble) and external life (outside the work bubble) (Lackovic, 2019). As photographs and visual media embody the world's materiality, they can help explore many aspects of work and connections to the external world. Work is intrinsically linked to the material world through technologies that mediate tangible services and production, albeit this materiality aspect has been underplayed in dominant graduate employability approaches (ibid.). This creates a familiar dichotomy between work life and life outside work, although time spent at work occupies a huge amount of most individuals' time, therefore life. Work is also life, but do we treat it as life? Current higher education policy imperatives and employability agendas are intensely individualistic and instrumental; they rarely include complexities relating to society and materiality, such as technological and ecological precarity (Peters, Jandrić, & Means, 2019). The relationalities between employees and the external local community (close and intimate proximity), global society, technology and ecology (Lackovic, 2019) are rarely inquired into or explored within prevailing graduate employability policy and agendas. Yet, these relationalities are more important than ever in the current times of global sociopolitical and ecological crises. Universities need to explore them.

# The Link to Images: Image-Related (Re)Action and Resistance

Most critical publications on the neoliberal university and its characteristics merely offer critiques of the condition rather than possible ways of acting (Tett & Hamilton, 2019). I here consider possible actions in relation to images, adopting Tett and Hamilton's (2019, p. 2) views on *neoliberal resistance* as having many forms—not just political, collective and public activity, but also physical, material or symbolic action, action that subverts dominant discourses or practices. Pictorial images can act as reflections and counter-neoliberal artefacts and learning signs. As mentioned above in relation to employability, they can "bring in" the world's materiality into higher education spaces for critical reflection. I should emphasize that this book argues for a relational approach in knowledge and learning, as well as a relational approach in academic and university interactions and practices (Burkitt, 2016). One depends on the other, one cannot develop without the other; they are inseparable. This chapter has sketched difficult, almost unhealthy, pressures in academia that obstruct innovation and caring relationality in higher education teaching, management and staff relationships, as those pressures promote a *non-relational organizational and staff being*. This means that competitive and individualist modes of functioning are dominant, fostered by policies and research-led culture that reward such modes. Without open-minded, caring and protective systems and practices it is hard to make progress in nurturing relational higher education, which will in turn nurture relational pedagogies.

There could be various ways to integrate images and graphics into university teaching, research and social interactions, to counteract crude managerialist and surveillance-like use of technology and disconnection of staff. The considerations here are humble, presented as possible role of images as connective organizational threads. Sharing images with colleagues and staff across faculties and university can mediate HE relationships and understanding. This could be done by having institutional and departmental platforms for socialization, chats and general social connectedness that would challenge inherent institutional hierarchies and meritocracy by sharing practices, hobbies, interests and values, cherishing connections between early-career and senior staff, between administration and non-managerial staff, and so on. This is especially the case with new entrants to the academic profession, who need this kind of supportive connectedness (Knight & Trowler, 1999). This could be also done at the level of innovation and methodologies, by having a dedicated methodological or innovation center or institute at the level of an HE institution. Imagine a regular teaching exchange with colleagues across disciplines structured around "big" societal issues and challenges, where everyone discusses the ways that different communication modes and learning objects are and can be used in teaching and research, what works, what needs to be improved, and how this could be done. Inquiry graphics (IG) would be a part of such exchanges, among a number of other practices. Imagine developing a visual trail map to explore the impact that *any production cycle, which can be connected to most disciplines,* has on the planet and societies globally, without highlighting just its efficiency or its economically profitable impact. Such map already exists in some form as a part of Professor Caroline Knowles' project that explored and mapped a flip-flop production trail[1] (Knowles, 2014; see also Lackovic, 2019). This kind of mapping scenario and IG method could be something for inter-program and interdisciplinary teaching and research collaboration, as it relates to several domains—geography, politics, geopolitics, history, engineering, sociology, art, environmental studies, economics, philosophy, languages, and the interdisciplinary field of education. Such maps could be inquired into in-depth via the Production–Signification–Consumption method (Lackovic, 2020) introduced in Chap. 9, building on the three sites of image meaning-making, to explore the places of image or object creation, the representation itself, and consuming audiences.

Educators can use images to create maps of ideational and material (sociomaterial) relationalities linked to the concepts they teach, across space, time, matter and conceptualizations, akin to Walter Benjamin's *constellations.* As Gilloch (2013) puts it, Benjamin asks readers or scholars to become "aesthetic engineers" when "objects, edifices, texts and images are fragmented, broken and blasted from their usual context so that they

---

[1] http://www.flipfloptrail.com/

may be painstakingly recomposed in critically contemporary constellations" (p. 3). A map with images and videos can be used to infer and develop various relational multimodal constellations, to advance subject-specific or interdisciplinary knowledge and programs. Such a map can provide a bird's eye view by linking the macro global system and governance to more micro sociomaterial practices, for example, the micro practices of flip-flop material sourcing, production, assembling, trade and eventual disposal (Knowles, 2014), that can be explored from a variety of disciplinary perspectives.

The point is, universities have undergone some big changes, such as massification (Guri-Rosenblit, Sebková, & Teichler, 2007), digitalization and unbundling of services. The accountability demand of audit focuses on the evaluation of teaching and research practices such as TEF (Teaching Excellence Framework) and REF (Research Excellence Framework) in the UK (Oancea, 2019; Derrick, 2018), as well as marketization (Hemsley-Brown, & Oplatka, 2010), internationalization, and predominantly human-capital driven graduate employability strategies. Such developments can raise concerns around the quality of teaching, the continual erosion and stifling of innovation, pedagogic (teaching–learning) practice and research, and the shifting role of students (as consumers) and teachers (as service-providers, who are monitored and evaluated more and more, more readily penalized for mistakes than acknowledged for good practice). The sketched landscape of contemporary HE links to concerns with images, as this book proposes a new way of approaching knowledge, communication, teaching and research, from interdisciplinary and multimodal perspectives, which seek a development of new holistic methods, philosophy and relational cultures. This is a big challenge when HE teaching–learning practices are bending under the burden of so many policy imperatives, institutional and administrative requirements and rules (Cartney, 2013). This is the case despite research findings that, time and again, prove that what most students value is first and foremost their teaching–learning *experience* and teachers' *care* (Anderson et al., 2019), meaning that the teacher and teaching takes a central role in nurturing students' relationship to the discipline and their growth as responsible, well-rounded citizens. As a recent review on digital innovation in higher education suggests, it is a massive challenge for online pedagogies to be both inclusive and innovative or efficient and innovative (Lee, 2020), especially practices that are new (and "alternative") in terms of their underpinning logic, resources or designs, such as an IG approach.

Some argue that organizational changes are slow to happen (Eason, 1989). However, the issue might rather be *what change is deemed important and why*, as some changes may indeed be rapidly introduced and applied: costly digitalization and digital management systems, new physical learning spaces (buildings), general construction and expansion are clear examples of higher education materiality. Some other changes, perhaps less costly, happen slowly, such as techno-pedagogical and cultural innovation and progress, as well as related training/ professional development and resourcing. Universities should strive to develop and support innovative and creative teaching and learning (Loveless, 2011). Innovative teaching is a practice that fosters creativity (Loveless, 2011) and critical inquiry (Lipman, 2003; Mason, 2008) via diverse communication modes, and operates as a type of relational cross-boundary thinking across sign systems and disciplines. It is a type of transformative thinking that challenges the status quo, breaks new ground, prepares students for complex futures and cultivates capabilities to zoom on minute detail and link it to something large-scale. Creative and critical also means seeing the interconnectedness of the whole system, between human and non-human things, and among people.

In this chapter I have sketched the challenges of, mostly, British universities, although these challenges are becoming global. However, I sincerely want to avoid providing just an exclusive picture of academic gloom, doom and apocalypse. On the contrary, I would suggest that this chapter serves to promote and focus on what is good about higher education and what we should cherish and love (Budd, 2019). In fact, this book is by and large about this love. Academic work is far from being just a challenging space. I personally feel great enthusiasm for working in academia and find it very rewarding. It is still a highly creative, independent, collegial and fulfilling job, where everyone is uniquely positioned to contribute to society and knowledge, and to support and nurture their students and their colleagues. This needs to be voiced and celebrated by all colleagues in places and spaces that are contributing with life-changing and inspiring research, management, teaching and administrative work.

What I have flagged up is the difficulty of making changes in teaching, management, and culture, as well as novel approaches to educational theory and practice. It is a challenge to incorporate a relational engagement to people and practices in the described context. Such engagements are not quick fixes or quick illustrations. It requires time to initiate and implement changes that foster deep and slow thinking, relational living and being, inclusive and supportive practices, an integration of related digital and multimodal resources, methods and assessment. Stakeholders' dialogue, management support and all-staff connectedness are needed to cherish relational approaches to higher education. An inquiry graphics is a humble part of relational approaches to help in academia healing, progress and celebration of the things we love about it. This might be challenging, but it is both needed and possible.

# References

Abbas, A., & McLean, M. (2003). Communicative competence and the improvement of university teaching: Insights from the field. *British Journal of Sociology of Education, 24*, 69–82.

Anderson, V., Rabello, R., Wass, R., Golding, C., Rangi, A., Eteuati, E., Bristowe, Z., & Waller, A. (2019). Good teaching as care in higher education. *Higher Education, 79*, 1–19.

Ashwin, P., Abbas, A., & McLean, M. (2014). How do students' accounts of sociology change over the course of their undergraduate degrees? *Higher Education, 67*(2), 219–234.

Attwood, R. (2009). Pedagogy a poor second in promotion. *Times Higher Education*, online version published on 10/12/2009. Retrieved from: https://www.timeshighereducation.com/news/pedagogy-a-poor-second-in-promotions/409511.article

Bacevic, J. (2019). With or without U? Assemblage theory and (de) territorialising the university. *Globalisation, Societies and Education, 17*(1), 78–91.

Bayne, S. (2008). Higher education as a visual practice: Seeing through the virtual learning environment. *Teaching in Higher Education, 13*, 395–410.

Blin, F., & Munro, M. (2008). Why hasn't technology disrupted academics' teaching practices? Understanding resistance to change through the lens of activity theory. *Computers & Education, 50*, 475–490.

Blunden, A. (2012). *Concepts: A critical approach* (Vol. 44). Leiden, Netherlands: Brill.

Breuer, E., & Archer, A. (Eds.). (2016). Multimodality in higher education. Brill, Boston.

Budd, R. (2019/accepted/in press). Looking for love in the student experience. In N. Hogson, J. Vlieghe, & P. Zamojski (Eds.), *Post-critical perspectives on higher education: Retrieving the educational in the university* (Debating Higher Education). Springer.

Burkitt, I. (2016). Relational agency: Relational sociology, agency and interaction. *European Journal of Social Theory, 19*(3), 322–339.

Cartney, P. (2013). Researching pedagogy in a contested space. *British Journal of Social Work*, 1–18.

Castells, M. (1996). *The rise of the network society, Volume I of The information age: Economy, society and culture*. Reading, MA: Blackwell Publishing.

Cooke, N. A. (2019). Impolite hostilities and vague sympathies: Academia as a site of cyclical abuse. *Journal of Education for Library and Information Science, 60*(3), 223–230.

Cranmer, S. (2019, April). How teachers' inclusionary and exclusionary pedagogical practices manifest in disabled children's uses of technologies in schools. In *Sustainable ICT, education and learning conference*.

Crook, C., & Lackovic, N. (2017). Images of educational practice: How school websites represent digital learning. In *Handbook on digital learning for K-12 schools* (pp. 75–90). Cham, Switzerland: Springer.

Derrick, G. (2018). *The evaluators' eye: Impact assessment and academic peer review*. Springer.

Eason, K. D. (1989). *Information technology and organisational change*. Hoboken, NJ: CRC Press.

Fuchs, C. (2008). *Internet and society: Social theory in the information age*. New York: Psychology Press.

Gabriel, M., Campbell, B., Wiebe, S., MacDonald, R. J., & McAuley, A. (2012). The role of digital technologies in learning: Expectations of first year university students/Le rôle des technologies numériques dans l'apprentissage: Les attentes des étudiants de première année universitaire. *Canadian Journal of Learning and Technology/La revue canadienne de l'apprentissage et de la technologie 38*.

Gao, Y. (2015). Constructing internationalisation in flagship universities from the policy-maker's perspective. *Higher Education, 70*(3), 359–373.

Gilloch, G. (2013). *Walter Benjamin: Critical constellations*. New York: Wiley.

Gornall, L., & Salisbury, J. (2012). Compulsive working, 'hyperprofessionality' and the unseen pleasures of academic work. *Higher Education Quarterly, 66*(2), 135–154.

Grey, S. J. (2013). Activist academics: What future? *Policy Futures in Education, 11*(6), 700–711.

Guri-Rosenblit, S., Sebková, H., & Teichler, U. (2007). Massification and diversity of higher education systems: Interplay of complex dimensions. *Higher Education Policy, 20*, 373–389.

Guthrie, S., Lichten, C. A., Van Belle, J., Ball, S., Knack, A., & Hofman, J. (2018). Understanding mental health in the research environment: A rapid evidence assessment. *Rand health quarterly, 7*(3).

Hallewell, M. J., & Lackovic, N. (2017). Do pictures 'tell' a thousand words in lectures? How lecturers vocalise photographs in their presentations. *Higher Education Research & Development, 36*(6), 1166–1180.

Hemsley-Brown, J., & Oplatka, I. (2010). Market orientation in universities: A comparative study of two national higher education systems. *International Journal of Educational Management, 24*, 204–220.

Henderson, M., Finger, G., & Selwyn, N. (2016). What's used and what's useful? Exploring digital technology use (s) among taught postgraduate students. *Active Learning in Higher Education, 17*(3), 235–247.

Henderson, M., Selwyn, N., Finger, G., & Aston, R. (2015). Students' everyday engagement with digital technology in university: Exploring patterns of use and 'usefulness'. *Journal of Higher Edu-cation Policy and Management, 37*(3), 308–319.

Hill, Y. (2017). Loneliness as an occupational hazard. Narratives of loneliness. In O. Sagan & E. D. Miller (Eds.), *Narratives of lonileness: Multidisciplinary perspectives from the 21st century*. London: Routledge.

Jandrić, P. (2017). *Learning in the age of digital reason*. New York: Springer.

JISC. (2009). Higher education in a web 2.0 world [WWW document]. http://www.jisc.ac.uk/publications/generalpublications/2009/heweb2.aspx#downloads

Johnson, L., Adams, S., Cummins, M., Estrada, V., Freeman, A., & Ludgate, H. (2013). *The NMC horizon report: 2013 higher education edition*.

Knight, P. T., & Trowler, P. R. (1999). It takes a village to raise a child: Mentoring and the socialisation of new entrants to the academic professions. *Mentoring & Tutoring, 7*(1), 23–34.

Knowles, C. (2014). *Flip-flop: A journey through globalisation's backroads*. London: Pluto.

Kuo, H. M. (2009). Understanding relationships between academic staff and administrators: An organisational culture perspective. *Journal of Higher Education Policy and Management, 31*(1), 43–54.

Lackovic, N. (2010a). Creating and reading images: Towards a communication framework for higher education learning. In *Seminar. Net: Media, technology & life-long learning* (pp. 121–135).

Lackovic, N. (2019). Graduate employability (GE) paradigm shift: Towards greater socio-emotional and eco-technological relationalities of graduates' futures. In M. Peters, P. Jandrić, & A. Means (Eds.), *Education and technological unemployment* (pp. 193–212). Singapore: Springer.

Lackovic, N. (2020). Thinking with digital images in the post-truth era: A method in critical media literacy. In *Postdigtial science and education*. Springer.

Lawless, B., & Chen, Y. W. (2017). Multicultural neoliberalism and academic labor: Experiences of female immigrant faculty in the US academy. *Cultural Studies↔ Critical Methodologies, 17*(3), 236–243.

Lee, K. (2020). Openness and innovation in online higher education: A historical review of the two discourses. *Open Learning: The Journal of Open, Distance and e-Learning, 24*, 1–21.

Lipman, M. (2003). *Thinking in education*. Cambridge, UK: Cambridge University Press.

Loveless, A. (2011). Didactic analysis as a creative process: Pedagogy for creativity with digital tools. In *Beyond fragmentation: Didactics, learning and teaching in Europe* (pp. 239–251). Verlag Barbara Budrich.

Lynch, K. (2006). Neo-liberalism and marketisation: The implications for higher education. *European Educational Research Journal, 5*, 1–17.

Mason, M. (2008). *Critical thinking and learning*. New York: Wiley.

Molesworth, M., Nixon, E., & Scullion, R. (2009). Having, being and higher education: The marketisation of the university and the transformation of the student into consumer. *Teaching in Higher Education, 14*, 277–287.

Oancea, A. (2019). Research governance and the future(s) of research assessment. *Palgrave Communications*. Palgrave Macmillan (part of Springer Nature). doi:https://doi.org/10.1057/s41599-018-0213-6

Palmer, M., Simmons, G., & Hall, M. (2013). Textbook (non-) adoption motives, legitimizing strategies and academic field configuration. *Studies in Higher Education, 38*(4), 485–505.

Parker, L. (2011). University corporatisation: Driving redefinition. *Critical Perspectives on Accounting, 22*, 434–450.

Passey, D., Shonfeld, M., Appleby, L., Judge, M., Saito, T., & Smits, A. (2018). Digital agency: Empowering equity in and through education. *Technology, Knowledge and Learning, 23*(3), 425–439.

Peters, M. A., Jandrić, P., & Means, A. (2019). *Education and technological unemployment*. Singapore: Springer.

Robertson, S., & Komljenovic, J. (2016). 13 Unbundling the university and making higher education markets. *World Yearbook of Education 2016: The Global Education Industry*, 211–239.

Ryan, J. (2011). Teaching and learning for international students: Towards a transcultural approach. *Teachers and Teaching, 17*, 631–648.

Ryan, J. (2012). Internationalisation of doctoral education: Possibilities for new knowledge and understandings. *Australian Universities' Review, 54*, 55–63.

Scardamalia, M., & Bereiter, C. (2006). Knowledge building: Theory, pedagogy, and technology. In K. Sawyer (Ed.), Cambridge Handbook of the Learning Sciences (pp. 97–118). New York: Cambridge University Press.

Schlichte, J., Yssel, N., & Merbler, J. (2005). Pathways to burnout: Case studies in teacher isolation and alienation. *Preventing School Failure: Alternative Education for Children and Youth, 50*(1), 35–40.

Selwyn, N. (2011). *Education and technology: Key issues and debates*. Continuum International Publishing Group.

Selwyn, N. (2014). *Digital technology and the contemporary university*. London: Routledge.

Shore, C. (2008). Audit culture and illiberal governance: Universities and the politics of accountability. *Anthropological Theory, 8*, 278–298.

Speight, S., Lackovic, N., & Cooker, L. (2013). The contested curriculum: Academic learning and employability in higher education. *Tertiary Education and Management, 19*, 112–126.

Srnicek, N. (2017). *Platform capitalism*. Wiley.

Teichler, U. (2004). The changing debate on internationalisation of higher education. *Higher Education, 48*, 5–26.

Tett, L., & Hamilton, M. (2019). Introduction: Resisting neoliberalism in education. In L. Tett, & M. Hamilton (Eds.), *Resisting neoliberalism in education: Local, national and transnational perspectives* (pp. 1–13). Policy Press.

Themelis, C., & Sime, J. A. (2020). From video-conferencing to holoportation and haptics: How emerging technologies can enhance presence in online education? In *Emerging technologies and pedagogies in the curriculum* (pp. 261–276). Singapore: Springer.

Tight, M. (2016). Examining the research/teaching nexus. *European Journal of Higher Education, 6*(4), 293–311.

White, E. J. (2014). Bakhtinian dialogic and Vygotskian dialectic: Compatabilities and contradictions in the classroom? *Educational Philosophy and Theory, 46*(3), 220–236.

# 3

# Educational Semiotics and Peirce's Triadic Sign in Higher Education

Why approach higher education practices with digital images from a semiotic perspective, and what does that mean? What is a sign? What is educational semiotics? What is a photographic sign building on Peirce's relational tripartite sign model? What is an inquiry graphic sign that incorporates digital photographs and concepts (in a disciplinary domain)? This chapter tackles these questions. It introduces a semiotic approach to education with inquiry graphics (IG). It illustrates an inquiry graphic sign, its roots in educational semiotics and Peirce's triadic sign model of meaning making, proposing a new approach to communication and learning in higher education.

## Communication and Meaning Making Beyond the Verbal

Language-centered theories, teaching and research have been adopted as normative in higher education studies and research, in most postgraduate courses and practices in Education (at MA, EdD or PhD level, commonly located at schools and departments of education or educational

© The Author(s) 2020
N. Lacković, *Inquiry Graphics in Higher Education*,
https://doi.org/10.1007/978-3-030-39387-8_3

research). Semiotic and multimodal underpinnings of communication are new to most students in higher education studies, as they are not often presented with higher education practices that are at the same time graphic/ pictorial from one side and deep, reflective and critical from the other. This is my experience within postgraduate education modules I have either led or assisted on for more than nine years at the moment of writing, with a large number of international and British students. When first encountered, the approaches of semiotics, visual and multimodal knowledge development and exploration are new to most, though certainly not all, learners in postgraduate education programs. These approaches can create strange, subaltern and liminal feelings. This is not surprising, because pictures and non-verbal modes of communication are still positioned as alternative rather than equally intellectual "higher" modes of communication in higher education (Lackovic, 2016). At times, these forms of engagements are even viewed as "non-academic" and "unnecessary", or an area for people who are *artsy* or creative or, at least, artistically inclined. This is the common legacy of our generally and widespread symbols-driven (verbal and numerical) educational background and traditions in the field of higher education studies or teaching practices. They mostly exclude rather than combine pictorial and other modes of communication and the importance of semiosis/interpretative mind work in education and life (recall Table 1.1). Yet, semiotics is not something new.

C.S. Peirce arrived at a mature version of his semiotics at the beginning of the twentieth century. Many schools of semiotics sprang up in the twentieth and twenty-first century (e.g. the French or Nordic strands). I do not intend to reinvent the wheel but I do intend to re-imagine and develop Peirce's semiotics in relation to images as signs beyond icons or indices, not inferior signs but compound icon-index-symbol signs, in the context of higher education practice and education studies, which is a new approach. It is a part of a semiotic theory of learning, which includes language and expands into other modes of communication. Simply put, semiotics is the study of signs, which can also be understood as a theory of meaning, tackling how signs exist (make meaning) in society (Hodge & Kress, 1988, p. 1). Kress argues that one cannot have a theory of learning without a theory of meaning, however implicit that may be; a theory of learning always entails a theory of meaning; meaning is the stuff of semiotics. Semiotically, sign-making is meaning-making, and learning is the result of these processes. (Kress, 2009, p. 28)

This means that meaning-making is central to learning. Images and graphics are signs in communication. Therefore, they are signs in and of education. Knorr-Cetina and Amann (1990) show that even a reading of a conventional image sign, such as radiograph in medicine, involves much meaning negotiation and sociocultural conditioning. They point out that the reading of medical radiographs evokes many other spaces and contexts which are virtually present at the moment of reading: the past (what caused it) and the future (what to predict), embodied practice (the description of personal experience relevant to the understanding of it), and scenic descriptions and behaviors (Knorr-Cetina & Amann, 1990). The natural sciences developed exponentially due to the improvement of realist drawing techniques in the Renaissance (today we have the development of 3D computer modeling). But meanings, as argued earlier, even if derived from conventional images, are not fixed (recall the discussion in Chap. 1). This is particularly so if we consider how the meaning of an abstract concept is expressed. By an abstract concept I mean a concept used to signify a scientific and generalised theory/ idea/ concept /experience/ feeling/ understanding rather than a *concrete* thing, activity or materiality. In social sciences, such concepts are terms such as social justice, habitus, power, economy, liberty, democracy, and so on.

Abstract concepts are central to most higher education disciplines. To remind the reader of the point made in Chap. 1, an image can only illustrate an aspect or instance of any abstract concept and can never embody the wealth of conceptual possibilities that a concept contains by its character of being "abstract." Subject and disciplinary concepts are not closed but open-ended concept entities with a wide variation of how they can exist via material and social events or instances (this view of concepts will be explained in Chap. 5). Therefore, sharing diverse images and image interpretations of abstract concepts (e.g., empiricism, cognitive load or constructivism), as will be empirically illustrated in this book via inquiry graphics (IG) designs in Chaps. 7 and 8, can enrich concept understanding and exemplify heterogeneous and plural concept character. Images can bring insights about relationships of concepts to many aspects of our world life and stress the multiplicity in the variations of concept meanings. Such an understanding of relationality and plurality of meanings is essential to understand the plurality of life, personal and collective experiences, thus challenging divisive rhetoric and otherness of any kind (Greer & Jewkes, 2005; Kull, 2008; Olteanu, 2019), by fostering a relational approach to knowledge and ultimately, life.

When students express their thoughts using pictorial representations and, subsequently, discuss them in a form of multiple representations as applied in the learning design presented in the empirical part of the book (Chap. 8), they are engaging in an act of communication. Communication is properly seen as the process whereby participating actors *produce and exchange meanings* (Hodge & Kress, 1988, 1), this exchange being the subject of interpretation and the crucial activity for the existence of human culture (Hall, 1997, 2). Apart from communication as the active reading of and reaction to others' signs and messages, communication has been also defined as a "social process, within a context, in which signs are produced and transmitted, perceived, and treated as messages from which meaning can be inferred" (Worth & Gross, 1974, 30). The communication process is not understood in my view as a straightforward input–output mechanism or knowledge "acquisition," the view that dominated teaching-learning designs for a long time under the influence of strongly behaviorist and cognitivist approaches to learning, but as an expansive and contextualized thinking process that depends on semiotic inference, interpretation and prior experience. If by communication in education we indeed mean, in part, that we infer messages by "reading" each other's signs, we need to evolve an understanding of what signs are and provide opportunities for students to express their own sign systems and interpretations of educational signs.

## What Is a Sign?

Ferdinand De Saussure and Charles Sanders Peirce (commonly referred to as the 'fathers' of semiotics (Crow, 2003), albeit different in their semiotic theories), provided the basis of what the sign is and how it works to produce meaning. De Saussure (2011)'s linguistic reasoning divided the sign into a "signifier" and "signified" (see also Kress & van Leeuwen, 1996, p. 5). According to De Saussure (2011), a signifier is the *form* of the sign, and the signified is what the sign *means* (the *concept* it represents). Together, the signifier and the signified form a sign (De Saussure, 2011; Chandler, 2002, p. 53).

However, this is not an unproblematic distinction, which is where Peirce's semiotics is very revealing. Our knowledge of the sign's Object (what a word or a picture refers to) is not the same as the sign form and is always specific to our prior experiences and subject to our interpretation (Interpretant). In that way, the sign has three components, as introduced in Chap. 1: Representamen, as the sign vehicle (e.g. the form), the meaning (Interpretant) and what the sign vehicle/ form refers to (its Object). In an illustration of de Saussure's sign (Fig. 3.1 above), Chandler (1994) shows de Saussure's (2011) semiotic view, by explaining the meaning stemming from the word "tree," by virtue of its linguistic structure (a specific combination of letters written or pronounced vocally), acting as a *signifier*. The *signified* is for de Saussure an understanding of what that word relates to (represents, signifies)—it would be a mental awareness (image scheme) that it is a specific plant (a tree in this case). However, "tree" on its own (either as a word or a drawing of a tree, or an existence of a tree in the world) contains elements with a potential for many other meanings related to the word such as branches, leaf, and trunk and what these mean in different contexts and for different organisms,[1] which

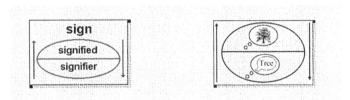

**Fig. 3.1** De Saussure's sign: digital illustration of signifier and signified. (Source: Chandler, 1994, building on de Saussure, 2011, p. 61)

---

[1] The work by Jakob von Uexküll (1982) and other semioticians (e.g., Thomas E. Sebeok, Kallevi Kull and John Deely) tackles the notion of *Umwelt*, the world and its meaning as experienced by a particular organism; the main premise of this approach is that organisms can have different *Umwelten*, even of the same environment, which accounts for an environment having a pluralistic

allows further exploration of what a tree is. Each of its constituent parts has its own meaning-making potential. Exploring the sign's form for further meanings is different with a picture of a tree than when encountering the writing or the verbal utterance of a "tree." This is because pictorial representation can immediately depict the "details" of the tree (the mentioned branch, leaf and trunk; the state of branching or leaves' changing color, bark texture, ants on the bark, and so on) which can in their own right act as sources of creative reflection and innovative insight, not that quickly and overtly brought to our awareness by the linguistic/verbal form "tree." This character of the depicted form to represent a potential for various meanings explorations when a picture is associated with a concept is at the core of inquiry graphics.

De Saussure's dyadic sign does not assert the actual reality and existence of the Object that the form relates to, even if the existence is imaginary (e.g., we can imagine a unicorn). By including this assertive component of meaning, Peirce's semiotics represents a holistic, philosophical, logical and encompassing take on *meaning-making*, or *semiosis*. The triadic approach allowed for the formation of Peirce's entire system of semiotics, logic, philosophy, ontology and epistemology.[2] Essential to Peircean semiotics is the principle of *semiosis*, "the triadic nature of the operation of the sign or the unceasing action of the sign" (Chandler, 1994, p. 39). By introducing a triadic relationship of sign-action, Peirce emphasizes the fact that a sign has some form (Representamen) to represent something else (its Object, which can be an idea or a concrete sensed thing) to some mind that interprets it (Interpretant). The concept of Interpretants is particularly insightful for education. It is useful for explaining the coming together of many minds to interpret educational texts, or images or scientific experiments, hence this heterogeneity of meaning and mind's prior knowledge and experience must be taken into consideration in educational environments. Inquiry graphics methods

---

character (as an environment of different beings). This can also apply for a group of humans, even if the differences in observing the same environment are minute. Differences of interpreting the same environment by a diverse group of people can also be rather big.

[2] Such as the three basic categories of sign as icon, index, and symbol, or views on truth, progress, knowledge and fallibilism (e.g. truth of the Object as an unreachable sign to human interpretation) (Almeder, 1980, p. 47).

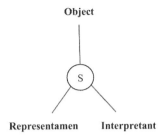

**Fig. 3.2** C.S. Peirce's triadic sign model

aim to externalize learners' interpretations and highlights the collective and sharing component of knowledge, in line with Peirce's ideas of science as collective endeavor (CP, 1.549; 2.537; 2.428; 5.569; 6.494). Interpretants need to be expressed in education, not just by the teacher but by learners[3] to support externalization of learners' prior and current knowledge and world views and sharing and negotiating of meanings in communities of inquiry.

Peirce's semiosis can be shown as a diagram with a central node, different from the commonly used triangle (Olteanu, 2019), such as the one shown in Fig. 3.2, building on Merrell's (2005, p. 28) diagrammatic sign triad. In any case, whether represented as a triangle or three tentacles with the central sign node representation, it is important to acknowledge that the three entities happen simultaneously, not sequentially. The pictorial (e.g. photographic) sign tripartite semiosis thus can be represented via the three sign elements (themselves also signs) building on Fig. 3.2, which are the constituents of an inquiry graphic sign and analysis:

- **Representamen** (the existence of the sign potential for meaning-making, such as some form or sensation. Peirce's representamen[4] is not just an

---

[3] A common criticism of semiotics is that it is subject to *individual* interpretative faculties, for talented individuals, e.g., Barthes or Eco, with a knack for interpretative and imaginative writing; however, one of the goals of inquiry graphics is to engage learners or research participants in interpretation, so that *multiple sign interpretations* are externalized to some extent and shared to develop knowledge or support research results stemming from those diverse interpretations.

[4] Peirce's Representamen does not only refer to the form of a sign but, more generally, to the sign's relation to itself, which could be expressed as form. The three ingredients of the schematic sign are interconnected.

embodied representational form, but my interpretation will focus on pictorial signs as embodied signs with embodied representamen.

- **Interpretant**, namely the interpretation/ meaning (conclusion) of the sign, as made by an interpreter, including emotions/reaction/action, and
- **Object** or that what the sign (or Representamen) refers to (Hodge & Kress, 1988, p. 20; Crow, 2003) (e.g., an object in the external or imaginary world, or an abstract concept).

Smith (2010, p. 38) provides another definition of sign that appeared in a 1908 letter from Peirce to Victoria Lady Welby (Hardwick, 1977, pp. 80–81):

> I define a Sign as anything which is so determined by something else, called its Object, and so determines an effect upon a person, which effect I call its Interpretant, that the latter is thereby mediated by the former. (Smith, 2010, p. 38)

Although these explanations include a person involved in the process of semiosis, Peirce made it explicit that the sign is a universal phenomenon in the world, and not just an entity subject to interpretation by the human mind (Smith, 2010). Therefore, the same sign or environment can have different meanings to different organisms and humans, the view aligned with von Uexküll's (1982) notion of *Umwelt*, the same environment that can have different meanings for different organisms. Peirce's semiotics allows for a view of education and knowledge development beyond anthropocentrism; hence it carried the germs of post-humanism before the term was even coined.

Merrel (2001) describes Peirce's triadic sign model (in Fig. 3.2) with these words, to emphasize the interpretative character of knowledge and understanding the world:

> I will allude to Peirce's object as the "semiotic object", for it is that to which the sign relates. The semiotic object can never be identical to the "real" object, since according to Peirce our knowledge is never absolute. Our knowledge can be no more than an approximation to the "real" world exactly as it is, or better, is becoming. Hence, in a manner of putting it, the

"semiotically real object" we smell, taste, touch, hear, and see is never identical to the "really real object." We simply can't know the world just as it is becoming: our minds are too limited, and it is too subtle and complex. Consequently, since this "real object" cannot be completely known once and for all, it can never be more than "semiotically real" for its interpreters. The third component of the sign is the interpretant. It is, roughly speaking and sufficient for our purpose, close to what we would usually take as the sign's meaning.

One of Peirce's definitions of a sign often quoted is: "A sign, or representamen, is something which stands to somebody for something in some respect or capacity" (CP 2.228). In this definition Peirce draws a clear parallel between a sign and representamen. Peirce's own definitions of the sign and representamen have varied over time (see Benedict, 1985, and Nöth, 2011). The Representamen in the present work focuses on the materially visible, identifiable and qualitatively describable content of a photographic representation (Fig. 3.3), adapting Peirce's definition of representamen as "the concrete subject that represents." (CP 1.540). My interpretation closely relates to Elleström's (2014) interpretation of representamen for the study of media and arts, focusing on pictorial materiality as a material instance, *an aspect of Representamen*. It also relates to Peirce's definition of iconic sign as "any *material image*, (such) as a painting (MS, 478, pp. 45–6)" quoted by Freadman (2001 n/a; my

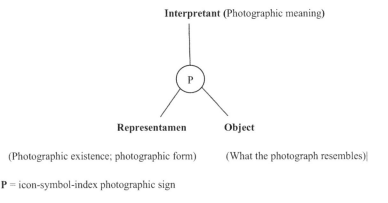

**Fig. 3.3**  A triadic model of how photographs (P) signify, building on C.S. Peirce

emphasis). As such, it could be also proposed that the Representamen version adopted here is to some extent closest to semiotic terms "tokens" and "replica" (Parker, 1998), as: "(a) replica is the vehicle of the sign. It is composed of ink, sound waves, or some physical stuff (Nöth, 2011, p. 456; Parker, 1998, p. 153)". I focus on the quality of a digital photograph to represent its object by embodying it (the form observed on the screen or the printed photograph). I acknowledge that this is a specific and focused interpretation of Representamen. Perhaps the term to be used here for Representamen is sign's embodiment, as suggested by Nöth (2011, p. 461). I continue the discussion with reference to such an embodied, photographic representamen.

In terms of the elaborately explained Peirce's triadic meaning-making model or diagram, how then do pictures make meaning? Let us consider a photographic picture as the main semiotic sign explored in this book as thinking mediator, presented earlier. The Peircean triadic model (CP 1.541) of meaning-making can be translated into the photographic meaning-making (Fig. 3.3), revealing the iconic sign therein as consisting of: (1) Representamen, the pixels of digital image form that to human eyes look like observable shapes and "things," an embodied representamen, or embodied sign vehicle; (2) similar in looks to the Object that the photograph stands for; and (3) Interpretant, the *meaning* which an interpreter concludes from the observed photograph in context.

Applied to photographs, Peirce's triadic sign can help understand the difference between the sign's object itself and the embodied representamen. These three sign nodes are interpretative, inseparable, emerging and relational. A photograph acts as a compound sign in digital communication, an *icon–index–symbol sign*. A photograph is iconic, because it signifies according to the similarity (near-to-isomorphic resemblance) between its object and its embodied representational form (representamen). Such type of signification by similarity is a characteristic of an iconic sign. In addition, a photograph is also an indexical sign, as it signals the existence of the object it shows (CP, 4.447), a kind of physical and existential relations to it. If there is a photograph, there exists a physical photographic object that it represents, unless the photographic representation is manipulated. Furthermore, when entering and supporting communication purposes, a photograph acts as a symbol, to signify a conventionally assigned and habituated idea/concept. A symbolic photograph that plays with collective desire (e.g., by constant repetition and reuse in the media), is what Barthes (2009/1972) called a "myth", such as a photograph of some woman being a symbol for femininity. This view of a compound communication sign also echoes Nöth's (2011, p. 461) reference to Santaella (2003, p. 51), who posits that "without its indexical ingredient, the symbol would have no power of reference, and without its iconic ingredient it would have no power to signify."

To further exemplify photographic sign's embodiment and meaning, I would recall some of the arguments from Chap. 1 on media images: photographs are often used in the media to embody abstract concepts. The concept of climate change can be embodied via a variety of photographs that can stand to represent something about the climate change. An abstract concept is imagined by humans via linking it to its concrete manifestations (Tateo, 2018), for example via photographs. The photograph itself shows something concrete that has happened or can happen in the world. In the case of the present concept example (climate change), this can be a melting ice floe. However, the embodied representation is not the concept itself. A photograph of an ice floe embodies an actual ice floe existing in the world and a general concept of an ice floe as its object. If this photograph is used to represent the concepts of climate change or global warming, then it has an assigned conceptual object, used to illustrate an existing or possible manifestation of that abstract concept, an aspect of the concept. The conceptual (symbolic) object is integrated into the embodied iconic object, turning the photograph into a symbolic representation of the concept. In other words, when a viewer sees a photograph of melting polar ice, the viewer can adopt the interpretation of this embodied representamen as a symbol of the climate change or global warming, accompanied by an affective reaction linked to it, such as anger, indifference or sadness. Concepts such as ice floe, rivers, water, soil, oil, trousers, house are all concrete concepts that exist in our sensed physical reality. However, a vast number of concepts, perhaps the majority of concepts that humans use in communication and place affective and ontological importance on, are abstract concepts. These are the concepts such as love, happiness, security, belonging, democracy, economy. In society, we learn to imagine and conceptualize abstract concepts, building on our personal, environmental, and educational background, as well as our corporeal and affective experiences (Tateo, 2018). Educators need to support learners to engage with these interpretative nuances and how images and concepts are consistently linked in life, education and the media.

## Peircean Semiotic Signification: More on Truth, Fallibilism, and Non-anthropocentrism

As introduced above in relation to Peirce's "semiotic object," as humans, we always interpret what we see, hence we cannot know and grasp an absolute truth of the sign (its object). It is so because we only know a semiotic reality, as "our knowledge is never absolute, but always swims, as it were, in a continuum of uncertainty and of indeterminacy." (Almeder, 1980, p. 47) This is important for tackling the meaning of any sign in communication. By understanding the primacy and limitation of our interpretative faculties and their intrinsic connection to corporeality through affect and other physical sensations (Tateo, 2018), we can acknowledge and explore corporeality/embodiment of interpretation (Olteanu, 2017). We can focus on inquiry of a sign in as many details as this is possible, to cultivate semiotic awareness. By claiming that all human knowledge is fallible, Peirce does not reject the pursuit of truth as scientific fact and goal (Almeder, 1980). Rather, he stresses the continuity of scientific and other types of knowledge and consistent growth thereof via signs, emphasizing the constant evolution and indeterminacy of meaning, what he calls *synechism* (Almeder, 1980, p. 47; CP, 1.549; 2.537; 2.428; 5.569; 6.494). By their triadic constitution, the primary goal of signs is evolution. As signs change over time, a view of signs' and concepts' fluid, pluralist and developmental character is central to Peirce's semiotics and an IG approach to concepts and conceptual development (elaborated in Chap. 5). What is possible (albeit still difficult) for humans is to reach an agreed "irreversible" opinion about the sign-object and provide factual statement (interpretant) about the sign that is accepted as some law or theory or scientific concept. This would preferably be reached by most diverse research and scientific communities in one field, across disciplines, including diverse public. If there are two competing interpretations of, and approaches to, one thing, it means to ask why it is so, and what can be done to reach an informed conclusion.

Contemporary signs, such as digital media information, are mainly anthropocentric, made by, for and about humans, even when they talk about nature, chemicals or animals. They are also dominant. This means that they promote a dominant and preferred concept interpretation by some humans, rather than a well-researched concept interpretation. They also often disregard the layered meanings of the visible and invisible forms of the world and life that contribute to meaning making. A photograph shared in the media commonly shows some material things captured in the world. By representing things existing in the world, digital photographs, in the context of media captions and texts and on their own, can suggest meanings about those things and can suggest action in relation to those things (to interpreters). An embodied representamen of a photograph can adopt conceptual–symbolic meaning, which differs for different interpreters. Even concrete, physical objects do not have singular meanings.

If I am in front of a house, the existence of that house at that moment in my world is true, as an object made of hard material with specific compositional characteristics, its existential material form (the embodied representamen). I can treat a house as a sign that I can use in communication. The definition of house represents an agreement (among assigned scientific and linguistic community) on what the most general and supposedly most widely accepted meaning of house is to call it a house. The English Oxford dictionary says that it is "a building for human habitation" (a part of the definition), but we know very well that animals and plants can and do dwell in houses: pets, plants, tiny animals like spiders and ants, different forms of matter, invisible things such as microbes, and so on. We also know that house is connected to many affective and aesthetic meanings assigned to it. When considering an emotional attachment to the house, the house becomes a home. Whether it has high ceilings or low ceilings makes a difference in terms of how it feels. Therefore, by being embedded in the complex sociomaterial world (Fenwick, Edwards, & Sawchuk, 2015), the house is so much more than the existential truth of its matter or its dictionary definition. Things and visual signs that embody them carry complex and varied meanings. What humans can grasp and define is very much like truth, but not the very truth itself:

> we are so far from ever being authorized to conclude that a theory is the very truth itself, that we can never so much as understand what that means. Light is electromagnetic vibrations, that is to say, it is (something) very like that. In order to say that it is precisely like that, we should have to know precisely what we mean by electro-magnetic vibrations. Now we can never know precisely what we mean by any description whatever. (Almeder, 1980, p. 47)

Knowledge is always in a continual state of development and flow, with current scientific knowledge and facts being relatively fixed knowledge in and of the time-up-to-now. This is aligned with the definition of a concept or conceptions put forward by Dewey and Bentley (2005/1960) as something that is a current state of accumulated knowledge in a field. Description involves meaning-making. Concepts in disciplines are agreed/ authorized descriptions of theoretical views in disciplines. Science and education evolve to give way to new truths, as pictures and science develop aligned with the spirit of historical eras. For several centuries the Earth was believed to be flat, and the center of the universe. Even today some hold on to this belief, although it is not accepted science. Once, diseases were treated with bloodsucking leeches as a dominant scientific truth and medical method of the time. Even contemporary approaches to how the body and mind work have been evolving and changing in last few decades.

The above stated fragility of knowing the truth of the object or the true object of a pictorial sign can be exemplified as a possible theme of *The Treachery of Images* (Fig. 3.4), the painting by Belgian artist René Magritte. The artist produced a plethora of paintings that blurred the boundary between words and images, real and imaginary, concept and picture. In *The Treachery of Images*, the painter created a clear-lined, simple realistic image of a pipe, centrally placed on the canvas, with the legend beneath it proclaiming *Ceci n'est pas une pipe* (This is not a pipe). The painting itself is probably an overused reference, but it might be familiar to the widest readership.

**Fig. 3.4** A drawing of Magritte's painting *The Treachery of Images*. (Courtesy of Andi Setiawan, © 2019 Andi Setiawan, all rights reserved, modified to black and white)

This is a good example of how meaning making works in by tackling the relationship between the representamen and its object that is openly disturbed, and therefore our certainty of knowing the object gets openly challenged. A drawn pipe resembles something, an object that we call a pipe. The painting is not a pipe though, as it is a representation of a pipe. The viewer knows this analogy, but the label in the painting might have been intended to shake our knowledge of things. Evans (2005) explains this as:

the "anchor" of resemblance, the object being depicted, hasn't in fact disappeared (as Foucault would have it ) from Magritte's drawing but that instead Magritte has used this "anchor" to remind us just how limited our ability to apprehend the object actually is. Namely, that our categorization of a really existing object with such and such physical qualities is based on habit, custom, and experience, and not because the object is the actual essence we give it (i.e., this object we call a pipe, because it was built in the manner that it was, facilitates the act of smoking but can never be wholly defined as being that and only that).

The viewers could feel caught "hanging"—"stripped of both the depicted object's human-given essence and the possibility of defining an objective existence for it—thus forcing us to confront the ambiguity of existence." (Evans, 2005, n/a). This further illustrates the arguments of not being able to know the absolute truth, as it is unreachable to humans.

It is not to claim that this interpretation of the painting is the only one, of course not. It emphasizes that "the relation between what we see and what we know is never settled" (Berger, Blomberg, Fox, Dibb, & Hollis, 1972). This illustrates Peirce's argument for the impossibility of knowing absolute truth, as the essence of things.

# A Semiotic Approach to Educational Philosophy and Theory, Edusemiotics[5]

The aim of education is to introduce new signs and sign systems to embed those in the minds and environments of learners in ways that facilitate the development of more complex systems. Recent seminal research in semiotics as a philosophical underpinning of education (Semetsky, 2017; McCarthy, 2005; Midtgarden, 2005; Semetsky, 2010; Stables, 2005, 2006; Semetsky & Stables, 2014) paved new pathways for educational philosophy and theory. Such approaches have been interchangeably labelled "edusemiotics" (Danesi, 2010, p. vii), "semiotic philosophy of education" (Semetsky & Stables, 2014), or "semiotic theory of learning" (Stables, Nöth, Olteanu, Pesce, & Pikkarainen, 2018). They aim to tackle the mentioned crisis of the humanities (Nussbaum, 2010; Jay, 2014; Martinelli, 2016; Cobley, 2017) by proposing sustainable solutions by their integration in general science, without ignoring the complexity of human societies in times of globalization and epistemological relativism (e.g. Lyotard, 1984). The contemporary literature in this regard (e.g. Danesi, 2002; Pesce, 2011, 2013, 2014; Pikkarainen, 2011, 2018; Olteanu & Campbell, 2018; Stables, Nöth, Olteanu, Pesce, & Pikkarainen, 2018; Pietarinen, 2006; Stjernfelt, 2007, 2014, Olteanu, 2016; Lackovic, 2018; Lackovic and Olteanu, forthcoming) represents a fertile ground for rethinking education and educational theory, philosophy and methods. This rethinking takes a new turn in the philosophy of education, detaching from the grip of analytic philosophy perspectives of the twentieth century Enlightenment (e.g. Dearden, Hirst, & Peters,

[5] The first two paragraphs of this section incorporate as yet unpublished work co-written with Dr. Alin Olteanu, which is acknowledged as our joint development.

1972; Hirst, 1974; Hirst & Peters, 1970). This is not to undermine the contribution of the Enlightenment era to the development of scientific reasoning and knowledge, but to challenge and expand its legacy and commitment to dominantly linear, numerical and logocentric (Derrida, 1978, pp. 246–248) and glottocentric (Cobley, 2016) construals of knowledge, learning and teaching.

Edusemiotics is an emerging philosophical and theoretical approach to learning, knowledge and education. It recommends semiotics as providing the core conceptualization for a philosophy of education liberated from the rigid assumptions of analytical philosophy, which have dominated this area for some decades (Stables & Semetsky, 2014; Semetsky & Stables, 2014; Stables, 2012, Stables, 2006; Semetsky, 2017; Olteanu, 2014, 2016; Suhor, 1984; Unsworth, 2008; Olteanu & Campbell, 2018; Lackovic & Olteanu, under review). It could be seen to bridge American pragmatism, European semiotics (e.g., Nordic), Vygotskian constructivism and continental post-structuralism, building on a range of thinkers besides C.S. Peirce, such as J. Dewey, G. Deleuze and J. Kristeva. Other schools of thought can be associated with edusemiotics, in relation to observing the relationship between humans and others (other humans, biosphere and artifacts). The consideration of meaning-making in this book also links edusemiotics with non-Western perspectives to power, culture, identity and control, as it focuses on meaning pluralism and the questioning of meanings and dominance of meaning authority. Such interest expands Peirce's semiotics.

Here I build on and contribute to this developing field and philosophy, particularly focusing on Peirce's (1991) tripartite sign. Via Peirce's triad, I adopt an edusemiotic view of relationality between material and conceptual/abstract entities in communication (Sebeok, 1991, 2001; Stjernfelt, 2011). Semetsky (2017, p. 704) argues that:

Charles Sanders Peirce's philosophy did not limit signs to verbal utterances (…) Peirce's perspective (…) emphasized the process of sign growth and change called semiosis, representing the action, transformation, and evolution of signs across nature, culture, and the human mind. In contrast to isolated substances such as body and mind in philosophy of Descartes, a Peircean genuine sign as a minimal unit of description is a tri-relative entity.

Peirce developed a rather elaborate system of semiotics rooted in pragmatist relations between the mind, the world of concrete existence and representation (Peirce, 1991). Inquiry graphics and the present work build on a selected and small part of this grand oeuvre, specifically developing Peirce's tripartite sign as an inquiry graphic sign for and of educational practice. Edusemiotics and Peirce are inseparable (Olteanu, 2014). Inna Semetsky (2007), who has done foundational work on formally launching a semiotic approach to education (edusemiotics[6]), in collaboration with and building on the word by Andrew Stables, emphasizes that (the) semiotic dimension is "implicit in philosophy of education, since signs are tools of/for human knowledge, learning and development" (Semetsky, 2007, p. 180). Semetsky adds that "(h)uman beings are sign-users" (Semetsky, 2007, p. 180). Indeed, as exemplified above, many authors and semiotic thinkers have argued in favor of the semiotic approach to education and an adoption of semiotics in educational theory and practice, as semiosis, sign using and sign action is a shared force of social and educational progress. At the EARLI[7] multiple representations SIG in 2012, Wolfgan Schnotz, who has developed research in multiple representations, called for a recognition and application of semiotics in the circles of cognitive sciences and psychology, which commonly does not delve into semiotics.

# Semiotics and Education Inter-Connectedness

Although edusemiotics and semiotics as an educational theory gained traction more recently, efforts and reflections on semiotics as an approach in education started much earlier, of course with Peirce in the nineteenth century, and in the twentieth century with propositions concerning semiotics in education and pedagogy argued, for example, in the 1970s by Bense (1977) as noted by Nöth (2010) or in the 1980s by Cunningham (1987a, 1987b) and Sebeok et al. (1988), also Nöth (1994) in the 1990s. In 1987, in the book *The Semiotic Web* (Sebeok, Umiker-Sebeok, &

---

[6] Institute for Edusemiotic Studies: http://edusemiotics.org/index.html
[7] The European Association for Research on Learning and Instruction (EARLI).

Young, 1988), Donald Cunningham reflected that it was surprising that semiotics had not informed educational practice more (Cunningham, 1987a). An obstacle to that might be that Peircean semiotics observes knowledge in a deeply *interdisciplinary manner*, in addition to a very complex language, sets of concepts as well as Peirce's peculiar terminology, writing style and variations in explanations. As such, this is a challenging approach, especially when most academic individuals, communities and tertiary education institutions still position themselves firmly within disciplinary belonging and boundaries. Although there is a constant talk about and calls for interdisciplinarity (e.g., by UK government bodies and research councils), disciplinary-based research is still highly salient and confirms strong disciplinary forms of organization (Trowler, Saunders, & Bamber, 2012).

Interdisciplinarity from a semiotic perspective is not some chosen or random pairing of different disciplinary subjects by students, e.g. offering to students to choose from different disciplinary subjects or courses, such as nursing and media studies, although this can be done in a comprehensive and inspiring manner. It means approaching disciplinary knowledge and programs as an *interdisciplinary body of inquiry*. Obviously, with any approaches there are gains and losses. The envisaged challenge of interdisciplinary inquiry graphics method for example is how to link its strength of often fine-grain micro level analysis with a theoretical approach or concept it is combined with, *not to underplay the scope given to either*. However, semiotics, if taken as a theory of meaning, makes a distinct contribution to knowledge and can stand on its own theoretically, as it promotes education development via semiotic theory and philosophy of meaning, intention and action.

Nöth (2010) makes a case for semiotics as foundational in education, echoing Kress's earlier quote at the beginning of the chapter, claiming that:

(s)emiotics and education are research fields with mutual interest and overlaps. The study of signs and sign processes help to understand how teaching means to communicate by means of signs and how learning means to interpret and to grow in the capacity of interpreting signs. (Nöth, 2010, p. 1)

Semiotics also challenges the linear, hierarchical, and deterministic approach to the curriculum. It can help diversify it by content and teaching practices to include traditionally marginalized modes of communication as well as content. Cunningham (1986, p. 369) observed something that still holds true: (most) education policy makers and educators, higher education included, regard curriculum as a set of discreet entities, such as learning outcomes, selection (of resources) and structure. Learning outcomes refer to sets of intended knowledge, attitudes and skills. Although this is practical and helpful, it is a partial view of education and learning. Cunningham (1987a) mentions the influential model by Robert Gagne (e.g., Gagne & Briggs, 1974), which is explicitly hierarchical and differentiates between high-level mastery (the learning of a rule) and simpler component skills mastery (of a concept that leads to the rule). Such an approach, akin to an acquisition metaphor of learning (Sfard, 1998) suggests that the knowledge, concepts and skills can be neatly hierarchically ordered and exist independently from the learner, contextual changes and multimodal senses, and therefore need to be and can be acquired.

> Curriculum thus becomes the knowledge propositions contained in our textbooks and teacher guides, with heavy emphasis on mathematical and verbal content, since they are conveniently represented as hierarchical propositions. (Cunningham, 1987a, p. 370)

A semiotic approach to education differs significantly. Aligned with the concepts such as semiosis (meaning-making process), sign-induced action, reflexivity and abduction (infinite process of teaching-learning via creative scientific insights and feelings), knowledge is a process of human adaptation and growth; it is developmental and open-ended, hence scientific concepts are also developmental and open-ended (these ideas will be further discussed in Chaps. 5 and 6). As Cunningham (1987a, p. 370) imagines, within a semiotic education paradigm,

> (t)he curriculum would stress ways of knowing, not knowledge acquisition. The possibilities for knowing would be expanded beyond the traditional verbal/mathematical modes to include the visual, musical, social and bodily-kinesthetic modes (…) Knowledge would be "decompartamentalized".

Therefore, *ways of knowing and collective knowledge creation, sharing and exchange* would become central, where assessment practices such as summative assessment might lose their present meaning or dominance and firmly link to formative assessment and learners' creative actions of engaging with knowledge and related practices. Cunningham's vision of interdisciplinary programs is in some ways being realized in more recent initiatives, such as the development of interdisciplinary programs familiar to me in the UK context, at a postgraduate level, at Edinburgh Futures Institute at the University of Edinburgh or interdisciplinary programs as Lancaster University's Institute for Social Futures, as well as increasingly interdisciplinary doctoral programs and centers (e.g., the Wire doctoral center or The Leverhulme Doctoral Scholarships Programme in Material Social Futures at Lancaster University), bringing together diverse disciplines in pursuit of knowledge. The leading focus for such interdisciplinarity is placed on exploring global and/or very particular problems, questions, themes, challenges, approached from various (disciplinary/ empirical/ epistemological) angles, rather than a simple pairing of two or more disciplines and subjects. These are important and exciting developments in education, still in developmental phases and having a futuristic flavor. We shall see what the future brings.

Nöth (2010) quotes Charles Morris to emphasize how a semiotic approach to and within education, an education as *semiotic engagement*, could finally bridge the separation of the arts and humanities from one side and the so called hard sciences from the other: "an education which gave due place to semiotics would destroy at its foundations the cleavage and opposition of science and the humanities." (Nöth, 2010, p. 4) He further refers to the work by Thomas (1987, p. 296), who writes that

> to understand the value of semiotics is to understand and appreciate its capacity to cut across established disciplines without losing the power of its insight. To value semiotics is to recognize the growing need for integrating current curricula towards some unified end.

J.O. Regan, in conversation with Sebeok, underlines the importance of semiotics to teaching as it "examines fundamental and highly abstract concepts that are at the basis of education, namely mind, learning, and information," adding that semiotics has provided a new perspective to pedagogy by the "*broadening of interest beyond the verbal into the nonverbal*" (Nöth, 2010, p. 2). In relation to this non-verbal perspective that incorporates the verbal but goes beyond it in a manner of multimodal communication, this chapter and this book address how teaching communicates by means of graphics as signs of communication for learning in higher education, and how graphic sign interpretation contributes to knowledge development and growth.

Whereas there is good scope for compelling arguments for semiotics as a core theoretical and philosophical underpinning for educational inquiry, as shown in this section and in a range of publications (e.g., in a collection of essays and chapters by a number of scholars in semiotics in two books edited by Inna Semetsky: *Semiotics Education Experience* (2010) and *Edusemiotics–A handbook* (2017)), semiotics-informed empirical inquiry with graphics or images in the field of higher education and education programs at universities has not been present to any notable extent. Indeed, empirical semiotic inquiries (that involve more than one interpreter) with graphics of any kind in higher education studies and the field of educational research are scarce. This is, perhaps, not surprising, as Nöth (2010) states that most teachings of semiotics are positioned in language, communication and media studies at university level, hence not in education departments, although they have a lot to do with education.

Another aspect of a semiotic theory of learning and edusemiotic is that learning is a *collective process* (Stables, 2010), not a property possessed or obtained by an individual. This is simply because everything newly learnt is learnt through an engagement with knowledge that comes from outside the individual. This happens via some collectively accumulated knowledge fields with sociocultural and historical meanings and applications, together with the material environment, interacting with existing individual knowledge schemata (built from prior experiences). These schemata are not some hierarchical neatly ordered mosaic; their boundaries are fuzzy, expandable and in flux. Learning is a form of being, a form of developing as a person relational to the social, cultural and ecological environment one is embedded in. In this way, learning is a development of a special relationship between the learner and the knowledge field, with all the complex environmental and sociocultural (economic, political and other) factors that inform this relationship and the field.

# Synthesizing Perspectives in Inquiry Graphics: A Triadic Image–Concept Sign

I adopt Peirce's semiotic and logical sign diagram as the basis for the analytical deconstructing of inquiry graphics, which are image-concept ensembles acting as learning resources. By doing so, I contribute to the body of knowledge not only in the semiotic theory of learning or educational semiotics, but also to general theorizing of knowledge, pedagogy and research philosophy, and to methods in higher education as well. The legend underneath Fig. 3.5 introduces key relational constituents of an inquiry graphics sign, aligned with Peirce's tripartite schematic sign model.

An IG is a complex, compound sign. PI (Picture Interpretation) and CI (Concept Interpretation) are brought together and expanded by critical interpretation of the CI-PI relationship. PI focuses interpretation on describing pictorial elements and their pictorial descriptive meanings. CI focuses interpretation on how these meanings gain an extra conceptual meaning, for example to represent an aspect of an abstract concept, idea

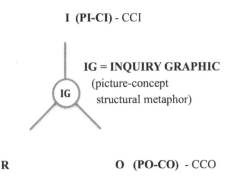

Fig. 3.5 An inquiry graphics (IG) sign with elements of its signification. R = Representamen, mainly the embodied form of the picture that is chosen to represent a concept; I = Interpretant (interpretation): PI = Picture/image Interpretant and CI = Concept Interpretant; PI is layered into denotation and connotation; CCI = Critical Concept Interpretant (critical inference/thinking); O = Object; PO = Picture/image/pictorial Object (what the picture embodied form refers to); CO = Conceptual (assigned, integrated) Object, what the picture is chosen to refer to for targeted communication and/or learning purposes; CCO = Critical Concept Object (what is critically known about the concept and the potential and character of the whole sign to be inquired critically) (IG = R+PI-CI-CCI+PO-CO-CCO)

or theory. CCO is a critical approach or idea that has been and can be assigned to an IG sign, it is a principle of criticality in relation to an IG object, not an analytical element per se.

Although Peirce devised a few classifications of signs, I introduced above the three types of signs that an IG sign incorporates: icon, index and symbol (CP 2.247–249). Reiterating, icons as signs function by the virtue of similarity between their form and what the form refers to (its object, either existing or not in the world, a concrete thing or an idea or sensation). A symbol refers to its form by some socioculturally agreed conventional system of signification, such as an agreed linguistic system, a number, or an image that symbolizes an idea or concept by convention to a large number of culture/ society members. An index has a diagnostic quality, as it signals the existence of something else connected to the sign form, but the form is not that thing signaled, also referring to an existential connection between these two (a smoke is an index for fire, a sneeze an index for particular processes of the human body). Most signs in communication are complex and compound signs as they act at the intersection of modalities and types, operating as icons, indices and symbols at the same time. I also view spoken and written language as multimodal, compound sign, as processing it and thinking about it involves more than verbal modality, a kind of spatial operation that involves the environment and external sensation (e.g., sound, trace on the screen or paper) (Malafouris, 2013). It links to the role of non-verbal things such as multimodal conceptual blending and metaphors that include references to external experiences (Lakoff & Johnson, 2008). This view of thinking could be called "multimodal intertextuality" (Lackovic, 2017) to emphasize the different modality implied in the word "text" and also thinking, not only verbal. An inquiry graphics process accounts for this multimodal sign complexity and hybridity, as it focuses interpretation on its iconic quality via image embodied Representamen and denotative image descriptions, and on its indexical–symbolic quality via conceptual object (CO)–conceptual interpretant (CI) in relation to pictorial object–interpretant (PO; PI) explorations for reflection and inquiry purposes.

Via inquiry graphics, I argue that a pictorial representation of a concept and its image–concept object of reference provide a vehicle bringing together the material and abstract aspects of thinking and knowledge development. This coupling needs to be interpreted and importantly, inquired in a learning community of inquiry, in order to deepen learners' (but also teachers') multimodal concept understanding. Inquiry graphics signification as a compound image-concept sign is illustrated in Fig. 3.5, and further explained in Chaps. 4, 5 and 6, each taking specific focus, on images, concepts, and learning. Via an IG sign, pictures' interpretations (PI) are related to concept interpretations (CI) and vice versa. When these two different modes of expression and reflection are brought into relationship, what happens is Multimodal Anchorage (MA) (Fig. 3.6). The main point of an inquiry graphics is that pictorial details offer a

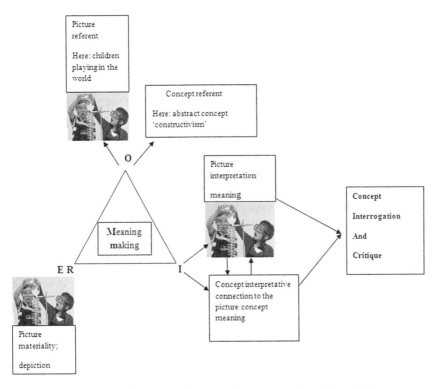

**Fig. 3.6** Image-embedded example of an inquiry graphics (IG) analytical model. ER = another term for embodied Representamen, here: External Representation; O = Object; I = Interpretant referred to as interpretation and the integrated concept–image character of an inquiry graphics sign; the drawing of the photograph is shown in a larger format in Fig. 3.7. **MA** = multimodal anchorage (the meeting point of the PI and CI from the I (interpretant) node in the diagram)

meaning potential that can be connected to the concept superimposed over the picture. Therefore, a learner has an opportunity to interrogate both the meaning of individual pictorial elements and their individual relationships, as well as a meaning of the picture as a whole, with the meanings the concept. Interpretations related to the concept can either start with considering the concept and how its meaning relates to the picture or by considering what is seen in the picture and how to connect the observed to the concept. Such thinking is challenging simply because general (not all) education at schools but also at universities does not treat images as thinking-integrated signs, hence this approach is novel to most learners. It can open many creative avenues of thinking and concept exploration, and an exercise in innovative and pluralistic idea generation.

Peirce's Representamen for an image can be labeled with different, perhaps more widely accessible, terminology (than the semiotic terminology), such an "External Representation (ER)" as in Fig. 3.6, or simply a "photographic depiction," which signals picture content *repertoire,* or in other words, the naming via listing of observed elements as nouns (Representamen's rhemes) and descriptions (Interpretant) of the elements it contains.

What is unique about an inquiry graphics approach? It proposes a novel approach to and method of learning concepts in higher education by introducing a different view of concepts, bringing in the neglected materiality and iconicity of the world (Barad, 2003) via external graphic signs. Picture's depictive materiality offers various elements that can be interrogated on their own, as part of a composition in relation to the concept within the learning context, constituting an IG sign.

# Inquiry Graphics Example: A Scientific Concept Integrated with a Pictorial Image

The image of the children with goggles, presumably showing children doing an experiment at school (the original image is a stock photograph) was chosen by a student to represent an aspect of the concept "constructivism", in the empirical study introduced in Part II of this book. A drawing rendering of this image is shown in Fig. 3.7.

**Fig. 3.7** A drawing to represent an aspect of "constructivism". (Courtesy of Andi Setaiwan, 2019 © Andi Setiawan, all rights reserved

This image, or any image, becomes an inquiry graphics when a conceptual/ thematic/ theoretical inquiry object is coupled with it, and thus integrated with the pictorial sign for the purposes of analysis and learning. Inquiry graphics are therefore pictorial images that are deliberately used for teaching–learning or any thematic and conceptual inquiry (also applicable in research and wider) so that they become what Lakoff and Johnson (2008) call structural metaphors. Structural metaphors happen when two things that do not have any so-called "natural" link are brought together to be linked (ibid.). The idea of metaphors as central for semiotic diagrammatic reasoning is also suggested by Danesi (2017). To explain further, what this image shows is two children doing something. It does not show "constructivism" in its pictorial form or its pictorial Object—it shows young human beings and some objects; yet, it can show by an effort or analogical and imaginative thinking an aspect of how constructivism can possibly work or be materially manifested in the world, in an educational context through sociocultural action and material relationality. This image, showing some children playing with particularly shaped dishes and liquids in an environment at denotative level, could connotatively mean that pupils are participating in an act of experimentation in a lab environment to understand a concept (e.g., a chemical reaction). The iconic (pictorial) Pictorial Object represents or refers to the children who were photographed and their described action in the world, at the moment of photographing. However, an assigned analytical/ conceptual Object (or Research Object in research applications (Lackovic, 2018)), bridges the Iconic and Symbolic meanings (via denotation–connotation) for this photograph to further contemplate meanings of a concept, in this case, for this photograph, "constructivism." The constructivism meaning is conventionally assigned to this image, thus also making the image a symbol of constructivism.

In accordance with Pietarinen and Bellucci's reading of Peirce, an inquiry graphics analysis in some way evokes the Peircean concept of diagram, where the concept connotation is symbolic and linked to an Iconic denotation:

> Peirce's claim that in a diagram "the signification of the symbol becomes the object of the icon" is really revealing. A symbol is a sign that carries information. Any proposition does so; any term or predicate does so, at least virtually; any argument does, and in a peculiar way (carries information that in its turn will become a source of further information). An icon, on the contrary, is a sign "from which information can be derived" (MS 478, 51–57, 1903). An icon represents the information contained in the symbol in such a way as to render further information derivable from it. In traditional terms, the Icon denotes what the Symbol connotes.

An IG analysis considers all sides of the IG sign meaning-making equal and treats image content details as serious conceptual inquiry elements, to encourage thinking beyond the boundaries of interpreting only what the picture means holistically at a configural level—as an interpretation that would say: "the children are doing a chemistry experiment" (with reference to Fig. 3.7). It invites an interpretation by paying attention to details, from micro level noticing and descriptions to macro level inferences, theoretical and creative insights and relationalities. The picture (see Fig 3.8) contains details such as: goggles, apron, test tubes, and

**Fig. 3.8** Inquiry graphics micro(image elements)–macro(meanings/ theory/ history) relationality. (Courtesy of Andi Setaiwan, 2019 © Andi Setaiwan, all rights reserved)

liquids in different colors. It also shows a particular type of interaction between two children of different gender, and so on. All these elements can contribute to concept exploration and inquiry. It integrates the rich data and elements that the picture shows to expand understanding and knowledge of the concept, what the concept that is linked to the picture means (building on the available literature), and what it could mean.

For example, apron and goggles are worn for different types of protection, but would the children put them on their own? Would they spontaneously put on goggles, or would they need adult supervision to do so? Therefore, what is the role of protection measures in constructivism and typical idea of constructivist learning, for example when it involves children (as goggles and aprons can signify different types of "protection")? What does that mean for constructivism as an independent inquiry? Is the adult's presence or adult's instruction necessary for health and safety reasons (much referenced in the UK context for example)? What is the role of various material artifacts, such as specialized equipment (to do something such an experiment) in constructivism? To what extent is school financial power to afford specialized equipment important in the provision of constructivist experiences? What happens when learners do not have access to such equipment, would they make alternative artifacts? What would it mean to explore where the goggles and the items the children wear were produced, and what happens to them afterwards? How does the outsourcing of resources effect anyone's engagement with it? What is the role of liquid colors in this case, and how would it feed into constructivist experience? What is not seen here but could be explored in relation to this picture and setting and a constructivist experience? What could happen before and after this type of interaction to support experiential knowledge development? What is the role of these children's prior knowledge? What is the role of the situated, surrounding environment (which, in the photograph is a blank space, which is of course unlikely in the physical world of a school lab environments)? What socio-cultural factors affect the children's interaction and understanding of what is happening? How is this learning and how is this not learning?

If we observe a photograph as *an assemblage of* individual *elements* (Fig. 3.8) that all contribute to the meaning of the holistic photograph representation (part–whole relations) linked to the key concept, then it makes sense to reflect on the meanings commonly and rarely (yet possible to be) attached to these elements and their histories, provenance, characteristics (objects or people or bodies). All things have production and consumption history, uses and meanings. By teasing these out in relation to various conceptual meanings that they can refer to, new insights can be developed, and specific perspectives and new meanings brought to the surface. An object or element evokes its historical existence and related material, biological, or sociocultural character, which is the basis of new significations, hence these characteristics are not fixed but fluid, and they evolve with any new use. In this way, any idea of fixed or a priori visual or multimodal "affordances" is contested.

Figure 3.8 shows this idea of "noticing" and naming individual elements by showing them individually to consider their common historical uses, characteristics and meanings, and the ways that these elements can relate to the pictorial and conceptual meanings in a given context. These elemental and configural meanings (all elements together) can invite reflections on both some more common or "obvious" meanings and inspire new meanings for exploring the concept ("constructivism" exemplified here).

An inquiry graphics analysis could then focus on both material elements and actions shown, switching between the observed (what is shown), the experienced (what is personally known about the shown), the authoritative (what has been written or produced in academic studies of the concept) and the imagined (how to connect all those, finding similarity). It is envisaged to work in the following way across Peirce's triadic model constituents, each subject to *interpretation*. These analytical ingredients relate to the finding of the two stages of action research in Chap. 8:

- **Embodied Representamen-led inquiry** (naming and listing basic interpretation): this involves listing of all elements observed as "nouns" to signal a presumed character or "name" of something observed (e.g., a boy); the naming is presumed as we cannot be sure that what looks to us as something it is indeed that thing; it has Peircean "rheme" quality, as it asks for listing of observed elements to consider their meaning making *potential*, before each one is considered in relation to the meanings of a holistic image-concept IG sign.

- **Interpretant-led inquiry** (descriptive interpretation): I here adapt semiotic distinction articulated by Barthes between *denotative and connotative meanings* for the purpose of systematic analysis to make distinction between qualitative descriptions of what we see (denotation) and how the observed qualitative phenomenon or action is assigned a particular sociocultural meaning (connotation). For example, I see a face with eyes open wide and eyebrows raised in specific shape (denotation) which can signal that the person is afraid or bewildered (connotation, depending on the eyebrows look). Learning how to interpret such and a variety of other sign cues has been critical for human evolution at a biological, sociocultural, and historical level.
- **Conceptual Object-led inquiry** (how can elements and their descriptions support inferences and insights about the concept that has been linked to the image? How does this inform a tentative research object (questions) or link to a specific theory or conceptualization?)

In simpler words, these could be:

- naming (of individual details),
- describing things (what qualities these details have, what they are like/ what is happening),
- the meanings of descriptions (what the described means socioculturally in the represented context),
- conceptual link (how those above link to the assigned (or spontaneously inferred) concept).

Such seeing-for-learning or research-related inference is not an easy process. It requires a training of the eye and the mind. When it comes to an inquiry into the concept which is to be understood and learnt, it is presumed that students need to be supported in doing an image-based inquiry, before they develop confidence. As Ormond (2011, p. 3) argues, "expecting students to be able to glean meaning from images without a supportive pedagogy generally leads to simplistic interpretations and discussion rarely goes beyond what is literally 'seen' or interpreted in any singular way." The point of inquiry graphics is not of just what is literally seen or what is interpreted, but how these can be elaborated and integrated by merging the image-signifying character with conceptual knowledge, reflection and development. This is to explore and develop how an image stimulates/inspires/leads thinking in various ways, providing various possibilities for inquiry, hence it becomes an integral part of thinking, as the studies in Part II will show. Indeed, pictures are often viewed as "easy," supportive and illustrative material that could be tackled by learners as mere depictions or illustrations (Carney & Levin, 2002). This is not because learners cannot do a deeper analysis linked to the picture, but because they have not encountered such pedagogies before, and because they need support to expand concept thinking in such a way.

The interpretative triadic cycle explained in this section is embedded in a larger holistic framework of meaning-making. Objects are interpreted under the influence of the cultural, historical, habitual and contextual particularities and goals that limit the infinity of interpretation (Hodge & Kress, 1988). Interpretations also need to consider situational and representational structure and agency (of sign makers). Namely, an interpretation and understanding of a sign depends on the culture where that sign functions and the context and time it occurs in (place, space, purpose, historicity), on localized conditions—such as the task, its goal, and the state of the agents or the environment (Reed, 2008), relational to larger systemic and global conditions.

Therefore, critical sign inquiry encapsulates an exploration of all those factors. For example, consideration of social agents' intentionality (an exploration of sign maker's or sign promoter's intentionality and the interpreter's intentionality) is important for critical thinking development. It is related to those views of social semiotics which are mainly concerned with the human-created, suggestive and transformative power of signs and their "ideologies." This, in turn, contributes to critical thinking and critical pedagogy development. Consideration of the Representamen and Interpretant—everything that is depicted and what it means in a given context (micro, meso, micro-meso) and could possibly mean in a larger society or culture context (macro level) as intrinsically related—is important for analytical thinking development, creative, encompassing and critical practices in higher education.

This chapter introduced the selected and focused edusemiotics aspects that inform an inquiry graphics sign. The chapter explained the semiotics "behind" an IG sign. It presented a variation of Peirce's and IG sign models/ diagrams and how they make meaning to mediate learning and knowledge in higher education. The book proceeds to focus on images for learning in higher education.

# References

Almeder, R. (1980). *The philosophy of Charles S. Peirce: A critical introduction.* Oxford, UK: Blackwell Publishing.

Barad, K. (2003). Posthumanist performativity: Toward an understanding of how matter comes to matter. *Signs: Journal of Women in Culture and Society, 28*(3), 801–831.

Barthes, R. ([1964] 1967). *Elements of semiology* (Annette Lavers & Colin Smith Trans.). London: Jonathan Cape.

Barthes, R. (2009/1972). *Mythologies* (Annette Lavers, Trans.). New York: Hill and Wang, Vintage Classics; Revised edition (3 Sept. 2009).

Benedict, G. A. (1985). What are representamens? *Transactions of the Charles S. Peirce Society, 21*(2), 241–270. Retrieved from: https://www.jstor.org/stable/40320088?seq=1

Bense, M. (1977). Die semiotische Konzeption der Ästhetik. *Zeitschrift für Literaturwissenschaft und Linguistik, 7*(27), 188.

Berger, J., Blomberg, S., Fox, C., Dibb, M., & Hollis, R. (1972). *Ways of seeing.* London: British Broadcasting Corporation & Penguin.

Carney, R. N., & Levin, J. R. (2002). Pictorial illustrations still improve students' learning from text. *Educational Psychology Review, 14*, 5–26.

Chandler, D. (1994). *Semiotics for beginners.* Retrieved from: http://www.aber.ac.uk/media/Documents/S4B/

Chandler, D. (2002). *The basics: Semiotics.* London: Routledge.

Cobley, P. (2016). *Cultural implications of biosemiotics.* Dordrecht, Netherlands: Springer.

Cobley, P. (2017). What the humanities are for – A semiotic perspective. In B. Kristian & P. Cobley (Eds.), *Semiotics and its masters* (pp. 3–23). Berlin, Germany: de Gruyter Mouton.

Crow, D. (2003). *Visible signs: An introduction to semiotics* (AVA Academia). London: AVA publishing.

Cunningham, D. J. (1986). Good guys and bad guys. *Educational Communication and Technology, 3*–7.

Cunningham, D. J. (1987a). Semiotics and education–strands in the web. In T. A. Sebeok & J. Umiker-Sebeok (Eds.), *The semiotic web* (pp. 367–378). Berlin, Germany: Mouton de Gryuter.

Cunningham, D. J. (1987b). Outline of an education semiotic. *American Journal of Semiotics, 5*, 201–216.

Danesi, M. (2002). *Semiotics in education*. Dresden, Germany: Thelem.

Danesi, M. (2010). *Foreword: Edusemiotics. Semiotics education experience* (pp. vii–vxi). Sense/Brill.

Danesi, M. (2017). Semiotics as a metalanguage for the sciences. In B. Kristian & C. Paul (Eds.), *Semiotics and its masters, 1* (pp. 61–83). Berlin: Walter de Gruyter Inc.

De Saussure, F. (2011). *Course in general linguistics*. New York: Columbia University Press.

Dearden, R. F., Hirst, P., & Peters, R. S. (Eds.). (1972). *Education and the development of reason*. London: Routledge & Kegan Paul.

Derrida, J. (1978) [1967]. *Writing and difference* (Alan Bass, Trans.). London: Routledge.

Dewey, J., & Bentley, A. F. (1960). *Knowing and the known* (No. 111). Boston: Beacon Press.

Elleström, L. (2014). Material and mental representation: Peirce adapted to the study of media and arts. *The American Journal of Semiotics, 30*(1/2), 83–138. https://doi.org/10.5840/ajs2014301/24.

Evans, G. S. (2005). *This could be a pipe: Foucault, irrealism and Ceci n'est pas une pipe*. The Cafe Irreal: International Imagination. http://cafeirreal.alicewhittenburg.com/review5.htm. Accessed 14 January 2020.

Fenwick, T., Edwards, R., & Sawchuk, P. (2015). *Emerging approaches to educational research: Tracing the socio-material*. London and New York: Routledge.

Freadman, A. (2001). *The classifications of signs (II): 1903. Digital encyclopedia of CS Peirce*. Retrieved from: http://www.digitalpeirce.fee.unicamp.br/190fre.htm

Gagne, R. M., & Briggs, L. J. (1974). *Principles of instructional design*. Oxford, England: Holt, Rinehart & Winston.

Greer, C., & Jewkes, Y. (2005). Towards "them", the people that are not like "us". Extremes of otherness: Media images of social exclusion. *Social Justice, 32*(1(99)), 20–31.

Hall, S. (1997). *Representation: Cultural representations and signifying practices.* London: Sage.

Hardwick, C. S. (Ed.). (1977). Semiotic and Significs: The Correspondence between Charles S. Peirce and Victoria Lady Wellby. Bloomington: Indiana University Press.

Hirst, P. (1974). *Knowledge and the curriculum.* London and Boston: Routledge and Kegan Paul.

Hirst, P., & Peters, R. S. 1970. *The logic of education.* London: Routledge and Kegan Paul.

Hodge, B. R. I. V., & Kress, G. R. (1988). *Social semiotics.* Cambridge, UK: Polity Press.

Jay, P. (2014). *The humanities "crisis" and the future of literary studies.* New York: Palgrave Macmillan.

Knorr-Cetina, K., & Amann, K. (1990). Image dissection in natural scientific inquiry. *Science, Technology & Human Values, 15,* 259–283.

Kress, G. (2009). Assessment in the perspective of a social semiotic theory of multimodal teaching and learning. In *Educational assessment in the 21st century* (pp. 19–41). New York: Springer.

Kress, G., & van Leeuwen, T. (1996). *Reading images: The grammar of visual design.* London: Routledge.

Kull, K. (2008). The importance of semiotics to University: Semiosis makes the world locally plural. *Semiotics,* 494–514.

Lackovic, N. (2016). MultiMAP: Exploring multimodal artefact pedagogy in digital higher education. *Proceedings,* 148–162.

Lackovic, N. (2017). Book review: Collective knowledge arises from multimodal, dialogic intertextuality: Learning in the age of digital reason (2017) by Petar Jandrić. *Knowledge Cultures, 5*(05), 131–135.

Lackovic, N. (2018). Analysing videos in educational research: An "Inquiry Graphics" approach for multimodal, Peircean semiotic coding of video data. *Video Journal of Education and Pedagogy, 3*(1), 1–23.

Lackovic, N., & Olteanu, A. (under review). New approach to educational theory and method in the postdigital world: Bridging the separation between the concept and the image. *Educational Theory and Philosophy.*

Lakoff, G., & Johnson, M. (2008). *Metaphors we live by.* Chicago: University of Chicago Press.

Lyotard, J. F. (1984). *The postmodern condition: A report on knowledge* (G. Bennington & B. Massumi, Trans.). Minneapolis, MN: University of Minnesota Press.

Malafouris, L. (2013). *How things shape the mind.* Cambridge, MA: MIT Press.

Martinelli, D. (2016). *Arts and humanities in progress: A manifesto of numanities.* Cham, Switzerland: Springer.

McCarthy, C. L. (2005). Knowing truth: Peirce's epistemology in an educational context. *Educational Philosophy and Theory, 37*(2), 157–176.

Merrel, F. (2001). Charles Sanders Pierce's concept of the sign. In P. Cobley, (Ed.), *The Routledge Companion to semiotics and Linguistics* (pp. 28–39). London and New York: Routledge.

Merrel, F. (2005). Charles Sanders Pierce's concept of the sign. In P. Cobley, (Ed.), *The Routledge Companion to semiotics and Linguistics* (pp. 28–39). London and New York: Routledge.

Midtgarden, T. (2005) Toward a semiotic theory of learning. In I. Semestky (Ed.), *Semiotics, education, experience* (pp. 71–82). Rotterdam, The Netherlands: Sense Publishers.

Nöth, W. (1994). Semiotic foundations of the cognitive paradigm. *Semiosis, 73*(1994), 5–16.

Nöth, W. (2010). The semiotics of teaching and the teaching of semiotics. In I. Semetsky (Ed.), *Semiotics education experience* (pp. 1–19). Rotterdam, The Netherlands: Sense Publishers.

Nöth, W. (2011). From representation to thirdness and representamen to medium: Evolution of Peircean key terms and topics. *Transactions of the Charles S. Peirce Society: A Quarterly Journal in American Philosophy, 47*(4), 445–481. https://doi.org/10.2979/trancharpeirsoc.47.4.445.

Nussbaum, M. C. (2010). *Not for profit – Why democracy needs the humanities.* Princeton, NJ: Princeton University Press.

Olteanu, A. (2014). The semiosic evolution of education. *Journal of Philosophy of Education, 48*(3), 457–473.

Olteanu, A. (2016). The implications for education of Peirce's agapist principle. *Semiotica, 2016*(212), 59–79.

Olteanu, A. (2017). Reading history: Education, semiotics, and edusemiotics. In *Edusemiotics – A handbook* (pp. 193–205). Singapore: Springer.

Olteanu, A. (2019). *Multiculturalism as multimodal communication.* Cham, Switzerland: Springer.

Olteanu, A., & Campbell, C. (2018). A short introduction to edusemiotics. *Chinese Semiotic Studies, 14*(2), 245–260.

Ormond, B. (2011). Pedagogy and pictorial evidence: Interpreting post-reformation English prints in context. *Curriculum Journal, 22*, 3–27.

Parker, K. A. (1998). *The continuity of Peirce's thought.* Nashville, TN: Vanderbilt University Press.

Peirce, C. S. (1991). Peirce on signs: Writings on semiotic. UNC Press Books. Edited by James Hoopes. (volumes 1-3 of The Writing of Charles S. Peirce: A Chronological Edition, edited by Edward C. Moore, Mz H. Fisch, Christian J.W. Kloesel et al. 1982

Pesce, S. (2011). Institutional pedagogy and semiosis: Investigating the link between Peirce's semiotics and effective semiotics. *Educational Philosophy and Theory, 43*(10), 1145–1160.

Pesce, S. (2013). Teachers' educational gestures and habits of practical action: Edusemiotics as a framework for Teachers's education. *Journal of Philosophy of Education, 48*(3), 474–489.

Pesce, S. (2014). From Peirce's speculative rhetoric to educational rhetoric. *Educational Philosophy and Theory, 45*(7), 755–780.

Pietarinen, A.-V. (2006). *Signs of logic: Peircean themes on the philosophy of language, games, and communication.* Dordrecht, Netherlands: Springer.

Pikkarainen, E. (2011). The semiotics of education: A new vision in an old landscape. *Educational Philosophy and Theory, 43*(10), 1135–1144.

Pikkarainen, E. (2018). Adaptation, learning, Bildung: Discussion with edu- and biosemiotics. *Sign Systems Studies, 46*(4), 435–451.

Reed, I. (2008). Justifying sociological knowledge: From realism to interpretation. *Sociological Theory, 26*, 101–129.

Santaella, L. (2003). Why there is no crisis of representation, according to Peirce. *Semiotica, 143*, 45–52.

Sebeok, T. A. (1991). *Semiotics in the United States.* Indianapolis: Indiana University Press.

Sebeok, T. A. (2001). *Signs: An introduction to semiotics.* Toronto: University of Toronto Press.

Sebeok, T. A., Umiker-Sebeok, D. J., & Young, E. P. (Eds.). (1988). *The semiotic web 1987.* Mouton de Gruyter.

Sefton-Green, J. & Sinker, R. (1999). *Evaluating screativity: Making and learning by young people.* London: Routledge.

Semetsky, I. (2007). Introduction: Semiotics, education, philosophy. *Studies in Philosophy and Education, 26*, 179–183.

Semetsky, I. (Ed.). (2010). *Semiotics education experience.* Sense/Brill.

Semetsky, I. (Ed.). (2017). *Edusemiotics – A handbook.* Singapore: Springer.

Semetsky, I., & Stables, A. (Eds.). (2014). *Pedagogy and edusemiotics: Theoretical challenges/practical opportunities* (Vol. 62). Rotterdam: Sense Publisher/ Springer.

Sfard, A. (1998). On two metaphors for learning and the dangers of choosing just one. *Educational researcher, 27*, 4–13.

Smith, H. A. (2010). Peircean theory, psychosemiotics, and education. In Inna Semetsky (ed.) *Semiotics education experience* (pp. 37–52). Brill/Sense.

Stables, A. (2005). *Living and learning as semiotic engagement: A new theory of education.* Lewiston, NY: Edwin Mellen Press.

Stables, A. (2006). Sign(al)s: Living and learning as semiotic engagement. *Journal of Curriculum Studies, 38*(4), 373–387.

Stables, A. (2010). Semiosis and the collapse of mind-body dualism: Implications for education. In Inna Semestky (Ed.), *Semiotics education experience* (pp. 21–36). Brill/Sense.

Stables, A. (2012). *Be(com)ing human: Semiosis and the myth of reason.* Rotterdam, Netherlands: Sense Publishers.

Stables, A., Nöth, W., Olteanu, A., Pesce, S., & Pikkarainen, E. (2018). *Semiotic theory of learning: New perspectives in the philosophy of education.* London: Routledge.

Stables, A., & Semetsky, I. (2014). *Edusemiotics: Semiotic philosophy as educational foundation.* London: Routledge.

Stjernfelt, F. (2007). *Diagrammatology. An investigation on the borderlines of phenomenology, ontology and semiotics.* Dordrecht, Netherlands: Springer.

Stjernfelt, F. (2011). On operational and optimal iconicity in Peirce's diagrammatology. *Semiotica, 2011*(186), 395–419.

Stjernfelt, F. (2014). *Natural propositions: The actuality of Peirce's doctrine of Dicisigns.* Boston: Docent Press.

Suhor, C. (1984). Towards a semiotics-based curriculum. *Journal of Curriculum Studies, 16*, 247–257.

Tateo, L. (2018). Affective semiosis and affective logic. *New Ideas in Psychology, 48*, 1–11.

Thomas, D. W. (1987). Semiotics: The pattern which connects. *American Journal of Semiotics, 5*, 291–302.

Trowler, P., Saunders, M., & Bamber, V. (Eds.). (2012). *Tribes and territories in the 21st century: Rethinking the significance of disciplines in higher education.* New York: Routledge.

Unsworth, L. (Ed.). (2008). *Multimodal semiotics: Functional analysis in contexts of education.* London: Bloomsbury Publishing.

von Uexkull, J. (1982). The theory of meaning. *Semiotica, 42*, 25–82.

Worth, S., & Gross, L. (1974). Symbolic strategies. *Journal of Communication, 24*, 27–39.

# 4

# Approaches to Images In/For Learning: A Move to Inquiry Graphics

Inquiry graphics signs contain external images (e.g. pictorial graphics; photographs) as well as mental images (conjuring up a pictorial image in one's mind), positioning them as equal modes of expression in learning designs, pedagogy, and knowledge development, equal to the dominant verbal mode. Jewitt (2008) observes that:

> Where image is acknowledged in educational settings it is often celebrated for its potential to interest and motivate learners and the link between visual forms of knowledge and learning is seldom made. (p. 15)

The present work is about making and exploring that link. Despite gaining special attention recently through the development of visually salient digital media (Jewitt, 2008), visual expression has been around for a long time. It is evident in the prehistoric era, apparent in early cave paintings (Prosser, 1998). For example, there are Patagonian "Cuava de las Manos"—hand stenciled cave art (Prosser & Loxley, 2008), and polychrome cave painting in the Lascaux caves that were estimated to be painted around 17,000 BCE. In addition, pictorial storytelling/pictography similar to modern day comics and graphic novels (e.g. Tan (2007)) were used to provide a narrative in ancient Egyptian wall paintings and

© The Author(s) 2020
N. Lacković, *Inquiry Graphics in Higher Education*,
https://doi.org/10.1007/978-3-030-39387-8_4

some 150,000 pitoti rock-carved figures in northern Italy narrating the life of the community living in the region in the Copper/ Iron Age. The Codex Zouche-Nuttali, a pre-Hispanic Mexican manuscript from the fifteenth century is another example of pictorial narrative, describing the life of rulers in the eleventh and twelfth century (McCloud, 1994). Another expressive use of images and words is evident in the eleventh-century Bayeux tapestry: a visual description of the battle of Hastings created in a combination of sequential pictures and woven words (McCloud, 1994). In sum, expression via images has been an ongoing human endeavor since the dawn of civilization. Yet, the invention of the printing press and the practicality, sheer power and symbolic conventionality of the alphabet (the existence of grammar) placed language literacy at the foreground of the necessary competencies for human communication. There is no expectation in any enthusiasm here for the "visual turn" to overthrow or endanger language and language literacy. However, I argue in favor of greater and more serious acceptance of images and multimodal character of communication, the role of images in learning designs and, consequently, the importance of re-considering language literacy as related to visual literacy, hybrid literacies such as multiliteracies and a semiotic interrogation of images for learning.

In contemporary digital society, the image has vigorously inhabited technology space, but, as argued in Chap. 2, this has not invigorated transformative digital practices with it in higher education. The nature of digital technologies and the shift from book to the *image-prominent* screen (Jewitt, 2002, 2005) and mixed media (Mitchell, 2002), have generated a need to understand how learners tackle such *image-salient technologies* for learning purposes. Consequently, this generates a need to understand what kind of new literacy practices learners can engage with (since screen communication practice is different from print communication practice). Discourse organized around books, articles, notebooks, and the blackboard comprised, and still seem to be the leading, resources for student learning. However, in today's culture, students are as likely to engage with the screen as with paper (Jewitt, 2008). Websites browsed on the screen are learning resources where reading does not flow in a linear fashion any longer—modular and granular designs of websites take reading experience to a new level. In this granularity, images hold an important place.

New technologies and media have rendered the production, exchange and access to images easier than ever before. They have initiated a fresh interest in image-based communication and meaning-making, due to the structural and representational changes in everyday communication and the emergence of new learning artifacts. Hence, images do matter, although the progress of teaching–learning to embed various modalities of communication is slow. How they matter for educational purposes is the focus of this chapter. I am aware, nevertheless, that this book is also logocentric in its primary expression form. Therefore, I also contribute to the situation I am weary of, but I have few options and opportunities to pursue a different form of expression in the context of the present book. I hope to contribute to changing this status quo, inspired by the work of colleagues such as Nick Sousanis, who completed the first PhD thesis in Education and English language in the graphic (narrative) form. This is not easy while situated in academic cultures that marginalize, resist, fear and even obstruct images, lacking in any support with and recognition of visual expression in knowledge development, for instance with regard to photographs, illustration, video or graphic narratives. For this book I had to exclude many images provided by students digitally modified many images that were provided by the students (due to copyrights and other publication challenegs). I developed an illustration idea drawn by Dr. Andi Setiawan, who deserves my gratitude and praise for supporting and enriching the book with few of his custom-made illustrations. Ideally, many points in this book would be expressed multimodally and with images, and this is something I hope to do in some of my future endeavors. In my hope and vision for educational futures, higher education institutions and journal publishers would have dedicated artists and trained artist-academics who would create pictorial, graphic and other modalities based academic resources. These could be done with drawings that simulate a material and embodied 3D world on a 2D surface, for an unflattened interpretation of a flat paper representation, to encourage seeing the world's non-flatness on a flat surface. As such, I relate to Sousanis's (2015) idea of "unflattening" (see Appendix 1 for drawings by Nick Sousanis and Andi Setiawan, as an example of visual expression that can be an integral part of an Inquiry graphics (IG) inquiry—the vast potential and power of drawing and sketching for education deserves a book of its own, but the IG inquiry can also account for using ilustrations to mediate learning).

I do not tackle here some well-known and exemplary works in psychology such as Stephen K. Reed's (2010) *Thinking Visually* and Rudolf Arnheim's (1969) *Visual Thinking* that bridge psychology and art. These books are relevant and can be used for future explorations of IG. In a nutshell, they provide arguments why images are important and how they function in relation to perception and reasoning (Reed, 2010; Arnheim, 1969). The perspectives chosen here are selected and selective, as there are many approaches and avenues that could have been taken, and, as in every approach, there are gains and losses with these practical decisions. In this chapter I focus on the argued trajectory of image uses in HE, from exploring images as *exposition* tools (to represent, to illustrate) toward their creative, integrated, and relational character and uses in higher education via IGs. Therefore, the chapter will consider the move in image uses and applications from the prevalent expository uses (Lackovic, Crook, Cobb, Shalloe, & Cruz, 2015) toward more integral uses in higher education, as proposed via IG. The expository use means using images mainly to *show* or illustrate something, rather than *inquire* into something, e.g. building on visual features. Expository images usually act as illustration tools or summaries, for the main purpose to be viewed, consumed or support verbal text, rather than to be engaged with creatively and critically, in order to be developed, changed, collaged, re-created, shared, challenged and adopted as constituents of an educational and scientific inquiry, such as an IG sign.

# Expository Images: Information Graphics and Multiple Visual Representations

To start with, the function of IG (inquiry graphics) stands at the different end of the spectrum to the widely practiced function of infographics (information graphics). This does not mean that one is better or worse than the other, but to consider their different key functions and purpose. Infographics belong to the expository uses of images, aligned with the notion of information visualization. Many researchers have explored information visualization: for example, Tufte's (2001) *The Visual Display of Quantitative Information* has been widely cited. One definition of "information visualization" is that "(i)nformation visualization is about gaining insight into data through a visual representation" (Ellis & Dix, 2007, p. 1). Ware (2000, p. 2) explains that

Until recently, the term visualization meant constructing a visual image in the mind (*Shorter Oxford English Dictionary*, 1972.) It has now come to mean something more like a graphical representation of data or concepts. Thus, from being an internal construct of the mind, a visualization has become an external artifact supporting decision making.

Therefore, "visualization" and "data (information) visualization" can be used interchangeably. There are various types of "data visualization" according to Ware (2000, p. 7): ranging from cave paintings to mathematical equations, and today there is a wide range of digital visualisations. With regard to interpretation, information visualization and information graphics are mainly concerned with an impactful summary of data visually, that is, how to present data effectively, so that it is easier for users to interpret them or learn how to do so, without much active interpretative and interrogating work taking place—the easier to decode (quickly), the better. Of course much effort is invested from infographic designers to create a compelling infographic.

In the research branded as "technology enhanced learning (TEL)," information visualization has been taken mainly to cover image types such as graphs, diagrams, maps and charts, rather than depictive, pictorial images or visual affordances of digital technology, tools and platforms, especially in terms of how they mediate learning. In medicine and biology related research (e.g., chromatography), visualization serves the aim of representing data (such as the DNA helix). The character of all visualizations is that there is no representation (embodied Representamen) that is identical to what it represents (its Object)—such isomorphism can be discussed just in case of cloning; otherwise, it is always a representation, a depiction, not the represented Object, and therefore subject to interpretation.

Infographics are species of multimodal information visualization and hybrid graphics as they actively use pictorial images in the design of visual information. An infographic is defined as "a type of picture that blends data with design, helping individuals and organizations concisely communicate messages to their audience" (Ware, 2000, p. 1). Many books about infographics have appeared since the rise of this communication medium. Often they are directed toward the beneficial market potential of "standing out" and putting a message across in a concise and animating way, to fit into the world of rapid data consumption, where all social media and services are competing for audience's attention (Lankow, Ritchie, & Crooks, 2012). Information visualization and graphics research are mainly concerned with designs that can most successfully and rapidly achieve cognitive data communication impact. This means that visualization allows immediate recognition of errors, an understanding of large-scale and small-scale features of data, and the perception of properties which are not easily anticipated just in descriptions and explanations of phenomena (Ware, 2000). This "depictive" quality of visual information, and of pictorial signs in general, is its unique character that differentiates it from verbal signs. But infographics do not have to necessarily serve only for quick information impact on viewers. All the elements of the depiction can act as triggers for creative reflection and insight, leading onto new ideas and solutions. As of more recently, infographics have also been considered as tools in political persuasion, not a minor function that they can have:

> digital political infographics are hybrid communicative forms, characterized by three influence trajectories between political persuasion, infographic conventions, and digital environments: "politicizing" infographic traits, "infographing" political tactics, and creating a new common ground, featuring a rhetoric of "tactile data experience." (Amit-Danhi & Shifman, 2018)

This only illustrates a hybrid persuasive character of digital media and image signs, as they can adopt various functions, and therefore need to be analyzed not just serve the presentation of data and data analysis. Infographics have been almost seamlessly embedded into everyday social media communication. Without any mechanisms to make learners aware that we need to stop and inquire all graphics, including infographics, HE will continue treating visual information mainly as data visualization and embellishments, rather than visual learning tools in the society and learning, using them primarily as illustrations, summaries and decorations. These uses can support a piece of information about research data to reach out to diverse audiences in an effective manner, for greater outreach and impact. However, they need to be counterbalanced, as we also need to consider the "slow thinking" with visualizations and graphics, not just fast impact. Although there exist free downloadable applications that offer teachers and students tools to create their own information graphics, images in these research traditions have functioned more as expository artifacts (whereby students are presented with visual material), rather than creative opportunities (whereby students are asked to infuse, design, re-design, re-create and create information). Inquiry graphics is similar to information visualization and infographics research as it is also a way of visualizing information or concept, albeit for a very different purpose—it requires an in-depth analysis. It focuses on student agency as exercised in creating or selecting an image and engage in a critical and creative interrogation of it.

Strategies for managing and "optimizing" learners' experience with expository images and visualizations is found in cognitive theories of multimedia image co-coordination and combination. The work by Mayer in multimedia learning is widely recognized as the author had produce a pioneering work on how different forms of visual and multimodal information affect viewers' short-term attention and memory capacity (most notably in relation to cognitive load theory when too many modalities are processed at the same time, the information is media-oversaturated, thus it overloads cognitive processing channels). But this is not the focus of inquiry graphics: IG is not about processing visual information in cognitive or psychological sense to address memory, as Mayer's and others' work focus on.

It is worth mentioning the work in the area of multiple representations as another type of expository visualization for learning study field. Ainsworth (2006) developed a widely recognized and applied framework of multiple representations functions in terms of how learners integrate different types of representations cognitively, which include, for example, complementary, constraining and deeper understanding functions developed across multiple (types of) representations (Ainsworth, 2006, 2008). These representations could be a video, a drawing and a photograph, all aiming to represent differently one key concept, phenomena, function or activity to be explored for learning. This is similar to the aims of the learning activity design developed in the empirical Projects 2 and 3 as they also require presentation and multiple display of images selected by learners for their critical discussions, albeit with different key aims. With inquiry graphics activities the focus is not on "appropriate" representation or fixed scientific goal as this might often be the case with multiple representations learning and its situatedness in "hard" sciences, but learners are free to choose whatever they find suitable from their own experience, which then provides a source and trigger for both individual and collective reflection. Ainsworth (2006) suggests, among others, rules for learning with/from a representation: (1) Learners should understand the form of representation, and (2) Learners should understand the relation between the representation and the domain. These are relevant to inquiry graphics: a drawing or photograph or mural as a type of graphics are all different forms of representations (the present focus is on digital photographs), and it is important to define how the image represents the domain (scientific domain or scientific concept). For example, learners would decide if a photograph represents a real-life possibility of its occurrence or it is a metaphor or symbolic representation, and what kind of content variations it could represent that can be relevant to the explored concept. This helps students engage with and understand the diversity of images and thinking with images possibilities.

The work on multiple representations is also relevant to inquiry graphics and related methods as it explores *learning* with multiple representations, concerning external visual representations. However, the aim of inquiry graphics is not centred on measuring the learning improvement (or the lack thereof) in hard sciences, as it is common in multiple representations research. IG differs from multiple representations research as it focuses on a "structural metaphor," that is, both an unlikely and predictable/logical/ possible *coupling* of a concept and an image for the purpose of learning with and beyond concept definitions, as a novel, creative insight. In multiple representation research, visual representation mainly represents a phenomenon to explicitly illustrate the concept aiming for as "scientifically correct" way as possible, such as medical drawings or illustrated diagrams (e.g., of heart functions), animated videos and drawings in physics or chemistry, and so on. The researchers are focusing on how a visual representation supports an understanding of a pre-determined scientific rule, law or conception, not meant to be conceptually challenged and expanded, and critically and metaphorically explored. An IG approach can expand multiple representations research, and the other way around.

IG empirical studies presented later share an interest in the *function of images for learning with multiple representations research*. In the present IG concerns, this is not to define or measure exact learning outcomes but to conceptualize student behavior and artifacts' characteristics within a specific interdisciplinary and edusemiotic framework. The focus is on the theory of meaning and teaching–learning practice with graphics and image–concept sign interpretations, as well as defining acts of such visual and multimodal learning.

## Visual Literacy as a Move toward Interpretation Fluidity and User-Created Images

Visual literacy moves the concern with visual exposition learning in Section "Expository Images: Information Graphics and Multiple Visual Representations" to the concern with visual interpretation learning, relevant to inquiry graphics. It relates to the general concept of visual communication and could possibly cover any form of activity that includes exploring visual interpretations. Academic concern with visual literacy and the term itself has existed since the late 1960s (Debes, 1969). It is hard to satisfy all the demands for an adequate definition, and it is understandable why the field of visual literacy and the term itself has been questioned and disputed as an appropriation from language literacy (e.g., by Cassidy and Knowlton, 1983). Debes' (1969) early definition views it as essential for human learning and for creating, appreciating, and understanding visual information (Debes, 1969, p. 27). The definition is useful but emphasizes perceivers' competencies and underplays the role of the visual form itself (Avgerinou & Ericson, 1997). Moore and Dwyer (1994) have written one of the most encompassing and eclectic accounts of what can be considered as visual literacy, covering the subjects of perception, perceptual rules, communication models, memory, design, creativity, aesthetics, interpretation, thinking, politics, moral and visual research—to name but a few themes. Thus, the concept of visual literacy covers many, perhaps all, sciences: communicating with representations can be a part of any scientific endeavor.

The American Association of College and Research Libraries took a big step in acknowledging visual literacy in higher education in their "Visual Competency Standards for Higher education" document in 2011 (ACRL, 2011). They offer the following definition:

> Visual literacy is a set of abilities that enables an individual to effectively find, interpret, evaluate, use, and create images and visual media. Visual literacy skills equip a learner to understand and analyze the contextual, cultural, ethical, aesthetic, intellectual, and technical components involved in the production and use of visual materials. A visually literate individual is both a critical consumer of visual media and a competent contributor to a body of shared knowledge and culture.

These standards are the response to a decades-long attempt by many educational researchers and thinkers to draw the attention of education policy makers and curriculum makers to the importance of visual literacy. The need for a more serious understanding of images in human communication has been argued throughout this book, especially in Chap. 1. Martin Jay (2002), one of the founders of visual studies, in his interview for the *Journal of Visual Culture*, contends that:

> Insofar as we live in a culture whose technological advances abet the production and dissemination of (…) images at a hitherto unimagined level, it is necessary to focus on how they work and what they do, rather than move past them too quickly to the ideas they represent or the reality they purport to depict. (Jay, 2002, p. 88)

The message in favor of developing visual literacy, or the more recent construct of "visual competence" (Müller, 2008), has been articulated for decades. It seems that the call for researching visuals seriously in education (higher education showing a particular neglect) has been repeated ever since the consideration of visual instruction and audiovisual methods in the 1920s and 1930s (e.g., Hoban, Hoban and Zissman's *Visualising the Curriculum*, published in 1937 (Reiser, 2001)). Alongside Sless's plea for exploring learning with visuals in higher education, another appeal was made in the 1980s by Krane and Dyson (1981): "What has not yet happened in education, in general, is the full recognition of pictorial conceptualization" (p. 21).

The visual literacy movement sparked some negative reaction though in the 1980s, such as Cassidy and Knowlton's (1983) verdict that the entire movement exercises a failed metaphor by mainly drawing on the view that the term "literacy" is most appropriate where it originated—in literature and linguistic studies. Without disputing the importance of stable scientific entities (e.g., literacy fundamentally stems from and is connected to linguistics), history teaches us that any existing concept is constantly being reshaped, re-understood and modified as time passes. The present book rejects conceptual determinism. Hence, "literacy" can involve the exploration of images (external or mental) and other communication modes, alongside language. The present work specifically delves into the semiotic aspect of visual literacy as semiotic thinking and learning designs that incorporate external and internal images.

In response to Cassidy and Knowlton's (1983) critique, Sless (1984) contends that visual literacy could be the case of a "*failed opportunity*," rather than a "failed metaphor" (Avgerinou & Ericson, 1997). The author claims that:

> Visual literacy is any sustained activity that treats visual material and its uses as worthy of intelligent consideration. This is the heart of the matter and the reason for retaining the metaphor. (Sless, 1984, p. 226, cited by Avgerinou & Ericson, 1997, p. 282)

Indeed, our experience might have taught us that there is much intelligent rationale for investigating visual materials (depictive images in this case) for and within human learning. Braden (1996) finishes his encompassing review of visual literacy stating that "there is much research yet to be done" although "the literature about visuals and visual literacy is overwhelming" (p. 511). The literature on visual literacy remains overwhelming today, but empirical research in higher education studies is still lagging behind the general compelling scope of visual literacy research. Avgerinou and Ericson (1997) identified the practical value of developing visual literacy in education at all stages (p. 289). They sought the benefits of developing visual literacy in the 1990s, just as in the late 1970s, by revisiting Ausburn and Ausburn's (1978) benefit list. The list is just as valid now, more than 20 years after Avgerinous and Ericson's revisiting. The first four learning benefits of visual literacy from the list show its connection to the verbal modalities and thinking:

1. increase in all kinds of verbal skills,
2. improved self-expression and ordering of ideas,
3. increase of student motivation and interest in subjects of all types at all levels,
4. reaching students not being reached in traditional ways.
(Avgerinou & Ericson, 1997, citing Ausburn & Ausburn. 1978, p. 295)

In connection to the fourth benefit, which is particularly relevant in international higher education context (as in the USA or the UK, where postgraduate international students form a large proportion of the student body) Sinatra, Beaudry, Stahl-Gemake, and Guastello (1990) argue in favor of visual approaches in teaching and learning with diverse international groups of students. Such groups represent a major part of the constituency for Master's degree courses (such as is the context for this book). Braden (1996) cites Baca and Braden (1990) list of what visual literacy research needs to do as a part of educational development and knowledge building:

• identify the learnable visual literacy skills;
• identify the teachable visual literacy skills;
• develop implementation of visual literacy constructs;
• validate implementation of visual literacy constructs;

- provide a rationale for visual literacy implementation in our society;
- provide a rationale for visual literacy implementation in our educational system;
- supplement research conducted in other fields, including psychology, education, learning, visual perception and eye movement studies, print literacy. (p. 70)

In line with these recommendations, I have been providing insights so far and will provide empirical findings that relate to these needs for visual literacy in education, via inquiry graphics and digital photographs. The word "supplement" above is problematic, as it still reinforces the alternative and marginal status of visuals and visual literacy as added rather than integrated constructs.

The term "visual competence" has been suggested as necessary by Müller (2008, p. 101) in terms of its relevance to social sciences, which is the context of the empirical studies in Part II: "the necessity for introducing a new research paradigm—'visual competence'—in the social sciences (anthropology, communication science, media and social psychology, political science, sociology).

The author goes on to argue that this necessity has been generated since "the actual transformations of reality triggered by processes of globalization and digitization require *a closer scrutiny of the visual*" (Müller, 2008, p. 10, italics added). These developments in the new millennium echo Sless's (1981) "old" concerns about the urgency of exploring the potential of images in higher education, and other reflections stated in Chap. 1. Other recent developments in the field clearly acknowledge the necessity of visual literacy in higher education. For example, Bleed (2005) claims in an Educause initiative report that:

Visual literacy must not be viewed as just another education "add-on" and "frill" (…) offers educators an opportunity to connect with learners and enhance the quality of their learning (…) deserves a significant focus in higher education.

The Educause report and the acknowledgement by The American Association of College and Research Libraries represent cases in the

United States. The UK still seems to leave visual literacy to creative industries, art, design and media, as a distinct, additional approach that might not be seen as integrative across disciplinary domains (e.g., The Digital Britain Report (BIS, 2009, p. 175), the Higher Education Academy Employability paper and at a school level in the Ofsted Drawing Together report (2009)).

According to the Visual Competency Standards for Higher Education (ACRL, 2011), in an interdisciplinary, higher education environment, a visually literate individual is able to:

- determine the nature and extent of the visual materials needed;
- find and access needed images and visual media effectively and efficiently;
- interpret and analyze the meanings of images and visual media;
- evaluate images and their sources;
- use images and visual media effectively;
- *design and create meaningful images and visual media*;
- understand many of the ethical, legal, social, and economic issues surrounding the creation and use of images and visual media, and access and use visual materials ethically.

Only the sixth of the points above relates to creative image practices (italicized for emphasis), requiring students to create an image or artifact for learning. An IG activity can support the development of a number of visual literacy "skills and competences," for example, all of the seven points above, although the goal of an IG activity is not observed through the terms "skills," "efficiently" or "effectively," but rather to support critical reflection and conceptual learning as relational and pluralistic. There have been a number of recent studies in visual literacy in the context of higher education. A recent review of the topic (Kędra, 2018) provides an overview of visual literacy definitions, between 1996 and 2013, with useful mapping of visual literacy categories clusters such as skills and types of visuals, concluding that instead of continuing to ask for a definition of visual literacy we should proceed to doing visual literacy studies and assessment, as definitions are already out there, generally presented in very similar ways (as can be also seen above). A special issue of the *Journal of Visual Literacy* (Kędra & Žakevičiūtė, 2019) provided a set of articles on visual literacy methods for learning and engagement with images in higher education, a few of them akin to an IG learning designs researched in the empirical studies in Part II (e.g., Chai (2019) focuses on the role of photo-elicitation in learning; Thompson (2019) suggests a critical method of reading digital images). However, there is still a scarcity of studies that explore learning in relation to postgraduate programs in education and higher education.

One design with images for learning that incorporates visual literacy cannot address all the points mentioned above. In addition, I am aware that the use of the terms literacy and visual literacy is contested, as visual forms of communication are different from verbal forms upon which the traditional literacy movement developed, and IG does not just support "visual literacy," but also multimodal and edusemiotic literacy and multi-literacies, including digital and critical media literacy. An alternative term to that of literacy is graphicacy. Yet, I do not think that deepening this debate on names and types is helpful, as many goals are shared among these terms, and terms, representing concepts, are not fixed, but evolving entities.

The present concern with visual literacy shifts the "images in learning" review from learning as either matter of outcomes or a concern with optimal learning design using images as illustrations or aids as in cognitive studies of representations, toward considering a more communicative, critical and creative approaches to images in learning in the following sections. The main visual literacy focus with IGs is placed on the potential of images to support creative practice with image-based resources, where such images serve reflexive and critical inquiry, analysis and discussion, which invites considerations of power, truth, provenance, visual message consumption, production, history, and so on, not just the interpretation of image content *per se or concerns with accuracy.*

## Criticality and Critical Media Literacy

Visual literacy is closely related to (or perhaps extended by) critical visual and critical media literacy (Kellner & Share, 2007). There is a glaring necessity to introduce a new research paradigm that embed these literacies and the so called "visual competence" into the social sciences (anthropology, communication science, media and social psychology, political science and sociology) to include the essential exploration of power, identity and representation, justice and equality, intersectionality and agency in relation to the visual and media (Share, 2005; Lackovic, 2020). This section is an acknowledgement of education as a political space that can also act as a normalizing machine.

Inquiry graphics is an approach that can be useful in considering power, ideology and other social issues, such as inequalities, structure, and agency via explorations of image–concept meanings. In that ambition, it is related to social semiotics as an ideological deconstruction of signs, a direction that also evokes developments toward critical semiotics, critical multimodality and critical inquiry graphics, when critical theory and pedagogy are related to inquiry graphics analysis. Semiotics and IG approaches can be cross-fertilized with critical theory approaches to media, as in the work of the Frankfurt school and its representatives— Adorno, Habermas and others. Social semiotics also actively embraces the often-volatile social dimension of meaning-making, focusing on the power relations that underlie the processes of sign creation and use in order to mold individuals and societies (Chandler, 2002). In *Social Semiotics*, Hodge and Kress (1988, pp. 2–4) argue that this social science deals with how people design and interpret meanings in texts and how those semiotic entities are formed and reshaped by social ideologies, interests and intentions. Social semiotics fuses M. A. K. Halliday's central idea on the social roots of language with Marxist theory to understand ideology in sign formation. Social semiotic views by Kress and van Leeuwen (1998) in *Reading Images: A Grammar of Visual Design* are framed by exploring the materiality of signs, how they signify in society and how they are motivated by human intentionality and volition. The reading of images they propose is informed by Halliday's linguistics; linguistic theory and characterizations are translated into the realm of images.

To re-visit the argument in Chap. 1 on the persuasive strength of visual input, the discussion here refers to Michael Apple's (2004) analysis of the power of media-created imagery on an audience's mind. The author states that he himself questioned his own foundation of reality when something happened for real, which he used to see only via media-created imagery beforehand. He is referring to his experience of 9/11 footage at the very moment of seeing the footage on the TV. He was surprised to realize that he could not believe the "real" as he expected more explosion, fire and smoke, in the manner of *Die Hard* movies, when fabricated explosions are shown. Therefore, the real event seemed unreal since it did not match his visual expectations. This disbelief, it should be noted, was felt by a leading scholar in critical (hidden) curriculum and ideology, very much aware of how images work; visual media affects all viewers. His argument is that visual media can shape our consciousness and influence our thinking, but we get on with our lives often unaware of this happening, with rare opportunities or none to tackle and analyze images in educational experiences.

Scholars have investigated visual representations and meaning making as related to semiotic and multimodality studies, placing their focus on different modes, such as CD ROMs (Jewitt, 2002), monuments (Kruk,2008), music (van Leeuwen, 1999), photographs in presentation slideware (Hallewell & Lackovic, 2017), and video clips (Martinec, 2000). They all suggest critical examination of meaning-making, which might contribute to further development of social justice, citizenship and activism. Although Peirce's semiotics was not concerned with ideology or exploring power relations overtly, these are implicit in the triadic sign structure which is obscured in everyday communication, but speaks volumes in terms of how representations work in societies. As such this meaning-making triad is often a hidden sign underlining communication in a society where individuals or groups rarely take time to pause and ask: "Is this really what this means (questioning the Interpretant of the Representamen) or the very Representamen-sign—Is what I see that what I think it is? How does this sign mean what it means to me, or how is it described in a scientific community and how the two can be brought together? Where did the sign come from?" and so on. The interpretative (Interpretant) and thus intentional and motivated character of sign when used in the society subsequently leads to considering the intention, motivation, interpretation, applications and the effects of human sign actions. I acknowledge that these considerations cannot be divorced from power, ideology, structure and agency. This book embraces these contestations of meanings characteristic as a part of critical theory and pedagogy but does not provide an extended consideration of that side of IG signification, treating it only as a part of student interpretative work.

I maintain that critical media information pedagogy or training is needed in any subject, discipline and program, to support higher education's civic role and duty in building more socially just societies. However, there is a tension in academic understanding of what this "training" and critical engagement entails. This tension is connected to approaches to media format, characteristics, analysis procedures and aims, as well as the effects of appraising them through theoretical and conceptual lenses (Pangrazio, 2016). Therefore, different terminologies are used to connote the need for critical engagement with media, foregrounding new notions of "literacy." Some of the terms include: critical media literacy (Kellner & Share, 2007), critical digital literacy (Pangrazio, 2016), critical information literacy (Elmborg, 2006), and critical media pedagogy. Shared messages of all these approaches could be summarized and presented to varying extents for each approach, as:

1) Media and social media messages are not neutral, but deeply entwined with socio-cultural histories, systems and ideologies, hence they need to be questioned and examined critically.
2) Media and social media critical examination require training and active practice.

In addition to these approaches, a "civic media literacies" approach foregrounds the role of critical pedagogy and theory in students' social media literacies (Mihailidis, 2018). One of the definitions of critical media literacy and pedagogy that I wish to emphasize, adapting Ellsworth's (1989, 324) definition, is the one that acknowledges teachers' and everyone else's "knowledge of me, the world and 'the Right thing to do' will always be partial, interested, and potentially oppressive to others." Mihailidis (2018) criticizes media literacies skill-building as a transactional approach, claiming that, although very useful, it needs definitional and practical expansion ("practical" meaning pedagogy, action and change). McArthur (2010) similarly identifies the need for and challenges in moving from critique to desired change. However, she also rightly emphasizes the importance of coming together, whether one sees herself as critical thinker or critical pedagogue. Inquiry graphics studies in Part II mainly support critical thinking, but they also have elements of critical pedagogy, acting as possible resistance arteficts and resources for organizational and pedagogical practice change (Tett & Hamilton, 2019). Only a union of many international pedagogues and the formation of critical mass could bring about some change, rather than pockets of thinkers and approaches that criticize each other, although they subscribe to the same broader strivings toward critical awareness (McArthur, 2010). Therefore, to cherish this culture of critical awareness, images of educational spaces and places, images on educational platforms, web sites, digital media, buildings and campuses need to be subject to critical inquiry. One such critical inquiry that IG approaches relate to is called critical graphicacy.

# Graphicacy, Critical Graphicacy and Photographs

Graphicacy is defined as "the ability to communicate using still visual images, such as graphs, maps, drawings etc." (Danos & Norman, 2011). This definition does not encompass moving and animated images, multimedia artifacts sand hybrid multimodal constructions. These authors appeal for considering the place of graphicacy in education in ways compatible to the present thesis:

> The power of images has great possibilities and potentials. It can change one's perceptions and decisions. It can be used as a tool for learning and for recording thinking. In our schools' curricula, we find literacy, numeracy and articulacy being the main focus areas across the subjects, placing no substantial efforts toward graphicacy. However, in all subjects, lessons are primarily taught with the use of verbal and visual communication. Despite this, the teaching of understanding and working with different types of images takes up little space in the curriculum.

Graphicacy can be related to visual literacy, but the concept of critical graphicacy is also related to both interpretation and critical learning with images. Roth, Pozzer-Ardenghi and Han (2005) give the name "critical graphicacy" to the critical analytical and semiotic scrutiny of pictorial representations. Roth and colleagues argue that:

Learning authentic science and other subjects would have some likeness with adaptation to particular settings and the structures that characterize its social and material characteristics. The way students thereby adapt is by means of developing structured dispositions... However, even within the different sub-fields of science, practitioners do not agree with all assumptions and question the very pedagogy used to bring new members into the culture... Pierre Bourdieu advises the practice of "radical doubt" with which his students are to get hold of and critique their own prejudice and commonsense notions that they had previously acquired without being aware of them. Education for critical graphicacy, paralleling education for critical literacy, means providing students with the opportunities to interrogate the different means of representing the world and to question the different power relations that are thereby constructed. (Roth et al., 2005, p. xiii)

Roth and colleagues extensively developed the critical reading of graphs, illustrative diagrams, and photographs, mainly in the natural sciences. Again, this differs from an inquiry graphics method that concerns mainly social sciences, but it can add a layer of critical inquiry to natural or the "hard" sciences. Notably, they provide classroom-based cases in favor of graphicacy. Their framework is grounded in semiotics (together with anthropology and critical phenomenological hermeneutics). The authors contend that:

Conceptualizing verbal texts, graphs, drawings, photos, and other communication devices as texts provides the basis for a notion of critical graphicacy that applies across the curriculum. We would therefore expect students to be empowered if they engaged not only in learning the subject matter of history, language, science, and mathematics but also in (semiotic) analysis of different forms representing. (Roth et al., 2005, p. 23)

They continue with arguing a considerable citizenship value to critical graphicacy using the term "border pedagogy" which goes hand-in-hand with the critical perspectives adopted in this book:

Students no longer learn only the "right stuff," but also learn how sign forms (inscriptions) support particular readings, argument, and politics.

They also learn that changing sign forms will carve up the world in different ways and, therefore, that meaning is neither transcendental nor fixed or terminable. Critical graphicacy thus defined becomes epistemological and discursive praxis; literacy becomes part of a broader project of border pedagogy and a construction of democratic public life.

It could be said that IG is a type of critical graphicacy orientation and activity, which develops critical graphicacy through Peirce's semiotic triad.

The main ingredient of an IG is a digital photograph (although it could be a physical photograph). Much has been said about the photograph, notably that it can function as icon, index or symbol (Goldstein, 2007), as mentioned earlier in Chaps. 1 and 3 when explaining photographs as signs. The hybrid communicative function of photographs further illuminates their contested. Goldstein (2007, p. 64) contends that "(t)he most trivial reason that a photograph can never represent reality is that it's a two-dimensional representation of a three-dimensional world." (p. 65). However, our mind makes a connection between that flatness and 3D world and understands that one represents the other, via our ability to understand perspective and depth in a photograph or drawing, its foreground and background. What matters is to *interrogate its content*.

The trouble is that photographs have a contested relationship with "truth" in society, as Hine (1909) cited by Goldstein, (2007, p. 61) warns, albeit the nature of his "average" person is unclear:

> The photograph has an added realism of its own; it has an inherent attraction not found in other forms of illustration. For this reason the average person believes implicitly that the photograph cannot falsify.

Questioning the "truth" value of pictures has had a long tradition. I build on Nöth's (2002) view that semiotics can provide tools for analyzing the truth or lie in pictures without a logocentric bias. Nöth (2002) reflects that pictures have been scapegoats for those who "foresee an apocalypse in the domain of media studies" (Nöth, 2002, p. 133). He argues that this is a long-standing bias, referring to Gustav Le Bon, who, in his work *Psychology of the Masses*, "accuses" the picture of their lowly character to serve the deception and manipulation of the (quote) "primitive ones" (Nöth, 2002, p. 133, quoting Le Bon (1895)). Nöth criticizes Le Bon's attitude toward pictures as the currency of the "masses," referring to Le Bon's words:

> The masses can only think in images and can only be influenced by means of pictures. Only pictures can frighten and persuade them and become the causes of their action (…) To them, the unreal is almost as important as the real. (LeBon, 1895, and 3.2 in Nöth, 2002, p. 133)

This association of pictures with mass thinking, as a derogatory, "primitive" form of thinking, is highly problematic. It is as problematic as exaggerating the virtues of pictures as vehicles of high level "visual thinking" by invoking Einstein's or Tesla's quotes and visualization techniques, or the proverbial claim that a picture tells a thousand words (so what, and how?). This does not amount to an understanding of what it means to think with images, such as photographs, and to take them as a legitimate means (signs or mediators) of communicating knowledge.

Certainly, photographs and our sense of vision need to be considered with caution. For example, we can see something that is not there. We often rely on our vision, as per the proverb "seeing is believing," although our vision can be tricked. Our individual sense of vision can trick us about the way the world seems to be or is. The concept of perceptual and optical illusion should be familiar to all. We can be "tricked" by images at the mere optical level, for instance the warning to car drivers that "objects in the mirror may be closer than they appear," hallucinations such as fata morgana, or at a more every day and therefore accepted case of visual lie, seeing a "broken" spoon in a glass of water, and so on. A recent example is the work of media artist Øyvind Kolås, who superimposed colored grids over black and white photos, giving the whole black and white photograph a colored feel to the eye, so that it seems that parts of the photograph are colored. "Tricks" can also be considered at the pictorial information consumption level. When viewing films, videos, advertisements or any pictorial representation, these representations are meant to be doing something—evoke an emotion, a perspective on the world, persuade. Evoke the examples and arguments from Chap. 1. Digital photographs as symbols of socio-cultural characteristics and concepts act to evoke ideas and feelings in humans. What it means to be respected, professional, sexy, poor, disabled, powerful, marginal and so on can be all encoded in photographic and media images (Hall, 2001, p. 19) occupying the digital.

In terms of representational truth of photographs (or its depicted form), it means to define the highest or nearest level of isomorphism of a photograph to its Object, or what it represents (Nöth, 2002). The invention of the camera obscura was a pivotal move in mimicking the objects' form from its 3D reality form onto a 2D form, by the manner of its closest possible representational isomorphism (as a photograph is never isomorphic to its Object in reality). Due to such mechanisms that create projected likeness, photographs look so real and believable, like frozen past moments. Over time, photographs have evolved with technology and arguably changed, and as such infiltrated everyday life to blur the boundary between the real and fabricated. The nearest-to-truth photograph is the one that corresponds to what it depicts factually, that is, a point- by-point representation (here taken as photo Representamen) of what it shows (its Object) (Nöth, 2002). That is, no aspect of its projected point-by-point form has been modified within and just after the first photographic processing. This also depends on the type of photoprocessing and how it works, as there exists mechanism today to alter (filter) photo rendering even during the process of taking a photograph, an issue which will be unpacked later. In legal proceedings, photographs can be used as documentary evidence that something happened (Nöth, 2002). Image types such as x-ray and radiograph are used in medical diagnosis as a type of visual truth. Yet, reaching some interpretational truth in terms of the most widely scientifically agreed meaning is not an easy endeavor, as it requires work and agreement by a larger scientific community. As science is in constant state of synechism (evolution), object meaning per se can never be fixed, other than agreed to the highest level of scientific consensus. Problems arise, of course, when the conditions around meaning-making are not well explored, stated or understood.

The urge to "accuse" photographs of "lying" is compelling (Goldstein, 2007). However, I suggest that what Goldstein (2007) is arguing by saying that all photos lie is that all photos can represent a framed and modified representation of reality (not necessarily by its users), and there are many ways they can be and are used by humans. If a lie is taken to be something that it is not what it stands for (Eco, 1976), which is any sign, for instance, then if we follow that logic all pictures and all language and all communication practices could be rightly called lies. Goldstein (2007) provides an example of a photographer's bent for photographic framing and how a photograph can look very "real" to our mind although it is manipulated and shows an event that could never happen in the real world. Photographs can be modified, and this modification can go to various extents, and to serve various purposes. Techniques such as cropping decide what is shown and what is not. These negotiated meanings reside at the crossroads of producer's and promoter's intent, the image signification and its contextualization, as well as the viewer's stance, prior knowledge and context of viewing. When tackling pictorial meaning, Rose (2011/2006) talks about three sites of image meaning-making: the production, the image itself (its materiality and composition), and the audience site, rightly positing questions in visual methods about the production, image signification properties, and image consumption.

Some dominant (encoded) meanings that could be interpreted as such (and hence proven to be dominant) by most intended viewers in pictures can be recognized and identified (Hall, 1973, 2001; Lackovic, 2010b). We can empirically "test" that by giving a diverse range of people an opportunity to code and analyze images with a set of identical questions (Lackovic, 2010), but any "one" fixed meaning is simply not there. Human intent and picture use is important in defining the level of truthfulness of pictures. Yet, in today's post-digital landscape, where the boundaries between offline and online are blurred (Jandrić et al., 2019), with its photographic upload frenzy, it can be hard to trace the digital life or birth and re-authoring of photographs, as they are readily appropriated, re-purposed, modified, collaged, and/or labeled with new texts. In this frantic digital production and dissemination medley, the visual has become a part of a power game, of media wars, where careful orchestrations of film, television and advertisement production goes around in global circles (Mirzoeff, 2002). One possible way forward in exploring the life of photos is to try to devise photo trails and understand how they are circulated —how and where they appear and reappear, for example by using the reverse photo search provided by Google Images search engine.

This also means to explore clusters of pictures, for example the ones that are labeled in similar way or occur in clusters on the media, such as institutional websites or news media.

If we further consider, as an example, a photograph filtering method that is now widely and almost by default used by anyone who owns a mobile phone, the discussion of the truth of the image gains a new layer of complexity. Is it the intention of the user of a selfie filter to tell a lie about the photo object or the representation of it, or is it to beautify the truth about the Object or its representation, or both; is there actually a difference between these intentions, and what does that difference mean, and how does it matter? Or is it about a specific degree of modification that makes an image a lie and turns it into a harmful or even oppressive representation? Can we define and agree where precisely to draw the line and how? Different arguments could arise. Someone might argue that some color beautification is not necessarily a change of the form, for instance red eyes in photos are corrected almost by default, for the very reason that they are unlike the real eye color. Someone else might point out for example that erasing under-eye circles, as in most cover magazine pictures, is certainly not telling the truth (either of object or its representation) and is not an innocent act of beautification in its idealization of the representation. Such modification idealizes the human subject-object, setting almost unachievable standards of beauty. But then there might be arguments that the filtering is art, or perhaps such a photograph is an art object that shows a new portrait style. Polish scientist-artist Prof Andrzej Dragan takes the use of Photoshop to a completely different extreme end—instead of erasing fine lines and smoothing out the look of the skin, he uses Photoshop to amplify and change facial and bodily shapes and lines, making the photograph looks visually extreme and often rather strange and disturbing at the level of detail and idea, to counter the dominant airbrushing "beautification" technique.

To summarize this exploration of photo truth, it could be said that trying to identify the intent and intentionality encoded in a picture by exploring its signifying properties, authoring, re-authoring, circulation, mediation, consumption and related context is important in appraising the use and role of photographs in everyday life. Engagement via edusemiotics can help such an exploration of images in education. A semiotic perspective on meaning-making is here considered to suggest a new focus on exploring photograph interpretations and their relationship to concepts across disciplines and in interdisciplinary spheres, such as the post-digital. Their ontological vagueness makes it even more appropriate to analyze and interrogate photographs in terms of their content, just as other pictorial forms, taken to be less "truthful." The benefits of such interrogation are not only in developing an understanding of the concept an image stands for, but also in developing critical and analytical awareness more generally and exploring the life of digital images as technosemiotic artifacts and post-digital signs.

# Photo Elicitation and Photovoice: Eliciting Thinking, Ideas and Prior Knowledge

There is a long tradition of mobilizing photographs as data within the social sciences. Unsurprisingly, this is particularly the case for anthropology, where photography is a common descriptive method for reporting (Collier, 1967). However, Collier took the step of treating pictorial material as more than mere records of cultural practice and social life. He suggests that they may be used to animate interview exchanges through a process he terms "photo elicitation," the elicitation of responses from the photo-viewer by using the photo in relation to certain interrogations of interest. Prosser and Loxley (2008, p. 22) illustrate the power of the photo elicitation method by stating that "images provide projective and iterative stimuli through which they reveal thoughts, behaviors, narratives and anecdotes."

Collier contrasts interviews he conducted this way with those in which he used traditional talk-only methods, stating the benefits of eliciting response by photographs: "The pictures elicited longer and more comprehensive interviews but at the same time helped subjects overcome the fatigue and repetition of conventional interviews." (1957, p. 858)

If we substitute student dialogue and communication for an anthropological interview, images appear as potent resources for fostering communication, at least if they are relevant to the concepts needing to be understood. In addition, it is noted that "what is important about the picture is determined, in part at least, by what people say about it" (Prosser & Loxley, 2008, p. 21, citing Walker & Weidel, 1985, p. 143). Since Collier's pioneering work, other investigators have compared various modes of media elicitation for interviewing (e.g., audio, photo and object), finding that photography is the most potent format (Samuels, 2004). Hurworth (2003) has traced the history of anthropological research exploiting the potency of photo-elicitation. Harper (2002) has provided a literature review that further promotes the case for interviewing in this way. He (2002, p. 22) presumes that photo-elicitation uncovers deeper layers of human consciousness and meaning-making in communication than words alone.

Some researchers pass the responsibility of the photography over to their participants. Therefore, participants create photographs in order to express their relationship to the topic assigned by the researcher. Prosser and Loxley (2008) claim that "there is greater potential in photo-elicitation when informants create or 'find' photographs that have significance for them" (ibid., p. 19). Heisley and Levy (1991) and Clark (1999) refer to this as "autodriving." Wang and Burris (1994) elaborate this to a form of photo-interviewing that they term "photo novella" or "picture stories," in which their participants use images to reconstruct everyday routines and events. Oliffe and Bottorf (2007, p. 850) term this method "photovoice." They argue that "Overall, there is strong agreement that photovoice can provide unique insights into diverse phenomena, as well as empowering and emancipating participants by making their experiences visible." Starr and Fernandez (2007) carry such reflexive photography to the extreme of equipping participants with head-mounted webcams, thus resourcing them to capture videos of everyday situations.

The studies cited above are based in anthropology or consumer research. However, such photo-elicitation interviewing has been employed in the context of education. It has proved particularly valuable for soliciting *students' personal understandings* of school and schooling (Agbenyega, 2008; Agbenyega, Deepler, & Moss, 2008; Epstein, Stevens, McKeever, & Baruchel, 2008). The strategy has also been employed for shaping conversations that refer to the design demands of school rebuilding projects such as the UK's BSF program (Woolner et al., 2010). One benefit of the method that these authors identify is the overcoming of stereotyped and unthoughtful responding that can characterize an interview. The visual and spatial nature of the mediating activities also seemed to help participants avoid more formulaic or over-rehearsed responses (Woolner et al., 2010). Chai (2019) argues in favor of a learning activity that includes photo-elicitation and creative and interpretative engagement around photographs in higher education.

I adopt an "*autodriven*" photo elicitation method (photovoice) as a pedagogic strategy for student agency and authoring, and for eliciting students' opinions and prior knowledge. In particular, this is exemplified in my empirical studies in Part II, students will select images themselves which would, according to their own understanding and exploration, represent the assigned concept to be explored, eliciting their concept interpretations.

# User Agency with Images: Engaging Students with Visual Materials in Higher Education

The traditional cognitive multimedia strand of research mentioned earlier as the expository approach to images has given little agency to students in tackling multimedia materials in the way that, for example, research on creative multimedia learning does (e.g., Sefton-Green & Sinker, 1999; Sefton-Green, 2005; Mitchell, 2003). Creative multimedia and multimodality research promotes student-generated content which is also the intention of inquiry graphics. For example, Mitchell (2003) presents a case of EdD students' creative engagement with *LiveSlideShow* software to deepen their engagement with academic themes. The software allows students to use images and sound to create a presentation on a topic. For example:

> Written demonstration of knowledge only projects a singular, verbal orientation toward the content. The projects required demonstration of knowledge through a multimedia orientation which not only required the learner to understand the concepts through these orientations as well, but to integrate these perspectives appropriately. (Mitchell, 2003)

In addition:

> Many students noted that these projects challenged them in new ways, demanding them to rethink how they communicate essential ideas. Most students thought that they would not have taken on these challenges themselves outside of a classroom setting. (ibid.)

The empirical examples in Part II aim to engage students in a manner similar to the above example from Mitchell (2003). They are engagements with *multimodal artifact assemblage for the purposes of interrogating disciplinary concepts*. The issue they tackle is defining conditions for stimulating depth of engagement *by the learner taking on an active critical inquiry role*. So, the core question is how to design a pedagogic scenario that orchestrates such image-based inquiry in a way, or by the virtue of design, which could be called optimal. Any approach to such a challenge requires consideration of the analytic skills that might need to be cultivated along the way.

Therefore, the empirical work adds another dimension to existing theories on learning with and from images: it contributes by *providing a narrative of engagement and a set of personal analytic awarenesses and inquiry dispositions* (fostering the development of the student's "scrutinizing eye" as Sless (1981) puts it in relation to images). The necessity of helping students to move from "glancing" to "productive observation and analysis" is also urged by Schnotz (2002, pp. 115/116) who claims (referring to the work of Mokros and Tinker & Weidenmann):

> Visual displays can support communication, thinking, and learning. However, they do not provide this support automatically. Learners often underestimate the informational content of pictures and believe that a short look would be enough for understanding and for extracting the relevant information.

The central educational and empirical concern of inquiry graphics practices is toward a particular design where student interpretation could lead to deeper engagement with the concepts, doing so through concept-relevant inferences, questioning and critique.

# Beyond Images: Creative Multimodality of Inquiry Graphics

New media development has encouraged approaches to learning which acknowledge an image emphasis on the screen (Jewitt, 2002, 2005). Kress and van Leeuwen (1996) rightly argue that, "given the importance of visually displayed information, there is an urgent need for developing adequate ways of talking and thinking about the visual" (p. 33). The rise of screen culture and practices—the so-called "digital turn" (Mills, 2010)—has extended interest in visual communication and communication realized in forms other than language. This interest encompasses approaches that judge communication to include not just language, but image, gesture, gaze, posture, sound and the relationships between them. Such approaches have been termed "multimodal" (Jewitt, 2009). Although this book focuses on photographs and graphics, inquiry graphics are multimodal artifacts, certainly a part of and contributing to the multimodality movement.

In the last two decades, the approaches of multimodality (Jewitt, 2014; Jewitt, Bezemer, & O'Halloran, 2016; Iedema, 2003; Jewitt, Kress, Ogborn, & Tsatsarelis, 2001; Kress & van Leeuwen, 2001); new literacies (Freebody & Luke, 1990; Knobel & Lankasher, 2006; Lankshear & Knobel, 2006); multiliteracies (Anstey & Bull, 2006; Cope & Kalantzis, 2000; New London Group, 1996) and academic literacy have been paving the way for a renewed understanding of communication and education processes, especially in relation to technology mediation. Such renewed understanding emphasizes that those processes go beyond language. They include various modes of meaning-making, and, consequently, new definitions of "literacy," "communication," "learning" and methods for researching them. This means that communication acts, including communication in education and at educational institutions, are fundamentally multimodal and now recognized as such (Bezemer & Kress, 2015).

The modes of "multimodality" include body movement and posture, gestures, gaze, print or computer screen layout, design, sound, tactile senses, material resources such as diagrams, photographs, illustrations,

3D models, liquids, video—any material thing that mediates teaching–learning interactions. Therefore, to understand educational processes beyond language, it is useful to apply approaches and methods that consider more modes than just language in meaning-making (Metcalfe, 2015; Norris, 2004; Bezemer & Kress, 2015; Jewitt et al., 2016; Breuer & Archer, 2016), such as video.

Higher education research has commonly applied methods that are language-driven (Metcalfe, 2015), such as interviews. The tactile and visual aspects of learning can be seen as prominent in some disciplines (e.g., medicine, engineering, applied arts and media and communication), but all disciplines include such aspects. If we accept that teaching–learning acts and interactions are multimodal, then capturing them in their multimodal nature, via a video recording, provides an opportunity to understand these teaching–learning interactions more fully. Such multimodal nature of communication is complex and layered. It can take much time to do an encompassing analysis. Therefore, more often than not, multimodal research focuses on particular modes or specific combinations of and relations among modes, including language. This focus needs to be clearly acknowledged. For example, multimodality studies have focused on, among others, hand gestures/ movement (Sakr, Jewitt, & Price, 2014), PowerPoint features (Zhao, Djonov, & van Leeuwen, 2014; Kress & van Leeuwen, 2001), and the relationship between speech and photographs in lectures at a range of universities (Hallewell & Lackovic, 2017), to mention but a few. In general, when applying any method, it is useful to consider and acknowledge what the analysis covers exactly.

A great swathe of multimodality studies has been done in the context of media and communication and in analyzing publicly available artifacts, such as advertisements (e.g., Thibault, 2000). However, there is a paucity of multimodal studies of higher education teaching–learning. Some exceptions include the work of Archer (2010) and the edited collection on multimodality in higher education by Breuer and Archer (2016). This book addresses the higher education studies gap by providing a multimodal and edusemiotic analysis and analytical approach.

Interest in multimodality as a recognition of communication signs consisting of other that verbal modes is not a product of the modern age.

As was argued in Chap. 3., Peirce's semiotics went beyond the verbal mode and the multimodal study has only been gaining pace since the mid-1990s, due to the rapid development of digital technology. The seminal work by the New London Group (1996) offered a "multimodality manifesto" that paved the way to development of broader views on literacy that surpass the purely linguistic. Authors such as Gunther Kress, Carey Jewitt, Theo van Leeuwen, Kay O'Halloran, Sigrid Norris and Arlene Archer, to name just a few, carried out seminal work in multimodality, with the field consistently expanding. Hull and Nelson (2005) claim that the power of multimodal expression lies in the mix of different modes and their relationships. This is also the "power" of IG. In discussing the combination of pictorial and language meaning-making as richer and more potent than the meaning realized through only one mode (e.g., language), they state that "(p) ictures, for instance, do not convey meaning in the same way that language does (…) As Kress (2003) notes, 'the world narrated' is a different world to 'the world depicted and displayed'" (Hull & Nelson, 2005, pp. 1–4). Therefore, it is fruitful to bring these two worlds together, not to continue treating them separately. In stating what is so powerful about using more modes of representation than language, Fosnot and Perry (2005) explain that different features of the same object or concept/ theme are depicted depending upon whether that object/ concept/ theme is represented through language, photography, drawing or clay etc. These authors argue that "(t)he very act of representing objects, interactions, or meanings embedded in experience, within media such as language, painting, or mathematical modelling appears to create a dialectical tension *beneficial to thought*." (Fosnot & Perry, 2005, p. 26, italics added).

Therefore, the dialectic is not to be overcome, but explored and expanded on. Since each communication medium has different affordances and limits, using more than one can enrich the formation of knowledge. As Archer (2010, p. 211) argues, "it is clear that using one mode to reflect on another can open up interesting spaces for reflection." In line with this multimodal quality of communication, new forms of "literacy" have been conceived in relation to the affordances of digital tools: such as those literacies termed "digital" or "media" literacies (Buckingham, 2010), multimodal literacy (Jewitt & Kress, 2003), information literacy (Eisenberg, Lowe, & Spitzer, 2004), multiliteracies

(Cope & Kalantzis, 2009), screen literacy (Brown, 2000), visual literacy (Avgerinou & Ericson, 1997) and digital visual literacy (Spalter & van Dam, 2008).

Acknowledging the need to investigate a range of modes in any learning act, the present book has one particular multimodal focus—the one of *image–language* joint use for learning, alternatively called image–concept unity. This dictates that inquiry graphics teaching–learning and associated IG learning design require students to make/ select images and then write explanatory narratives. They thus create an image–concept sign, a multimodal artifact (ensemble). Much more can be said of multimodality (for a comprehensive introduction see Jewitt et al., 2016). As this book focuses on graphics in learning, the book's scope is focused on the visual side of communication, as a specific focus within multimodality, tackling thinking, concepts and designs that integrate graphics. The multimodal aspect of it deserves further attention, and this is planned to be dealt with in another publication. This book's focus is the visual, semiotics, learning, concepts and knowledge development.

The proliferation of visual information has generated the so-called "visual turn." According to Jewitt (2008, p. 6, citing Castells, 2001):

(T)he visual turn can be understood as a response to this newly configured global and networked landscape marked by the social, cultural, economic trajectories of late (post)modernity: fluidity, speed, saturation, frenzied pixilation, and immediacy.

Jewitt claims that "The terrain of communication, creativity and education is changing in profound ways" (Jewitt, 2008, p. 6). The visual turn and its relative "pictorial turn" (Mitchell, 1995; Curtis, 2009) have initiated a more serious approach toward how images both shape and are shaped by culture and society. Indeed, our everyday life is "entwined with practices of representation" (Jewitt, 2008, p. 10). Pictures need to be understood as valid and equally potent sources of meaning-making artifacts and symbols, alongside language.

If teachers/ tutors encourage students to engage and produce learning artifacts in different modes (sign systems), and especially by combining two modes, one of them being verbal, this can be beneficial for learning.

The focus on "production" moves the student from consumer to producer (Neary, 2010): an inquiry graphics engagement encourages students to be creative and critically aware producers. The process of exploring the meanings of one disciplinary or program or module concept/ theme/ unit via a different sign systems is similar to "transmediation" (Short & Kauffman, 2000; Schmit, 2013), and akin to multimodal "transduction" (Kress, 2010). The benefits of transmediation are strongly argued by Short and Kauffman, (2000, p. 45):

> Transmediation is the process of taking understandings created in one sign system and moving them into another. Because the meaning potentials in each system differ, this process is not a simple translation of meaning from one system to another. Instead, learners transform their understandings through inventing a connection so that the content of one sign system is mapped onto another's expression plane. (Siegel, 1995)

Learners search for commonalties in meanings across sign systems, but their search creates anomalies and tension because each system has different meaning potentials and lacks one-to-one correspondence. This tension encourages learners to invent a way to cross the gap as they move to another sign system and, in so doing, to think generatively and reflectively. They create a metaphor that allows them to create new connections, ask their own questions, and open new lines of thinking (Siegel, 1995). Transmediation is thus a generative process in which new meanings are produced and the learner's understandings are enhanced.

*IG are integrative multimodal artifacts and signs that integrate images into conceptual thinking,* not as an addition but as key to creative and critical insight. As such they move the positioning of an image in learning from an expository artifact to an integral artifact in a learning design, and a mediator of students creative practice as well as their concept thinking externalization and expansion. IG processes are similar to transmediation if we consider the linguistic explanations of the concept coupled with pictorial materialization of the same concept. It is indeed not the case of some straightforward translating or transferring things from one system to another, but of creating a multimodal unit, connected via *multimodal anchorage,* which is the term coined in this book, explored in the empirical part. Multimodal anchorage (or just anchorage) brings together the meaning of image with the meaning of the concept for the consideration of conceptual forms and boundaries and especially for *probing those*. Interpreting the sign in detail helps understand its structure and how it makes meaning. Knowing the structure of the sign is seen as beneficial for students' learning, in harmony with Bruner's (1984, p. 183) statement:

> Learning is, most often, figuring out how to use what you already know in order to go beyond what you currently think. There are many ways of doing that. Some are more intuitive; others are formally derivational. But they all depend on knowing something "structural" about what you are contemplating—how to put it together. Knowing how something is put together is worth a thousand facts about it. It permits you to go beyond it.

This argument in favor of the knowledge of "something structural" therefore suggests that students would benefit from carefully "deconstructing" the inquiry graphics sign in their academic quest for a meaning that goes beyond its surface (Smagorinsky, 2001), in-between individual image elements and the whole image–concept IG sign.

# Integrating Approaches to Images Via Inquiry Graphics Practice in Higher Education

All the approaches discussed in this chapter are considered in the build-up of inquiry graphics as they share an ambition to bring serious attitude toward and acknowledgment of images in its various forms. As explained earlier, IG focuses on turning pictorial images and other graphics into inquiry artifacts to support relational and integrative ways of teaching and thinking that bridge the gap between the concept and the image, as will be further unpacked in the following Chap. 5. This inquiry with pictorial signs is envisaged to be developed into various pedagogical designs, and also as a part of a larger relational model. With IG, I acknowledge expository uses of images, but I strongly want to move images beyond such uses and suggest that they are not just there for reading and interpretation, for example, to establish whether they are "good" or "bad" (deceptive, manipulative). It can be said that my approach of inquiry graphics brings together critical graphicacy and photovoice with earlier presented photographic tripartite sign building on Peirce's triadic modeling, to argue the embeddedness of images in knowledge and concept development and its link to creative learning engagement. An inquiry graphic is a relational multimodal artifact as it contains an image and a conceptual narrative that is not supposed to treat image only as illustration, but as a source of imaginative analogical thinking to connect the image and the concept in many ways, for example as depending on interpreters (learners). This is what distinguishes inquiry graphics from other approaches such as infographics, critical graphicacy or visual literacy or methods, albeit IG activities can be related to and can incorporate these approaches and their ambitions.

In particular, IG encourages concept–image relational analysis and analogical thinking (a type of multimodal, iconic "intelligence"), for seeking concepts and ideas that were not originally "intended" in an image representation, but can nevertheless be related to the concept and body of knowledge (literature) that the image is positioned to relate to. As such, it can inspire new ways of thinking and modelling the world. The concept-image relationship can be changed for an artifact–concept exploration to encompass a wide variety of artifacts. It is important to include visually impaired people as iconic intelligence does not impose an iconic external image, but a mental diagrammatic and spatial modelling of understanding when learners interact with the world that surrounds them (environment, context).

An IG pedagogy means embedding graphics (iconic, visual sign) into inquiry thinking and pedagogical dialogue, by developing reflective and critical narratives around these graphics. Such a pedagogical or learning design can use, as a ground for analysis, an iconic image, for example a student-selected photograph chosen to represent an idea or concept. The method could inspire students to contemplate links between pictorial characteristics and any assigned concept upon the picture. This exemplifies thinking as "world-making" (Bruner, 2009), that bridges intuitively and logically known worlds with possible worlds (Pieterinen & Bellucci, 2016). It is the type of creative thinking mentioned in Chap. 1 that avoids conceptual determinism but seeks links across concepts and modes, refusing to close the chain of semiosis and possibilities. It seeks potential solutions, options and relations, awaiting to be discovered and acted upon. One can ask when this elaboration and chains of associations stop. This is for users (e.g. teacher and students) to decide and define the boundaries themselves.

# References

ACRL (Association of College & Research Libraries). (2011). ACRL Visual Literacy Competency Standards for Higher Education. *American Library Association*, October 27, 2011. http://www.ala.org/acrl/standards/visualliteracy (Accessed May 15, 2020).

Agbenyega, J. S. (2008). Developing the understanding of the influence of school place on students' identity, pedagogy and learning, visually. *International Journal of Whole Schooling, 4*, 52–66.

Agbenyega, J., Deppeler, J., & Moss, J. (2008, January). Knowing schooling, identity and pedagogy visually. In *AARE 2008: Changing climates: education for sustainable futures. Proceedings of the 2008 Australian Association for Research in Education conference* (pp. 1–12). Australian Association for Research in Education.

Ainsworth, S. (2006). DeFT: A conceptual framework for considering learning with multiple representations. *Learning and Instruction, 16*(3), 183–198.

Ainsworth, S. (2008). The educational value of multiple-representations when learning complex scientific concepts. In J. K. Gilbert, M. Reiner, & M. Nakhleh (Eds.), *Visualization: Theory and practice in science education* (pp. 191–208). Dordrecht, Netherlands: Springer.

Amit-Danhi, E. R., & Shifman, L. (2018). Digital political infographics: A rhetorical palette of an emergent genre. *New Media & Society, 20*(10), 3540–3559.

Anstey, M., & Bull, G. (2006). Teaching and learning multiliteracies: Changing times, changing literacies. International Reading Association. 800 Barksdale Road, PO Box 8139, Newark, DE 19714–8139.

Apple, M. W. (2004). *Ideology and curriculum* (3rd ed.). London: Routledge.

Archer, A. (2010). Multimodal texts in Higher Education and the implications for writing pedagogy. *English in Education, 44*, 201–213.

Arnheim, R. (1969). *Visual thinking*. Berkeley, CA: University of California Press.

Ausburn, L. J., & Ausburn, F. B. (1978). Visual literacy: Background, theory and practice. *Programmed Learning and Educational Technology, 15*(4), 291–297.

Avgerinou, M., & Ericson, J. (1997). A review of the concept of visual literacy. *British Journal of Educational Technology, 28*(4), 280–291.

Baca, J. C., & Braden, R. A. (1990). The Delphi study: A proposed method for resolving visual literacy uncertainties. *Perceptions of Visual Literacy*, 99–106.

Bezemer, J., & Kress, G. (2015). *Multimodality, learning and communication: A social semiotic frame*. London: Routledge.

BIS. (2009). The Digital Britain report, DCMS (Department for culture, media and sport). https://www.gov.uk/government/publications/digital-britain-final-report

Bleed, R. (2005). Visual literacy in higher education, Maricopa Community Colleges, *ELI explorations*, August 2005, Educause Learning Initiative.

Braden, R. A. (1996). Visual literacy. In J. M. Spector, M. D. Merrill, J. Elen, & M. J. Bishop (Eds.), *Handbook of research for educational communications and technology* (pp. 491–520). Cham, Switzerland: Springer Nature.

Breuer, E., & Archer, A. (Eds.). (2016). Multimodality in higher education. Brill, Boston.

Brown, J. S. (2000). Growing up: Digital: How the web changes work, education, and the ways people learn. *Change: The Magazine of Higher Learning, 32*, 11–20.

Bruner, J. (1984). Vygotsky's zone of proximal development: The hidden agenda. New Directions for Child Development.

Bruner, J. S. (2009). *Actual minds, possible worlds*. Cambridge, MA: Harvard University Press.

Buckingham, D. (2010). Defining digital literacy. In *Medienbildung in Neuen Kulturräumen* (pp. 59–71). Springer.

Cassidy, M. F., & Knowlton, J. Q. (1983). Visual literacy: A failed metaphor? *ECTJ, 31*, 67–90.

Castells, M. (2001). *The internet galaxy: Reflections on the Internet, business, and society*. Oxford: Oxford University Press.

Chai, C. L. (2019). Enhancing visual literacy of students through photo elicitation. *Journal of Visual Literacy, 38*(1–2), 120–129. https://doi.org/10.1080/1051144X.2019.1567071.

Chandler, D. (2002). *The basics: Semiotics*. London: Routledge.

Clark, C. D. (1999). The autodriven interview: A photographic viewfinder into children's experience. *Visual Studies, 14*, 39–50.

Collier, J. (1957). Photography in anthropology: A report on two experiments. *American anthropologist, 59*(5), 843–859.

Collier, J. J. (1967). *Visual anthropology: Photography as a research method.* New York: Holt, Rinehart and Winston.

Cope, B., & Kalantzis, M. (Eds.). (2000). *Multiliteracies: Literacy learning and the design of social futures.* London and New York: Routledge (Psychology Press).

Cope, B., & Kalantzis, M. (2009). Multiliteracies: New literacies, new learning. *Pedagogies: An International Journal, 4,* 164–195.

Curtis, N. (2009). *The pictorial turn.* London: Routledge.

Danos X., & Norman E. (2011). Continuity and progression in graphicacy. In *Graphicacy and modelling IDATER 2010.* Design Education Research Group, Loughborough Design School, 103–120.

Debes, J. L. (1969). *The loom of visual literacy – An overview.* Audiovisual Instr.

Eco, U. (1976). *A theory of semiotics.* First Midland Book edition. Indiana: Indiana University Press.

Eisenberg, M. B., Lowe, C. A., & Spitzer, K. L. (2004). *Information literacy: Essential skills for the information age* (2nd ed.). Westport, CT: Libraries Unlimited.

Ellis, G., & Dix, A. (2007). A taxonomy of clutter reduction for information visualisation. *Visualization and Computer Graphics, IEEE Transactions on 13,* 1216–1223.

Ellsworth, E. (1989). Why doesn't this feel empowering? Working through the repressive myths of critical pedagogy. *Harvard Educational Review, 59*(3), 297–325.

Elmborg, J. (2006). Critical information literacy: Implications for instructional practice. *The Journal of Academic Librarianship, 32*(2), 192–199.

Epstein, I., Stevens, B., McKeever, P., & Baruchel, S. (2008). Photo elicitation interview (PEI): Using photos to elicit children's perspectives. *International Journal of Qualitative Methods, 5,* 1–11.

Fosnot, C. T., & Perry, R. S. (2005). Constructivism: A psychological theory of learning. In C. Fosnot (Ed.), *Constructivism: Theory, Perspectives and Practice* (2nd ed., pp. 276–291). New York: Teachers College Press.

Freebody, P., & Luke, A. (1990). Literacies programs: Debates and demands in cultural context. *Prospect: An Australian Journal of TESOL, 5*(3), 7–16.

Goldstein, B. M. (2007). All photos lie: Images as data. In G. S. Stanczak (Ed.), *Visual research methods: Image, society, and representation* (pp. 61–81). Los Angeles: Sage.

Hall, S. (1973). *Encoding and decoding in the television discourse.* Retrieved from: http://epapers.bham.ac.uk/2962/1/Hall,_1973,_Encoding_and_Decoding_in_the_Television_Discourse.pdf

Hall, S. (2001). Encoding/decoding. In M. G. Durham & D. M. Kellner (Eds.), *Media and cultural studies: Keyworks* (Vol. 2, pp. 163–174). Oxford: Blackwell Publishing.

Hallewell, M. J., & Lackovic, N. (2017). Do pictures 'tell' a thousand words in lectures? How lecturers vocalise photographs in their presentations. *Higher Education Research & Development, 36*(6), 1166–1180.

Harper, D. (2002). Talking about pictures: A case for photo elicitation. *Visual Studies, 17*, 13–26.

Heisley, D. D., & Levy, S. J. (1991). Autodriving: A photoelicitation technique. *Journal of Consumer Research,* 257–272.

Hine, L. (1980/1909). Social photography: How the camera may help in the social uplift. In A. Trachentenberg (Ed.), *Classic essays on photography* (pp. 110–113). New Haven, CT: Leete's Island Books. (Reprinted from Proceedings, National Conference of Charities and Corrections, 1909).

Hodge, B. R. I. V., & Kress, G. R. (1988). *Social semiotics.* Cambridge, UK: Polity Press.

Hull, G. A., & Nelson, M. E. (2005). Locating the semiotic power of multimodality. *Written Communication, 22*, 224–261.

Hurworth, R. (2003). Photo-interviewing for research. *Social Research Update, 40*(1).

Iedema, R. (2003). Multimodality, resemiotization: Extending the analysis of discourse as multi-semiotic practice. *Visual Communication, 2*, 29–57.

Jandrić, P., Ryberg, T., Knox, J., Lacković, N., Hayes, S., Suoranta, J., et al. (2019). Postdigital dialogue. *Postdigital Science and Education, 1*(1), 163–189.

Jay, M. (2002). That visual turn. *Journal of Visual Culture, 1*, 87–92.

Jewitt, C. (2002). The move from page to screen: The multimodal reshaping of school English. *Visual Communication, 1*, 171–195.

Jewitt, C. (2005). Multimodality, "reading", and "writing" for the 21st century. *Discourse: Studies in the Cultural Politics of Education, 26*, 315–331.

Jewitt, C. (2008). *The visual in learning and creativity: A review of the literature.* Arts Council.

Jewitt, C. (2009). *The Routledge handbook of multimodal analysis.* Routledge Chapman & Hall.

Jewitt, C. (2014). 12 Multimodal approaches. *Interactions, Images and Texts: A Reader in Multimodality, 11*, 127.

Jewitt, C., & Kress, G. R. (2003). *Multimodal literacy.* New York: Lang.

Jewitt, C., Bezemer, J., & O'Halloran, K. (2016). *Introducing multimodality.* London: Routledge.

Jewitt, C., Kress, G., Ogborn, J., & Tsatsarelis, C. (2001). Exploring learning through visual, actional and linguistic communication: The multimodal environment of a science classroom. *Educational Review, 53*(1), 5–18.

Kędra, J. (2018). What does it mean to be visually literate? Examination of visual literacy definitions in a context of higher education. *Journal of Visual Literacy, 37*(2), 67–84. https://doi.org/10.1080/1051144X.2018.1492234.

Kędra, J., & Žakevičiūtė, R. (2019). Visual literacy practices in higher education: What, why and how? *Journal of Visual Literacy, 38*(1–2), 1–7. https://doi.org/10.1080/1051144X.2019.1580438.

Kellner, D., & Share, J. (2007). Critical media literacy, democracy, and the reconstruction of education. *Media Literacy: A Reader*, 3–23.

Knobel, M., & Lankshear, C. (2006). Digital literacy and digital literacies: Policy, pedagogy and research considerations for education. *Nordic Journal of digital literacy, 1*(01), 12–24.

Krane, H., & Dyson, L. (1981). *Graphics communication*. Education Department Victoria.

Kress, G. R. (2003). *Literacy in the new media age*. London and New York: Routledge. Psychology Press.

Kress, G. R. (2010). *Multimodality: A social semiotic approach to contemporary communication*. Taylor & Francis.

Kress, G., & van Leeuwen, T. (1996). *Reading images: The grammar of visual design*. Routledge.

Kress, G., & van Leeuwen, T. (2001). Multimodal discourse. The modes and media of contemporary communication. (Cappelen, London 2001).

Kruk, S. (2008). Semiotics of visual iconicity in Leninist 'monumental' propaganda. *Visual Communication, 7*(1), 27–57.

Lackovic, N. (2010b). Beyond the surface: image affordances in language textbooks that affect National Identity Formation (NIF). In *Mapping minds* (pp. 51–65). Oxford: Brill.

Lackovic, N. (2020). Thinking with digital images in the post-truth era: A method in critical media literacy. In *Postdigtial science and education*. Springer.

Lackovic, N., Crook, C., Cobb, S., Shalloe, S., & D'Cruz, M. (2015). Imagining technology-enhanced learning with heritage artefacts: Teacher-perceived potential of 2D and 3D heritage site visualisations. *Educational Research, 57*(3), 331–351.

Lankow, J., Ritchie, J., & Crooks, R. (2012). *Infographics: The power of visual storytelling*. Wiley.

Lankshear, C., & Knobel, M. (2006). *New literacies: Everyday practices and classroom learning*. Open University Press.

Martinec, R. (2000). Construction of identity in Michael Jackson's Jam. *Social Semiotics, 10*(3), 313–329.

McArthur, J. (2010). Time to look anew: Critical pedagogy and disciplines within higher education. *Studies in Higher Education, 35*, 301–315.

McCloud, S. (1994). *Understanding comics.* New York: HarperCollins.

Metcalfe, A. (2015). Visual methods in higher education. *Research in the college context: Approaches and methods*, 111–127.

Mihailidis, P. (2018). Civic media literacies: Re-imagining engagement for civic intentionality. *Learning, Media and Technology*, 1–13.

Mills, K. A. (2010). A review of the "digital turn" in the new literacy studies. *Review of Educational Research, 80*, 246–271.

Mirzoeff, N. (Ed.). (2002). *The visual culture reader.* Psychology Press.

Mitchell, M. (2003). *IMEJ article – Constructing multimedia: Benefits of student-generated multimedia on learning.* Retrieved from: http://imej.wfu.edu/articles/2003/1/03/

Mitchell, W. J. (2002). Showing seeing: A critique of visual culture. *Journal of Visual Culture, 1*, 165–181.

Mitchell, W. J. T. (1995). Interdisciplinarity and visual culture. *Art Bulletin, 77*, 540–544.

Moore, D. M., & Dwyer, F. M. (1994). *Visual literacy: A spectrum of visual learning.* Englewood Cliffs, NJ: Educational Technology Publications.

Müller, M. G. (2008). Visual competence: A new paradigm for studying visuals in the social sciences? *Visual Studies, 23*, 101–112.

Neary, M. (2010). Student as producer: Bringing critical theory to life through the life of students. *Roundhouse: Journal of Critical Social Theory*, 36–45.

Nelson, B., Ketelhut, D. J., Clarke, J., Bowman, C., & Dede, C. (2005). Design-based research strategies for developing a scientific inquiry curriculum in a multi-user virtual environment. *Educational Technology, 45*, 21–27.

New London Group. (1996). A pedagogy of multiliteracies: Designing social futures. *Harvard Educational Review, 66*, 60–92.

Norris, S. (2004). *Analyzing multimodal interaction: A methodological framework.* London: Routledge.

Nöth, W. (2002). Can pictures lie? In *Semiotics of the media. State of the art, projects, and perspectives* (pp. 133–146). New York: Mouton de Gruyter.

Ofsted. (2009). *Drawing together: Art, craft and design in schools.* London: OFSTED.

Oliffe, J. L., & Bottorff, J. L. (2007). Further than the eye can see? Photo elicitation and research with men. *Qualitative Health Research, 17*, 850–858.

Pangrazio, L. (2016). Reconceptualising critical digital literacy. *Discourse: Studies in the Cultural Politics of Education, 37*(2), 163–174.

Pietarinen, A. V., & Bellucci, F. (2016). The iconic moment. Towards a Peircean theory of diagrammatic imagination. In *Epistemology, knowledge and the impact of interaction* (pp. 463–481). Cham, Switzerland: Springer.

Prosser, J. (1998). *Image-based research: A sourcebook for qualitative researchers.* Reprinted by Routledge in 2000. London: Psychology Press.

Prosser, J., & Loxley, A. (2008). *Introducing visual methods.* ESRC National Center for Research Methods (NCRM) Review Paper. Retrieved from: http://eprints.ncrm.ac.uk/420

Reed, S. K. (2010). *Thinking visually.* Psychology Press.

Reiser, R. A. (2001). A history of instructional design and technology: Part I: A history of instructional media. *Educational Technology Research and Development, 49,* 53–64.

Rose, G. (2011/2006). *Visual methodologies: An introduction to researching with visual materials.* Sage.

Roth, W. M., Pozzer-Ardenghi, L., & Han, J. Y. (2005). *Critical graphicacy: Understanding visual representation practices in school science.* Dordrecht, Netherlands: Springer.

Sakr, M., Jewitt, C., & Price, S. (2014). The semiotic work of the hands in scientific enquiry. *Classroom Discourse, 5*(1), 51–70.

Samuels, J. (2004). Breaking the ethnographer's frames reflections on the use of photo elicitation in understanding Sri Lankan Monastic Culture. *American Behavioral Scientist, 47,* 1528–1550.

Schmit, K. M. (2013). Making the connection: Transmediation and Children's literature in library settings. *New Review of Children's Literature and Librarianship, 19,* 33–46.

Schnotz, W. (2002). Commentary: Towards an integrated view of learning from text and visual displays. *Educational Psychology Review, 14,* 101–120.

Sefton-Green, J. (2005). Timelines, timeframes and special effects: Software and creative media production. *Education, Communication & Information, 5,* 99–110.

Sefton-Green, J., & Sinker, R. (1999). *Evaluating creativity: Making and learning by young people.* Routledge.

Share, J. (2005). Media Literacy in the US. *MedienPädagogik: Zeitschrift für Theorie und Praxis der Medienbildung, 11,* 1–21.

Short, K. G., & Kauffman, G. (2000). *Exploring sign systems within an inquiry system in what counts as literacy: Challenging the school standard*. Teachers College Press (pp. 42–61).

Siegel, M. (1995). More than words: The generative power of transmediation for learning. *Canadian Journal of Education, 20*, 455–475.

Sinatra, R., Beaudry, J. S., Stahl-Gemake, J., & Guastello, E. F. (1990). Combining visual literacy, text understanding, and writing for culturally diverse students. *Journal of Reading, 33*, 612–617.

Sless, D. (1981). *Learning and visual communication*. Halsted Press.

Sless, D. (1984). Visual literacy: A failed opportunity. *Educational Technology Research and Development, 32*, 224–228.

Smagorinsky, P. (2001). If meaning is constructed, what is it made from? Toward a cultural theory of reading. *Review of Educational Research, 71*, 133–169.

Sousanis, N. (2015). *Unflattening*. Harvard University Press.

Spalter, A. M., & Van Dam, A. (2008). Digital visual literacy. *Theory Into Practice, 47*, 93–101.

Starr R. G. Jr., & Fernandez, K. V. (2007). *A pluralistic examination of mall store patronage*. Retrieved from: https://anzmac.org/conference_archive/2007/papers/R%20Starr_1a.pdf

Tan, S. (2007). *The arrival*. New York: Arthur A. Levine Books.

Tett, L., & Hamilton, M. (2019). Introduction: Resisting neoliberalism in education. In L. Tett, & M. Hamilton (Eds.), *Resisting neoliberalism in education: Local, national and transnational perspectives* (pp. 1–13). Policy Press.

Thibault, P. (2000). The dialogical integration of the brain in social semiosis: Edelman and the case for downward causation. *Mind, Culture, and Activity: An International Journal, 7*, 291–311.

Thompson, D. S. (2019). Teaching students to critically read digital images: A visual literacy approach using the DIG method. *Journal of Visual Literacy, 38*(1–2), 110–119. https://doi.org/10.1080/1051144X.2018.1564604.

Tufte, E. R. (2001). *The visual display of quantitative information* (2nd ed.). Cheshire, CO: Graphics Press.

Van Leeuwen, T. (1999). *Speech, music, sound*. Macmillan International Higher Education.

Walker, R., & Weidel, J. (1985). Using photographs in a discipline of words. In R. Burgess (Ed.), *Field methods in the study of education* (pp. 191–216). Lewes: Falmer Press.

Wang, C., & Burris, M. (1994). Empowerment through photo-novella: Portraits of participation. *Health Education Quarterly, 21*, 171–186.

Ware, C. (2000). *Information visualization: perception for design.* Amsterdam: Elsevier/Morgan Kaufmann.

Woolner, P., Clark, J., Hall, E., Tiplady, L., Thomas, U., & Wall, K. (2010). Pictures are necessary but not sufficient: Using a range of visual methods to engage users about school design. *Learning Environments Research, 13*, 1–22.

Zhao, S., Djonov, E., & Van Leeuwen, T. (2014). Semiotic technology and practice: A multimodal social semiotic approach to PowerPoint. *Text & Talk, 34*(3), 349–375.

# 5

# Concepts Re-imagined: Relational Signs Beyond Definitional Rigidity

This chapter further unpacks the inquiry graphics (IG) theoretical under-pinnings of image–concept relationality and multiplicity by considering the traditional role of concepts in education, and how it can and needs to be expanded. The theoretical and conceptual considerations here come from an eclectic range of thinkers and approaches *relevant to learning sciences, learning processes and knowledge development,* aligned with the view that *concepts are relational, holistic, non-dualistic signs (which means they do not exclude pictorial images, either external or internal).* The chapter posi-tions itself against the dualist view of corporeal image sensation and lan-guage/ abstract concept separation, epitomized in Descartean body–mind dualism. In theorizing the notion of any particular "concept," I would first consider concepts at the functional, definitional and classification-sensitive level that has been explored mainly in the domain of cognitive psychology, which still by and large informs the design of educational programs. That is why the approaches that prevail even today are chosen as the starting point of unpacking concepts. This unpacking of what con-cepts are will not be historically encompassing, as others have done it well, providing compelling critical insights as to why concepts need to be linked to learning *activity and processes* (for an in-depth overview see

© The Author(s) 2020
N. Lacković, *Inquiry Graphics in Higher Education,*
https://doi.org/10.1007/978-3-030-39387-8_5

Blunden's (2012) book, *Concepts: A Critical Approach*). I will then make arguments and provide examples of why and how concepts need to be tackled from the perspectives of concept–image multiplicity, relationality, non-ocularcentrism, transformative thinking, creativity, sharing and criticality.

I consider any fixed definition of concept as problematic. However, I acknowledge the existence of conceptual definitions and related foundational texts as useful and necessary as the first step of concept exploration, a way of exploring and stating writers', teachers' and learners' epistemological or ontological positionality. My view of concepts is mainly multimodal–semiotic, that is, as a schematic manipulation/ modeling and adaptation across modalities, where "mental" is the mind both *inside and outside the body*, as an embodied and extended cognition, *including* the environment and its sociocultural, structural, agential and historical meanings and influences, which I'll further discuss in Chap. 6. I also view concept as evolutionary (in state of constant development) aligned with Peirce's synechism, echoing Dewey and Bentley's (1960, p. 192) concept/conception definition as "a current phrasing for subject matters designed to be held under steady inspection in inquiry."

# Defining a Concept: From Rigidity to Complexity and Relationality

To define a concept when developing knowledge is useful insofar that it can help an educational community introduce, and then discuss, debate, learn and expand that concept, get its various aspects explored and probed over time. To define a concept in writing is needed as it helps the reader, and it positions the one who defines it in their epistemological and ontological stance. From the perspectives of cognitive sciences, Merrill, Tennyson, & Posey (1992) define a concept as "a set of specific objects, symbols, or events which are grouped together on the basis of shared characteristics and which can be referenced by a particular name or symbol (p. 6)." They suggest that concepts consist of "concept classes" and classes are observed to have "instances" (Merill et al., 1992). Providing concept instances is seen as beneficial for developing student conceptual understanding. They propose two kinds of instances: examples and non-examples. Examples help us define some instance, which is a member of the concept under consideration. Non-examples help distinguish members which do not belong to the concept in question, in order to avoid confusion and misunderstanding (they are usually the members of another concept observed to stand in some opposition to the target concept).

According to Merrill et al. (1992), "classification" means "identifying concept classes when there is an instance or providing instances for concept classes"; "generalization" invites the student to look for "common attributes which the new instance share with the previous examples"; "discrimination" happens when the student "stops generalizing" and makes "finer distinctions between very similar situations" (p. 14). What can be noted in each definition is that the property of first defining *similarity (the premise of iconic thinking)* is necessary for all operations. Another view rooted in verbal mentalistic psychology and widely adopted in planning educational programs and curricula today, adding to an elementary level understanding of concepts, is Howard's definition of the concept as "a mental representation of a category," and an abstraction from experience (Howard, 1987, p. 1). Whether this mental representation contains an image or not and how it relates to the external environment and the socio-cultural history is the question that have troubled thinkers since ancient times. I tackle this issue here by proposing an *image–concept unity, rather than dichotomy of* purely mentalistic representation approaches and their role in learning and knowledge development, the dichotomy that still prevails in higher education studies as a field of inquiry.

Concepts change meaning, however slightly, according to their interpreters, as argued in Chap. 1. To reiterate, despite the "agreed" scientific meaning of concepts, individuals will have their own, personal interpretation, dependent on prior experience and well-developed mind schemata. Chaps. 1, 2, 3 and 4 highlight the multiplicity and heterogeneity of concept or practice meanings and human experiences. When an act or a person is observed from a dominant angle (e.g. scientific or that of neo-liberal efficiency), the interpretations stemming from it will be partial as they will show one side of the "picture." A fellow-member of the same discipline may still have different meaning schema for a given concept, let alone members of different disciplines. The space of concept applications thereby may be fuzzy and contested. Hierarchical approaches of categorization and ordering of thinking in teaching and learning have been highly popular in education, the ubiquitous Kolb's cycle and Bloom's taxonomy, that focus on cognitive operationalization of learning, proposing discreet and ordered phases or taxonomies (including the distinct stages of human (child) development). Hierarchical taxonomizing and categorization of any kind of university-level learning that promote distinct categories (as compared to for example any non-hierarchical taxonomies whose units are specific but can include and relate to other units) is contested here. Learning happens across a spectrum of learning acts and ways of knowing and knowledge development, hence it is contested to extract any hierarchical, definitive stages or pyramids of it. Unless this fluidity is acknowledged, education will continue to promote highly hierarchical outlooks on learning and social system function. Perhaps some want it to remain so. It is possible and welcome to define some dominant characteristics within taxonomies, but the boundaries between these functions are always fuzzy, and always subject to sociocultural and material factors and influences. This also includes any boundaries or categories suggested in this book and its empirical findings. Knowledge-building is not only cognitive, and importantly, it is contested to view particular types of reasoning rated as higher and lower and as separate and distinct entities. The development of and contribution to knowledge lies in critical engagement, which includes concept boundary moving (Canning, 2007). Learning designs that apply images as inquiry graphics assign the role of "depicted experience" to images so that the depicted experience can be explored and abstracted, and the other way round, so that an abstract idea, concept or theory can be embodied. Abstraction, representation and exploration are viewed as a relational system within the inquiry, a sociomaterial assemblage of thinking, teaching and learning.

Like Howard's (1987) "experience–abstraction" distinction, Vygotsky might be seen in many Western interpretations as neatly dividing concepts into true (scientific) and spontaneous (everyday) (Vygotsky, 1987) as if they were distinctly separate entities. To some extent that might even have been the case. However, for Vygotsky, the underlining principle of a concept is that of a "whole," a holism of scientific–everyday concepts (Robbins, 2005), although he does make a distinction of what those are.

It could be that scientific concepts link to Howard's "abstraction" and everyday concepts to Howard's "experience." Yet the link can be made if the two are viewed as members of the whole, one underlying unity underpinned by *action and process*. An inquiry graphics (IG) artifact as building on Peirce's triadic sign and icon–symbol reasoning in knowledge advancement (iconic thinking/ diagrammatic imagination) could be connected to Vygotsky's relational approach to concept development (Robbins, 2005). It has to be noted that Vygotsky was primary concerned with language (and linguistic semiotics), but he viewed psychological action as unity of external and internal world bridged by language. Vygotsky's view does not entail divorcing abstraction from sensed experience (Robbins, 2003, 2005, 2007), which is also against dualisms of mind–body or concept–image in how human mind operates in the world. Understanding Vygotsky's scientific–everyday concept division in the tradition of a dualistic dichotomy is problematic. Western interpretations tend to take Vygotsky's theory too mechanically: it was not intended to provide a "lockstep" approach to human development but a more complex, unitary view on humans and concepts (Robbins, 2005), an approach that is also called non-classical psychology. Robbins (2007, p. 85) quotes Daniel Elkonin's (1989, p. 478) definition of Vygotsky's non-classical psychology as "the science of the way the subjective world of a single person emerges from the objective world of art, the world of production tools, the world of the entire industry." Dorothy Robbins studied with Vygotsky's student, Leontiev, in Moscow, where she also spent time in conversations with Vygotsky's family. She argues that Vygotsky's ideas are commonly misunderstood and misinterpreted in Western context (Robbins, 2005), as they fail to acknowledge that at the heart of Vygotsky's educational philosophy is an idea of "*holism*," the functioning of the whole and its unity *while acknowledging the functioning of its underlying structural elements, or units*. It is a specific unity–units relationship. This is similar to the relationality of IG, as IG stresses the functioning of the image–concept sign as a whole via its analytically framed units of Representamen, Interpretant and Object, exploring sign's underlying structural elements, but ultimately seeing it and theorizing it as a sign whole, a holistic unity of the three characteristics that affect semiosis and acting in the world.

In that way, the external world is important and not separate from the mental. They both form the mind. This is the definition that establishes relationality between inner (subjective) and outer world (sociomaterially objective, meaning of material objects) and the realization of objectives, intentions and volition in human concept development. Indeed, if we deal with two intrinsically linked aspects of one concept (such as its scientific meaning and the meaning through everyday manifestation), "(t)he goal, then, is to arrive to an account— a kind of "translation at the crossroads"—that would *make it possible to link*, but not reduce one perspective to another" (Wertsch, 1998, p. 7 quoted in Thompson, 2012, p. 10). Robbins (2007, p. 90) argues that "(i)n much of postmodern society, psychological and philosophical theories tend to focus on "parts" of a whole structure, often without understanding the all-encompassing nature of what "holism" refers to." Parts exist as identifiable parts but within a unity.

Whereas the dialogic work of Bakhtin and dialectics of Vygotsky are different (see White, 2014), inquiry graphics embraces both in order to go beyond this dichotomy, without subscribing exclusively to either of them, but focusing on ways of knowing that imbue thinking processes, which can involve both the dialectic and the dialogic (Thompson, 2012). From that perspective, concepts are linked to some authoritative knowing (tied to a figure of authority, e.g., a recognized thinker, book author, teacher or educational institution—teachers and educational institutions still have the power and authority of marking, assessment, learning designs and degree awards). To subvert the authoritative human knowing and taken-for-granted assumptions, concepts are explored via dialogical inquiry of concepts as open-ended, non-determinate entities, mediated by IG artifacts. This does not serve the purpose of transcending the difference as some dialectic goal (of differing voices and knowings, so that one is correct and the divergence is brought to an end), but to establish heterogeneity of voices and meanings, by providing enough room for authority to be acknowledged but also challenged and knowledge further reshaped. Bakhtin's (1981) work on language development and dialogue points at the inherently multimodal as well as relational social character of language and language learning. Private thoughts and writing are always in relation to something in the world. A written text or spoken language contains references and association triggers for other ideas, concepts and entities, that is, multimodal intertextuality (Lackovic, 2017), to emphasize the diverse modes of intertextual work in a piece of text or thinking processes. According to such logic, "texts" are not just written or spoken verbal accounts. Intertextuality, by the virtue of different modal associations is multimodal anyway, yet the construct "multimodal intertextuality" I proposed (Lackovic, 2017) is used to make an emphasis on text's modal diversity in relation to writer's ideas and reader's associations, analogy and experiences. Inquiry graphics focus on seeing the unity of multimodal thinking from both ends and understanding how the units within it work and inform each other, the units being both material/ natural, and sociocultural in their character, and importantly *interpretative (subject to interpretation)*. Any abstract thinking has its roots or its realization as sign-in-action in some concrete experience and "everyday" concept, and any disregard of this is compartmentalizing knowledge development, thus providing a partial view of a concept or knowledge in question. Concrete experiences are commonly mediated by concrete, material artifacts.

Such view of concepts also resonates with Andy Blunden's proposition in his book *Concepts: A Critical Approach*, of concepts as interdisciplinary and equally subjective and objective; he interprets Vygotsky's sociocultural and holistic approach to concepts similarly to Robbins's (2005) view of subjective–objective (everyday–scientific; bodily–material–cognitive) inseparability. Blunden (2012, p. 9) even contests the very concept of a concept stating that

> concepts do not fit together like the tiles of a mosaic, and nor can they be categorized into various types. They refuse to behave as if they were entities of any kind, even with blurred edges. These troublesome facts are often taken as reasons for abandoning the whole idea of concepts.

This view aligns with the views proposed here of concept as open-ended entities that may have a name, yet what they are and what they mean is subject to constant readjustment, bound by environmental, intentional, contextual and other sociocultural and historical factors. None the less, I maintain that to use the word "concept" as a concept is ubiquitous to all disciplines: "whether viewed from psychology, logic, history, social theory, anthropology or linguistics, there is something called a 'concept'" (Blunden, 2012, p. 10).

Van der Veer and Valsiner (1994) argue that thoughts are not born out of some sense-deprived void, but one needs to rise above the senses to reach a higher concept. However, can a living human being ever rise so far (above) as to be *separated from the* senses and their corporeal existence? I argue that in our gravity-bound life this is simply not the case, at least not for most humans. Humans live in the material body through which the world is sensed across spatial, pictorial, tactile, olfactory and other senses, that is, via corporeality (I do not want to privilege the sense of seeing), entwined with cognizing about that world. As long as we have bodies, we will cognize via, not separated from, that body and related senses. Human thinking and acting processes cannot be done (at least so far in history) in an isolated vacuum or "void" of nonmaterial entities.

## Concepts Beyond Ocularcentrism

The ocularcentrism paradigm can be usefully considered here to present the notion of the "higher education void" coined in this book, building on the keynote I presented at the 4th conference of the Association of Visual Pedagogies. Ocularcentrism is, simply put, giving primacy to the sense of vision and anything that connects to it, for instance visualization and pictures. I want to be clear that I am not proposing with IG signs and designs some ocularcentric doctrine. Rather, I consider ocularcentrism in relation to the persistent *separation between logical concept* and *image*, mind and matter, reason and intuition, in a manner of *either–or*, with the former concept in these pairs taken to be "pure" and the latter "impure" in the project of Enlightenment, and the other way round when it comes to postmodern thinking (Kavanagh, 2004). The concern with ocularcentrism dates back to Plato's and Descartes' rationalism, and the quest for "pure reason," in simple terms the reasoning abstracted and separated from experience and sense data (Kavanagh, 2004). A continuation of these dichotomies has created some disciplinary traditions that constitute what I term a higher education "void," defined as a space of higher education theory and research that excludes any serious acknowledgment or analytical engagement with material or sense-engaging objects and artifacts; that effectively means it is an abstract theoretical conceptual space that does not consider or link to world's materiality, artifacts, non-verbal modes and meanings that these mediate. This could also refer to academic publications or ways of teaching and learning.

There is no such *worldly space* that is a void. To illustrate that, I often refer to the US comedy series " *The Good Place*," which is (spoilers ahead) a story about an afterlife where The Bad Place (Hell) is presented as The Good Place (Heaven) to the four main deceased characters, until the doomed souls realize it, and manage to get the chief architect Devil onto their side, in a quest to correct the way that all this Good–Bad place business works. In one of The Good Place episodes the main characters find themselves in Janet's "void" (Janet being an all-knowing universal entity looking like a woman, an equivalent of ancient Greek oracle), which is a blank whitish space of nothingness, nothing material other than the humans who find themselves there. The void, where they still manage to stand on something (rather than float in it for example), can get easily populated by "things" at the whim of Janet's thought. In the scene when they arrive to the void, they all look like Janet; they have their individual minds and identity but Janet's body (Fig. 5.1). In a university context, teaching this popular film culture example can be compared to a state of affairs when teaching, policy and curriculum are enacted with no reference to the world's materiality, and treating all students and actors as if they were the same and would interpret the same concept in the same way (through the same corporeality, as if they were all one person, like the scene in Janet's void showing all main characters having Janet's form (Fig. 5.1), or in the case of an educational context, learners). The example evokes an idea of the development and implementation of curricula in a distinct separation from the senses and materiality of the world, the materiality that for example iconic pictures manifest and represent, and that related senses can evoke.

Important questions of "What is knowledge?" are not revisited while communication and visualization modes develop at ludicrous speed, becoming faster in every iteration. Evoking the reference in Chap. 1, labeling the institutional change as slow can be juxtaposed with the

**Fig. 5.1** Author's charcoal style rendition of Janet's "void" with Janet body clones. (Source: Created by the author, an interpretation of a scene in Episode 9 "Janets," season 3 of *The Good Place*)

massive and rapid financial investments in advancing the speed of visual technology and material infrastructure (e.g., at universities), and, more worryingly, at a level of global politics and state mechanisms, investments in visual military technology (Bartram, 2004; Kellner, 1999).

The higher education "void" is reinforced by reproducing the vertical "higher" knowledge that is equated with power, manipulating abstract concepts and having a higher social status (Bernstein, 2006). Arguably, to access such powerful knowledge and operate with it skillfully is indeed a prerequisite for academic and social success. To defuse this problem of access is important. But the very premise and the foundations of power-ful–powerless knowledge separation in the first place needs to be challenged. In order to allow for wider accessibility, educators can also challenge the more powerful knowledge in the first place, in a more knowledge–power diffused, yet still scholarly strong higher education. The point is that "scholarly" is often equated with the conceptual and the abstract, glorifying particular verbal and discourse competences. Although arguments for an increase of access to "higher" knowledge discourses are well founded and have contributed greatly to the scholarship around class-based access and success, we need to be careful about problematizing the socioeconomic issues surrounding access without problematizing the academic knowledge conceptualization, reproduction and practice itself, that reinforce conceptual abstractions in opposition to daily, embodied experiences. The problem arises when an inclusion of horizontal discourses is observed as watering (dumbing) down the intellectual strongholds and density of scholarly wordings and hard science (of the vertical discourse). Horizontal discourses are the ones present in the arts and humanities, and more everyday and lay interactions and experiences, which contain pictures and other non-verbal media to a considerable extent, commonly rated as a sign of lesser academic rigor. The point is, it does not have to be so, as pictures and words can be integrated into "higher" education, without being labeled as unscholarly or promoting ocularcentrism.

That is why the materialism of the world need to be interrogated, because humans are related, via both physical–bodily and symbolical–schematic-ideological links, to worldly sociomatter while alive in the world. The senses and abstract reasoning are entwined, they are the two sides of the same coin— of understanding, interacting with and shaping the world. Through perception, our mind transforms the physicality of the perceived into abstraction, meaning and, ultimately, a scientific concept (Dahlin, 2001), but does not separate the concept from its sensed root, as it has already been embedded in the mind–body schema at the beginning, and it stays as such. With this in mind, the scientific concept is a semiotic sign, an icon–symbol that can change context and thus meaning (Wertsch, 1985). The proof of the human mind's complexity and creativity, according to Fauconnier and Turner (2002), is its capability to blend concepts into icon–index–symbol hybrids that are appropriated to literally endless situational, ideational and dialogic nuances. We need to be aware that we (humans) have the capacity of unique unlimited semiosis (interpreting the world) that always leads to an *endless variety of new discoveries new things and ideas*. Contextual and systemic particularities and concept definitions limit the semiotic spinning off. This is useful and needed in terms of functionality, but we would need to keep in mind that there are limitless possibilities of ideas in life and subsequent scenarios. That is why, Fauconnier and Turner (2002) argue, an artificially intelligent humanoid mind is still a distant scientific dream in these very subtle semiotic terms of internal mind–external world *blending and entanglement.*

Bridging the abstract concept meaning and abstract models with its everyday manifestations and real life scenarios is not an easy endeavor, especially not for a student-novice in this type of thinking engagement; on the contrary, it has proved to be rather challenging, and that is indeed its value (images being not just pretty pictures), as will be shown in Part II, but such thinking is certainly possible and allows for a transformative learners' experience. The challenge of developing new concepts has been considered via an approach (also seen as framework or theory) termed *threshold concepts.*

## Threshold Concepts: Toward Threshold Graphics

Meyer and Land's (2003) "threshold concepts" provide a useful framework to further examine the relational notion of the Vygotskian everyday–scientific concept unity. An important aspect of threshold concepts is the difficulty that students encounter in linking everyday, familiar experience with abstract scientific knowledge and models. Meyer and Land define a "threshold concept" as a critical disciplinary concept for transformative learning to help a student move from the periphery toward belonging to a disciplinary community. A threshold concept is defined as:

> akin to a portal, opening up a new and previously inaccessible way of thinking about something. It represents a transformed way of understanding, or interpreting, or viewing something without which the learner cannot progress. (Meyer & Land, 2003, p. 1)

Semiotic thinking via notions of "strangeness" and "difficulty" as a prerequisite for deep learning, is just such a type of new and previously inaccessible way of thinking about something. Via IG, symbolic relations and meanings are drawn between aspects of the threshold concepts, until a recognizable element of knowledge, that is, its iconic quality, is established, as icons function due to the understood similarity between two entities, the familiar (e.g., image) and the unfamiliar and troublesome (threshold concept). This is why overcoming a threshold concept requires an engagement with semiotic icon–symbol–index thinking, such as an inquiry graphic.

Meyer and Land (2003) provide a list of examples of the transformative experience necessary for grasping threshold concepts in a discipline: at the core of each example is the notion of linking everyday experience to an abstract concept and drawing relations between the same concepts in different manifestations, the scientific and the everyday. However, threshold concepts are by no means easy: for students—discipline—they can be rather troublesome. The particular problem of abstract–everyday (familiar) separation is exemplified in a comment of a practitioner in the field of economics:

> sometimes students see abstract models as abstract models and don't see the link between them and the real world, so that students would be quite happy talking about problems of inflation, unemployment and soon, but as soon as you say "Good, let's have a look at the model," they sort of switch off. They think that's a completely separate issue. "I don't want to do the model, I just want to talk about inflation or unemployment." So the idea that models which look abstract—can be looked at —actually talk about the real world, perhaps that is a crucial factor. I mean they tend to put models into one box and then the discussion about the policy issues in another box. They don't necessarily see that the two must be linked. Perhaps that's a threshold issue. (Meyer & Land, 2003, p. 12)

The students would have their own views of how an abstract model "works" in real life in relation to some real-life issues, which might lead to what is considered to be misconceptions or simplification of scientific concepts in relation to the currently accepted knowledge of that concept. One thing that is missing in the above exploration is that everyday life concepts have some worldly *material* manifestations and effects, especially in the exemplified discipline of economics that has a lot to do with placing and determining *economic value upon material goods.* In an inquiry graphics scenario, students would start with considering what material and physical properties are linked to a concept and a model, and that would then be investigated. Therefore, students need to voice their understanding and tutors need to hear that voice (of students' interpretations) which opens discussion and lets in the tutors' support in overcoming the difficulty of grappling with troublesome concepts (Lackovic, 2010). In a nutshell, "abstracting" and connecting the meaning of a threshold concept across contexts and in relation to everyday experiences is challenging and therefore seen as marker of transformative concept experience (Wertsch, 1985). It is not easy at all to turn abstract concepts in disciplines into image instances, and the other way round in a cyclical process of inquiry, to weave so-called "higher order" ideas, and subsequent conceptualizations and theorizations from such icon–symbol image prototypes (Lackovic, 2016). This is contrary to the common take on pictorial images as illustrative add-ons, something extra, unnecessary.

What we know about a concept evolves—concepts as signs always evolve—so what we know at one moment gets appropriated into new, different or more complex context systems. This view is supported by a developing field of cognitive science called "distributed cognition," also known via the nation of the "extended mind," where inner mental development is fundamentally linked to the outer world (context, artifacts, actors, and so on). This approach argues that the mind extends into the environment, which is drawn into its mental work (Robbins & Aydede, 2009). These views need to be expanded by considerations of the mind as inherently related to its physical vessel, the body, as signaled in approaches of embodied cognition. Wyndhamn and Säljö (1997) assert that there is a risk of turning concept formation into a "pedagogical drug." This would mean that to think it is possible to "feed" something into students with an immediate testable result in a pharmaceutical input–output manner is contested. Along those lines, to avoid that "pedagogical drug" of a cognitive model that is more computational, a revised HE teaching–learning methods and practices (in a holistic form called pedagogy or andragogy) might attempt to connect everyday and scientific concepts by embedding available technology tools and pictorial image media and artifacts to be a part of students' "extended" mind, acting as mediators of students" creative endeavor. This aligns with the perspectives of edusemiotics presented in Chap. 3.

I propose that when inquiry graphics are explicitly applied in relation to and for tackling threshold concepts, they are called Threshold Graphics. Such a holistic, multimodal and dynamic semiotic approach to educational practice suggests and simulates "everyday concepts" as essentially embedded in "scientific concepts" and the other way round. A related inquiry can start with the consideration of material world, the body, the matter, and expand into the explorations at a theoretical, sociocultural, historical and ideological level of signification. In such a scenario, iconic images act as constituents of students' extended minds. They depict an opening of many possibilities of how the image might be interrogated via a concept, it is an opening for possible worlds formation, for the thinking that is never cut off from the immediate or wider circumstances it is situated in (e.g., of politics, culture, ideology, structure, agency or ecology). Image thus can support understanding of complex relations between objects, phenomena, environment, and circumstances.

Providing ideas on those externalized material, relational instances of abstract concepts could lead students toward better concept understanding. Building better concept understanding might then lead them toward (inter)disciplinary knowledge building (Scardamalia & Bereiter, 1993, 1994). Importantly, employing the pure power of perception and creative–analytical appreciation of the seen (aside from rising above it) can lead students to consider solutions and ideas which surpass narrow concept boundaries (Dahlin, 2001). To help students become innovative thinkers, educators need to help them in crossing disciplinary and other boundaries and determinisms that characterize the vocabulary and noniconic views of concepts. This view resonates with Meyer and Land's (2003, p. 13) concern with *whose* (threshold) concepts are students supposed to learn, who determines them and with what power and reason. Therefore, it is desirable to provide an opportunity where the origin and determinism of the concept and its representation is reflected upon. It might help students further develop into people who question what they see but are able to "see outside the box" of constraints, rather as in Blake's beautiful poetic invitation to see the big abstract concepts in small, concrete everyday objects or link large- and small-scale entities, micro and macro practice and world:

> To see a World in a Grain of Sand,
> And a Heaven in a Wild Flower,
> Hold Infinity in the palm of your hand
> And Eternity in an hour.

William Blake, from "Auguries of Innocence"

## Concept "Mindfulness": Plurality/ Multiplicity of Concept Aspects and Possibilities

If learning as changing as a person requires the development of new ways of seeing the world (Stables, 2010; Bruner, 1986; Robbins, 2005, 2007), this must encourage considering concepts in much wider terms that their definitions: those that allow "unimagined" solutions, varieties of instances, and critical examination of those complexities that lie behind concepts. Such complexities can be considered from an ecological perspective (Maran & Kull, 2014) through the prism of the various different systems that contribute to concept meanings: economic, political, educational, government, religious, personal beliefs, values, chronological-historical, family, institution/ workplace, and affiliations of peers/ groups/ subgroups. This assertion is compatible with the viewpoint of social semiotics which examines meaning from a critical perspective that questions hierarchies, power and ideologies (Hodge & Kress, 1988). Concept transfer (the view popular in approaches that favor the building of particular educational concepts and so-called soft skills, unlike typing or bicycle riding) can be done only partly, and immediately shaped by the new environment and context. In order to "enhance" any possibility of some sort of howere partial "transfer," it is necessary to avoid over-contextualization of information (Bransford & Schwartz, 1999), that is, to avoid encouraging the view that a concept is strictly bound to one context, although there are some contexts that it most readily occurs in, as defined in particular disciplines.

As Bransford and Schwartz (1999) argue, presenting and exploring concepts in multiple contexts "can increase subsequent transfer" (Bransford et al., 1990, quoted by Bransford & Schwartz, 1999 p. 64). This is here adapted as a possibility for a type of transfer as shaped by new circumstances, as a direct or complete transfer of concepts is either impossible or highly unlikely, since every new situation involves a level of adaptation, however minute (of signs, concepts, action, reaction). To reiterate previous arguments about concepts, it does not mean that defining concepts is unnecessary or not good—it is useful in society and education not to be overwhelmed with the chaotic network of inter-relatedness. We need to start from concept definition; concept definition is helpful. However, to revisit some earlier points, concept meanings are not locked in their definitions (far from that): they are slippery, changing, negotiable, personal, and context-dependent. Therefore, creating conditions in which students are invited to identify this slippery, negotiable and personal nature of conceptual understanding to explore multiple perspectives is suggested as a necessary approach to knowledge development and learning in HE.

Some approaches to thinking already strongly support the need for having *multiple perspectives* on concepts. For example Harvard Professor Ellen Langer's (1989) "mindfulness" thesis offered a useful framework for the development of multiple perspectives in thinking, ahead of the present time when "mindfulness" has become an omnipresent buzz word way too fashionable across domains (from exercise to mental health), and appropriated into popular culture. Although we cannot be exactly sure of Langer's "mindfulness" influences, it is important to state its core definition here as relevant to reflective thinking. Langer and Moldoveanu (2000) state that mindfulness "can be best understood as the process of drawing novel distinctions" (p. 1), and that is how I view it too in relation to education and learning. Langer developed her mindfulness theory after a long span of research capturing what she called human mindless and mindful behavior and identifying their consequences (Langer, 1989). According to Langer (1989), in order to be "mindful," human actors need to consider contextual multiplicity and develop perceptual and thinking mechanisms to transfer objects of inquiry into different circumstances, with different agents, aims and uses. This also calls for understanding the interdependency of life experiences and the multidimensionality of the concepts we work with. Such a view builds on this ongoing and previous chapters" argument in favor of seeing beyond concept boundaries, and in favor of cultivating *relational thinking*. Langer and Moldoveanu (2000, p. 2) argue that drawing novel distinctions has the following benefits, by allowing:

* a greater sensitivity to one's environment,
* more openness to new information,
* the creation of new categories for structuring perception, and
* enhanced awareness of multiple perspectives in problem solving.

It can be agreed that these are all worthwhile aims: goals that are worthy of directing higher education practices. As Langer and Moldoveanu (2000) caution, "education is an area that often abounds with mindlessness" (p. 3). As an example, the authors refer to the case of learning the basics of certain tasks such that they become second nature, without questioning who determines what those basics are, and why. If basics are learnt with an *inflexible frame of mind*, it is hard to adapt them when more and varied information about a task is available (Langer & Moldoveanu, 2000, p. 3). Langer and Moldoveanu (2000) argue in favor of pedagogical approaches that encourage mindful perspective-taking, where the learner is made interested in perspectives and their origin. This is in contrast to teaching that claims absolute truths. Instead, it employs methods that give agency to students, so as to make learning more meaningful (Langer, 1997). Such construct of "mindfulness" is claimed to alleviate the perpetuation of prejudice, stereotypes and archetypes (Demick, 2000). Categorizing concepts is useful at a basic level of life functionality, but such perpetuations can limit possibilities for the building of knowledge that allows plurality, equality, equity and social justice. This allowance is a worthwhile educational aim.

# Concept Multiplicity as Creativity and Sharing of Inquiry Graphics

This section considers "creativity" in relation to concept knowledge development (Peirce's *synechism* or evolution), resonating with the idea of multiple perspectives in concept learning. Paavola and Hakkarainen (2005) proposed a new metaphor for learning concepts as an addition to the two metaphors (acquisition and participation) discussed earlier (Sfard, 1998); the new metaphor is "knowledge creation." This view is also present in Scardamalia and Bereiter's (2006) knowledge-building theory. Their theory argues that the accent in education should be put on the creation processes, whereby "something new is created and the initial knowledge is either substantially enriched or significantly transformed during the process" (Paavola et al., 2002, p. 24). However, little research has been conducted to offer pedagogical possibilities and teaching–learning designs that would support learning as knowledge creation (Hong & Sullivan, 2009) to go beyond verbal creation.

There are uncertainties surrounding this concept of creativity as it has been defined in a myriad of ways. How do I define it? What is it to refer to, and how do we develop it? In this book, creativity is considered in relation to *making new connections* and relations among things that already exist in some form and/or are not "naturally" linked (Tan, 2002). Human imagination has the power to combine, change and create anything new, everywhere (Thompson, 2012 p. 4). This is compatible with Fauconnier and Turner's views on the everyday capability of mind to create formidable blends of concepts when seemingly unconnected and non-related concepts are blended and make sense dependent on the context, users and purpose. This is also compatible with a view on the infinite chain of meaning making (the world in the state of an endless semiosis). Kress (2004) argues that our everyday communication is creative since we *interpret* acts of communication all the time. However, how can we understand creativity better in relation to learning and therefore "practice" it with students?

This book offers the notion of creativity through addressing multiple perspectives and thinking about one idea in more than one mode, not just the mode of language. The notion of creativity, coming from artists themselves, build on their own experience as creative, productive agents (Tan, 2002). It emerges that creativity is not some mystical state of mind but is very close to having a "trained" mind able to see things from multiple perspectives and establish new connections toward an innovative and thus creative unity.

Paul Klee thought that an artist was like a tree, "drawing the minerals of experience from its roots—things observed, read, told and felt—and slowly processing them into new leaves" (Tan, 2002, p. 1). This is an interesting metaphor, pointing at the core of creativity as a generative and transformative endeavor where some sensory-mental experience is refined to take a new form. This view is connected to the act of understanding a concept by combining its everyday and scientific manifestations, as well as creating the zone of strangeness and challenge. One needs the other: focusing primarily on sensory experience may lead to superficiality; focusing just on abstract thinking might lead to impractical disconnection from the sensed environment and sociocultural conditions which constitute the living world.

Shaun Tan, the author of the award-winning wordless graphic novel "The Arrival", defines his artistic inspiration and creativity in the following terms:

> inspiration has to do with careful research and looking for a challenge and creativity is about playing with what I find, testing one proposition against another and seeing how things combine and react. (Tan, 2002, p. 1)

His picture books and graphic novels have been labeled "highly imaginative," "strikingly original" and even "magical" (Tan, 2002, p. 1). However, as the artist claims, there is:

> nothing mysterious about the way they are produced. Each work contains many thousands of ingredients, experiments, discoveries and transforming decisions… What is original is not the ideas themselves, but the way they are put together. (Tan, 2002, p. 1)

This is very similar to De Haan's (2009) definition of intellectual creativity as "the ability of individuals to generate new ideas that contribute substantially to an intellectual domain." (p. 173). Creative solutions are similarly defined by Gardner (1993), who sees creativity as forming "new questions in a domain in a way that is initially considered novel" that, in time, can get infiltrated into the culture as a common way of doing things (p. 35).

Creativity can and should be fostered in students. According to Loveless (2007, p. 9), digital technologies need to play role in fostering "(c)reative processes supported by opportunities for play, exploration, reflection and focused engagement with ideas... ." Hence, as mentioned earlier, educators need to motivate students to use digital technology and learning resources creatively. The argument for linking creativity and technology for innovative and creative educational scenarios (Loveless, 2002) links to the imperative on developing multiple perspectives through learning experience discussed earlier.

In a nutshell, creativity in educational context is primarily seen as *making new connections from available resources that contribute to the development of concept understanding and demand an effort in re-invention of the existing resources for the creation of new ones.* That is this book's working definition of creativity. It is also linked to the challenge of "translating" one mode into another in a generative fashion (concept idea into a selection of a concept image, concept image into concept exploration or writing a concept explanation), also known as semiotic "transduction."[1] The inquiry graphics learning design aplied in situ in the empirical part of the book (Projects 2 and 3) encourages students to first transform a concept definition and what they know about it into images and then narrate those images in relation to the concepts they were chosen to represent, recognizing a commonly accepted scientific notion of that concept, and then moving that concept definition boundary, breaking it, experimenting with it, challenging it. Such a task poses a creative challenge with a potential to generate creative solutions in terms of translating between modes and developing meaningful connections between the depicted and the concept. However, the goal of an IG approach in learning is

---

[1] http://multimodalityglossary.wordpress.com/transduction/

relation more than translation, hence I introduce the concept of **multi-modal anchorage**, when efforts are invested in coupling and relating an image and a concept.

Concept development happens through forms of sharing that take place within a disciplinary community. Universities support concept development by offering a variety of courses to enrich students' knowledge of particular disciplines. Courses may differ in how far they furnish such communities. As Parker (2002) states "to be engaged in a discipline is to shape, and be shaped by, the subject, to be part of a scholarly community, to engage with fellow students (p. 374)." Thus, an academic discipline is seen as "practiced and engaged with," as opposed to the notion of a "subject" which, as critiqued by Parker (2002), "can readily serve the purpose of learning outcomes and fall into the mode of valuing teaching and learning on the basis of student attainment" (p. 374). This distinction between "subject" as an "acquisition" term and "discipline" as a "participation" term relates to the well-established debate on acquisition and participation metaphors in learning, as reviewed by Sfard (1998). Acquisition metaphors see learning in the instrumental terms of "acquiring knowledge" while participation metaphors see learning in the more "vocational" terms of moving from being a novice toward being closer to the center of disciplinary expertise (where teachers can represent those community experts) (ibid.). From a more vocational and community-based view on knowledge development, learners would be starting from the periphery and going through stages of progression toward being members of an expert community (Sfard, 1998; Lave & Wenger, 1991). However, the periphery is not to be seen as meaning unequal or less important and valid. This book acknowledges the danger of choosing only one metaphor in educational practice—in this case, either just the metaphor of "concept acquisition" or of "concept building through participation" and interaction (Sfard, 1998). However, from the position in this book, I suggest that the debates around acquisition versus participation can be overcome if knowledge is observed from a semiotic perspective as a continual evolution of signs, a network of evolutionary semiosis, always relational to the material world and contextual circumstances. Both cognitive or participation approach to learning can be expanded and perhaps reconciled with the considerations of the meaning–form *relationality* in IGs.

# Critical Awareness in Concept Inquiry

Dewey believed that in order to develop knowledge we need to perceive deeply and to question that which is perceived (Dewey & Bentley, 1960; Dewey, 2009/1910). The "fallacy of intellectualism" is that experience itself stands for knowledge (Boisvert, 1998, p. 19). It can certainly develop into knowledge, but it is not learnt knowledge per se (otherwise, why people repeat the same mistakes); the learner needs to reflect on and question the experience and that which is perceived. This does not happen as often as it is wished for, and there are might be selective reflective practices that exclude the growth as a person. Growing happens by acknowledging one's own fallibilist reasoning (recall Chap. 3).

In Chap. 4, criticality was considered in relation to visual signs and media. There are many ways in which "criticality" and "critical thinking" and "critical pedagogy" has been defined, usually tightly connected to a critique of societal phenomena, power relations, representations, deconstruction of meaning. It is widely used in education and is commonly seen to be of paramount importance for developing awareness and reason to strengthen civil society, responsible citizenship (Lipman, 2003) and informed decision making; especially in response to information such as advertisements, popular fiction and political rhetoric.

The term "criticality" is often attached to many "critical theorists" such as, for example, the transformational work by Paolo Freire (1970/1993) or Gloria Jean Watkins better known for her pen name bell hooks (2014) and Henry Giroux (1994) and "critical theories" such as Marxism, feminism, post-colonialism and critical race theory. In general, the field of critical theory is much larger and spans across various terms, approaches and movements. What "criticality" means in this book, in its broader sense, is related to voicing students' diverse perspectives in the learning process (not just the teacher's); thereby creating a space for student agency in the learning process to problematize ideas (Brockbank & McGill, 2007), toward a possibility of socially just and inclusive action and change (Freire, 1970/1993). Importantly, it views all students, no matter their background or status, as capable learners whose perspective is needed and worthy of acknowledging and sharing (Cin & Doğan,

2020). It also means to develop a mindful approach to information consumption, rather than automaticity (Potter, 2004), especially as promoted by everyday imagery in the media, on the internet and even in educational literature.

Critical pedagogies argue that the root of disciplinary discourses and knowledge building is a critical stance on life and worldwide issues (Smallwood, 2002; McLean, 2006). This book asserts that the cultivation of critical pedagogies is necessary for the development of concept understanding. The massification and commercialization of HE risks disciplines being reduced to subjects which mainly offer a route into employability (McArthur, 2010, 2011). Instead, educationalists need to revitalize disciplines into displaying the "power to develop minds to contribute to understanding and knowing how to act in the world" (McLean, 2006, p. 67). That is, to encourage students to voice their opinions and experiences, explore evidence, reach conclusions about various concepts on their own (rather than be told what is the right concept and believe in that by default).

As argued so far, disciplines operate with disciplinary concepts which resource deep exploration and hence the creation of meaning for that discipline. It can then be said that a set of concepts forms a "conceptual framework": a network of concept meanings which, in turn, furnishes a "conceptual discourse" for some discipline, or disciplines. Finally, this discourse leads to acting and sharing within a disciplinary and/or interdisciplinary community (Lave, 1991; Wenger, 1998). To develop interdisciplinarity, which is in my opinion a much needed albeit challenging way forward in higher education, it is essential to accept that the same concepts names and labels will have different definitions and meanings across disciplines, teachers and students, therefore, having porous boundaries.

"Conceptual discourse" is what members of such a community do when they exercise the conceptual framework together. A concept within the framework can then be understood as: (1) its basic, functionalist and vertical classification-sensitive level (Merril et al., 1992; Howard, 1987) and as its expansion, desirably so, or as: (2) an entity that transcends narrow definition and disciplinary boundaries. The latter understanding positions concepts to support innovative and complex ideas, literacies and performances—this supporting role is seen as crucial to effective learning for the student-futurologist and their achievement of well-rounded personal and collective development in the contemporary fluid and destabilised world, ridden with big challenegs and uncertainties. Therefore, higher education should aspire to create conditions in which students experience an active and participatory development of their concept understanding via constant "critical acumen" (Tavin, 2003). Such conditions and engagements are prerequisites for student transformation. This transformation happens when one develops new ways of seeing the world (Marton, Dall'Alb, & Beaty, 1993). Although I do not focus in further depth on critical theory or pedagogy, these approaches merit further investigation.

Criticality in the present context is connected to what has been discussed as "mindful thinking"—opening opportunities to think about one's own and collective thinking, interpretation, doing and processes involved in that thinking in order to make (creative) insights and conclusions. Creativity is further connected to De Bono's idea of "lateral" and "parallel" thinking: "lateral" meaning not following conventional patterns of thinking but allowing mind to find all relevant points in a situation; "parallel" meaning to "allow different ways of thinking to coexist (rather than compete and cancel each other out), so that they can lead to solutions beyond the limits" of the stated problem or idea (Moseley et al., 2005, p. 135). In a single phrase, this thinking can be called an organic, inclusive, dynamic, granular relations-based thinking.

Critical inquiry is adopted as *concept problematization and imagination by not accepting concept definition at its face value but trying to explore it and think of various manifestations of the concept that require conceptual embodiment exposure and discussion.* It is hoped in the empirical studies in this book that the students will develop critical concept inferences and concept elaborations as integrated with images, engaging with IG. The main "criticality" focus in an inquiry graphics design and studies is to what extent and how students manage to elaborate on their ideas and develop critical concept inferences which go beyond concept definition, and to what extent and how the picture resources that inference as an integrated analytical sign. As conceptual inquiry supports the development of knowledge and learning, this leads to Chap. 6, which can be seen as an extension of the present Chap. 5.

# References

Bakhtin, M. M. (1981). *The dialogic imagination: Four essays* (Michael Holquist, Ed. and Caryl Emerson & Michael Holquist, Trans.). Austin, TX: University of Texas Press. *84*(8), 80–82.

Bartram, R. (2004). Visuality, dromology and time compression: Paul Virilio's new ocularcentrism. *Time & Society, 13*(2–3), 285–300.

Bernstein, B. (2006). Vertical and horizontal discourse: An essay. In *Education and society* (pp. 53–73). London: Routledge.

Blunden, A. (2012). *Concepts: A critical approach* (Vol. 44). Leiden, Netherlands: Brill.

Boisvert, R. D. (1998). *John Dewey: Rethinking our time.* New York: SUNY Press.

Bransford, J. D., Sherwood, R. D., Hasselbring, T. S., Kinzer, C. K., & Williams, S. M. (1990). Anchored instruction: Why we need it and how technology can help. In D. Nix & R. Spiro (Eds.), *Cognition, education, and multimedia: Exploring ideas in high technology* (112–138). New York & London: Routledge.

Bransford, J. D., & Schwartz, D. L. (1999). Rethinking transfer: A simple proposal with multiple implications. *Review of Research in Education, 24*, 61–100.

Brockbank, A., & McGill, I. (2007). *Facilitating reflective learning in higher education.* London: McGraw-Hill International.

Bruner, J. S. (1986). *Actual minds, possible worlds.* Cambridge, Massachusetts: Harvard University Press.

Canning, J. (2007). Pedagogy as a discipline: Emergence, sustainability and professionalisation. *Teaching in Higher Education, 12*, 393–403.

Cin, F. M., & Doğan, N. (2020). Navigating university spaces as refugees: Syrian students' pathways of access to and through higher education in Turkey. *International Journal of Inclusive Education*, 1–15.

Dahlin, B. (2001). The primacy of cognition–or of perception? A phenomenological critique of the theoretical bases of science education. *Science & Education, 10*, 453–475.

De Haan, R. L. (2009). Teaching creativity and inventive problem solving in science. *CBE-Life Sciences Education, 8*, 172–181.

Demick, J. (2000). Toward a mindful psychological science: Theory and application. *Journal of Social Issues, 56*, 141–159.

Dewey, J. (2009/1910). *How we think.* Lightning Source UK Ltd.

Dewey, J., & Bentley, A. F. (1960). *Knowing and the known* (No. 111). Boston: Beacon Press.

Elkonin, D. B. (1989). Ob istochnikakh neklassicheskoi psikhologii (On the sources of non-classical psychology). In D. B. Elkonin (Ed.), *Izbrannye psikhologicheskie trudy* (Selected psychological writings) (pp. 475–478). Moscow: Pedagogika.

Fauconnier, G., & Turner, M. (2002). *The way we think: Conceptual blending and the mind's hidden complexities*. New York: Basic Books.

Freire, P. (1970/1993). *Pedagogy of the oppressed* (Rev. ed.). New York: Continuum International Publishing Group.

Gardner, H. (1993). *Creating minds: An anatomy of creativity seen through the lives of Freud, Einstein, Pieasso, Stravinskv, Eliot, Graham, and Gandhi*. New York: Basic Books.

Giroux, H. A. (1994). *Disturbing pleasures: Learning popular culture*. New York: Routledge.

Hodge, B. R. I. V., & Kress, G. R. (1988). *Social semiotics*. Cambridge, UK: Polity Press.

Hong, H.-Y., & Sullivan, F. R. (2009). Towards an idea-centered, principle-based design approach to support learning as knowledge creation. *Educational Technology Research and Development, 57*, 613–627.

Howard, R. W. (1987). *Concepts and schemata: An introduction*. Cassell Educational.

Kavanagh, D. (2004). Ocularcentrism and its others: A framework for metatheoretical analysis. *Organization Studies, 25*(3), 445–464.

Kellner, D. (1999). Virilio, war and technology: Some critical reflections. *Theory, Culture & Society, 16*(5–6), 103–125.

Kress, G. (2004). *Literacy in the new media age*. London: Routledge.

Lackovic, N. (2010). Creating and reading images: Towards a communication framework for Higher Education learning. In Seminar. net (Vol. 6, No. 1).

Lackovic, N. (2016). MultiMAP: Exploring multimodal artefact pedagogy in digital higher education. *Proceedings, 148*–162.

Lackovic, N. (2017). Book review: Collective knowledge arises from multimodal, dialogic intertextuality: Learning in the age of digital reason (2017) by Petar Jandrić. *Knowledge Cultures, 5*(05), 131–135.

Langer, E. J. (1989). *Mindfulness*. Boston: Addison Wesley Longman.

Langer, E. J. (1997). *The power of mindful learning*. Boston: Addison Wesley Longman.

Langer, E. J., & Moldoveanu, M. (2000). The construct of mindfulness. *Journal of Social Issues, 56*, 1–9.

Lave, J. (1991). Situating learning in communities of practice. *Perspectives on socially shared cognition, 2*, 63–82.

Lave, J., & Wenger, E. (1991). *Situated learning: Legitimate peripheral participation*. Cambridge & New York: Cambridge University Press.

Lipman, M. (2003). *Thinking in education*. Cambridge, UK: Cambridge University Press.

Loveless, A. (2007). *Creativity, technology and learning – A review of recent literature*. Report 4 update, Futurelab. Retrieved from: http://www2.futurelab. org.uk/resources/documents/lit_reviews/Creativity_Review_update.pdf

Loveless, A. M. (2002). *Literature review in creativity, new technologies and learning*. Bristol, UK: Futurelab.

Maran, T., & Kull, K. (2014). Ecosemiotics: main principles and current developments. *Geografiska Annaler: Series B, Human Geography, 96*(1), 41–50.

Marton, F., Dall'alba, G., & Beaty, E. (1993). Conceptions of learning. *International Journal of Educational Research, 19*, 277–300.

McArthur, J. (2010). Time to look anew: Critical pedagogy and disciplines within higher education. *Studies in Higher Education, 35*, 301–315.

McArthur, J. (2011). Reconsidering the social and economic purposes of higher education. *Higher Education Research & Development, 30*, 737–749.

McLean, M. (2006). *Pedagogy and the university: Critical theory and practice*. New York: Continuum International Publishing Group.

Merrill, M. D., Tennyson, R. D., & Posey, L. O. (1992). *Teaching concepts: An instructional design guide*. Englewood Cliffs, NJ: Educational Technology Publications.

Meyer, J., & Land, R. (2003). *Threshold concepts and troublesome knowledge: Linkages to ways of thinking and practising within the disciplines* (pp. 412–424). Edinburgh, UK: University of Edinburgh.

Moseley, D., Baumfield, V., Elliott, J., Higgins, S., Miller, J., & Newton, D. P. (2005). *Frameworks for thinking: A handbook for teachers and learning*. Cambridge, UK: Cambridge University Press.

Paavola, S., & Hakkarainen, K. (2005). The knowledge creation metaphor–An emergent epistemological approach to learning. *Science & Education, 14*, 535–557.

Paavola, S., Lipponen, L., & Hakkarainen, K. (2002, January). Epistemological foundations for CSCL: a comparison of three models of innovative knowledge communities. In G. Stahl (Ed.), *Computer Support for Collaborative Learning: Foundation for a CSCL community, proceedings of CSCL 2002* (pp. 24–32). Boulder, Colorado, Hillsdale, New Jersey: Lawrence Erlbaum Associates.

Parker, J. (2002). A new disciplinarity: Communities of knowledge, learning and practice. *Teaching in Higher Education, 7*, 373–386.

Potter, W. J. (2004). *Theory of media literacy: A cognitive approach.* Thousand Oaks, CA: Sage.

Robbins, D. (2003). *Vygotsky's and AA Leontiev's semiotics and psycholinguistics: Applications for education, second language acquisition, and theories of language.* Westport, CO: Praeger Publishers.

Robbins, D. (2005). Generalized holographic visions of language in Vygotsky, Luria, Pribram, Eisenstein, and Volosinov. *Intercultural Pragmatics, 2*, 25–39.

Robbins, D. (2007, June). Vygotsky's and Leontiev's non-classical psychology related to second language acquisition. In *International Nordic-Baltic region conference of FIPLV innovations in language teaching and learning in the multicultural context* (Vol. 47057).

Robbins, P., & Aydede, M. (2009). A short primer on situated cognition. In *The Cambridge handbook of situated cognition* (pp. 3–10).

Scardamalia, M., & Bereiter, C. (1993). Technologies for knowledge-building discourse. *Communications of the ACM, 36*, 37–41.

Scardamalia, M., & Bereiter, C. (1994). Computer support for knowledge-building communities. *The Journal of the Learning Sciences, 3*, 265–283.

Scardamalia, M., & Bereiter, C. (2006). Knowledge building: Theory, pedagogy, and technology. In *The Cambridge handbook of the learning sciences* (pp. 97–115).

Sfard, A. (1998). On two metaphors for learning and the dangers of choosing just one. *Educational Researcher, 27*, 4–13.

Smallwood, P. (2002). "More creative than creation" on the idea of criticism and the student critic. *Arts and Humanities in Higher Education, 1*, 59–71.

Stables, A. (2010). Semiosis and the collapse of mind-body dualism: Implications for education. In Inna Semestky (Ed.), *Semiotics education experience* (pp. 21–36). Brill/Sense.

Tan, S. (2002). *Picture books: Who are they for?* Retrieved from: http://www.shauntan.net/images/whypicbooks.pdf

Tavin, K. M. (2003). Wrestling with angels, searching for ghosts: Toward a critical pedagogy of visual culture. *Studies in Art Education, 44*, 197–213.

Thompson, P. (2012). Both dialogic and dialectic: Translation at the crossroads. *Learning, Culture and Social Interaction, 1*, 90–101.

Van der Veer, R., & Valsiner, J. (1994). *The Vygotsky reader.* Oxford, UK: Blackwell Publishing.

Vygotsky, L. S. (Rieber, R. W., Carton, A. S.). (1987). *The collected works of LS Vygotsky: Volume 1: Problems of general psychology, including the volume thinking and speech.* Springer.

Wenger, E. (1998). Communities of practice: Learning as a social system. *Systems Thinker, 9*, 2–3.

Wertsch, J. V. (1985). *Vygotsky and the social formation of mind.* Harvard University Press.

Wertsch, J. V. (1998). *Mind as action.* New York: Oxford University Press.

White, E. J. (2014). Bakhtinian dialogic and Vygotskian dialectic: Compatabilities and contradictions in the classroom? *Educational Philosophy and Theory, 46*(3), 220–236.

Wyndhamn, J., & Säljö, R. (1997). Word problems and mathematical reasoning – A study of children's mastery of reference and meaning in textual realities. *Learning and Instruction, 7,* 361–382.

# 6

# Learning, Knowledge and Thinking Via Guided Image Inquiry

Previous chapters tackled the notion of learning from a variety of perspectives, but they all have in common that learning and conceptual development are processes that do not foster dualist separations of image and concept, calling for an integrated, multimodal approach to thinking, learning and conceptualizing with images, and other non-verbal modes. This chapter focuses on the learning concept or paradigm that inquiry graphics (IG) designs and activities promote and incorporate.

## What Is Learning? A Contested Pursuit

Learning is a complex activity both in and outside the body, embodied and relational. Learning is an adaptation toward a change as a person, hard to assess with any immediate testing and possibly not tested with summative assessment (as what is tested might be memorization that can evaporate into a thin air after some time). By defining learning as such, I relate to Andrew Stables's description of learning (2010, p. 27) as sign-mediated change/ becoming, being and *social judgment*:

© The Author(s) 2020
N. Lacković, *Inquiry Graphics in Higher Education*,
https://doi.org/10.1007/978-3-030-39387-8_6

"learning" is a term used to validate certain kinds and examples of personal, social and institutional change: generally speaking, those of which we approve (teachers and/or educational institutions, curriculum developers and policy). At times when we speak of learning, we mean social reproduction; at its most exciting it refers to something that at least feels new for the individual... The brains that light up in the psychologist's or neuroscientists laboratory do not learn: learning is part of being a person, and being a person is subject to social judgments.

Therefore, human learning is a development of semiotic awareness and consciousness that informs learners' future acts. It is not here viewed as only a change in memory, but an adaptation toward a change as a person that is hard to assess with any immediate memory testing. Many psychology-based cognitivist theories have implicitly encouraged a positivistic view of knowledge, whereby what is to be learned is "out there" (in the world) and the consequences of that learning are something that has to become replicated "in here" (in the mind). This encourages conceptions of learning as "acquisition" (Sfard, 1998): something whose successful presence is to be detected through structured testing. The question of what is learned in such acquisition sense is understood as some sort of "change in long term memory" (Kirschner, Sweller, & Clark, 2006). Knowledge as acquisition encourages an empirical approach to learning that stresses the effective design of outcome (acquisition) tests and, perhaps, a strong faith in prescriptive and "direct instruction" as the powerful force behind learning (ibid.). Practical psychology-driven studies of learning are still dominated by the apparent pursuit of discrete changes in something like long-term or short-term memory, although students might still resort to last minute pre-exam "binge learning" (reading for short-term memorization/memory change, which could be measured by testing).

Although the importance of research on instruction (in learning) is acknowledged, this term is transformed here into *"guidance"* and seen as embedded within an alternative approach to learning and knowledge development that incorporates edusemiotic principles of longitudinal growth of knowledge. This approach views the consequences of learning not in terms of inserting knowledge items into some memory space but in terms of *incremental elaboration or reconfiguration within some space of individual and collective meaning, as it unfolds over time in the world (as socio-cultural context) and material surroundings (as socio-material environment).* In line with this view, Kress (2009) argues that we must acknowledge thinking and learning "on the go"—otherwise we privilege particular autocratic forms of learning that stress outcome assessment and leave more useful signs of learning unacknowledged—as development, as effort, as interaction, as imagination, as creativity, as inquiry. This approach to learning invites educational practitioners to think more about those learning actions and efforts. It encourages thinking about more flexible and relational taxonomies that would acknowledge different forms of interaction that characterize the experience of learning. Therefore, learning is seen in terms of an unfolding—in terms of understanding as emergent, as idea development, as knowledge building (Scardamalia & Bereiter, 2006). This favors more the Vygotskian and Peircean notion of learning as evolutionary rather than a static approach to knowledge. The driving belief behind "knowledge-building" theory is the notion that we are a "knowledge-creating civilization" (Scardamalia & Bereiter, 2006, p. 97). In other words, knowledge-building theory calls for a pedagogic focus on knowledge selection, creation and innovation.

Given the plethora of learning theories and approaches, it is hard to ground design in a single approach, particularly since many overlap (I here highlight what different approaches have in common, as they do have distinct differences too), building on and adding to each other. In particular, we could be vigorous (social) constructivists, applying minimally guided, problem-based, or inquiry-based learning with our students, with minimal instruction, but then perhaps find ourselves frustrated—if students get lost on their way, or fail to achieve intended or deserved outcomes or our way of working clashes with any other demands at assessment or auditing level. Nevertheless, this certainly does not mean that inquiry-based learning cannot be designed in effective conjunction with instructional support, still preserving the open-endedness of concept and knowledge and an independent, creative and critical discovery quest.

The teaching challenge is how to orchestrate (or curate) learning activities (Crook, 2010) to embrace multiple and new perspectives on learning. This means thinking whether sufficient guidance, examples, and preparation have been provided to support autonomous inquiry in accordance with pedagogical purpose and learning goals. In my teaching practice, I usually change learning and teaching designs building on my previous experience. Online courses that I have engaged with for the last five years usually have cohorts who are already professionals working in higher education, many of them with years of experience in the field, pressing deadlines and commitments in daily life, hence it poses a challenge to balance strong support with minimal guidance in such environments. The point is that learning and thinking with images and semiotics are new and often surprising approaches to higher education for most students in the field of higher education research and studies. That is why most students need guidance and examples, which I hope this book can serve.

A question of what theories of learning are most relevant lingers in the air. However, we need not view learning theories in terms of competitive and exclusive choices. As Bransford et al. (2005, p. 49) argue, educators need to stop asking whose theories and views are right or better, but ask instead how learners can be resourced and orchestrated, building on the wide knowledge base that has been accumulated so far around learning, *various* theoretical inspirations for both growing and innovating to practice and be prepared for constant adaptation to change. In the empirical Part II, a proposed pedagogic/learning design builds on such approaches to learning and educational research, which are like threads in a tapestry of educational practice, as a more encompassing understanding of learning (Hammerness et al., 2005) than any singular approach to and theory of learning. As of relatively recently, researchers call for assessment that is a healthy mix of both formative and summative, positioning the former as related to process and innovation, and the latter to outcomes and efficiency (Bransford et al., 2005). Arguments for the social justice aspect of assessment are also gaining strength (McArthur, 2010), calling for a greater focus on the formative aspects of assessment and turning away from grading. I adopt a mindful and eclectic blend of theoretical themes and approaches that all share a view on knowledge and learning as a development, a creative and generative processes that include observing and reflecting on relations in unity and acknowledge plurality and multiplicity of conceptual and knowledge manifestations in the world. One useful theoretical position in relation to learning and the edusemiotic focus of synechism and learning processes (see Chap. 3) is the theory of "knowledge building" (Scardamalia & Bereiter, 2006), further discussed in next section.

# What Is Knowledge Building? Knowledge as Development in a Community of Inquiry

Knowledge-building theory could relate to edusemiotics to some extent (there are differences), as it draws from but goes beyond social constructivism to reflect the "contemporary emphasis on knowledge creation and innovation" (Scardamalia & Bereiter, 2006, p. 97). This focus on creation and innovation also requires seeing students as members of some knowledge-building *community*. Knowledge advancement, aligned with Peirce's edusemiotic views, means understanding that is *emergent and socially shaped*. Some of the relevant tenets of the knowledge-building theory are:

- idea improvement: knowledge advancement as idea improvement, rather than as progress toward some true or warranted belief and only through the reproduction of existing ideas;
- constructive use of authoritative information (not deterministic or oppressive);
- understanding as emergent.
  (Scardamalia & Bereiter, 2006, p. 98)

Thereby, knowledge in a field advances, rather than accumulates, hence the goal should not be regurgitation (of facts, text). It does not advance to a final state, again in agreement with Peirce's view on knowledge and truth fragility "there are three things to which we can never hope to attain by reasoning, namely, absolute certainty, absolute exactitude, absolute universality. We cannot be absolutely certain that our conclusions are even approximately true" (CP 1.141). Thus, pedagogy needs to focus on how ideas emerge, develop, improve and change (preserving the notion of the "scientific truths" we currently hold in disciplines but letting them be freely open to query and challenge, especially in the context of the post-human, beyond the Anthropocene and related to the materiality of the world). Scardamalia and Bereiter (2006, p. 99) refer to Rheinberger's (1997) "epistemic things", such as concrete models that are particularly important in education for the creation of further knowledge and they argue that there needs to be enough access to concreteness that represent the outside world, its visual and material culture and artifacts. Pictures or digital photograph as a part of IGs can act as those concrete models.

Another view that acknowledges the adaptive nature of knowledge in an age of uncertainty and complexity positions educational practice as "preparation for future learning", or so called "PFL" (Bransford et al., 2005). This means learners need to be well-prepared for demands in the various contexts and challenges of future learning (Bransford & Schwartz, 1999) and circumstances, therefore provided with opportunities to:

> try out hunches, receive feedback, and attempt to revise based on the feed-back. In contrast, typical tests provide few opportunities for feedback and revision. (Bransford et al., 2005, p. 53)

This idea of "trying out" and "receiving feedback" then is a needed ingredient of a pedagogic activity.

## Knowledge Development as Inquiry Graphics Integration and Mediation

Wertsch (1991) argues that, for learning to happen, the learner needs to master mediational means: the artifacts entering into learning interactions. These artifacts comprise any communicational means that are socioculturally produced by humans, from physical artifacts such as various machines, to psychological ones such as language, images, that have been here observed as signs, and so on. This mediated activity demands an "active learner". It is not that teachers should not be involved but when they are there, they are not passively transmitting some information, but supporting a set of conditions where more active exploration can take place. Learners' understanding is always developed in a dynamic relationship with the sociocultural particularities of the environment and learning contexts. As Bruno and Munoz (2010, p. 368) reflect:

> That means the student needs to deal with "what others say," and the way this is assimilated and accommodated in the subject… needs to construct a network integrating his internal existence with what the external world (society) offers and says about that knowledge.

The student's mind will constitute the student's complex and relational "identity" and "particularity" (Bruno & Munoz, 2010, p. 368).

One of key ideas of sociocultural constructivism is that our interaction with the world takes place through the mediation of tools (Kozulin, 2003). It is important to acknowledge that tools do not serve some simplistic act of function of mediation, but they are also integral for *reflective mediation* (Gillespie & Zittoun, 2010). When they become a part of the thinking process, they bring in their own characteristics and materiality that affects meaning rather than being just a "passive" meditative artifact or some crude tool. These authors challenge the use of the terms "tool" and "mediation" in order to consider instead the terms "sign" and "reflective practice"(Gillespie & Zittoun, 2010). This is not pursued in the spirit of activity–culture antinomy but activity–culture complementarity. For Gillespie and Zittoun (2010), "tools" are of a material nature and humans use them to achieve some (visible) change in the world, whereas "signs" are semiotic resources which humans "use" to cause some change in their own psychological state and/or the state of another person/group. Yet, a tool can be a sign and a sign can be a tool, and in many cases a sign and tool come together to make meaning, that is, the tool's materiality is a part of a symbolic sign making. Many material artifacts can function as sign-tools. Thus, their nature is fluid and determined by contextual use. Furthermore, each tool can be used either non-reflectively or reflectively: one "uses" tools or signs in a routine or intuitive manner (non-reflective use) or one takes time and effort to reflect upon their use. The use of IG foregrounds reflective use, but it goes much beyond it, to initiate unique insights on sign-tools, building on learners' experiences.

The designed pedagogic activity in Projects 2 and 3 is supported by technological resources, which implies that students would be using those resources as tool-signs, to produce a visible, end object (tool), operating

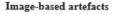

Subject (Learner) | Object (concept development)

**Fig. 6.1** The "Image artifact–Subject (learner)–Object" triad

with meanings as signs (in various levels of reflective or perhaps non-reflective ways, depending on how they use them). Due to this fluid nature of mediating resources, the term "artifacts" has been chosen to refer both to tools (visible artifact products) and signs that can mediate meaning change via an action of interpretation/ reflectivity/ criticality. Figure 6.1 illustrates the sociocultural Vygotskian triangle, commonly used in CHAT (cultural-historical activity theory) that applies to the focus of the application of IG in the empirical part of the book. In essence, the pedagogic activities explore the represented triadic relations: *how inquiry graphics as image-based artifacts affect the development of the subject's (learner's) concept understanding.*

The most important aim of an IG practice is to use the depictive image (graphics) as a resourceful mediating and integrative reflective artifact to engage learners in the building of knowledge, that will further evolve, as signs are evolutionary.

# Thinking as Reshaping of Cognitive Schemata and the Iconicity of Thinking[1]

At the cognitive process level of thinking and learning, constructivism concerns the nature of knowledge as "schematic" (Piaget, Brown, & Thampy, 1985). This means that a disciplinary concepts (e.g.,

---

[1] Last three paragraphs of this section incorporate joint work with Dr. Alin Olteanu on the iconicity of thinking.

"constructivism," "classroom," "learning") exist as individual schemata that are constantly reshaped by sociocultural interactions and artifacts. In that way, they have both individual and social character. Schemata are a kind of semantic filter of the mind (not the brain) through which any new experience is passed, whereby that new experience is integrated to what we already know (our existing schemata) and made a relevant item for them. Yet, a schema is simultaneously "accommodated" to take account of the demands of some new experience. When students learn about new concepts, those concepts might not easily fit within the existing schemata or the fit made might be done almost as a forced integration. That is when students struggle to grapple with new concepts and their schemata resist accommodation, creating what was discussed in Chap. 5 as a destabilizing state of grappling with a threshold concept. Students need to be encouraged to evoke prior experience and find a more familiar reflective ground in order to evoke interest and get in-depth with a field of inquiry. This might take time. What tutors can do is to apply teaching and learning methods which give agency to students and help stimulate creative effort, imagination and transformation. For any individual there is a personal representation of any concept being developed. That ownership of a concept reflects the individual's history of experience—which needs to be externalized and reflected upon with a particular intention to challenge the boundaries of the concept's schemata.

Here I turn to consider the thesis of iconicity of thinking that relates to these efforts of the mind to find similar or familiar aspects of any new conceptual field. By doing so, I am arguing that the iconicity in an internal environment (e.g., as represented in a photograph) is inherently linked to the iconicity of thinking itself. It builds on Peirce and has been proposed by a number of scholars in semiotics. It is the subject of a paper I have co-written with Alin Olteanu, whose reflections and references related to diagrammatic reasoning can be usefully related to the principles of inquiry graphics. This and the following two paragraphs incorporate our current co-writing efforts. The hypothesis that iconicity is seminal for meaning-making (cf. Elleström, 2014; Stjernfelt, 2007) and scientific reasoning (Pietarinen & Bellucci, 2016) implies that any apprehension requires observing certain similarities (via corporeality). Observing similarity involves operations of cross-modal translation by analogy and association that require establishing some common denominators between two "things", one new and one that have been experienced or learnt before. The link between phenomenological corporeality and iconicity is suggested foundational for the recent "iconic turn" in many areas of the humanities (Boehm & Mitchell, 2009, pp. 110–111). At a more physical level, by seeing or touching shapes, one can anticipate or know how an object could be grasped and handled, as the mind makes a connection between the shape and the function of grasping. Making sense of one's environment, thus, implies the discovery of useful similarities across entities, meanings and actions (how these connect), by practical or mental (simulation) experimentation, also called *diagrammatic reasoning* (Stjernfelt, 2007; Pietarinen & Bellucci, 2016). Given the plurality of sense perception channels of human corporeality, such experiments consist in mental manipulation involving iconicity across modes (see Stjernfelt, 2007, pp. 91–92) and are critical for imagining, even in scientific investigation. This is highlighted, for instance, in one of Peirce's diagram definitions (MS 616, 1906), as provided and used also by Pietarinen and Bellucci (2016, p. 474), as

> a concrete but possibly changing mental image of such a thing as it represents. A drawing or model may be employed to aid the imagination; but the essential thing to be performed is the act of imagining. (MS 616, 1906; quoted in Lacković & Olteanu, forthcoming)

Peirce used the term "diagram" to refer to the particular type of icon that signifies due to internal part–whole similarities, that is, through its schematic structure. The supposition of the iconic turn, following Boehm and Mitchell (2009, p. 110) and Stjernfelt (2007) is that a knowing subject can learn something (develop schemata) only if a sufficient level of similarity between what one knows at that given moment and what is to be learned is observable (or sensed). Such similarity (between the known and the yet unknown) is a prerequisite for knowledge development, understood as meaning expansion. For educational purposes, examples from real life and concrete instances are useful as they create a situation of comparison. As Legg (2017, 29) posits, the implications of scaffolding education iconically are profound: for providing learners with a navigable road-map of a subject matter, for enabling them to see further connections of their own in what is taught, and for supporting meaningful active learning.

Iconicity in education means that understanding things is a type of semiotic modeling of both verbal and nonverbal signs, which brings back the view of concepts by Dewey and Bentley (1960), that any concept is only the current state of knowledge (as developed and approved by some knowledge authorities). As such, concepts are not amodal mental entities, expressed only analytically, but also embodied and sensed schemata, using a terminology from cognitive semantics (Lakoff & Johnson, 1980). The iconic turn in semiotics is connected to the recent (re)discovery of Peirce's schematic and diagrammatic semiotics (Pietarinen, 2006; Stjernfelt, 2007; Pietarinen & Belluci, 2016), kick-started by Umberto Eco's (1997) reconsideration of Peircean iconicity and resulting debates on perception and conception. These extensive debates amount to the idea that meaning does not stem from conventional codes only (languages). Rather, human conventions are founded upon meanings and things that are both verbal and non-verbal that humans discover in and link to their environments throughout life and which facilitate the further development of more complex meaning. External artifacts and/or sensations are entwined with the mind in cognitive processes (Malafouris, 2013). IGs can act as *external scaffolding artifacts* that mediate acts of iconic (and also multimodal) reasoning.

# The Externalization of Thinking Processes with/via Images

One view related to the Peirce-inspired iconicity of thinking is "extended mind" perspective. It argues that humans operate in the world by exploiting the environment which "extends" their cognitive abilities into that environment: using a variety of strategies, external tools and representations (Scaife & Rogers, 2005, p. 181; Clark & Chalmers, 1998). The idea of externalization and external cognition therefore implies that when we think we do not do something that is exclusively private and internal. Beyond doubt, it partly is. However, the processes that go on in our minds typically incorporate useful elements in the external world that are available to us (there and then) through our senses. It is not to deny the operational functioning of the brain, but to observe cognition as extended into a cognition system that includes an immediate context and environment. Thinking happens not as a computational operation inside the head but it extends beyond the individual: inviting us to consider not just what is inside the head but also what the head is inside of (Hollan, Hutchins, & Kirsh, 2000), that is, its environment. Langer's mindfulness approach illustrated in Chap. 5 as well as sociomaterial approaches (Fenwick, 2010) mentioned in Chap. 1 gels nicely with the idea of extended mind as in both mind and cognition are not seen only in a narrow sense of some computational model of the brain, but where mind "extends" into the environment, providing myriads of possibilities for human–artifact–concept interaction. In short, our thinking is conceived as an achievement distributed over an environment of things, matter, designs, spatial structures, people and activity. We exist and our life makes sense in relation to and with other people, natural and non-natural things, contextual circumstances, conditions and artifacts. The cognitive work is done on/ with/ through both internal and external representational material. The main idea of this theoretical tradition is that we usually need external resources to support more effective cognition. Norman (1993) talks about external "aids":

> The power of the unaided mind is highly overrated. Without external aids, memory, thought, and reasoning are all constrained. But human intelligence is highly flexible and adaptable, superb at inventing procedures and objects that overcome its own limits. The real powers come from devising external aids: it is things that make us smart. (Norman, 1993, p. 43)

However, I would not want to reduce external artifacts to "aids" of cognition as it will be shown in Part II that they enter into the process of thinking at a much finer, dynamic and integrative way than being mere "aids". By being signs, they themselves direct thinking and action. Indeed, Card, Mackinlay, and Shneiderman (1999, p. 3) expand the aid into the "entwined" metaphor, also evident in the sociomaterial concept of "entanglement" (Orlikowski, 2007), stating that not only "visual artifacts aid thought; in fact, they are completely entwined." Yet, I think we can still focus on individual entanglement ingredients and resources to understand how they constitute it.

We all must have experienced how hard it can be to think spontaneously without an external point of reference—our mind might wonder off, jump from one idea to another. Our minds tend to be swarmed by unceasing thoughts. It can be hard to think in or for education without the thinking externalized or materialized in some relationship with the situated environment. The proponents of external cognition argue that it is not cognitive amplification that technologies and artifacts support: it is cognitive task *change* through new means of mediation (Norman, 1993; Arias-Hernandez, Green, & Fisher, 2012). This change is what is beneficial for learning, as it creates focus sand link with external surroundings. They suggest that mind changes its concern from focusing on mental task performance (abstract and symbolic reasoning) to perceptual and motor task performance (reasoning directly related to an external world and artifacts). This kind of change of focus, I would argue, does not happen in any structured of delineated fashion, to clearly separate when one performance ends and the other starts, hence the mental and external are inter-related, they coexist. It evokes the terms "transmediation" and "transduction", when thinking focus in an activity changes from one mode to another (e.g., from images to words and vice versa). This change makes a cognitive task more fluent and confident, since there is an external object which can be a point of reference and also act as an integrated sign in thinking and speaking.

According to Hutchins, external artifacts (which he calls cognitive artifacts if they are used for thinking and learning—such as visually represented information) help cognition and make it re-mediated, but not "amplified":

> it is not that the cognitive properties of individual minds get amplified; it is rather the effective coupling of individuals and cognitive artifacts that produces cognitive properties of a system that are more effective than those produced by the individual mind alone (Hutchins (1995), cited by Arias-Hernandez et al., 2012, pp. 10).

Therefore, thinking concerns an external physical and material as well as symbolic system where the mind is situated in (recall the idea of photographs as compound, icon–index–symbol signs introduced in Chap. 1). Sterelny (2004, p. 5) claims that the human ability to leave graphical records was revolutionary in terms of the impact of such "trail leaving" and provided the base of rapid human evolutionary development, at a nexus of cultural and biological forces, not one or the other. Passing on collective knowledge only by spoken reports, storytelling, songs, or rhymes is ephemeral and dependent on individual talent to pass it on, unless recorded. The creation of specialized epistemic artifacts gave rise to rapid societal development and "cognitive breakthrough" (Sterelny, 2004, p. 5). Such artifacts are those whose purpose surpasses functional and physical acting in the world of the spear or rudimentary tools to be integrated into thinking, aesthetics and idea-sharing. External visual representations integrated in IG act as highly specialized epistemic artifacts in that respect. But, surprisingly, only recently have psychology and learning sciences oriented to the external world (of signs, symbols, gestures, images or artifacts) in such a way that it can be incorporated into accounts of human mental life/ thought.

Once cognitive theory had embraced the idea that thinking is a system with material things as well as mental things, then it naturally followed that psychologists should try and understand the process of this incorporation of the material into the mental—this extension of cognition. For example, Kirsh (1995) looked at how we actively structure our external environments to be supportive in this way. He gave the simple example of setting out the food and tools on a kitchen surface to support in some sensory and visual way the procedure of cooking. This was offered as an example of managing the environment (for action) in the sense of distributing cognition introduced there. A more cognitive example (managing the environment for *thinking*) is his case of a Scrabble player setting out the letters on a Scrabble-piece holder—set so as to channel seeing word possibilities. The proposed thinking with IG is similar to this Scrabble layering as it asks the learner to bring parts (elements) of the image together in forms that carry new meanings, which can materialize some properties of concepts. This is also for externalizing learners' thoughts about it for a dialogic exchange with the teacher, and at the level of challenging concept definition, suggesting new interpretations of the concept manifestation and occurrence, again encouraged to be freely shared in a learning community.

In summary, external representations or artifacts (sign-tools) are of great benefit for cognition (Kirsh, 2013), as "people think more powerfully with external representations than without. *They allow us to think the previously unthinkable* (Kirsh, 2010, p. 441, emphasis added)". Therefore, any external graphic representation is an obvious example of an integrated external "resource" that we can deploy for thinking. For example, the traditions of "infographics" and information visualization discussed in Chap. 4 are forms of thought externalization via visual designs. Both traditions are trying to reduce the amount of "working out" or interpreting that the learner has to do: the effort of interpretation is brought off by the ingenuity of the visual design and its rules. This is the case with static infographics; these embrace websites that feature animated infographics, which can demand greater engagement from the viewer, However, this is typically through playing with the presented material rather than interrogating and exploring that material. One of the main tenets of these species of research (infographics and visualizations) is to increase the effectiveness and ease of information presentation. But for an in-depth learning, we can combine that summary function with the function of exploration and inquiry.

# Inquiry as a Key Action of Inquiry Graphics

I mentioned above that knowledge development foregrounds the role of externalization and sharing, and this happens in a community of inquiry. This section considers inquiry as educational strategy that is connected to guided knowledge building theory. It first reviews the notion of inquiry as traditionally researched. The book adopts inquiry learning as an option for *social* sciences learning, not just as commonly taken to be studied for the natural sciences—since "inquiry" is seen as a universal act of creative concept exploration, rather than only subject to experimenting in "hard" sciences. It proceeds by tackling inquiry through the lenses of reflective communication and meaning-making performed collaboratively in small groups.

## The Case for Guided Inquiry Learning

Inquiry and project-based learning have both been considered educational strategies related to constructivism and knowledge-building perspectives. Inquiry learning is mostly employed in natural sciences education, or any scientific discipline which mainly progresses through experimentation. One of the main features of inquiry learning is to develop a hypothesis which will then generate data collection, experimentation, analysis, inference, validation and conclusion. Through inquiry learning practice, students are expected, in a broader sense, to develop their knowledge about the natural world, understanding of generative processes, and an appreciation of the social and participatory nature of science (Lehrer & Schauble, 2006). This means, therefore, that it is also important for them to develop a sense of the processes whereby knowledge is shared, revised and elaborated. Therefore, there is another dimension of inquiry, namely, to approximate a genuine scientific community.

Inquiry learning is the pedagogic choice commonly traced back to Dewey's (2009/1910) pragmatism. Having had experience in teaching science himself, Dewey recommended that learners engage in active exploration of scientific phenomena, while tutors act as their guides (ibid.). Since inquiry-based learning and problem-based learning encourage the spirit of "discovery", they have been seen as belonging to the general species of non-guided "discovery learning" (Kirschner, Sweller, & Clark, 2006). However, inquiry and problem-based learning researchers view this as a misconception (Hmelo-Silver, Duncan, & Chinn, 2007). In fact, there are significant data and argumentation in inquiry and discovery learning research that favor inquiry learning to be *guided*. To reinforce that requirement, Kuhn (2009, p. 5) suggests that fluency in inquiry modes of learning requires "sustained engagement and support in order to attain the levels that are expected." In addition, Zimmerman (2007) and De Jong (2006) have both reviewed a range of specific difficulties experienced by learners that were related to inquiry learning and that clearly indicated that learners needed guidance. Even learners' collaboration can make inquiry harder: Lakkala, Lallimo, and Hakkarainen (2005) describe a case study where ten teachers found it hard to support inquiry knowledge building that was collaboratively managed, the findings also supported by Bell, Urhahne, Schanze, and Ploetzner (2010). Therefore,[2] there are obstacles to inquiry learning. One way forward is to *relate the discourse more to learners' lives outside the classroom*, as suggested by Songer, Lee, and McDonald (2003). It may also prove successful to allow inquiries to extend over longer periods of time (Lehrer, Schauble, & Lucas, 2008). Overall, it can be concluded that learners do need some sort of guidance while practicing inquiry learning. The type of guidance that is demanded in such educational tasks might correspond to "scaffolding" (Wood, Bruner, & Ross, 1976) and the term that expands it to consider the role of meaning-making as semiotic scaffolding (Hoffmeyer, 2015). This is a pattern of teacher engagement that recruits the learner's interest and externalize his/her meaning-making processes—through strategic intervention—allowing a teacher to manage a task. Hill and Hannafin (2001) point out how such a scaffolding relationship can support conceptual, metacognitive, procedural, and strategic aspects of some task. Explicating learning as semiotic scaffolding implies the iconic-turn standpoint introduced earlier in this chapter, as it reveals the former as "the piecing together of the semi-autonomous parts of a scaffolding," a process of diagrammatic reasoning which "has the character of meaning-bearing couplings as they support still more complicated versions of the basically significant perception–action cycle." (Cobley & Stjernfelt, 2015, p. 292). According to Gough and Stables (2012), this view of nature and culture opposes Enlightenment anthropocentrism, as the environment and all things and beings in it are considered seriously, demanding a semiotic approach to education.

The material–conceptual context/ environment at the moment of thinking, as well as the meanings shared by peers, contribute to the process of scaffolding. As such, signs must be considered open-ended entities, always in the process of evolving, with possibilities for alternatie meanings. This finds support in a range of theories of meaning, from Bakhtinian "dialogism" and Carroll's "anarchonovelization" (White, 2014) to Deleuzian "assemblag(ing)" as "a becoming that brings elements

---

[2] This paragraph incorporates the work on inquiry graphics and iconic thinking co-developed with Dr. Alin Olteanu.

together" (Wise, 2014, p. 91). "Scaffolding" can be labor intensive and it requires great sensitivity and attention from the tutors' side—when to intervene and when to pull back. On the other hand, it does not mean that the tutor's presence is always necessary. Preparatory exercises, worked examples, presentations and an activity script can act as "scaffold" for learners, providing them with space for more peer-to-peer collaborative inquiry without constant presence of a tutor, which is an ambition of the pedagogical study inquiry scenario in Part II.

Thus, a successful inquiry design and integration of scaffolding signs might usefully provide a cycle-script in order to guide and make transparent the process of inquiry. In such a case, the core structuring purpose of scaffolding is retained but in the form of a narrower species of support, one that has been termed "scripting" (O'Donnell & Dansereau, 1992; Dillenbourg & Jermann, 2007). A script for inquiry offers a pre-set sequence of steps and instruction that guides the learner(s) through some activity in an organized manner. Part II adopts the principle of two types of inquiry: a "scripted inquiry"(when students are provided with support resources and script for independent study and dialogue) and a "shared inquiry", when the inquiry is shared in some space (online or face to face), between peers and with the tutor. An investigation of data in the spirit of "inquiry learning" is seen as appropriate to all disciplines, no matter whether they are within the natural or social sciences, or the humanities. The pedagogical research design in this book adopts this guided inquiry outlook and views inquiry as related to the development of critical thinking and as a resource for the investigation of concepts in social sciences, not just the natural sciences. Arguably all disciplines need to encourage inquiring minds in learners. In particular, the empirical studies in this book explore the inquiry of concepts in educational studies and educational psychology and related visual representations (concept aspects materializations).

## Inquiry as Dialogic Meaning-Making

Many researchers of inquiry learning point to the importance of conversation and communication. Sharples, Taylor, & Vavoula (2007, p. 226) reinforce this point referring to Dewey:

To be a recipient of a communication is to have an enlarged and changed experience… It may fairly be said, therefore, that any social arrangement that remains vitally social, or vitally shared, is educative to those who participate in it. (Dewey, 1916)

In this basic act of communication, learners are invited to interpret the world and thereby have a dialogue both with others and with the world. Also, the discourse we produce in private is never a monologue, as Bakhtin (1981) argued for a dialogic and social nature of all texts, so every voice and thought is relational to some other (Todorov, 1984; White, 2014); it is always produced as a dialogue between the author and the artifact (e.g., a book, film, or website), the author and the existence of others, such as an expected audience (Friedman, 2005, p. 30). Hence, it is social in its core nature. Thus, the audience and purpose bear a significant place in the creation of any discourse and every such discourse can be viewed as a variation of dialogue. The point is that when educators set tasks for students to be carried out in private, this is not simply an isolated, individualistic and unsocial practice. On the contrary, there is always an expected audience for such a task; in the case of education, this is usually peers and tutors.

What this means in terms of educational design is that learning designs in higher education need to be conversational (Laurillard, 2002), where "conversational" implies something expressed and externalized (Sharples et al., 2007), turning the inner dialogue of the "audience" (with the seen/heard) into a visible thinking trace and expression. The more that learners have opportunities to express their opinions in various ways (perhaps using technology to support that expression), the more traces of learning are made. Leaving visible traces of thinking is one of the core opportunity of educational practice with (and without) technology. This view is supported by Sharples et al. (2007, p. 227):

Central to these learning conversations is the need to externalize understanding. To be able to engage in a productive conversation, all parties need access to a common external representation of the subject matter (an agreed terminology, and also notes, concept maps or other learning resources) that allows them to identify and discuss topics.

Reflection is arguably very important in an inquiry design. It provides an opportunity for the learner to slow down and stand back from their own thinking and perform the analytic and metacognitive activity of addressing the very nature of their inquiry process as well as the nature of the inquiry object.

In defining reflection, Mezirow (1990) cites Boud, Keogh, and Walker, using a number of reflective acts to describe reflection:

reflection is "a generic term for those intellectual and affective activities in which individuals engage to explore their experiences in order to lead to new understandings and appreciation." Importantly, this means that reflection would include making inferences, generalizations, analogies, discriminations, and evaluations, as well as feeling, remembering, and solving problems. It also seems to refer to using beliefs to make an interpretation, to analyze, perform, discuss, or judge—however unaware one may be of doing so. (Mezirow, 1990, p. 2)

Mezirow argues that in "communicative learning, meaning is validated through critical discourse" (ibid., p. 6). He defines communicative learning in the following way:

Communicative learning is less a matter of testing hypotheses than of searching, often intuitively, for themes and metaphors by which to fit the unfamiliar into a meaning perspective, so that an interpretation in context becomes possible. (Mezirow, 1990, p. 6)

Meaning-making communication and semiotics was discussed in Chap. 3 in relation to meaning-making, interpretation and image artifacts. Reflective learning (dialogue) is linked to emancipatory education. Through dialogue, participants create consciousness of the differences among themselves, so that they can practice tolerance and respect. In order to participate in an emancipatory education, learners need to develop a dialogue that helps them "challenge presuppositions, explore alternative perspectives, transform old ways of understanding, and act on new perspectives." (Mezirow, 1990, p. 6).

Furthermore, for successful communication between tutor and student, it is important that the tutor knows how his/her students make meaning. If we revisit the Pioneer Plaque from Chap. 1 (Fig. 1.1), Barlex and Carré (1985) also remarked that the picture message was created without knowing the audience, therefore without any knowledge of how they would make meaning. The reference to the Pioneer Plaque opened the discussion of conceptual–theoretical Part I in Chap. 1, and it is now nearly closing it in Chap. 6. To remind the reader, The Pioneer craft's mission was to search for other life forms in outer space. It carried a plaque with a pictorial message that was meant to "communicate" to any alien beings a depiction of humans and their "position" in the universe. However, in spite of their best try, the scientists could not have known what decoding and meaning-making mechanisms other life forms might have. In addition, the depictions were done in accordance to cultural particularities and beliefs which do not reflect the views of all humanity (that would be very hard indeed). The main point of evoking this example again (also noted by Sless, 1981, Chandler, 2002, and Kress & van Leeuwen, 1996) is that without knowing how message recipients make meaning and what meaning perspectives (beliefs) they have been "enculturated" into, "communicating with them might be problematic and futile" (Lackovic, 2010b, p. 126). Therefore, the tutor gains greater understanding of learners' reasoning and their paths to fuller concept understanding by uncovering their meaning-making processes, their interests and beliefs, rather than not asking for their interpretations. This is not to say that the messages disseminated from the tutors' side necessarily are fuzzy and ambiguous. This is to acknowledge differences in interpretations stemming from one single source (e.g., text, tutor's talk or images). Both students and tutors come to the classroom with different knowledge bases and meaning-making approaches (Lackovic, 2010b). They have different prior knowledge. The Pioneer example refers to the significance of providing students with opportunities to externalize and attend to their prior knowledge. The acts of externalizing opinions and interpretation set the scene for appreciation and exchange of opinions as well as their critical and analytical examination (peer to peer, or student–tutor).

# Integrating the Approaches in Part I: A Brief Summary

Chapter 1 provided examples and argument as to why images are important and should be considered as integral in higher education. This was done to emphasize how digital images, as parts of inquiry graphics, provide the necessary link between higher education and learners' experiences of daily life and its materiality and ideology, especially in the present world of constant technological advances and "virtual" materiality mediation via digital social media. It argues that communication via and with images needs to be considered seriously in higher education research and studies, as this is not yet the case, evidenced by the review of "top ten" journals in higher education studies. It set the scene for a relational approach to concepts in higher education, as image–concept relationality. Chapter 2 situated the IG activity in the contemporary landscape of neoliberal and digital university as a non-relational state of being and practices that prevailingly celebrate individual competitive advantage. Although it provided a critique, it also turned to position IG and related practices with images as possible creative, transformative and resistance practices, providing humble examples of remedial action that promote a larger concept of relational and caring university, aiming to foster cultural, organizational and practical changes. The examples were provided as triggers for action, which does not have to include images only but implies collaboration and support mediated by artifacts in order to connect university staff, and also reach out to the public. Chapter 3 introduced the semiotic and edusemiotic theoretical background of an IG sign. It provided definitions, examples and a few diagram versions of what a photographic sign and an IG sign is and how it works as a compound communication sign, emphasizing the value of interpretation science and philosophy underpinned by semiotics and edusemiotics. Chapter 4 turned to images as one of the two main modal ingredients of IG to consider visual signs in and for higher education learning, arguing how an IG sign and empirically explored IG activity designs relate to many approaches to image learning and competences, such as visual literacy, multiple representations, critical graphicacy, multimodality and photo elicitation. It established a relationality between these approaches and IGs. Then, in Chap. 5, IG were observed form the perspective of concept development, the concept being the other central relational mode of an IG, alongside the image. The chapter perspectives explored approaches to concepts, arguing for concept–image relationality, from definitional to multiple and alternative concept approach and understandings. This consideration was informed in good part by perspectives in educational psychology. In the last chapter of Part I, Chap. 6, the focus was placed on inquiry graphics as artifacts for mediating learning and knowledge inquiry mainly from the vantage point of sociocultural educational psychology and learning sciences, such as the perspectives of distributed cognition and extended mind, linking them to Peircean iconicity of thinking processes that IG artifacts can mediate as semiotic scaffolds. Part I set the scene to understand the **image-concept-inquiry** grounding of IG approaches (methodological and theoretical) and their character of relational and pluralist signs and practices; it provided a conceptual framework and theoretical–conceptual pillars for the empirical studies in Part II. It seeded a proposal for an (*edusemiotic*) *theory of learning with images or a relational theory of learning.* The explorations of IG for higher education reflection and learning designs to follow in the empirical part build on some key perspectives on IG discussed in Part I. The following Part II is strongly empirical and it explores how the coupling of an image and a concept is brought together and how it works in reflective thinking and learning, with what character and in what ways. It focuses on inquiring concepts via images in order to externalize students' thinking, support critical reflection and consciousness, and, hopefully and eventually, lead to transformative education.

# References

Arias-Hernandez, R., Green, T. M., & Fisher, B. (2012). From cognitive amplifiers to cognitive prostheses: Understandings of the material basis of cognition in visual analytics. *Interdisciplinary Science Reviews, 37*, 4–18.

Bakhtin, M. M. (1981). *The dialogic imagination: Four essays* (Michael Holquist, Ed. and Caryl Emerson & Michael Holquist, Trans.). Austin, TX: University of Texas Press. *84*(8), 80–82.

Barlex, D., & Carré, C. (1985). *Visual communication in science: Learning through sharing images.* Cambridge, UK: Cambridge University Press.

Bell, T., Urhahne, D., Schanze, S., & Ploetzner, R. (2010). Collaborative inquiry learning: Models, tools, and challenges. *International Journal of Science Education, 32,* 349–377.

Boehm, G., & Mitchell, W. J. T. (2009). Pictorial versus iconic turn: Two letters. *Culture, Theory and Critique, 50*(2–3), 103–121.

Bransford, J., Vye, N., Stevens, R., Kuhl, P., Schwartz, D., Bell, P., Meltzoff, A., Barron, B., Pea, R. D., & Reeves, B. (2005). Learning theories and education: Toward a decade of synergy. In P. Alexander & P. Winne (Eds.), *Handbook of educational psychology* (2nd ed.). Mahwah, NJ: Erlbaum.

Bransford, J. D., & Schwartz, D. L. (1999). Rethinking transfer: A simple proposal with multiple implications. *Review of Research in Education, 24,* 61–100.

Bruno, S., & Munoz, G. (2010). Education and interactivism: Levels of interaction influencing learning processes. *New Ideas in Psychology, 28,* 365–379.

Chandler, D. (2002). *The basics: Semiotics.* London: Routledge.

Clark, A., & Chalmers, D. (1998). The extended mind. *Analysis, 58,* 7–19.

Clark, C. D. (1999). The autodriven interview: A photographic viewfinder into children's experience. *Visual Studies, 14,* 39–50.

Cobley, P., & Stjernfelt, F. (2015). Scaffolding development and the human condition. *Biosemiotics, 8*(2), 219–304.

Crook, C. (2010). Versions of computer-supported collaborating in higher education. In *Learning across sites: New tools, infrastructures and practices* (pp. 156–171). London: Routledge.

De Jong, T. (2006). Technological advances in inquiry learning. *The Educational Forum,* 532–533.

Dewey, J. (2009/1910). *How we think.* Lightning Source UK Ltd.

Dewey, J., & Bentley, A. F. (1960). *Knowing and the known* (No. 111). Boston: Beacon Press.

Dillenbourg, P., & Jermann, P. (2007). Designing integrative scripts. In *Scripting computer-supported collaborative learning* (pp. 275–301). New York: Springer.

Elleström, L. (2014). Material and mental representation: Peirce adapted to the study of media and arts. *The American Journal of Semiotics, 30*(1/2), 83–138. https://doi.org/10.5840/ajs2014301/24.

Fenwick, T. (2010). Re-thinking the "thing" sociomaterial approaches to understanding and researching learning in work. *Journal of Workplace Learning, 22*(1/2), 104–116.

Friedman, M. (2005). Martin Buber and Mikhail Bakhtin. In *Dialogue as a means of collective communication* (pp. 29–39). Springer.

Gillespie, A., & Zittoun, T. (2010). Using resources: Conceptualizing the mediation and reflective use of tools and signs. *Culture & Psychology, 16*, 37–62.

Gough, S., & Stables, A. (2012). Interpretation as adaptation: Education for survival in uncertain times. *Curriculum Inquiry, 42*(3), 368–385.

Hammerness, K., Darling-Hammond, L., Bransford, J., Berliner, D., Cochran-Smith, M., McDonald, M., & Zeichner, K. (2005). How teachers learn and develop. Preparing teachers for a changing world: What teachers should learn and be able to do, 358–389.

Hill, J. R., & Hannafin, M. J. (2001). Teaching and learning in digital environments: The resurgence of resource-based learning. *Educational Technology Research and Development, 49*, 37–52.

Hmelo-Silver, C. E., Duncan, R. G., & Chinn, C. A. (2007). Scaffolding and achievement in problem-based and inquiry learning: A response to Kirschner, Sweller, and Clark (2006). *Educational Psychologist, 42*, 99–107.

Hoffmeyer, J. (2015). Introduction: Semiotic scaffolding. *Biosemiotics, 8*(2), 153–158.

Hollan, J., Hutchins, E., & Kirsh, D. (2000). Distributed cognition: Toward a new foundation for human-computer interaction research. *ACM Transactions on Computer-Human Interaction (TOCHI), 7*, 174–196.

Hutchins, E. (1995). How a cockpit remembers its speeds. *Cognitive Science, 19*, 265–288.

Kirschner, P. A., Sweller, J., & Clark, R. E. (2006). Why minimal guidance during instruction does not work: An analysis of the failure of constructivist, discovery, problem-based, experiential, and inquiry-based teaching. *Educational Psychologist, 41*, 75–86.

Kirsh, D. (1995). The intelligent use of space. *Artificial Intelligence, 72*, 1–52.

Kirsh, D. (2010). Thinking with external representations. *AI & SOCIETY, 25*, 441–454.

Kirsh, D. (2013). Thinking with external representations. In *Cognition beyond the brain* (pp. 171–194). Springer.

Kozulin, A. (2003). Psychological tools and mediated learning. In *Vygotsky's educational theory in cultural context* (pp. 15–38). Cambridge, UK: Cambridge University Press.

Kress, G. (2009). Assessment in the perspective of a social semiotic theory of multimodal teaching and learning. In *Educational assessment in the 21st century* (pp. 19–41). New York: Springer.

Kress, G., & van Leeuwen, T. (1996). *Reading images: The grammar of visual design*. Routledge.

Kuhn, D. (2009). Do students need to be taught how to reason? *Educational Research Review, 4*, 1–6.

Lackovic, N. (2010). Creating and reading images: Towards a communication framework for higher education learning. In *Seminar. Net: Media, technology & life-long learning* (pp. 121–135).

Lacković, N., & Olteanu, A. (forthcoming). Learning in times of visual technologies: A relational approach to educational theory and practice that integrates external and internal images. *Educational Philosophy and Theory*.

Lackovic, N., & Olteanu, A. (under review). New approach to educational theory and method in the postdigital world: Bridging the separation between the concept and the image. *Educational Theory and Philosophy*.

Lakkala, M., Lallimo, J., & Hakkarainen, K. (2005). Teachers' pedagogical designs for technology-supported collective inquiry: A national case study. *Computers & Education, 45*, 337–356.

Laurillard, D. (2002). *Rethinking university teaching: A conversational framework for the effective use of learning technologies*. Psychology Press.

Legg, C. (2017). 'Diagrammatic teaching': The role of iconic signs in meaningful pedagogy. In I. Semetsky (Ed.), *Edusemiotics–A handbook* (pp. 29–45). Singapore: Springer.

Lehrer, R., & Schauble, L. (2006). Cultivating model-based reasoning in science education. In *Cambridge handbook of the learning sciences* (pp. 371–388).

Lehrer, R., Schauble, L., & Lucas, D. (2008). Supporting development of the epistemology of inquiry. *Cognitive Development, 23*, 512–529.

Malafouris, L. (2013). *How things shape the mind*. Cambridge, MA: MIT Press.

McArthur, J. (2010). Time to look anew: Critical pedagogy and disciplines within higher education. *Studies in Higher Education, 35*, 301–315.

Mezirow, J. (1990). *Fostering critical reflection in adulthood*. San Francisco: Jossey-Bass.

Norman, D. A. (1993). *Things that make us smart: Defending human attributes in the age of the machine*. Boston: Addison-Wesley Longman.

O'Donnell, A. M., & Dansereau, D. F. (1992). Scripted cooperation in student dyads: A method for analyzing and enhancing academic learning and performance. In *Interaction in cooperative groups: The theoretical anatomy of group learning* (pp. 120–141).

Orlikowski, W. J. (2007). Sociomaterial practices: Exploring technology at work. *Organization Studies, 28*(9), 1435–1448.

Piaget, J., Brown, T., & Thampy, K. J. (1985). *The equilibration of cognitive structures: The central problem of intellectual development*. Chicago: University of Chicago Press.

Pietarinen, A.-V. (2006). *Signs of logic: Peircean themes on the philosophy of language, games, and communication*. Dordrecht, Netherlands: Springer.

Pietarinen, A. V., & Bellucci, F. (2016). The iconic moment. Towards a Peircean theory of diagrammatic imagination. In *Epistemology, knowledge and the impact of interaction* (pp. 463–481). Cham, Switzerland: Springer.

Scaife, M., & Rogers, Y. (2005). External cognition, innovative technologies and effective learning. In *Cognition, education and communication technology* (pp. 181–202).

Scardamalia, M., & Bereiter, C. (2006). Knowledge building: Theory, pedagogy, and technology. In *The Cambridge handbook of the learning sciences* (pp. 97–115).

Sfard, A. (1998). On two metaphors for learning and the dangers of choosing just one. *Educational Researcher, 27*, 4–13.

Sharples, M., Taylor, J., & Vavoula, G. (2007). A theory of learning for the mobile age. In R. Andrews & C. Haythornthwaite (Eds.), *The Sage handbook of E-learning research* (pp. 221–247). Los Angeles: Sage.

Sless, D. (1981). *Learning and visual communication.* Halsted Press.

Songer, N. B., Lee, H.-S., & McDonald, S. (2003). Research towards an expanded understanding of inquiry science beyond one idealized standard. *Science Education, 87*, 490–516.

Stables, A. (2010). Semiosis and the collapse of mind-body dualism: Implications for education. In Inna Semestky (Ed.), *Semiotics education experience* (pp. 21–36). Brill/Sense.

Sterelny, K. (2004). Externalism, epistemic artefacts and the extended mind. In *The externalist challenge* (pp. 239–254).

Stjernfelt, F. (2007). *Diagrammatology. An investigation on the borderlines of phenomenology, ontology and semiotics.* Dordrecht, Netherlands: Springer.

Todorov, T. (1984). *Mikhail Bakhtin: The dialogical principle* (Vol. 13). Manchester: Manchester University Press.

Wertsch, J. V. (1991). A sociocultural approach to socially shared cognition. In *Perspectives on socially shared cognition. American Psychological Association* (pp. 85–100).

White, E. J. (2014). Bakhtinian dialogic and Vygotskian dialectic: Compatabilities and contradictions in the classroom? *Educational Philosophy and Theory, 46*(3), 220–236.

Wise, J. M. (2014). Assemblage. In Charles J. Stivale (Ed.), *Gilles deleuze: Key concepts* (pp. 91–102). London and New york: Routledge.

Wood, D., Bruner, J. S., & Ross, G. (1976). The role of tutoring in problem solving. *Journal of Child Psychology and Psychiatry, 17*, 89–100.

Zimmerman, C. (2007). The development of scientific thinking skills in elementary and middle school. *Developmental Review, 27*, 172–122.

# Part II

## How and What

# 7

# What Is Thinking with Digital Images Like? Inquiry Graphics Potential

The empirical material reported and analyzed in this chapter provides insights into how adult learners think with images. The aim of the chapter is to provide fine-grain level details of learner's thinking patterns, processes and acts with inquiry graphics (IG) signs as learning mediators.

The chapter presents in detail an IG study, Project 1. This study engaged 12 doctoral students in education to represent aspects of an abstract concept of relevance to the research training that they are familiar with, via a pictorial representation. The project achieved this by closely scrutinizing a set of doctoral students' pursuit of this goal; they were all, with one exception, teachers, and hence well positioned to evaluate the pedagogic potential of an IG-based activity. "Pedagogical value" is here defined in terms of the potential of an external image to be integrated into concept-related reflection, criticality, and the development of multiple perspectives in reflective learning and learner's growth. These aspirations are fundamental in IG learning designs.

© The Author(s) 2020
N. Lacković, *Inquiry Graphics in Higher Education*,
https://doi.org/10.1007/978-3-030-39387-8_7

# Project 1 Study Aims

The aims of the study were:

*Aim 1: Investigating image-supported thinking processes: Externalizing thinking*

The study aimed to make visible the thinking processes shaped by the task of searching for an image to represent an abstract concept, using the Google Images search engine. It investigated how people linked abstract concepts to images and image representations spontaneously, whether, how, and to what extent that search and its consequences supported multiple concept ideas, reflection, and critical thinking about the concept.

*Aim 2: IG guidelines evaluation*

The study also sought participants' evaluation of the guidelines which the researcher (book author) and the module professor had designed to support students in developing more versatile approaches to concepts and relevant image choices. These guidelines provided illustrations of how one concept could be manifested in many different, but also non-exhaustive, pictorial formats.

*Aim 3: Inquiry graphics pedagogical potential and value*

Finally, the study sought participants' evaluation of the image-based task that they would perform in terms of its pedagogical potential and value. Participants are doctoral students with teaching experience, hence well-positioned to comment on this method from the point of pedagogical evaluation and teaching experience.

***Aim 1 Implementation: Investigating Image-Supported Thinking Processes*** Students were be asked to perform the activity of selecting an image to represent a concept. The study design (think-aloud interview) would make visible students' thinking processes in order to better understand how thinking about an abstract concept via images develops before, during, and after performing an image search with the help of the Google Images search engine. The method sought to make visible the following features of an image-based (or inquiry graphics) inquiry:

- participants' preliminary image associations (ideas) to the concept;
- subsequent search keyword strategies;
- approaches to integrating the concept and images: How the image search initiates concept reflection and how an image is articulated when talking about the concept.

*Aim 2 Implementation: Scenario Guidelines Evaluation:* Guidelines were specifically designed to address thinking about concepts with images. They address the diverse perspectives it might be possible to take on a concept and its pictorial representation, but they are, of course, not exhaustive. The guidelines are hoped to support future learning designs (and the following study) for the development of multiple concept perspectives and multiple angles for image interrogation. Asking students in this study to relate their search performance and image selection to the guidelines (and consequently evaluate the worth of guidelines for the image searching activity targeted at students) would provide insights regarding the pedagogical strengths and weaknesses of this support tool. More about the guidelines and their design rationale will follow.

*Aim 3 Implementation: Pedagogical Potential and Value* Students with teaching experience will be selected as participants and, as such, their opinion as educational professionals will help authenticate the design in terms of its perceived pedagogic potential. The opinion sought will concern how far they might endorse this method, and the logic of IG on the basis of their experience of interacting with it and performing the image search.

## Research Questions

The following list presents main research questions and sub-questions derived from the aims:

RQ 1: How do students imagine an abstract concept by invoking particular image instances?

> RQ 1.1: How do preliminary image associations relate to the abstract concept?

RQ 2: How are the concept and image articulated and related during the image search?

> RQ 2.1: How do participants use the image search engine?

(a) in terms of actual search words chosen;
(b) in terms of how their search word decisions relate to their concept and image thinking; and
(c) in terms of participants comments on the images they view or choose.

> RQ 2.2: How is the image content and interpretation articulated and related to the concept?

> RQ 2.3: To what extent do participants elaborate on the concept and develop critical and multiple perspectives on the concept during the search?

RQ 3: What pedagogical potential is there in this image search activity as identified by the participants?

> RQ 3.1: How do the participants evaluate the pedagogical potential of this activity upon their own completion of the whole task?

> RQ 3.2: How do the participants evaluate the IG scaffolding guidelines upon the completion of the reflective image task and image guidelines mapping exercise?

# "Thinking with Images" Study Method

The "Thinking with Images" mixed method for this study entails the conjunction of an adapted, gently scaffolded "thinking aloud" protocol—termed here "STA" (scaffolded thinking aloud)—along with a semi-structured interview. As used here, the thinking aloud method invited participants to report verbally on what they are thinking and doing while performing a cognitive task. There are instantiations of the method which accept the researcher's thoughtful interference as a legitimate part of the method. This method is termed "mixed," because the researcher had two different investigation foci: one concerned with the thinking processes active while the participants were performing the task (the thinking aloud method) and another focus concerned with participants' opinions and evaluation of the pedagogic task they have experienced (explored with the semi-structured interview).

## Scaffolded Thinking Aloud (STA) Method

To explain further the mixed method aspect of the study, mixed methods are common in social science research and they also gel nicely with my pragmatic and semiotic learning inquiry positioning: the researcher explores two or more methods in order to gather a richer corpus of data and to triangulate (Creswell & Clark, 2007). Hence, many researchers have turned to mixing methods within a single study; for example, combining various quantitative and qualitative methods, such as survey with ethnographic observation, or thinking aloud with interviews. By mixed methods I do not mean mixing of traditionally quantitative and qualitative but mixing two distinct methods.

The "Thinking with Images" therefore consists of:

1. scaffolded thinking aloud (STA) protocol with Google Images search engine, and
2. a semi-structured interview.

The STA method is designed to reveal the manner of *executing* thought, as an ongoing process, not the *reconstructing* thought when participants are requested to articulate their presumed thinking about some past task or experience (Nisbett & Wilson, 1977). The "thinking aloud" tradition has been widely applied to uncover, and thus understand, thinking processes during a task's completion. It is chosen here in order to unveil the thinking processes when an abstract idea is to be turned into a picture, as a pictorial idea and a concrete image chosen via Google Images search engine, and how concept ideas and images jointly influence thinking. The researcher is supposed to interfere as little as possible, providing occasional prompts when the participant stops talking for a prolonged period, such as: "What are you thinking/ doing now?" and "Could you say (comment) more?" I also had a scripted instruction/ questions prior to the thinking aloud activity that asked for participants' first image associations and reflections.

There is no uniform way of conducting a "thinking aloud" protocol. Van Someren et al. (1994) review a range of techniques. They are built around: observations, retrospection, introspection, questions and prompting, and dialogue observation. "Observation" means that the researcher's main role is to witness and document the process, "retrospection" is when participants are asked to think about an activity after its event, "introspection" is to ask reflective questions to the self, "questions and prompting" is when the researcher directly asks questions of interest, and "dialogue observation" is when the researcher observes a conversation between two (or more) participants. The "thinking aloud" method is most criticized when it is performed in retrospection (Nisbett & Wilson, 1977). That does not apply here; the present STA method allows participants to be introspective about what they are doing as they are doing it *while* their search is supported by researcher's questions and prompting. There are issues arising from the potential disturbance of cognitive processes (van Someren et al., 1994, p. 32) whenever the researcher intrudes with a comment or question within a "questions and prompting" technique. There can be a synchronization problem between the speed of thought and thought verbalization, in order to claim that the participant was indeed "thinking aloud" (Van Someren et al., 1994, p. 33). There may be problems with working memory (if there is a difficulty, a participant might overload working memory trying to verbalize the ongoing thoughts (ibid.)). This study admits these possible disturbance of thinking processes and suggest that any occurrence will be at an acceptable rather than obstructing level.

In the present study, I adopted a technique of occasional "questioning and prompting" while the user is performing "thinking aloud" during the task, giving encouragement to the effort as well. Questions and prompting in a thinking aloud method have their advantages and disadvantages (van Someren et al. 1994). An advantage is that the participant "does not have the chance to 'smooth over' the answer as she/he may in the case of retrospection, or to skip over it" (van Someren et al., 1994, p. 23). The main disadvantage is that the process of thinking can be interrupted, as mentioned before: it might be made difficult to continue the same thread. However, in the present case, as noted earlier, when interruptions to ask questions occur, they are desired or needed as there has been a long pause. In short, the aim of the STA method is to *investigate thinking processes and actions articulated by the participants when they engage with the "Thinking with Images" task.*

In sum, participants in this study were searching for images on Google images to represent the researcher-assigned concept. They were "thinking aloud" during that activity in order to explain what they were doing but also to reflect spontaneously on the actions and images but also to provide reflection when asked by the author. If the participant developed many concept ideas, or had more than one image idea or otherwise had a lot to say, the researcher's intervention would be minimal. Otherwise, the researcher interjected with encouragements, questions and explanations. Scaffolding of this kind would be taking place in a tentative learning scenario, but in a more extended format: that is, managed and distributed by the tutors and by peers over a period of time. The direction of thinking shaped by social questioning and prompting here will help in understanding what kind of instructions the researcher might need to provide (or avoid) for students in the subsequent pedagogic implementation.

## A Semi-Structured Interview Method

A second constituent of this "Thinking with Images" method is a semi-structured interview. It was deployed to investigate participant attitudes toward the proposed image-based concept inquiry guidelines and to the pedagogic value of the scenarios. According to Bryman (2008), two main types of interviews can be distinguished in qualitative research: unstructured and semi-structured (a structured interview has a fixed set of questions and unstructured allows for more freedom and open ended and flexible researcher-interviewee interactions). A researcher can creatively expand this core definition of semi-structured interview and add various artifacts that can lead interviewees' reflection, such as photographs (turning it into photo-elicitation and photovoice interviews), drawings or any artifact, it could be a video, or interviews can be conducted while walking (a walkabout interview) and so on. In this case, the interview was partly organized around an artifact—the guidelines on pictorial diversity when representing concept aspects. An unstructured interview develops around the themes and topics that the interviewees find important or feel compelled to talk about. Since this Project 1 study focuses on attitudinal (perspective) judgements in order to answer particular research questions, alongside the "thinking aloud" concerned with thinking processes, a semi-structured interview was chosen an appropriate participant-accounting method. It included a set of predefined questions that I would ask participants, but I had freedom to provide clarifications, re-shape the predefined questions, and ask new and sub-questions following up on participants' responses. The main concerns of the semi-structured interview phase were to understand participants' opinions on the pedagogical value of the "Thinking with Images" activity and its potential for concept learning. More specifically, the interview sought to uncover participants' response to the guidelines that were created to support students' versatile thinking.

## Research Ethics

Participants were provided with a "project information sheet" in order to understand the nature of the project and to respect both the approved ethical research procedure and compliance with BERA's "Revised Ethical guidelines for Educational Research" (BERA, 2004). Participants were informed as to the reasons and nature of the project and the extent of engagement that was expected from them. The information provided explained that the participants would be performing a task related to a broadly defined research area. The task as it was designed did not compromise participants in any way (e.g. asking to disclose sensitive information or provide any personal details to be analyzed or reveal their names (I used pseudonyms when addressing them) and they were free to withdraw at any stage of the process. Participants' names provided in the following sections are fictional. Participants' research topic and place of birth are not disclosed, since that was considered to be too close to revealing their identities: saying "UK" or "international" was chosen to be informative, yet protective.

## Participants

The participants comprised an opportunity sample of PhD students in Education at the University of Nottingham. PhD students were chosen as participants because I, the researcher, shared with them the experience of a "Research Methods" course which had explored abstract disciplinary concepts. Thus it was possible to choose one such concept from this course with a personal awareness of those concepts which were regarded as difficult or easy by the students. I sent an invitation e-mail to PhD students: that is, all those whom I knew had been engaged in teaching. Fifteen invitations were sent and 12 students consented to participate in the project and be interviewed, nine males and three females. Table 7.1 summarizes participants' gender, age and their status as a home or

**Table 7.1** "Thinking with Images" study participants

| Participant (P) Male–Female | PhD participant pseudonym | Age group | UK/International |
|---|---|---|---|
| P1, M | David | 20–30 | UK |
| P2, M | Brian | 20–30 | UK |
| P3, M | Patrick | 30–40 | International |
| P4, F | Jessica | 30–40 | UK |
| P5, M | Shaun | 20–30 | UK |
| P6, M | Mathew | 30–40 | UK |
| P7, M | James | 20–30 | UK |
| P8, F | Elisabeth | 20–30 | UK |
| P9, M | Christian | 30–40 | International |
| P10, M | Oscar | 30–40 | International |
| P11, F | Natalie | 20–30 | UK |
| P12, M | Andrew | 40–50 | UK |

international student. All participants were involved in educational research. They also had diverse disciplinary training, such as: mathematics, media and communicating, psychology, primary school teaching, languages/linguistics, English as foreign language (EFL), English and literature, computer sciences and programming, and physics, which adds to the strength of their pedagogic evaluation.

## Chosen Concept for Thinking with Images: "Empiricism"

I assigned a concept to participants for them to perform the task, asking: "Please search for an image to represent an aspect of the concept." The concept assigned needed to be abstract, semantically challenging, potentially controversial, yet familiar to the students (in this case, as a part of their PhD generic "Research Methods" course). These conditions were sought because the IG pedagogic method planned for the subsequent studies presupposes that a tutor would assign such concepts to their students so that they would share their opinion about the concepts by representing them via images, and unpacking both image and concept meanings (how they are connected). Furthermore, the participants would have the greatest interest in a concept if it was chosen from the research methods course that the PhD participants experienced in the very recent past, and that I knew was a concept that rendered some discussions and

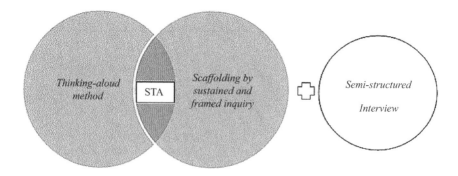

**Fig. 7.1** "Thinking with Images" Project 1 study mixed method. (STA (scaffolded thinking aloud) and semi-structured interview)

debates. I therefore chose the concept "Empiricism". The task of looking for an image to represent an instance of such a broad abstract concept as "Empiricism" was sufficiently difficult not to be solvable in an automated manner, yet it was current enough to be a recent and familiar concept to the PhD student participants.

## The Guidelines for Image Search and Selection

In collaboration with the module professor, a set of guidelines was designed for considering diverse perspectives for pictorial representation of disciplinary concepts. The guidelines identified a variety of ways in which a concept might be articulated. Those ways drew upon the theoretical approaches to learning and concepts discussed previously in the book: namely, that teachers need to provide varied concept examples to support students' understanding and find ways to support diversity and multiple perspectives on concepts, including the challenging of concept boundaries. The core rationale for the guidelines was that *concept understanding is enhanced if formulaic and definition-based ideas can be "enriched" with a range of related examples as well as "alternative" and "challenging" ones* to support multiple perspectives and creative thinking via images.

In designing the guidelines, those perspectives were considered, together with the basic principles of Pierce's Embodied Representamen–Interpretant-Object, that is, what is depicted in a picture, and its basic level content and meaning that can constitute an image–disciplinary concept example, a pairing that is a multimodal structural metaphor. Therefore, the guidelines were designed with the aim of supporting future students to think more widely about concepts, to do this by developing more versatile ideas, image choices, and angles of image-concept interrogation.

Central to guidelines design is that they would function as a worked example for the subsequent pedagogical intervention study. The module professor was asked to suggest candidate concepts which could be assigned to students in a follow up study, relevant to the already planned curriculum. One abstract concept—"Constructivism"—was chosen to be explored as an exercise to understand how the guidelines might work. These illustrations were designed to see how they "work." The module professor and the researcher had a series of meetings supported by e-mail correspondence in which they discussed and identified a variety of approaches in relation to the concept "Constructivism" and relevant image possibilities. They first considered solutions individually in accordance with approaches to a concept as relational and multiple concept perspectives, trying to think about how this concept can be manifested or pictured in the world in various ways. The aim was to consider different perspectives on what the concept meant, how it would generate a set of possibilities for its exploration, and how those perspectives might be represented via diverse pictorial content.

Charts, graphs, symbols, story boards, flow and spider diagrams as species of graphics (Danos & Norman, 2011) were excluded for being either non-depictive (containing numbers and/or words) or adding unnecessary complexity to the core idea of choosing depictive images, mainly digital photographs, although drawings were considered—those which depict scenes, events. PhD student participants would be initially prompted to choose a depictive image, which meant it could be an illustration. Therefore, the researcher and the tutor provided concept and image examples via the guidelines planned to act as possible "working examples" on concept and image versatility for students. The solutions ranged from the conventional or formulaic (here termed "iconic" to mean iconic meaning not iconic sign, hence stereotypical—a different meaning from Peirce's icon as sign type) toward those that embodied more diverse and challenging perspectives, addressing different contexts and perspectives for the concept. The guidelines first show a concept-image approach (e.g. ICONIC, CONTRAST, METAPHOR) followed by a question or questions that the students might ask themselves (concept question/s), which is then followed by an image content example of how this ideational aspect of the concept could be linked to an image.

## Guidelines for Concept Thinking and Image Representation Diversity

(1) **ICONIC** (here iconic is used as adjective to describe symbolically salient, recognizable, stereotypical meaning)

- Concept question: How can we express what is the stereotypical, conventional definitional, formulaic meaning of the concept?
- Image content: A depiction that can embody a classic instance of the concept understanding, tightly connected to the concept definition. It is presumed that most people's first associations would be some stereotypical representation of how that concept would "manifest" in an image.

(2) **CONTRAST**

- Concept question: What is the opposite of the concept/ its meaning? What are the concepts that are in some way oppositional to the concept under consideration? How do they help us understand the concept considered?
- Image content: A depiction that brings out and embody in some way that oppositional concept; it challenges the core and stereotypical meaning by showing the opposite to it.

(3) **METAPHOR**

- Concept question: Can we think of a metaphor for an aspect of the concept; can we think of a concept aspect in symbolical and metaphorical way?
- Image content: A depiction that shows a metaphorical/ non-literal/ symbolic representation of the concept as things, events or entities that can symbolize an aspect of the concept or the concept itself, such an image of books for representing knowledge.

## (4) CHALLENGING (UNCONVENTIONAL)

- Concept question: How can we define and subsequently challenge the concept boundaries? What are alternative versions, explanations or instances of the concept?
- Image content: A depiction that shows less obvious and unusual realization and embodiment of the concept; although it is not that obvious, it can be argued that it is linked to the concept. It will be an alternative unconventional episode or event where the concept might be happening.

## (5) OUTCOME

- Concept question: What follows from the application of the concept?
- Image content: A depiction that shows what might happen as a goal, result or outcome exercising or applying the concept, e.g. an action, reaction, context, artifact.

## (6) CAUSE/ PREREQUISITE

- Concept question: What conditions are the prerequisites for the concept to develop or occur or be experienced and/or understood?
- Image content: A depiction that shows the conditions or prerequisite context or actions or artifacts that lead to the concept realization, occurrence, surfacing.

## (7) EVERYDAY ACTIVITY or PERSONAL EXPERIENCE

- Concept question: Can the concept be identified in some everyday or very familiar routine, event, place, activity, state or artifact? Perhaps some activity very familiar to the learner.
- Image content: A depiction that would show a familiar context, a snapshot, thing or situation from personal experience or episodes; something very familiar personally to connect this experience to the concept.

## (8) OBJECT or FOCUS

- Concept question: Is there one aspect or object or focus related to the concept that can be extracted for consideration?

- Image content: A depiction that shows one object or ingredient or something that can be a focal point for scrutiny, for example one tool or equipment. The focus can also be placed on people (what we know and do not know about them—either as present in an image or as image creators, manipulators and consumers. The focus can be on animals, nature, etc.

(9) **CONTEXT or PLACE**

- Concept question: How is the concept influence by different by different contexts and places, how does it change depending on changing context or place?
- Image content: An image that reminds or suggests possible settings where concepts may occur: social, natural, work, leisure and other environments and settings, events

(10) **TIME**

- Concept question: How has the concept changed over time?
- Image content: A depiction that shows something about the historical development of the concept, an approach or scene from the past that relate to it, now and imagining the future.

(11) **CULTURE and IDENTITY**

- Concept question: How is the concept manifested in different cultural settings and influenced by cultural particularities?
- Image content: A depiction that shows that a concept might exist differently in different cultural or national contexts, in a different profession, community country, identity profile and so on. A depiction might also be linked to difficulty/ struggles to realize the concept.

Tables 7.2 and 7.3 image source information, credit and resources:

- ICONIC: Flickr. https://www.flickr.com/photos/vfwnational-home/7790696536 Attribution 2.0 Generic (CC BY 2.0): the image provided on Flicker by Flickr user VFW National Home for Children, labelled as New Science Lab 031.

**Table 7.2** A table with images to exemplify the guidelines for the concept "constructivism"—1

| Examples for the concept "constructivism," following the guidelines—1: |
| --- |

ICONIC: A depiction for "constructivism" showing children independently engaging with materials in a lab, the so-called "hands-on" experience. The teacher is not visible, presumed to be present, supervising/observing.

CONTRAST: A depiction showing a supposed opposite idea to learners" "hands-on" active learning experience: a teacher (traditionally represented) "transmitting" information via blackboard; the "sage on the stage" teaching to the presumed learners' audience.

METAPHOR: A depiction showing a building construction and a team of workers working together that can metaphorically represent strategic action such as "scaffolding" in constructivism. It provides triggers to consider relevant but also misleading aspects of such an explicit scaffolding metaphor.

CHALLENGING: A depiction showing a nineteenth-century cadaver dissection lesson. The learners are not apparently participating in the principled action; are they vicariously doing so via the principled actor and via observation? Could this be a constructivist experience? How?

OUTCOME: A depiction of an assembled DNA model from component parts. Different colors of the model could provide aspects of DNA characteristics. The students who created it might have constructed (developed) deeper knowledge of genetics by engaging in its construction.

Note: One image can and usually does fall under *more than one category*. The categories are offered to trigger diverse ideas about the concept and the depictions of concept aspects. They serve to help the versatility in approaching concepts and images. They are not exclusive or exhaustive

**Table 7.3** A table with images to exemplify the guidelines for the concept "constructivism"—2

| Examples for the concept "constructivism," following the guidelines—2 | |
| --- | --- |
|  | CAUSE/ PREREQUISITE: A depiction of a school laboratory. For a constructivist learning to occur, the resources, space and equipment that support this engagement need to be in place/ secured. The equipment mediates constructivist activities, acts as its prerequisite. |
|  | PERSONAL EXPERIENCE: A depiction of a gardening activity. If learners themselves and/ or someone they know engage in gardening, this involves specialized knowledge and routines, that develop by learning, action and reflection, for example mediated/scaffolded by YouTube videos. |
|  | FOCUS: A depiction of a Logo programming output. Logo is a computer programming activity deeply influenced by constructionist educational philosophy; how does it support constructivist learning experience? |
|  | CONTEXT: A depiction of a classroom context and teacher–student interactions. A typical context where the students are engaging with artifacts, actively participating, with the guiding presence of the teacher not visible, but presumed. |
|  | TIME: A depiction of a human–screen interaction in the 1980s. Learning has over time migrated to the screen and digital interaction, with the rise of computer-mediated education. This poses questions of the extent to which screen time is constructivist, how it can be, how it has changed, and what the role of technology advancement is in constructivist learning. |
|  | CULTURE: A depiction of a different cultural learning setting of learners in a natural setting. How is the setting constructivist or not, how it can be, and what role do resources play? What does this mean in terms of resources distribution and equality globally, e.g. global schools and their lab equipment? |

- CONTRAST: Pixabay; https://www.pexels.com/photo/man-in-black-and-white-polo-shirt-beside-writing-board-159844/, free to use.
- METAPHOR: Unsplash. https://unsplash.com/photos/qvBYn-MuNJ9A Image by Josue Isai Ramos Figueroa on Unsplash @jramos10
- CHALLENGING: Anonymous Engraving of an anatomy taking place at the Leiden Anatomy Theatre (1609) after a drawing by J. C. vant Woudt (Woudanus)); https://extra.shu.ac.uk/emls/si-13/billing/index.htm; source: Billing, C. (2004) "Modelling the anatomy theatre and the indoor hall theatre: Dissection on the stages of early modern London" Early Modern Literary Studies Special Issue 13 (3).1–17 <URL: http://purl.oclc.org/emls/si-13/billing
- OUTCOME: Wikimedia Commons; DNA Lego Model; Author: Michael Wade, from Berkley, CA, USA; Creative Commons Attribution 2.0 Generic license; https://commons.wikimedia.org/wiki/File:DNA_Lego_Model.jpg
- CAUSE/ PRE-REQUISITE: Pixabay. Pixabay License; Free for commercial use; No attribution required: https://pixabay.com/photos/lab-classroom-school-study-class-1075972/
- PERSONAL EXPERIENCE: Pixabay. https://pixabay.com/photos/hard-working-gardener-gardening-4083485/; Free for commercial use, no attribution required
- FOCUS: Attribution-ShareAlike 3.0 Unported (CC BY-SA 3.0); Example Output of Logo (turtle graphic). Logo source code to create this graphic: to n_eck:ne:sz repeat:ne [rt 360 / :ne fd:sz] end to mn_eck:ne:sz repeat:ne [rt 360 / :ne n_eck:ne:sz] end Start Program with: mn_eck 36 20; remi—graphic created by remi, logo source code created by Arbol01; https://en.wikipedia.org/wiki/Logo_(programming_language)#/media/File:Remi_turtlegrafik.png
- CONTEXT: Pxfuel. Url: https://www.pxfuel.com/en/free-photo-jxdnq. Creative Commons licence.
- TIME: Wikimedia Commons: https://commons.wikimedia.org/wiki/File:Cpc464.computer.750pix.jpg; Amstrad CPC464 computer. Data and programs were input with the built-in tape reader on the right of the keyboard.<br> Photographed by Adrian Pingstone in 1988 and released to the public domain. {{PD-user Arpingstone}}; Public domain

- CULTURE: Piqsels. License to use Creative Commons Zero—CC0; hoto license: CC0 public domain; Url: https://www.piqsels.com/en/public-domain-photo-jjohl

## "Thinking with Images": Procedure Steps 1–4

This section describes the overall procedure as defined for participants.

The procedure deployed the STA method first (to study image-based thinking processes) and then the semi-structured interview procedure (to study the evaluation of guidelines and pedagogic potential). The total scenario was organized loosely into five parts, in accordance with the defined research questions and aims (although this five-part structure was not made explicit to participants). The first three parts fall within the STA method and the second two ("the activity's pedagogical potential," and "guidelines evaluation") fall within a semi-structured interview method:

1. *Activity introduction*

The participants were invited to sit in front of a computer and to open Google Images search site in a web browser. The researcher had a scripted talk for the activity.

Scripted talk: "I am going to ask you to think about and search for an image which would, in your opinion, represent an aspect of the concept I shall reveal in a moment. So, you will search for and choose an image for an educational purpose of encouraging an animated discussion, either to discuss it with your peers or to prompt your students' discussion. Could you also try to talk me through what you are doing?"

This was a consistent presentation repeated in every interview. When needed, the author would provide variation of the above scripted task if the participant had any questions in order to clarify the task further, but the core instruction remained.

## 2. *Eliciting participants' first association*

Scripted talk: "The concept is "empiricism." I know you studied the concept within your Research Methods course."

Question: "What is your first image association when you think about the concept of empiricism?"

Sub-Q: "Are any other pictures coming to your mind?"

After the participants thought about their first image associations, they were provided with a definition reminder.

Scripted talk: "Here is a short paragraph taken from Wikipedia as a digital reference to remind you of what the internet offers as concept definition:" (reading the definition was optional, a participant was offered the chance to read a Wikipedia definition):

> Empiricism is a theory of knowledge which states that knowledge comes only or primarily from sensory experience. One of several views of epistemology, the study of human knowledge, along with rationalism, idealism, and historicism, empiricism emphasizes the role of experience and evidence, especially sensory experience, in the formation of ideas, over the notion of innate ideas or traditions; empiricists may argue however that traditions (or customs) arise due to relations of previous sense experiences.
>
> Empiricism in the philosophy of science emphasizes evidence, especially as discovered in experiments. It is a fundamental part of the scientific method that all hypotheses and theories must be tested against observations of the natural world rather than resting solely on a priori reasoning, intuition, or revelation.

Sub-Q: "Are any other pictures coming to your mind now? Feel free to interpret or challenge this definition in any way you may want to do so."

The reason for choosing the above Wikipedia definition merely lies in Wikipedia's popularity and on an assumption that many students might turn to Wikipedia to find answers.

## 3. *The search: Image–concept interrelation*

"Thinking aloud inquiry" Question: Can you now use the Google Images search engine and find an image or images to represent an aspect of the concept? You are welcome to provide more than one image by considering more aspects and issues you can connect to the concept or the image(s) you have selected. The point is indeed to think with images, not just one image.

Instruction variation: The author asked participants to find one image only in the first two "Thinking with Images" encounters which piloted the method (with participants David and Brian). Nevertheless, the first two events are included in the present analyses but to a limited scope. Starting with the third "Thinking with Images" encounter (Patrick), the researcher encouraged participants to come up with more images in order to explore possible development of novel and versatile perspectives.

During the search, participants would also be prompted to think of "an image which would challenge the typical view on the concept" and "an image that would contribute to a useful debate."

Possible prompts: "What are you doing?" "Which search words are you using?" "Any other ideas?"

The "scaffolding" is mainly *directional*—keeping thinking on the relevant path—and keeping up the *motivation* of reflection.

4. *Semi-structured interview schedule*:

At this point in the encounter, the mode of conversation shifted toward a more traditional interview. The purpose of this was to explore students' perspectives on two aspects of the process they had just experienced: the pedagogic potential of image–concept mapping and the clarity of the guidelines that might direct future students in such a task. The guidelines were only shown to the participants after they completed the task. The lead questions for each of these are given below.

A. Pedagogical value

"Can you comment on pedagogical potential of this activity?"
Additional:
"Would you apply it with your students?"
"Have you done something like this before, as a student/as a teacher, can you describe it?"

B. Guidelines evaluation

"Could you look at the guidelines I designed to support more versatile approaches to concepts and image choices? Could you map your images against the guidelines?"

After the participants thought about their image choices relating to the guidelines, they were asked:

"Do they make sense?" "Are they clear enough?" "What do you think about the guidelines?" "Are they useful or not?"

Scripted talk about the guidelines and categories:

"One category is not exclusive; images usually can be placed within a few categories—the guidelines offer ideas and multiple perspectives rather clear-cut boundaries. There is no finite set of approaches."

## Data Analysis: A Thematic Visualization Analysis

This section describes the qualitative analysis applied. It builds on the method of "thematic analysis" described by Braun and Clarke (2006). I call it "thematic visualization analysis" as the creation of maps and diagrams adopts a specific data visualization approach that structures thematic units. Thematic analysis is a method for identifying, analyzing and reporting patterns (broadly, "themes") within data (Braun & Clarke, 2006, p. 6). An important responsibility in such analysis is to provide the reader with a clear account of what the researcher did, and why (a thick description of analytical moves). This means making fully visible the methodological procedure (as above) and the way that the analysis was conducted (Attride-Stirling, 2001). Qualitative thematic analysis is often criticized for making the themes seemingly "emerge" from data, as if they simply resided there (Taylor & Ussher, 2001). Hence, it is always important to explain clearly how the analysis was performed, how the themes were derived, and the reasons behind those steps—so that readers can feel confident that they could do very similar analytic moves themselves. Participant thinking is conceptualized in terms of "acts of inquiry." This visible talking and acting is coded and located in relation to proposed "thematic clusters."

## Familiarization and Transcription

The 12 "Thinking with Images" encounters were audio-recorded and then transcribed. Transcription was verbatim. That is, the researcher transcribed all verbal utterances and thereby developed a close familiarity with the data. These 12 transcripts will be termed the "data set." Each individual case transcription will be termed a "data item." The term "instance" is employed interchangeably with "image." The data were read and re-read before moving to the Braun and Clarke's (2006) "Initial Coding Stage" which is here termed the "Topicalization Stage."

## Topicalization

Sections of conversation in each data item were differentially highlighted (in different colors). These divisions reflected the schedule of questioning in the STA conversations. They furnished a pattern based on intended task structure, as specified in the five parts of the STA and semi-structured interview methods comprising the "Thinking with Images" task.

The resulting topics sections reflect the activities carried out by participants in accordance with the task's scenario, as: *Grounding* (where the participant is providing first image associations, reading a paragraph on the concept and briefly reflecting on its nature), *Instance selection* (where the participant is searching for images), *Instance reflection* (where the participant is thinking about the concept in terms of the instance(s) selected), *Searching reflection* (where the participant is articulating processes of image search and selection—either executed or contemplated search and selection), *Guidance mapping* (where the participants react to the guidelines, particularly in relation to their own chosen image instances and by evaluating the usefulness of the guidelines) and *Pedagogic evaluation* (where participants reflect on the potential of this method for pedagogic practice.

The content of each transcribed data item was thereby allocated to one of six relevant topics identified above. These topics do not map cleanly onto those periods of the conversation that were structured by the researcher's involvement (that is, the STA exchange and the guidelines and pedagogic potential exchange). That is because participants would occasionally anticipate the concerns of later sections (or echo the concerns of earlier ones) within periods of the exchange that were not planned to be about them. For example, a participant might spontaneously comment on the pedagogic potential of the activity while engaged in searching during the STA period of the task. That is why the researcher identified and bolded key instances that "belonged" to each of the defined six sections and placed them under the relevant section.

## Defining and Naming Thematic Clusters and Codes

The highlighted sections in the Topicalization phase were further scrutinized for the formation of tables with final themes and critical examples. A "theme" was identified as: "something important about the data in relation to the research question" (Braun & Clarke, 2006, p. 8) the nature of that "importance" is shaped by research questions. It must be noted however that research questions here do not seek themes in particular but rather occurrence of instances that answer the research questions.

"Critical examples" were key transcription extracts from data items relating to the themes named in this phase and relevant research questions. These will be tabulated and thereby serve as the bases for participants' "thinking pathway maps," which will be explained later in this section. In this phase research questions were used as the leading force in defining the items within thematic clusters. The researcher engaged and re-engaged with data items and further clarified these analytical themes to derive the coding and structure described next.

The thematic coded material was segmented into four thematic clusters named to mark different thinking processes in relation to the research questions concerning image-supported concept thinking:

• Imagine-ation, (RQ 1.1.)
• Searching images (RQ 2.1.)
• Concept articulation (RQ 2.2 and 2.3)
• Retrospective reflection (RQ 2.4)

These are reviewed below first as positioned in relation to the associated research questions they bear upon and then by explaining the meaning of each thematic cluster:

*I: "Imagine-ation" Code (RQ 1.1)*

This analytical code notes occurrence of preliminary first thoughts about how to represent the concept via an image prior to search. They are later grouped in accordance with what they refer to (e.g. object, person).

*RQ 1.1*: How do preliminary image associations relate to the abstract concept?

*IA: Instance (Image) Association(S) Code*

This refers to the instance (image) association, or group of associations, that a participant generated. Their preliminary, very first image associations are labelled as "IA1." All the following instance associations, occurring prior to or during the actual search, are numbered as "IA2," "IA3" and so on.

*S: "Searching Images" Codes Cluster (RQ 2.1)*

*RQ.2.1*: How do participants use the image search engine?

This second cluster relates to the process of active image search and how it is managed. Items in this cluster address how the search engine is used:

a) in terms of actual search words;
b) in terms of how their search word decisions relate to their concept and image thinking;
c) in terms of participants comments on the images they view or choose.

The following analytical categories were identified illustrating these three search process foci:

### *SW: Search Words*

The exact search words entered into the search engine in order to find images. In organizing the data and in subsequent tables here, these were put in bold—arranging them in the order that they arose. Search words' instances were numbered, for example: SW1, SW 2, and so on.

### *SE: Searching Explanations*

Participants' comments which illustrate reasoning around the search process itself, in particular, comments around insertion of particular search words or responses to "Why those words?"

### *SI: Search Image*

Participants' comments on images during the search process itself, commonly a description of an image or images.

### *C: "Concept Content Articulation" Codes Cluster*

This cluster concerns concept ideas, elaborations and refinements that were inspired by the outcome of searching and thinking. Thus, it reveals how images prompt participants' reflection. The codes are scrutinized against the following research questions:

*RQ 2.2*: How is the image content and interpretation articulated and related to the concept during the search?
*RQ 2.3*: To what extent do participants comment on the concept and elaborate on it (develop critical and multiple perspectives on the concept) during the search?

After careful engagement with the transcripts, the following theme categories were derived:

### *CI: Concept Idea*

Any idea(s) on the concept articulated, this is an idea introduction or mentioning and not an elaborated or reflective account of the idea.

What constitutes a *concept idea*: it is taken to be any idea which represents an angle for looking at the concept, albeit as part of some dominant theme the participant might choose to pursue.

### CIE: Concept Idea Elaboration
The participant reflects on an idea or tension relating to the concept during the search, going beyond just providing an idea but comments on what it means in relation to the concept, commonly unpacking an issue or tension in relation to the concept, often in a critical manner.

To answer RQ 2.2, the researcher looked at each coded map, in particular how the code SI (search image) and IA (image association) are related, or not related, to any comment on the concept that preceded or followed up image content articulation. How the content image was voiced within the CI and CIE thematic code was also considered.

*RR: Retrospective Reflection Code*

*RQ 2.4*: To what extent do participants elaborate on the concept and develop critical and multiple perspectives on the concept, after they decide to terminate their search for images and when asked to reflect on the images?

This is not a cluster since it tackles one concern: comments made regarding the concept or the concept in relation to images that were made while looking back over the conduct of the task. That is, after the searching is complete and is under review.

### CRR—Concept retrospective reflection:
Critical reflection on the concept that is articulated after the search, when the participant has stopped searching for images and starts reflecting on how the images found are useful for exploring concept meaning and particular aspects of it in relation to the chosen images.

In keeping with the principles of good qualitative analysis, the intention here has been to make the "raw" data as visible as possible, so that the

**Table 7.4** Coding table for research question theme clusters

| Thematic code cluster | Code abbr. | Meaning (summary) |
|---|---|---|
| Imagine-ation | IA | Instance association: image ideas prior to research; numbered in order of occurrence (IA1, IA2 etc.) |
| Searching images | SW | Search words: exact search words entered in Google Images search engine |
| | SE | Search explanations: explaining searching for an image, generally commenting on the search process |
| | SI | Search image: comments on images during the search process itself, commonly a descriptive account of an image |
| Concept articulation (mediated by image search) | CI | Concept idea: any idea(s) on the concept articulated |
| | CIE | Concept idea elaboration: more reflective talk on some concept idea, going beyond providing an idea by unpacking an issue or tension in relation to the concept, in reflective and often critical manner |
| Retrospective reflection | CRR | Concept retrospective reflection: articulated after the search, a reflection on how the images found and the whole process mediated the exploration of concept meaning |

reader may confirm the researcher's interpretations as they become built upon it. Because it is important to capture across-participant variability, findings will be presented for each data item (participant). For each such "case" a table was constructed that presented key illustrative material in terms of, where possible, the actual words employed by participants in relation to theme categories (Table 7.4).

The coding above was used to generate maps of participants' thinking pathways. Retrospective reflection is not presented in the map as the map refers to the search in progress rather than this concept reflection which happens *after* the search.

The following coding clusters are taken from the semi-structured interview part, when participants provide their opinions on the activity and IBCI guidelines in order to answer RQ3.

"Application" cluster (how the solutions are seen as relevant to supporting pedagogic discussion)

*RQ3.1*: How do participants evaluate the pedagogical potential of the activity upon completion of the whole task?

*RQ3.2*: How do participants evaluate the IBCI scaffolding guidelines upon the completion of the reflective image task and image-guidelines mapping exercise?

For this thematic section, the transcripts were scrutinized for the selection of material that illustrated an ability to see the generative potential of the images in a pedagogic setting and evaluate the value of the guidelines.

## Reporting: Narrating image Thinking Pathways

Data reporting requires systematization of themes and the entire data set into a coherent story of findings in accordance with research questions. Because it is important to capture across-participant variability, findings will be presented for each data item (participant) first and then they will be commented in light of the whole data set and in accordance with RQs.

1. First, data visualization of the participants thinking will be presented via:

   • **Image–concept narratives** on participants thinking pathways to present an organic thinking

   Image–concept narratives show how participants' thinking develops in relation to the coded stages of "imagine-ation," Search, and Concept articulation *during the search* (see the main coding Table 7.4). The narratives were developed in relation to research questions.

2. Second, different data visualization forms will be used to illustrate particular inquiry foci:

   • **Spider diagram on first IA** (image ideas/ associations) for the whole data set
   • **Spider diagram on Google Images** SW (all search words) for the whole data set

3. Third, descriptive and reflective narratives will comment on:

- Participants' evaluation of a) pedagogic value of the activity and b) the guidelines looked from a holistic perspective.

# Findings: Thinking with Images Pathways

This section presents the findings. It narrates each participant's thinking pathway, and in case of one participant (Shaun), it exemplifies a visual thinking pathway map I created for each participant to map how their thinking processes developed in relation to conceptual ideas and images. These are *thinking trajectories organized around coding and research questions.*

Each narrative follows research questions and code clusters:

- First associations (RQ 1.1)—IA
- Initiating and performing search (RQ 2.1)—SW, SE, SI
- Concept–image articulation and relation (RQ 2.2. and 2.3)—CI, CIE
- Critical and manifold concept perspectives (RQ 2.4)—CRR

To remind the reader of the codes (as in Table 7.4), these are:

IA = instance association
SW = search words
SE = search explanation
SI = search image
CI = concept idea
CIE = concept idea elaboration
CRR = concept retrospective reflection

The Image-Concept Thinking Pathways narratives that follow contained **numbers** in parenthesis/brackets as they were originally accompanied with maps (such as Fig. 7.3 in Shan's Image-Concept Thinking Pathways). These numbers referred to the image coding maps I created during the coding process, and the coded map segments with codes IA, SW, SE, SI, CI, CIE, and CRR.

## Patrick's Image–Concept Thinking Pathways

### First Associations

Patrick's preliminary image associations, after reading the concept definition, were abstract associations about the concept: "science," "people's ideas of science, psychology", rather than an image idea. Hence, this participant first responded with an abstract idea to the abstract concept.

When asked about an image idea, Patrick provided two: "grey pictures of Einstein" (similar to Fig. 7.2) and "some dusty books". He later critically referred to these as his own "stereotypical" views on science, he noted that this surprised him, how stereotypical the images that popped up in his mind were. These ideas were then followed by spontaneous and more alternative thinking about the everyday and personally familiar application of science, "empirical" as related to academic study such as a PhD or master's degree. This concept thinking was related to a new image idea: "Google scholar screen shot." Finally, before searching for an image, Patrick offered an alternative concept idea in terms of tackling "hands-on activity teaching and learning" as a process of empirically built knowledge. This evoked an image idea to represent "the acts in classroom" ("when kids are doing whatever they are doing"), a departure from more definition-bound concept and image ideas in the beginning. In summary, Patrick would first think about a concept idea and then try to turn that idea into a concept image; he exhibited a varied set of ideas about the concept and used images to exemplify these ideas, which also provided new ideas for reflection.

### Initiating Search

Patrick "found" an image in the mind first and then looked for the best fit, customizing the image search words inserted in the Google Images engine to that image in the mind. First, for the image to represent "science," Patrick wanted to find a black and white image of a scientist, and so inserted "a scientist," for the "black and white" search option in Google. Although this was not following a particular scientist's image, Patrick chose the image which matched his first image idea of a "a grey picture of Einstein" (Fig. 7.2).

**Fig. 7.2** A photograph of Einstein as a stereotypical image of an empirical scientist. (Image information and credit: Albert Einstein, half-length portrait, seated, facing right; Inscribed on mat: Mrs. Eugenie Meyer zum Andenken an ihren Besuch in Caput [i.e. Caputh] am 15.VIII.31. Albert Einstein. Date:1931: Source: Library of Congress, Prints & Photographs Division, [reproduction number LC-USZC4-4940]. Author: Doris Ulmann (1882–1934); Wikimedia Commons)

Explaining why he chose that image, Patrick commented that the choice of "black and white" was intentional and had a particular metaphorical meaning revealing "black and white" view on scientists and science that he held:

I suppose because that's maybe my view on science. Black and white. Just my image of scientists. How strait-laced they are … for example even in psychology I prefer the more quantitative side of things rather than social psychology where there are those competing ideas.

## Concept–Image Articulation and Relation

The "black and white" picture quality helped Patrick to confront his own bias and stereotypical views on scientists and science. This is an example of how a picture and its characteristic manifest metaphorical projections of the concept ("black and white picture" were chosen to represent "black and white views on science/ scientists"). This picture was also echoed later in the reflection, when he talked about his second (and final) chosen picture, having searched for it carefully as the photographs of children that he was seeing did not match the image idea he had in his mind. Referring back to this first black and white photograph of Einstein, he wanted to stress how important it is to challenge stereotypical images of science and scientists among children, encouraging them to feel like scientists by doing empiricism in a form of a hands-on activity. Basically, the first picture provided a concrete example of a stereotypical idea (of scientists) which, due to its static presence and depictive character, was an immediate, concrete reference for his metaphorical association, and subsequent critical scrutiny and awareness of personal bias.

The quality and elements in picture 1 (Einstein) brought new concept reflections which might not have occurred otherwise (without the picture)—black and white view on science, stereotypical view on scientists, and later questioning whether Einstein was actually a stereotype (a stereotypical scientist) or not (when thinking about him as an example). However, Patrick did not unpack further picture details, for example the blackboard and chalk shown behind Einstein in the photograph he chose could be a reference for exploring the notion of time, relating to learning tools and data presentation, considering how these things change or get preserved over time, and why.

The second picture (showing play-doh) was not used as a platform to find more possible concept associations but as a projection of Patrick's idea. He had an idea of what he wanted the picture to show so did not spend time looking at it in any interpretative manner but using it to illustrate his idea. However, he did refer to other pictures he was viewing during the search, interpreting their content. For example he initially was interested in one image but when opening it for closer scrutiny, he realized that the children did not look happy in the image, and he preferred kids to be enjoying themselves in the classroom. Then, when he saw what he thought was an image of happy children, they looked to him as if they were doing nothing, so again that was not the image he was looking for, as they had to be both happy and doing something, a hands-on activity. Obviously, Patrick had a very particular image idea for his second image choice: he wanted to find it for particular reasons—to represent happy children, doing something in the classroom, using their hands, being messy and busy. In the end, he picked one which was the closest match to his idea.

## Critical and Manifold Concept Perspectives

In terms of concept reflective thinking, Patrick's dominant concept theme during the search was the idea of empiricism as experienced by children via a "hands-on" teaching strategy. This is an alternative approach to the concept which departed from initial concept ideas and images and represents a good example of critical and alternative thinking about the concept. By considering representations of empiricism in the classroom and focusing on its messy, busy character, Patrick shifted significantly from the straightforward, "black and white" image of a science he provided in the beginning.

The participant made an effort to think about alternative approaches to empiricism. He first provided a more stereotypical concept idea and representation that evoked empiricism as a representation of a famous male scientist, therefore, a scientific actor representing empiricism, a science "celebrity." He then developed four concept ideas, three related to the dominant alternative theme mentioned:

(a) empiricism as doing an academic study;
(b) empiricism as hands-on knowledge creation
(c) empiricism as group and collaborative knowledge creation (as opposed to solitary endeavor); and
(d) —in relation to critical thinking skills—empiricism as the grounds for challenging stereotypes (rather than perpetuating them).

His ideas b, c, and d were elaborated, hence coded as CIE—this differentiates them from just an articulation of an idea which is marked as CI (CI 1). It was explained in each code definition that there was a difference when a participant simply articulated an idea (=CI (concept idea)) and elaborated on it (=CIE (concept idea elaboration)). In a nutshell, the "Thinking with Images" process supported Patrick to express critical and new perspectives on the concept, questioning his own views/bias, and shifting from stereotypical to alternative ideas that he linked to the concept.

# Shaun's Image-Concept Thinking Pathways

## First Associations

This narrative section shows how I coded narratives via "thinking with images" maps (Fig. 7.3). Shaun's narrative is an example of how each narrative was coded with numbers in parenthesis/brackets that represented some key codes (e.g. IA (instance association), SW (search words), as

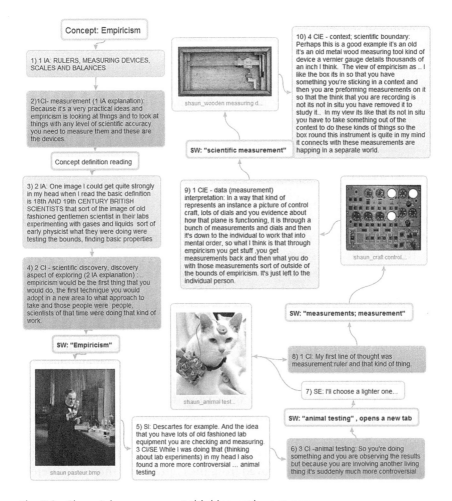

**Fig. 7.3** Shaun's image–concept thinking pathways map

explained above; see Fig. 7.3). Shaun's first image ideas were: "measuring devices": "rulers," and "scales and balances" (1) 1 IA). These were derived from ideas of scientific accuracy (2) 1 CI).

Having read the definition, Shaun developed one more image idea prior to the search: namely, "Eighteenth- and nineteenth-century male British scientist, in the lab experimenting with gases and liquids" (3) 2 IA) "*finding the basic properties of things*" (30 2 IA).

## Initiating Search

When turning to search for an image, Shaun decided to type the concept "empiricism" first rather than match an image idea he had identified. He wanted to "*to see what comes out.*" He chose an image of a painting of Louis Pasteur which actually matched his image of the nineteenth century male scientist in a lab.

## Concept–image Articulation and Influences

While looking at the images of scientists and labs, his thinking suddenly turned a new direction: he noticed an image of a cat and came up with the idea of "animal testing" as a controversial scientific empirical practice (8) This case illustrates how viewing a search display of images can inspire new thoughts and image ideas—Shaun was looking at images of labs and the context of experimental settings. The act of viewing such image content, together with his intention to find something intriguing (controversial), triggered the idea of "animal testing," as animals are used in lab tests.

After the controversial image and questioning the ethics of animal testing, he turned to his original concept idea, the measurement devices. Shaun did use particular picture elements (details) to draw inferences about the concept: the image of a measuring device placed within a clear wooden boundary of a box provided the base for inferring the metaphor linked to this image that pointed at "empirical research boundaries," with empirical firmly linked to the lab experimentation, and how it was problematic when results were removed from the context and then interpreted outside those boundaries (10). Hence, the picture content served as a

**Fig. 7.4**  Airplane control panel dials. (Free image source Peakpx: https://www. peakpx.com/531030/photo-of-airplane-s-instrument-panel)

platform for inferring concept ideas. Furthermore, details in the picture of the airplane control panel dials (Fig. 7.4) reminded Shaun that the dials have numbers and show some measurement, but it is up to the person (the pilot) to interpret and hence manage the system. The picture supported important thinking about individual measurement (data) interpretation, which opened a consideration of the importance of interpretative process.

## Critical and Manifold Concept Perspectives

With regard to concept ideas, the selected images provided the platform for three key critical ideas on the concept. Shaun connected the image of the scientist in the lab to (a) put forward the idea of empiricism as default scientific method of discovery in natural science two centuries ago (4) 2 CI):

the discovery aspect of exploring would be the first thing that you would do, the first technique... scientists of that time were doing that kind of work. (4)

During the search, the participant criticized (b) the removal of context from scientific investigation (10) 4 CIE)—the box boundary in the image of a wooden measuring device, as mentioned earlier, provided a framework for the metaphor for empirical study as being a world with its own boundaries created to study another one:

> You are performing measurements on it so that the thing that you are recording is not in situ you have removed it to study it... you have to take something out of the context to do these kinds of things, so the box round this instrument is quite in my mind: it connects with these measurements as happening in a separate world (10) 4 CIE).

The picture of the dials on the air craft control system was related to (c) the importance being placed on the individual subject who reads those dials (the measuring) and what he/ she does with that, rather than the measurement tool. Hence it provided a trigger for thinking about data (measurement) interpretation and context in empiricism (9) 1 CIE):

> That kind of represent an instance, a picture of control craft, lots of dials and your entire evidence is there (...) and then what you do with those measurements, sort of outside of the bounds of empiricism, it is just left to the individual person. (9) 1 CIE)

## Jessica's Image–Concept Thinking Pathways

### First Associations

Jessica's preliminary image association was connected to the concept word's phonetic quality "When I think of empiricism I think of sounding like an empire." After reading the concept definition, this idea of empire was linked to the definition and an image of "19th century Raj" and "enlightenment science." Her image associations then narrowed down to a particular image, an image she knew, hence familiar to her, of "quite famous 19th century oil paintings" with "the horary, the vacuum, a bird or animal in a glass." In connection to that image idea, Jessica developed a reflection about the past time when there were *"certainties relating to evidence and knowledge,"* which dictated the concept ideas that Jessica explored, mainly focusing on the notion of data interpretation and bias in classical empiricism that is rarely acknowledged.

## Initiating Search

The participant generated an image idea first and then tried to map her search onto the idea and, thereby, customized the searching to her own image. She first inserted the following sets of search words which were a mix of abstract ideas and concrete picture characteristics expected to lead her to the image she wanted to find: "art, vacuum painting," " nineteenth century art, oil painting," "nineteenth-century painting, science" and "nineteenth century, painting, science, vacuum, enlightenment" and the name: "Vesalius." She picked an image that, according to her memory, matched best the image she wanted to find—an image of the Leiden Anatomy Theatre (Fig. 7.5).

## Concept–Image Articulation and Relation

Jessica's case showed that the act of searching can (serendipitously) redirect the thinking about the concept and evoke new image ideas and further concept elaboration. The images which she saw as results of the search word insertion suddenly evoked the memory of an image she analyzed when she was an undergraduate student and she decided to re-focus her search to find that image instead:

> As we have been looking at these, I have been thinking about science in the notion of an observation and kind of sensory observation and knowledge; it reminds me of the work of the Vesalius which is… if I have spelled that right… his work on anatomy. (Fig. 7.5)

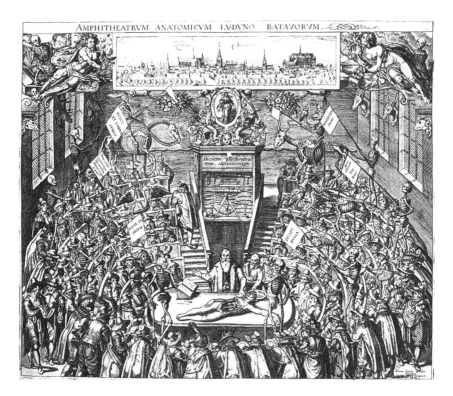

**Fig. 7.5** Anonymous Engraving of an anatomy at the Leiden Anatomy Theatre (1609). (Image information and credit: After a drawing by J. C. vant Woudt (Woudanus)). Source: https://extra.shu.ac.uk/emls/si-13/billing/index.htm; Source: Billing (2004))

From the very start, Jessica had particular ideas of what images she would like to search for—she sought the images she was familiar with and seemed confident about how she could relate them to the concept of empiricism, mainly in critical fashion. Her search and her image ideas were focused and elaborations were built on her prior knowledge of the pictures. She used the knowledge she had about the Vesalius picture to make new connections and creative ideas in relation to empiricism and the image of the anatomy theatre. It provided her with an opportunity to re-interpret the image again in new light.

Jessica used some picture elements to make interesting and creative concept related points: she referred to the *depicted Shakespearean theatre setting* and *the action of corpse examination as ways of how empiricism was practiced in the past*—these depicted elements were related to the historical value and origin of modern terms, such as 'operating theatre' (as early corpse examinations were done in theatres), which then was connected to the term empiricism. She was talking about a practice of dissecting female bodies as a specific disturbing form of empirical practice, which bothered her as a feminist scholar. At a certain point after she stopped searching, she examined the picture more closely by enlarging it, and noticed that the corpse examined in the picture she selected was not a female corpse, as she had thought it was, in order to make a point how female corpses examined were interpreted in relation to sociocultural values of the time, such as the women's chastity and associated worth. That made her critically reflect about her own expectations and how her expectations were leading her interpretation of the image.

This could signal that if participants select pictures that they already have a solid knowledge of, it might allow them to be more articulate and creative in re-interpreting it in relation to a new concept being explored. Also, if participants decided to take a photo themselves, this effort might provide better opportunities for concept engagement and consequently elaboration. However, details in very familiar images might be "overlooked"; that is, the student might stick to some views which they wanted to pursue (dissection of female bodies, although the picture does not actually show that), using pictures as a support to what they wanted to argue about. However, Jessica was very observant and introspective, and she did point at this possibility herself. This is an illustration of how participant's knowledge connected to some image lead and influence image interpretation in light of the concept. Its strength is that the participant might have a lot of interesting ideas and comments to make, based on their prior knowledge of the image. This can be very useful for concept reflection and discussion. Familiar images still provide a potent source for a participant's reflection, hence there is more to gain than lose from them in terms of possible concept reflection.

The argument that Jessica "infused" into the image was around the problems of *data interpretation* and *the power of seeing*. Indeed, she herself showed how beliefs can guide an interpretation of what we are seeing. Yet, making such situations and processes visible was and can be a valuable transformative experience.

## Critical and Manifold Concept Perspectives

Jessica provided an elaboration of the concept through the picture, articulating different ideas (angles) to elaborate the main concept of data interpretation; contesting it to claim connections between evidence and knowledge. Being familiar with the picture, this allowed her to provide a thorough picture narrative, although the picture did not show a female corpse as she had it in her memory of the image she intended but did not find. Nevertheless, it was relevant enough; it could have been used as a reference to female corpses too and proved a potent trigger for concept thinking, as well as the realization of how her expectations were influencing what she was seeing.

Jessica expressed the following critical ideas on the concept: a) evidence–knowledge link and causality, b) empirical data interpretation, c) historical character of meaning and practice, d) culture influencing knowledge epistemologies and e) the act and power of seeing/ looking. However, it can be said that the issue of data interpretation is the strongest thematic thread in her thinking, showing an overarching critical approach to the concept. For example, her picture interpretation was underpinned by critiquing empirical investigation as asserting knowledge based on observation taken out of the cultural context, and how interpretation was immediately taken to mean scientific reasoning:

> It's a picture of literally an operating theatre… very much like the old style Shakespearean theatres and it's…. And what I found really interesting…was the ways in which the person dissecting the body would interpret the body with and likely add meaning to what was meant to be a very scientific reason.

## Mathew's Image–Concept Thinking Pathways

### First Associations

Having skimmed the concept definition, Mathew's first image associations were abstract ideas of the "classics and scientific method". Then he provided a concrete image idea: "test tubes," adding further image ideas: "the great scientists," such as "B. F. Skinner" (*"That's come into my head now, I don't know why. I think it's because I was reading him not long ago"*) and "lab benches." The comment he made on the image idea of B. F. Skinner signals that the participant might evoke images related to something they have recently seen or experienced since that is "fresh" in their memory.

### Initiating Search

When he started to search for an image, Mathew typed the word "empiricism" into the search engine in order to explore what Google Images offered. He commented on this act, showing critical awareness that by typing "empiricism," he had deprived himself of an opportunity to shape the image search with his own search words:

> I'll type in empiricism; see what they think... That's gone against what perhaps I should be doing. Because I should be I think looking for the things that empiricism forms in my head. If I just type empiricism into the search engine I'm going to see the ideas suggested by Google and suggested by others, the most popular ideas. But I bet if I put that in I'm going to get test tubes, that kind of thing...

### Concept–Image Articulation and Relation

The image search and selection did not provide much reflection for Mathew and there was little elaboration on the concept. However, he showed a fascination for image aesthetics (black and white photos) and images of people. People portraits were really interesting and important to him, their histories and how their portraits suggested what kind of people they were, not just as scientists, but as 'everyday' people. Having done a Master's degree in Digital Photography, image aesthetics might have overpowered attempts to develop ideas about the concept, and made him focus on photographic aesthetics ("*I'm really interested in photography*"). Mathew nevertheless showed awareness that image aesthetics could affect his choice without seeing a clear link between his choice and the concept of empiricism: "*I'm automatically attracted to it (a photograph), but, what's that got to do with empiricism?*". In a way, Mathew's like and dislike for particular images (preference toward black and white photographs showing portraits and dislike for cartoons) proved to be an obstacle to concept reflection rather than a trigger. But it also did lead to some quite important insights. While viewing the images which were shown as the result of the search word "scientist," Mathew expressed critical awareness on stereotypical imagery he had when thinking of first image associations and that what he might endorse by selecting an image of a stereotypical lab scientist:

> There's a classic image. And that's the kind of thing I see in my head and it's horrendous looking. It's absolutely awful but that's what came into my head. The clichéd scientist and the test tube with some bizarre potion in it. So I think we've got to save it just because that's what I visualized… And there you go a test tube. Microscopes and test tubes. It's bizarre.

In that way, the search and selection process provided him with an opportunity to confront his own stereotypical ideas and hence question stereotypes and typecasting in general: similar to what had happened in Patrick's case. However, Mathew did not provide any elaborate concept ideas: although he could have commented on the biographies of the people whose images he selected (Aristotle, Hume, Pappert, Heidegger), or how they contributed to empiricism, he did not do that. He would mainly comment on picture content, expressing like or dislike or describing its photographic quality, style, light and attractiveness. His photography degree was overtaking his reflection. It was hard for Mathew to infer any substantial concept reflection from the viewed or selected pictures, other than concept-led ideas on empiricism as related to science, labs and measurement. Indeed, it is hard to do so looking at people's portraits—they might not offer more than triggering details of, and insights on, key people's biographies and contribution. Depending on the narrator's knowledge of scientists' biographies, this can actually be animating and interesting. A good knowledge of people's biographies is essential to relate them to the concept. This is the case when images did not serve that well as a platform for Mathew's concept inference, exactly because there was a particular fascination with photography and portraits. This might have been because they were images of particular genre (people's portraits) and he either did not know enough about the people's biographies to comment in light of empiricism or he thought that it was well enough explained/ self-explanatory why he had chosen those pictures and those people as great thinkers in human history who had pivotal ideas on empirical science (as mentioned, he chose pictures of Aristotle, Hume, Pappert, Heidegger), so it was not necessary to comment on them in light of the concept. His pursuit of image aesthetic and fascination with aesthetic quality of photographic portrait was a constraint on the quest for concept meaning. In addition, like Patrick and Shaun, he focused on male scientists, that he did critically reflect on as a clichéd scientist image, and commented how this subconscious image cliche was: "absolutely awful."

*Critical and Manifold Concept Perspectives*

Mathew's search did not result in any elaborate image idea, other than having general ideas around "science" and "measurement" (CI). In summary, his comments were more an account of his opinions on image search process (SE) and image content (SI) rather than thinking about the concept, but his critical awareness about subconscious bias was a notable contribution to critical thinking with images.

## James's Image–Concept Thinking Pathways

### First Associations

James's first visual idea was an image of "John Locke", "some sort of old man from 17-something." So his image idea went into the direction of representing a famous person in relation to empiricism, in a way similar route to Mathew's, again stereotypically imagining a male scientist form the past. After reading a definition, he added definition-led concept ideas of "measurements and stuff like that," and image ideas of "people measuring things, studying things and putting numbers on things, so something like a thermometer."

## Initiating Search

When he started his search, James did not try to map his search words onto his image ideas, but inserted the word "empiricism" instead into the search engine to "*see what people think of it.*" He chose an image which represented five senses (this was a drawing that symbolically showed eye for vision, hand for touch, nose for smell, etc.), unrelated to the image ideas he had contemplated beforehand.

## Concept–Image Articulation and Relation

The browsing and selection process proved useful for James to articulate concept ideas and elaborate on them in relation to image content and his interpretation of that content. He approached the image search as an exploration rather than something to map onto a pre-imagined idea of how his image should look. After he chose his first image, since it reminded him of "senses" and the importance of sensory experience in empiricism, he went on to establish a very personalized approach—that of an opposite concept—existentialism. It can be said that his thinking of the senses and what is not in the image of the senses he was viewing (the mind, being), triggered a novel approach to empiricism via considering its opposite, what he saw as Cartesian thought. It was a new direction in thinking (Fig. 7.6).

Since he expressed a liking for cartoons, he went on to search for particular cartoons which would illustrate this innovative approach to the concept where he wanted to find first a representation of two opposite concepts juxtaposed, as if fighting with each other (Empiricism vs. Descartes) and then he wanted an illustration of the opposite concept

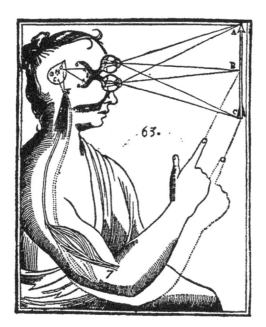

**Fig. 7.6** Descartes' mind and body dualism. Diagram from one of René Descartes' works. (Image information and credit: Public domain. Source: Wikimedia Commons: https://commons.wikimedia.org/wiki/File:Descartes_mind_and_body.gif Scanned from Dagfinn Døhl Dybvig & Magne Dybvig (2003). Det tenkende mennesket. Oslo: Tapir akademisk forlag. ISBN 8251918642. Page 173. Which had it from Descartes: The World and Other Writings. Cambridge U.P. 1998. Date: between 1596 and 1650)

alone. Suddenly, he had a new concept idea which happened as he finished commenting on the senses image.

At times, James' reflection on the concept in relation to picture content had more the character of cartoon verbal and pictorial "content mirroring" and elaboration rather than, for example, in Shaun's case of image–concept content interpretation. To put it in differently, he read what was said in the cartoon and re-told that in his own words, sometimes elaborating on that content. James was skillful in doing so and he was a good conversationalist in general. Therefore, this case pointed at the possibility of participants rephrasing the content of the cartoon, since cartoons contain words which limit the image ambiguity and "anchor" its meaning. This strategy can be successful though, as in James's case, if the participant continues to re-interpret the content further and infer concept meanings. But a student might possibly stay at the basic level of "re-telling" the cartoon rather than inferring concept–image relations.

With regard to another image of his choice, Dr. Horrible, James was very aware of his "evil" gaze and used this descriptive image element to question the notion of empiricism as "evil," positioned against the "soul" and "religion" which he disagreed with. His explanation of why he thought of Dr. Horrible (since he recently watched Dr. Who) echoed Mathew's explanation on why he thought of B. F. Skinner—since he had recently read about it:

> I chose Dr. Horrible because I was trying to think of famous mad scientists or famous crazy scientists and Dr. Horrible sprang to my mind, I watched it last week.

This case identifies participants' personalized image associations in terms of something very familiar that they can relate to, either as a part of a very recent experience (James and Mathew) or a memorable experience (Jessica's image with which she became familiar with while an undergraduate).

## Critical and Manifold Concept Perspectives

Speaking of concept reflection and elaboration, James developed three concept ideas: (a) understanding through senses, (b) the opposite concept (existentialism) and (c) the view of empiricism as "evil" juxtaposed to the notion of soul and religion. Understanding through senses:

> This picture of the senses represents everything what I think of empiricism… It's just things you can see, hear, taste, touch, smell that are all outside the body.

It can be said that his thinking of the senses and what is not in the image (the mind, the being, thinking and interpretation) triggered a novel approach via considering what he deemed its opposite, Cartesian thought:

> What about the antithesis of that argument?… It's never about what goes on in the mind or the thinking process.

In addition to his criticism of empiricism, James also displayed a critical view on Cartesian thought, and of existentialism as well in relation to the cartoon picture of a humanoid cat questioning its existence, as well as a critical view on the stereotypical image of an empirical scientist (here, the one engaged in experiments) as someone evil, cunning and almost insane, working against the soul and trying to measure everything—he challenged this "popular view in some circles", referring to Dr. Horrible image:

> I think that's a good evil scientist picture. So, evil…. Because the idea that empiricism…. There's an idea from some quarters that I don't agree with at all but it's quite popular in some ways that empiricism leads you to ignore the soul and people… I suppose it's a big deal and it's part of a debate.

In summary, the image search provided a powerful platform for James to explore and critique the concept. He started his search to see what was offered by Google but departed in a personalized direction, prompted by the images he was seeing as the result of the search.

## Elisabeth's Image–Concept Thinking Pathways

### First Associations

Elisabeth's first image associations were abstract ideas related to the concept: "scientists, men in coats with beards," followed by image ideas on "test tubes," an idea of "systematic and structured study," and a concrete image of "Einstein, blackboard and chalk." She did not read the definition, just glanced at it.

## Initiating Search

Elisabeth wanted to explore empiricism through the notion of social research and decided to match this abstract concept idea to her search word decision. She inserted the following words into the search engine: "social experiments cartoon" which led her to choose her first image that showed a mouse size maze resembling an office environment with cubicles and mice in these spaces, with a human scientist above it making notes. The speech bubble comment (made by the scientist) was in Turkish, which was not her native language.

## Concept–Image Articulation and Relation

Elisabeth expressed a particular intention in terms of the image genre, similar to the one James expressed: she decided to focus on comic cartoons, having seen a few comics as results of the first search words typed. She noted picture ambiguity and favored what she called a concise and clear narrative quality of cartoons:

> think I'll be better off with cartoons in there because it's more like a scenario rather than a picture, yes, I think they get the message across really. And they are quite concise and it's more of a scenario than just a picture that could mean anything so it guides you more.

This is an interesting comment since picture ambiguity might be its advantage too (i.e., not always a disadvantage), since it can create productive cognitive tension; that is, an effort to think about its meaning and a creative effort to infer possible concept-related meanings. On the other hand, a cartoon might not be as clear as it seems to be and the words that it contains might limit creative image exploration. However, Elisabeth did not pay attention to what the cartoon was actually saying (the words)—as mentioned, one of her cartoons (the first one) was in Turkish. She was more concerned about what it depicted, which is a surprising reaction (as James did carefully read the captions).

She was thinking about customizing every single image she chose to the idea and issue she wanted to discuss. This customization illustrates this participant's intention to "personalize" the image and change it in some way. It may be that seeing the comment (in bubbles) might inspire participants to change those comments, at least if they do not match their interpretation of the depiction or what they intend to argue. In that way, even cartoons (and not only traditional depictive images) can serve as a platform for projecting meanings, although one would think that their meaning is more fixed due to the words they contain. But, as shown in this case, those words can be ignored.

Elisabeth wanted her images to elicit a particular emotional response—she wanted to find an image which would be humorous and thought-provoking. This shows her rhetorical ambition in image selection (emotional response wanted):

> Looking for something that's kind of funny but gets you thinking about it (…) because you want it to be something provoking.

Furthermore, Elisabeth tackled the images' depictive quality and referred to what was happening in her opinion in each image to infer concept ideas, but after she decided to stop the search and asked to reflect on the images chosen: for example, a scientist pointing at the blackboard made her think of scientists always pointing at some results which are presented as if "set in stone," hence pointing at surprising inflexibility in how some results are discussed and presented. A drawing of a doctor or scientist looking at an x-ray image of the head that showed a television instead of the brain, and showed another person was seated in front of him, supposedly the one whose head was x-rayed prompted her to think about using inappropriate methods for answering research questions and how what we see influence what we think.

It seems that she was also not satisfied with the choices and felt more like drawing an image herself rather than finding it. The images chosen provided her with some reflection on the concept during the search, but she did reflect on them after the search in further depth though, when prompted.

## Critical and Manifold Concept Perspectives

In general, during the search, Elisabeth's thinking was more descriptive in relation to the image rather than concept reflective or explanatory—she was thinking aloud about the image content as the source for concept inference as related to the meaning of the whole picture (as she commented on the mice picture):

> Maybe he's looking at the office politics of mice? I don't know. This one (mouse) is obviously looking over something and maybe talking to this one here. He (the scientist) is looking at interactions between these different people because it's in an office environment, here you've got a box cubicle to yourself and that's all that you've got and that brings about questions about work.

Elisabeth was mainly interested in thinking about empiricism in connection to social sciences, in particular social research and empirical research involving humans, and she was thinking how hard it was to observe sociocultural aspects/factors in a lab environment, which is a critical approach to the concept. She followed this core theme developing three ideas during her search: (a) the issues of "empirical" meaning seen as "scientifically rigorous," (b) empiricism as scientific structuring, and (c) the role of context in social research. Therefore, she did have valuable concept ideas (CI) which she did not elaborate on enough during the search, but when prompted after the search, she did so.

# Christian's Image–Concept Thinking Pathways

### First Associations

Christian's first image idea in relation to the concept was "*a scientist in front of a blackboard giving proof of an equation*" in relation to the idea he had provided beforehand of "*finding proof, proving something.*" Hence, he first thought of an abstract idea and then mapped an image onto that idea. However, having read the definition, the wording affected him to change his mind and shift to an idea of "experimentation": "*experimenting with actual things like, for instance, in chemistry or physics or trying things out in biology, experimenting with tubes*" (3), so this idea defined his image of a "scientist mixing chemicals and using test tubes in a chemical laboratory." Then he provided a more concrete concept image idea in order to illustrate a concept idea, "*to find an actual historical or well- known example that might be a little bit thought-provoking.*" He related this intention of a concept idea example to a concrete image of "Pavlov's dog" (Fig. 7.7).

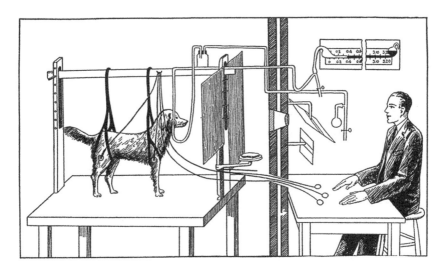

**Fig. 7.7**  Pavlov experiments with dog. (Image information and credit: Public domain licence CC-BY-4.0; Photo number: M0014738; Full Bibliographic Record: http://catalogue.wellcomelibrary.org/record=b1291205;  Source/  Photographer: Wellcome Trust; https://wellcomeimages.org/indexplus/obf_images/f8/89/793ca2 1e30dd29687f45f36c8078.jpg;  Gallery:  https://wellcomeimages.org/indexplus/ image/M0014738.html Wellcome Collection gallery (2018-04-01): https://wellcom-ecollection.org/works/t82myw43 CC-BY-4.0)

## Initiating Search

Christian decided to do a customized search in accordance with the image ideas he had, so he typed the following words which were mapped into his image ideas: "Pavlov dogs" and he chose a drawing of Pavlov dog as his first image (Fig. 7.7). He chose two more images, a set of 6 test tubes with different liquid colours, and a black and white photograph of someone measuring a man's cranium, wearing what resembles some uniform.

## Concept–Image Articulation and Relation

When thinking of experiments during the search, he decided that it would be good to think of a controversial experiment, something more thought provoking, unethical. He came up with an image idea of "humans measuring humans," "*an image of a scientist measuring a cranium of a human being to say something about that human because I think that's a little bit problematic.*"

Christian thought that having more time for thinking might result in better image ideas and choices: "*I could come up with some very interesting images if I'm thinking for a long time.*"

After the search, Christian commented that picture content simplicity (meaning that the picture do not show many details) might not provide enough triggers for reflection and exploration of the concept. He remarked that, commonly, one would find picture contents lacking details to unpack. So, he thought it was difficult to find images rich in content using Google image search:

> One of the problems of finding an image like I just did perhaps is that I put in a single search term so very often I would find an image with one specific, what would you call it, one specific thing going on. For instance, I typed measuring head and this is a guy measuring a head and nothing else. So in many cases there wouldn't be a lot of details if you know what I mean. And perhaps if I wanted to find a really, really thought-provoking image with a lot of potential for discussion then it would be a bigger image with more things going on at the same time. And that's a little bit difficult to find on Google.

On the other hand, this participant also thought that the search result could actually render image examples which one would not consider and thus, might find new and surprising concept ideas in them:

> But it's also nice just to search and see what you find because I knew that I wanted something with the cranium being measured but now I have found this picture where they are wearing uniforms so that gives a different, extra dimension to the image and that is actually good. I didn't think about that but that's good, I actually like that.

Therefore, the picture content detail—uniforms—provided a new possibility for thinking about the context and purpose of measuring, which might not have been thought of otherwise without a pictorial detail. Christian used pictures as illustrations of his concept ideas. He approached the image search as looking for an example which would be inspiring for the participants to think about and debate the concept—this illustrates Christian's focus on image functionality to support discussion.

## Critical and Manifold Concept Perspectives

In terms of concept reflection, Christian elaborated concept meaning through the chosen pictures in relation to two main themes: "experimentation" (dog and test tubes) and "measurement" (measuring cranium). Within these guiding themes, he articulated clear and precise concept ideas which he wanted the viewers to debate: a) experimental method—the process of setting an experiment, b) experiment generalizability and transferability, c) data interpretation, d) ethics, e)—senses and data interpretation and f) universality of measurement method.

In relation to the dog picture, he questioned experiment generalizability and transferability:

> ..to think about that particular experiment whether or not the knowledge gained from that experiment can be transferred to other domains because if you can get a dog to react that way, can you get a human being to react in the a similar way? What does an actual experiment show? What are you able to say when you have the results?

In relation to the cranium image, Christian raised an issue of data interpretation in terms of mensurability, that is, questioning what can be measured:

> We don't know what's going on and I think most people, well at least me, I would think a lot about what is going on here. Perhaps a criminal person having his head measured. They're trying to find out if there are any patterns I guess… People's personalities and people's intelligence are very, very difficult to measure, if not impossible….

Christian displayed an unusual ease and clarity in relation to the task, possibly because he teaches in the field of Media and Communication. Therefore, he can be seen as being more aware and sensitive to image affordances and significations. He termed the test tube image as being *iconic for empiricism* before viewing the guidelines (where this term is indeed listed) and he showed particular sensitivity to how image can serve as a platform for concept thinking and debate. Christian did provide more critical thoughts and suggestions after the image search—which are not reported here as the data described are sufficient to exemplify critical and analytical concept elaboration.

## Oscar's Image–Concept Thinking Pathways

### First Associations

Oscar's first image association was an image of "*a funnel.*" "This image reflected Oscar's concept idea on empiricism as something which is a restrictive and directional approach; he mentioned the words "guided" and "streamlined." Connecting this image to the read definition, Oscar thought about the concept in terms of guided and restricted norms, empiricism as an inflexible and unidirectional investigation.

### Initiating and Performing Search

When he started searching, Oscar decided to insert the word "empiricism" first rather than looking for an image of "funnel" for example. He saw it as an action he was required to do:

I'm doing that because you asked me about empiricism so that I could explore using those words.

## Concept–Image Articulation and Relation

Oscar chose an image drawn by Descartes, exactly the image shown earlier (Fig. 7.6) that accompanied James' thinking about senses and his reference to Descartes (note that James did not choose that image presented earlier, but Oscar did). Oscar inferred concept meanings from the pictures and some details in those pictures—the Descartes picture was linked to knowledge as confined to the boundary of the head, the second illustration of a monkey at a desk and an English-speaking character in suit and tie triggered off ideas of language and communication and the microscope in one image he saw but did not choose made him think that the characters were looking at the cell and thus he thought about how knowledge is passed on by people and interpreted individually, so that observation is contested in claiming truth. His final image choice was an illustration that showed a person who had a funnel instead of head that was being filled with colourful note papers, as he also wanted to find an image linked to his first image association.

Just like Elisabeth, he wanted to customize the cartoon, hence to change the words in the image, as he commented on the monkey and microscope image:

> I would change certain things in it yes. I would change something like, maybe the dialogue saying "are you seeing what I am seeing"? Or something like that because that's the whole idea.

He was paying more attention to the cartoon representation rather than what it was saying, just as Elisabeth did, but unlike James (but James's cartoon search was more personalized and specific).

## Critical and Manifold Concept Perspectives

Oscar pursued his initial concept ideas throughout his search through five concept ideas: a) restriction and boundaries of scientific method/ tradition, b) knowledge as being in the head, c) the issue with observation leading to truth, d) the issue of data interpretation and language, as being value-laden, and e) data interpretation as bound by prior knowledge.

He provided an elaborated reflection of the image, noting the contested issue of empirical research claiming the truth and being value-free, raising the issue of interpretation and language, and the disregard for the role of language in particular:

> Does monkey speak English, does he speak monkey? .....So there's that kind of hidden meaning behind things that's loaded. So it's not value free. So one of the things I would want to lean on is that something that is empirical is not necessarily free of values.

Oscar focused on subjectivity and value-laden empirical research. He reflected on scientists being bound by their disciplines and knowledge, thus approaching everything within those boundaries, with particular mindsets, frameworks of thinking, tools, environments, and so on. The third picture showing two characters—one looking through a microscope—was abstracted to the concept aspect of "knowledge consumers" as he termed it reflecting how what we see is a sort of "recycled knowledge," the knowledge of other people we have "consumed" and now assigned with our meaning:

> He's now believing what he's saying but is it actually the truth? So that's the whole idea of empiricism is that testing is based on the assumptions of his values, what he knows. … he knows what a cell looks like....

## Natalie's Image–Concept Thinking Pathways

### First Associations

Natalie's first image ideas on the concept were: "*books, just piles of books*"; "*on my desk, general books, out of the library.*" She related that image to research: "*I think I relate that term to research and work and where you start off with research is the reading. So I think that's why I thought of lots of books.*"

## Initiating Search

When starting to search for an image, Natalie decided to type the word "empiricism." She did so because she wanted to be cautious and was concerned about embarrassing herself in a group discussion if she "interpreted it wrong." So, she pointed that it was a safe decision to see what was offered by Google. The images she chose were a venn diagram (knowledge was at the overlap of 'truth' and 'belief' circles), a child dressed up in a lab coat in front of test tubes, a lab environment with rows of people engaging with microscopes, an empty lab environment, two children engaging with a globe model.

## Concept–Image Articulation and Relation

Image content provided ideas for Natalie. She actively commented on search and images in terms of their genre (diagrams and charts are good) and whether they meant anything to her or not. During the search, while looking at the lab images, she came up with the image idea of "a child as researcher, in a lab coat, in a science lab." Seeing two children and the globe—directed her to think about the role of age in being entitled to be authoritative and do "credible" research—so, can children be researchers?

Natalie's search went from the concept itself and exploring what was on offer into a more and more personalized exploration: so from the concept, to concept idea/ aspect, and to an image-led idea to match her image content expectation. Seeing the image of two children looking at the globe after she typed "empiricism" evoked her interest and concept focus on children which she revisited at the end of her search.

Natalie commented that "some images don't mean anything to me" which suggests that the participants will select images which they feel capable of interpreting, basically which send some sort of meaning or message they could use and unpack. In relation to that, an image which would "not mean anything" to the viewer might generate viewers resistance to interpret.

The diagrams that Natalie chose were basically tackled in terms of repeating the word labels they show. Natalie dealt with the images at a holistic level—looking at what the representation as a whole means to her.

## Critical and Manifold Concept Perspectives

In terms of concept ideas, Natalie developed five: (a) empiricism as reading and doing research, (b) as connected to traditional sciences, (c) empiricism in relation to knowledge and age (children's contribute to knowledge?), (d) education research vs. natural sciences research and (e) pupils as researchers.

Natalie was concerned about the relationship between knowledge and empirical study and how this relationship works and is determined. She exhibited an interest in children and their perception of the world and how age influences empirical understanding:

> two boys looking at a world: that would be quite good for starting a discussion how empiricism and knowledge relates to children.... children at different ages will have different concepts and different ways of thinking about things and what is truth and their understanding of it. (Fig. 7.8).

The chart and diagram that Natalie chose seemed not to provide a source of reflection, since she mainly provided a descriptive account of them (repeating what was written on the chart and diagram). This participant thought about empiricism in terms of her own research, namely in terms of giving the role of researchers in relation to children in schools and difficulties arising from that. She raised an interesting issue of contribution to knowledge "allowed" only to be performed by certain individuals and groups, dependent on age and hierarchy:

> The pupils as researchers... you could talk about the pros and cons to do with that, whether that is research and what knowledge you would be gaining.... The teachers don't really understand it. They don't understand how it can work. ... It's kind of the adult teachers don't really see that the children can really contribute toward research so I suppose for me that's something that you could talk about. (16)

**Fig. 7.8** Interacting with a big globe. (Image information and credit: Free public images, web iste Pikrepo; it shows two people interacting with the globe. URL link: https://www.pikrepo.com/ffkvb/boy-wearing-blue-t-shirt-learning-globe-during-daytime; the image modified to black and white)

## Andrew's Image–Concept Thinking Patterns

### First Associations

Andrew's first image association was *"English Victorian scientist working in a physics laboratory or a general natural sciences laboratory"* as an illustration of his thinking about empiricism: *"empiricism is something of the past for me, last 110 years have moved away from empiricism so I've situated it in a Victorian England."*

### Initiating Search

When starting to search for images, Andrew inserted the word: "empiricism" first, and then chose the image of Louis Pasteur (Fig. 7.9) as *"consistent with my image,"* referring to the Victorian gentlemen he imagined beforehand. That image was previously chosen by Shaun.

**Fig. 7.9** The image of Louis Pasteur chosen by both Shaun and Andrew. (Image information and credits: Albert Edelfelt—Photograph originally posted on Flickr as Albert EDELFELT, Louis Pasteur, en 1885. Date of generation: 27 August 2009. Photographed by Ondra Havala. Modifications by the uploader: perspective corrected to fit a rectangle (the painting was possibly distorted during this operation), frame cropped out. Wikimedia commons licence: https://commons.wikimedia.org/wiki/File:Albert_Edelfelt_-_Louis_Pasteur_-_1885.jpg; modified to black and white)

## Concept–Image Articulation and Relation

During the image search, he was fascinated by the opportunity provided by images to explore his own research in education and his thesis, so he decided to shift the focus of exploration to that research. This is an example of how the images can shift the focus of the main concept exploration into exploring other areas of the participant's interest. Image browsing and image search seemed to inspire Andrew to critically reflect on image content and functionality (e.g., contest the "truthfulness" of what photographic images of classrooms show). He seemed to have enjoyed the search so much that he decided that he wanted to explore his own thesis concerns via this image search, finding all the results Google image offered interesting and intriguing, a cause of reflection.

After the Pasteur images, he chose a lab image. Interestingly, again, it was the image previously chosen by Oscar. The lab image initiated thinking about educational research:

> To retain on that image.... I was thinking from that it prompted me to think about more specifically empiricism in the field of educational research

This led Andrew to insert the words: "empiricism in educational research" which did not show any images he would choose. Andrew was looking for a representation of classroom. Then he shifted his focus on classroom and typed "classroom":

> I'm looking at classrooms now. It would be the place in which I would be interested in secondary education research. I'm interested in classrooms and schools and a lot of them are empty classrooms or staged images.

He was struck by images showing individual tutorials or one-to-one relationships when it came to search words relating to "learning." His focus was slowly shifting away from the concept concerns toward his own thesis concerns and he typed: "learning in schools."

Then, he decided he wanted to go back to tackling the "teaching" concept search. Then he went into the direction of his own interest and typed: "teacher's professional development" commenting on this topic digression: "*I'm actually indulging myself through this in exploring visually my own thesis.*"

He then came back to consider the concept "empiricism" again and his final search was "empirical evidence." He was interested in the issue of validity and evidence in empirical research and the importance placed upon them.

Andrew eagerly engaged in critical interpretation of the images he was seeing in terms of both image meaning and imaged details, although this enthusiasm made him go off the topic (of concept exploration) for a part of his search. Still, this was a case when a participant really felt inspired to do image-based search and concept-meaning exploration.

## Critical and Manifold Concept Perspectives

In terms of concept elaboration, Andrew developed the following concept ideas: (a) empiricism as a paradigm from the past, (b) the difficulty of doing research in classrooms, (c) one-to-one learning in schools (not relating it to empiricism, just exploring) and (d) the deception of the senses—he saw an intriguing image while searching that showed a person looking in the mirror that showed the person in the mirror having a more attractive body than the person looking at that mirror image. He also unpacked the staged, posed images in contrast to what is experienced in practice, paying attention to picture content.

He pointed at the difficulty of doing research in classrooms due to the mere notion it being "research," so behavior and interactions that might happen in everyday circumstances might not surface. He showed a critical attitude toward the image itself: considering intentions of the image-maker and the process of image-making:

> I'm looking for evidence of a real classroom. I know when people go in and photograph a classroom everyone behaves in a way that they think they should behave for the photo so it's very difficult to find a genuine photo of a classroom… I think that just shows how difficult it is to research classrooms and teaching practice because the moment you enter into that intimate space everyone behaves slightly differently. I suspect that happens when you video them as well. People say it doesn't, but I don't believe it. Because… I can't find an image of a real…. They've been told to look busy.

He seemed to be fascinated by a realization that exploration of Google Images about the classroom and teaching can usefully contribute to critical examination and reflection on those concepts.

# Findings Overview: Concept–Image Ideas, Patterns and Characteristics

Having presented ten participants' thinking pathways map, this chapter proceeds to drawing conclusions from the presented analysis. As was shown in individual participants' thinking maps populated with key code instances, participants exhibited a reflective and critical attitude toward the concept and its meaning and/or their own thinking. Although there was a uniformity and similarity in their first image associations and concept thinking, participants quickly provided concept ideas in distinctive ways, developing the search in accordance to their interests, prior knowledge and experiences. Individually, they did approach the concept relating it to some more or less dominant *personal interest*:

- Patrick: "hands-on" teaching and learning
- Jessica: data interpretation—history, art and culture
- Shaun: data interpretation—numbers, measures
- Mathew: photography, biographies
- Elisabeth: social research context
- Christian: data interpretation—communication/ media and discussion
- James: playful, humorous "upside-down" positioning of ideas
- Oscar: data interpretation—language
- Natalie: children (as researchers, in research)
- Andrew: educational research and professional development

Overall, four participants were challenging the empirical claim to "truth" and "objectivism" in relation to *data interpretation* issue. Although I did not explain to them anything about IG prior to the task, this attitude was aligned with IG principles. Participants' interpretations were influenced by their disciplinary and doctoral research background, prior and personal experiences, which images triggered explicitly. Overall, their individual image choices and ideas were diverse and potent resources for concept exploration, discussion and the enhancement of concept understanding. There was a variety of thinking approaches across participants, who did display unique and personalized concept ideas, mainly reflecting their background and interests.

All in all, the participants developed *two distinctive sets of concept ideas*:

1) *Definitional*: ideas that were more linked to the concept definition, and
2) *Alternative*: approaching empiricism from a different angle other than the definition-led.

However, when they mentioned definition-led ideas, those were typically critical accounts of the concept and its definitional aspects. So, participants were concerned with the objectivity and validity claimed by empirical research, mainly in relation to subjective nature of data interpretation and context dependency. Commonly, natural sciences were juxtaposed with social sciences and education research. Their account in most cases made a separation of these sciences, but it did also challenge the dichotomy, although not that overtly.

Participants developed alternative concept approaches during the search such as: children as researchers, classroom activities, knowledge-building through collaboration and prior scientific achievements as opposed to solitary scientist, thinking about the concept through the lenses of culture, beliefs and time (history), considering ethical issues in experimentation (animal and human testing) and exploring the concept via biographies of key people.

There is a rich set of insights stemming from the results that point at various ways and characteristics of exploring the concept via an image that can form ways of knowing. These different thinking acts can be summarized as follows:

- **Image as projective surface and as launch pad**: A picture serve to "illustrate" concept ideas: the participant projected ideas onto the image – there was an intention regarding concept meaning that the image would show, and also, the seen images can trigger a new idea (act as an idea launch-pad).
- **A whole-picture response**: The participant would not do any semiotic reading of the selected images and its details but would interpret the picture meaning as a whole, what the whole picture meant to them, other than involving details in the image search.

- **Image as reality check and truth claims**: The activity exposed the participant's bias and/or prejudice which the participant was aware of and confronted it—it made an impact in terms of challenging stereotypical views; the participants questioned any truth value assigned to what was seen as well.
- **The potential of affect**: Searching for an image with emotional tone (e.g. animal testing pictures), thus identifying the significance of affect for stimulating debate around images.
- **Semiotic potency of picture elements/details**: Images can furnish details (e.g., the dials in a control system, the box's wooden boundary) that, if interpreted with an intention to create the link to the concept, trigger and inspire nuances of conceptual meaning and support creative concept inferences. This means that the picture details were considered as reflection triggers, alongside an overall idea for the meaning of the picture (a whole picture response).
- **Benefits of personal image familiarity**: Working with a familiar image might result in more confident and richer concept narrative and exploration.
- **Constraints of personal image familiarity**: But working with a familiar image might bound thinking to ideas that are too rigidly preset, so image depiction might be "overlooked" or misinterpreted.
- **Genre preferences**:

  - may constrain image–concept reasoning (e.g. black and white photographic portrait formats might narrow opportunities for concept mapping and reflection),
  - may result in sticking to one graphics genre, for example the comic/cartoon genre.

- **Exaggerated focus on image aesthetics** may also constrain image–concept reasoning.
- **Extraction of opposing features.** An image may be read in terms of features that are the opposite of those shown and thereby invite novel approaches to the concept: considering the concept opposite.
- **Re-telling of cartoons**: cartoons invited image description and re-telling of what the caption says—it takes a skillful and capable narrator

to go beyond re-telling—thereby focusing on the words in cartoons might compromise the range of possible interpretative work, but they can also open new avenues for interpretation or learners can draw them.

- **From abstract to concrete search strategy**: image search word strategies would generally go from abstract (the concept, idea) to more concrete (a pictorial representation).
- **Cartoon word customization**: when participants wanted to change the words in chosen cartoons, this was an opportunity for re-imagining the cartoon in light of the concept.
- **Describing the picture rather than inferring concept meanings**: some participants had a tendency to describe the picture during the search rather than explore concept meaning.
- **Concept Google exploration**: participant might stick to the word "empiricism" in search approach, and potentially remain driven by images which were tagged as "empiricism" on Google images search engine, although the doctoral researchers in the study managed to use such images as idea launch-pads, that is, an image seen triggered a new idea about the concept.
- **Image functionality as social, cognitive and affective**: picture choosing was performed to satisfy their: social role (how they will support animated discussion with peers), cognitive role (how they will support concept understanding) and affective role (initiating controversy, stirring emotions).
- **Visualized image mapping**: search led by the visualized object or description ("funnel").
- **Selective interpretation**: Participant might resist thinking about and interpreting images which at first sight haves "no meaning" to them, which confuse them; this might be expected from the students as well.
- **Distracted by other interest**: Once the idea of recruiting images to concept understanding has been established, some participants may become distracted by the idea and drawn into other themes that are of personal interest and link with what they are familiar with, as suggested by found images.
- **Representational criticism**: an exploration of how what is shown in photos corresponds to the experienced reality of that context.

# Thinking with Images: Image Ideas and Search Words

Having presented the key instances or incidents in each data item, the analysis next addresses the data in a holistic manner, considering the emerging picture in accordance with research questions. This part of the analysis provides further data reporting and visualizations on first image ideas and search words, further illuminating research questions 1.1. and 2.1:

*First image ideas* (from the concept utterance into the first image association (IA)): RQ 1.1. How do preliminary image associations relate to
   the abstract concept and what are they?) and.
*Search words*: RQ 2.1 (concept and image thinking is transformed into
   image search and search word formulation (SW)): How do participants use the image search engine in terms of actual search words?

## First Image Ideas

Participants' first image ideas and associations uncover whether there are any patterns across participants' initial and spontaneous image ideas when thinking about the concept and what content that image idea takes (what it represents: e.g., an object, a person, or an event). These results will explore how diverse or unique are individual first image associations. The findings will carry implications for the pedagogical potential of the activity provided to the students in Project 2. Pedagogical potential is defined based on knowledge enrichment by considering and exploring different views, aspects and inputs related to the concept, ranging from more definition-driven image ideas to more challenging and alternative ones. Figure 7.10 shows all first image ideas that the participants had during the search, grouped in accordance to their content, followed by an explanation.

I shall proceed to describe the map (Fig. 7.10) for the readers who cannot see the map and its text. The first image ideas/associations that participants had were: 1) **Abstract ideas** informing image ideas: science,

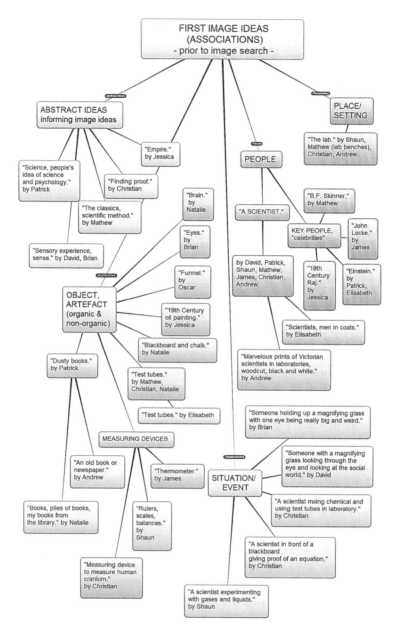

**Fig. 7.10**  Map of first image ideas

people's idea of science and technology; empire; finding proof; the classics, scientific method; sensory experience; sense. 2) **Object/artifact** (organic/non-organic) image ideas: brain; eyes; funnel; nineteenth-century oil painting; blackboard and chalk; test tubes; thermometer; rulers, scales, balances; measuring device to measure human cranium; dusty books; an old book or newspaper; book, piles of books, my books from the library, 3) People of different profiles: scientist (a general idea, expressed by seven participants) and more specific profiling as men in coats, a Victorian gentleman (marvelous prints of Victorian scientists in laboratories, woodcut, black and white, and concrete people: B.F. Skinner, Einstein, John Locke, and nineteenth-century Raj, 4) **Place/setting**: the lab, lab benches, 5) **Situation/events**: someone holding up a magnifying glass with one eye being really big and weird (Brian-pilot participant), someone with a magnifying glass looking through the eye and looking at the social world (David-pilot participant), a scientist in front of a blackboard giving proof of an equation, and a scientist experimenting with gases and liquids. Participants' image ideas were grouped according to what kind of content those ideas were related to, as shown in the diagram. Image ideas which were not generated in relation to reading the concept definition are presented in bold and bigger font (e.g., "John Locke," "Empire"). When asked for their image associations, participants developed four different image-content ideas to represent an aspect of the concept "empiricism" for concept exploration and discussion: people, objects and artifacts, situations/ events, and place/ setting.

Sometimes, the participants' first image idea (e.g., "science" by Patrick, or "physical senses" by Brian, the two pilot testing participants) was actually another "abstract idea" about the concept that guided the formation of image ideas or the search. This case is labelled as "Abstract ideas informing image ideas": although it is not an image idea *per se*, it informs the image ideas that proceeded and hence is also an image idea content category.

When it comes to "people" image ideas, the participants thought of the professions related to empiricism—"scientist"—and "key people" relevant to the concept in some way, "celebrities" to use a modern term. In terms of "objects and artifacts" image ideas, the participants thought of the artifacts that are related to empirical knowledge generation, experimenting and measuring devices as a particular subgroup. In relation to "situation/ event," a participant would describe an activity or a situation. Considering the setting idea, a participant would point at a particular setting where an activity might take place: in this case, it was the lab and classroom.

## Core, Definitional Meaning

It can be concluded that the participants' first image ideas and associations to the concept were largely reflecting the "core" meaning of the concept in terms of reliance on physical senses and scientific experimentation and measurement. Even when participants provided somewhat different and unconventional image ideas ("Empire, British Raj," or a particular "nineteenth-century oil painting" by Jessica and "funnel" by Oscar), those ideas were connected to scientific experimentation and laws that underpin it. But that was expected, and still showed a great versatility in ideas and imagination.

The first image idea was guided by thinking about the concept utterance (the word "empiricism") and reading the concept definition. It is apparent from the presented narratives that before reading the definition, participants provided more idiosyncratic image associations (empire; piles of books; rulers, scales and balances; a scientist giving a proof of equation; funnel; John Locke).

While and after reading the concept definition, many participants followed up on the concrete words they had read, developing image ideas around experimentation, such as test tubes, scientists (eighteenth-, nineteenth-century scientists, any scientist, famous scientist), lab, lab benches, doing an experiment. This is an interesting point, as some students might turn to Wikipedia and Google search to find explanations of the concept they need to think about and it might be that their images will be strongly influenced by concept definitions found, here such images are defined as stereotypical iconic.

What this means for IBCI implementation is this: if students do not go on to read and search further, their concept ideas, if they are not confident about them, may be definitional and the images may reflect such ideas as well as the narratives, possibly projecting ideas onto an image. This signals the need for guidelines to help students who do not feel confident to probe the boundaries of concept definition and therefore might stay within the boundaries. This is not to say that such ideas and images are not useful or needed: on the contrary, they are definitely needed as a starting point in concept thinking, since they point to standard definitional characteristics of the concept and these characteristics can still yield very creative and insightful ideas and image examples.

## Stereotypical Scientist

An image of a "*scientist*" was prominent among first image association (nine out of 12 participants clearly identified the term; two signaled to it implicitly (the person holding the magnifying glass by David and Brian who acted as first two pilot participants); four participants also named particular scientists (Mathew, James, Patrick and Elisabeth)). Only three out of 12 participants did not mention "scientist" as one of their first image ideas: Jessica, Oscar and Natalie.

As commonly admitted by the participants, their image of a scientist came in a form of a very stereotypical, clichéd image (an old man from the past). For example, Patrick and Mathew clearly expressed an uncomfortable awareness of providing some clichéd image ideas and commented on how important it was for the students to challenge such views. There were no modern-day scientists, women scientists, or young scientists in participants' image associations.

This shows that the participants provided image associations to concepts which were traditional, historical (here: mainly from the past), uniform and stereotypical from the outset. This might point to two possibilities: the participant simply saw the concept as inherently traditional and "old fashioned" and thus had a similar image conception of it ("an old man in a lab"). or the participant's first ideas which happen without much thinking show the images and ideas embedded in our schemata, as they echo the images most prevalent in the society, in particular dominant representations constantly promoted in the media to represent a concrete or abstract concept, for example a scientist.

It is useful to contrast this convention with the range of images produced, which offers possibilities for inferring different concept reflections and critiques in students' image-concept narratives and discussions in Project 2.

## Challenging Stereotypes
## and Supporting Metacognition

I argue that people's/students' clichéd and stereotypical (iconic[1]) image associations needs to be uncovered and articulated so that it can be discussed, explored and critiqued. Recall that the question the participants were asked was "What is *your* first image idea/ association?" If such first, spontaneous individual ideas and associations are indeed related to the definitional, common and/or stereotypical images and meanings, actually as expected, then the students will benefit from uncovering and discussing those meanings.

This is one way of helping students to be metacognitive, that is, to think about their own thinking. That is exactly what happened during the search—the participants commonly reflected critically on their own attitudes and behaviors during the search. Once such beliefs and behaviors are identified, the participant can unpack the concept further in the more critical and reflective way required in a serious academic inquiry.

Indeed, revealing and confronting first image associations provided an opportunity for the thinker to challenge them and think critically about them. Even if the participants did not go much beyond the core definition, they were all approaching the search and their thinking critically. Having a concrete example of an image to look at was a support for their reflectivity. Arguably, the image as a point of reference acted as an external trigger for metacognition.

Some participants did manage to provide more alternative concept ideas during the search as their thinking was developing (animal testing, Shaun; classroom, teaching, Andrew; researching the social world, Elisabeth, Oscar). Some developed more alternative and innovative image ideas (children painting, play-doh and shapes—Patrick, child in a coat lab—Natalie, measuring a cranium—Christian, Vesalius" woodcut of an operating theatre—Jessica). Those image ideas are not in the first image

---

[1] Note the difference between (1) iconic as socioculturally "iconic associations," such as a film or fashion icon, hence a widespread and widely adopted sociocultural symbol (linked to a person or thing), a stereotypical idea, and (2) an iconic sign and thinking in semiotics, where the iconic sign, an icon, is a type of sign.

associations diagram but can be found in individual thinking maps. The more alternative image ideas were developed as a part of the scaffolded "Thinking with Images" task, therefore, it can be expected that the students might not go much beyond the initial definition-led image ideas unless scaffolded (helped/ prompted to do so) and unless investing time in the search and concept exploration and familiarization.

## Search Words

This section approaches search from the perspective of search words inserted in the Google Images search engine by the participant. The diagram shows the participants' decisions on what search word to use in the image search process. Identifying participants' search word decisions is important, since this provides an understanding on participants behavior with technology in terms of their search strategies when using the Google Images search tool. As previously argued, there is insufficient understanding of how technology is used by students for inquiry. Therefore, this transduction will uncover how it happens in the "Thinking with Images" activity.

The diagram in Fig. 7.11 was developed as search word groupings in accordance with each participant's *first* search words inserted (the diagram lines are assigned participants' names, the diagram includes all 12 participants' search words). The students' search strategy has been defined in terms of the first search words and whether the participants follow up the concept word itself, the concept idea, or an image idea. Therefore, the diagram has three main groups created in accordance with first search words:

- **the concept** (typing the concept itself—"empiricism"—in the search engine);
- **concept idea** (typing a concept association: a term or phrase other than the word "empiricism");
- **image idea** (trying to find a particular image, mapping the search onto an image idea).

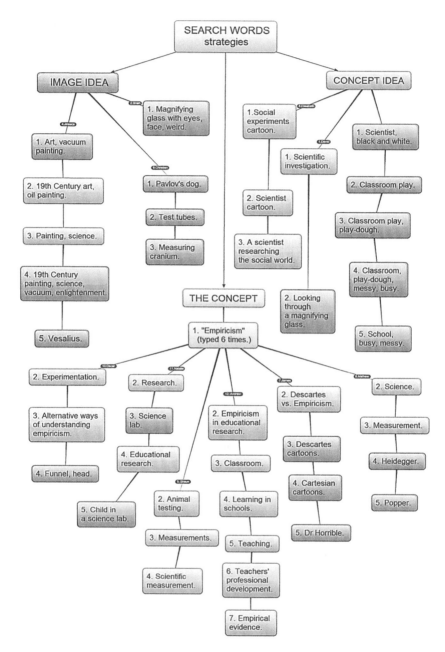

**Fig. 7.11** A variety of image search words entered by participants. (Presented in accordance with the strategies for their first entries: The concept—yellow, concept idea—pink, and image idea—orange)

I shall proceed to describe the map (Fig. 7.11) for the readers who cannot see the map and its text or distinguish colours; also, if the diagram print is monochrome, the intended diagram's colour-coded meanings would be lost. There were three key image search strategies with regard to the word(s) inserted in the search engine: image idea, concept idea, and the concept itself. **Image idea examples**: art, a painting of vacuum; magnifying glass with eyes, face; Pavlov's dog; test tubes; measuring cranium device; nineteenth-century painting showing vacuum, the period of enlightenment, Vesalius (anatomist); science lab; funnel, head; child in a science lab; looking through a magnifying glass; scientist, black and white; classroom play; classroom, play-dough; classroom, play-dough, messy, busy; school, messy, busy; Descartes cartoons; Cartesian cartoons; Dr Horrible; Heidegger; Popper. **Concept idea examples**: nineteenth-century art, oil painting; painting, science; social experiments cartoons; scientist cartoon, scientific investigation; a scientist researching the social world; experimentation; alternative ways of understanding empiricism; research; educational research; empiricism in educational research; classroom; Descartes vs. empiricism, animal testing; learning in schools, measurements, scientific measurement; teaching; teachers' professional development; empirical evidence; science. **The concept itself** meant typing "empiricism".

## Search Word Strategies

Half of the participants decided to start their search by inserting the concept word itself: "empiricism." This is interesting, since these six participants did provide some particular image or concept ideas prior to the image search, but they decided not to start the search by customizing the search in accordance to their ideas. The reason behind this, as most of them explained, was to explore and see what the engine offered. This means that they wanted to see what images had been tagged and connected with the word "empiricism" on the internet by other people. Natalie provided a particular explanation in relation to the concern as to whether her interpretation of the concept was wrong and how other people who would view her image would react, whether they would be able to relate to it or not. This is an interesting point in that it suggests that some very personalized image choices might be too challenging for interpretation.

Only Jessica, Brian and Christian started with customizing the image search to their image idea, mapping the search against the idea, whereas David, Patrick and Elisabeth decided on inserting a concept idea they wanted to explore as a starting point of their image search.

There are 49 search word entries altogether, 21 image-idea led ones, 22 concept idea/ concept aspect led ones and six "empiricism" entries. In total that means that there are 28 search words which represent some concept (including six entries which repeated the starting concept) and 21 entries altogether which were inserted with a particular image content on mind. Therefore, mapping image idea onto the search happened in fewer cases that exploratory "concept" type entry, although the difference is not great.

In the diagram, there is a great variety of search word entries produced by the 12 participants and similar choices among them happen but are rare. As they went on with their search, the participants developed more and more defined and, importantly, diverse ideas and focus of what kind of image they would like to find and/or what concept aspect to explore and consequently entered more personalized and versatile search words.

If we also consider the "concept reflection" reported via the narratives presented earlier, it can be said that the process of searching for images and viewing the result of the image search entry usefully supported the participants' reflection on the concept, concept idea development and its critical exploration.

Furthermore, the diversity of search entries to find an image as shown in the diagram provided potent opportunities for developing and exploring different concept perspectives, from the ones which are seen as "core" and "basic" (not claiming that they do represent "core" concept meanings but they strongly reflect a concept definition) to the ones that go beyond concept boundaries and explore the concept from angles other than those taken to be core. First spontaneous image ideas and associations usually had the character of reflecting the core concept meaning, whereas the participant came to novel or unconventional aspects after engaging with the process of concept and image thinking and search.

# Pedagogical Value of Thinking with Images, an IG Practice

This section reports on participants' evaluation of the pedagogical potential of the activity and the activity guidelines. All the participants endorsed the pedagogical value of the activity, with particular participants reflecting on different aspects of that value. Participants' comments were assigned with overarching themes and sub-themes which show what strength the participant saw in the activity (refer to Appendix 2 for participants' quotes that support the concluded themes)—these themes are not exclusive but relational; for example, criticality is intrinsically linked to knowledge development:

*Criticality and Critical Pedagogy, Transformative Ways of Thinking*

- Challenging stereotypes
- Deconstruction of historical artifacts
- Initiating novel way of seeing things
- Exercising students' creativity
- Showing multiple concept perspectives via representations
- Considering taken-for-granted concept aspects

*Learning and Knowledge Development*

- Acting as discussion and presentation scaffolding
- Enhancing visual literacy
- Good for learning from comparison
- Supporting personalized learning
- Acting as a memory prompt
- Selected pictures easier to critique than drawn pictures
- Developing concept understanding
- Suitable for dyslexic students
- Engaging and thought-provoking

*Challenges That Were Mentioned*

- The activity is less suitable for some disciplines
- Group dynamics: talking about images in a group was commented on as not driven by individual opinions and interpretations but more by the group dynamics
- Assessment: developing an assessment system for the activity was seen as tricky.

## Participants' Evaluation of Guidelines

This section reports participants' opinion on the image search guidelines after they looked at their image choices and tried to relate them to the guideline categories. During the process of mapping, it became clear that the guideline categories were mostly helpful but could be confusing and that they were definitely overlapping since one image could commonly fall into more than one category.

Participants' evaluations were grouped into the following categories (refer to Appendix 3 to see example of participants' quotes which support the categories below):

*General Positive Attitude: Guidelines were Useful*

Of the 12 participants, ten thought it was useful to be supported by the guidelines.

*Necessary vs. Unnecessary*

Two participants thought of them as unnecessary and one thought the opposite: that they were necessary.

*Prior vs. After the Search*

One participant thought it best to give the guidelines to the students prior to the search and one thought it best to give them to the student after the search.

*Supporting Image Interpretation*

One participant thought that it was good to use guidelines to support students' multiple perspectives during image interpretation.

# Findings in the Light of the Project's Research Questions

1. *How do Preliminary Image Associations Relate to the Abstract Concept?*

Upon hearing the abstract concept, most participants provided similar concept ideas related to science, scientists from the past and experimental method (test tubes, lab context). Their image ideas were strongly related to the core concept definition. In this case the concept was empiricism and it was largely related to experimental scientific method and sensory experience, especially so upon reading the concept definition. However, participants provide more idiosyncratic, particular concept and image ideas before they read the concept definition (e.g. "books"; "John Locke"; "funnel"; "empire"; "rulers"; "scales and balances"). With the exception of Patrick, no participant had an alternative image idea that departed from the core concept definition before starting the search.

## How Does this Inform a Pedagogic (or Learning) Design?

This suggests that it can be expected that students' first thinking and association to a concept will be strongly connected to widely used, definitional interpretation of concepts, and hence to images which illustrate those core definition meanings. It is speculated that the students in Project 2 might first read some concept definitions (from journal papers and the internet in general (e.g. Wikipedia)) in order to gain better familiarity and confidence in relation to the concept. Then, they might decide to illustrate, via an image, an aspect of the concept strongly connected to its working definition.

This is not seen as bad or unwelcome—such examples are an opportunity to strengthen students' understanding of core concepts' meanings. However, this is also seen as the first step in concept understanding, and students might need support to approach the concept from different angles in order to enhance pluralist and critical thinking.

The implication for the IBCI activity design is that the results proved the provision of IBCI guidelines reasonable for encouraging alternative ways of thinking since first associations and ideas are expected to be strongly related to core definition interpretations. The search shows how a *motivated* student would develop the search, that is, a motivated student is the one who invests time and thinking in the search, without the researcher/ tutor being there to encourage such behavior. It can be argued that the researcher's presence and prompting scaffolded the search development. When a student is alone, he/ she needs to be motivated to get into the search procedure to explore the concept, as was shown as possible. In Project 2 the students will be doing the image search exercise in private, therefore, it can be predicted that if they are supported by clear and appropriate scaffolding (task guidance and guidelines for search), they can then better positioned to develop their search and concept thinking, if motivated. Providing support and guidelines is desired but will need to be carefully planned and executed at an appropriate time and pace which will be considered and developed in Project 2.

## 2. How do Participants Use the Image Search Engine?

*(a) In terms of actual search words typed? and (b) In terms of how their search word decisions relate to their concept and image thinking?*
The participants displayed three distinct intention strategies in starting their image search, as apparent in the search words they typed:

### Concept Repetition (The Concept)
When they start their image search by typing the concept ("empiricism").

### Concept Idea-Led
When they start their search by typing an abstract idea related to the concept.

*Image Idea-Led*
When they start their search by typing the words which can be related to the description of the imagined image content (a particular image content they expect to find).

## How Does this Inform a Pedagogic Design?

None of the predispositions above promises better (or worse) reflective and critical processes; it predicts the occurrence of starting patterns in the search that the students might have in an IG activity that presupposes a digital image *search*. This is also not to say that any of the dispositions exclude the processes mentioned in the other cases.

However, it can be said that the concept-idea and image-idea led dispositions are more search engine independent than the concept-repetition one. All strategies can be developed into a substantial effort of concept exploration and thinking. It remains to be seen how the students will do it. The researcher and tutor will need to consider how to encourage all three dispositions when searching: exploring what is on offer, thinking about the concept and visualizing possibilities, as well as inferring information from visually presented information (a depiction). This is a demanding and sensitive task and the researcher would need to provide support carefully without trying to impose some sort of semiotic training or instructional spoon feeding. One way is to show those possibilities in action implicitly, during the plenary session when results and ideas are shared between students and the tutors.

3. *When Participants Browse (View) Images and Select an Image, How Does This Enable Them to Articulate Concept and Image Ideas?*

The way participants treated the images in relation to the concept and concept idea has been defined as follows:

- *Projective: image for concept idea projection/ illustration*: this happens when a participant has a particular idea that he/she wants to illustrate via an image, so the attitude toward the image is to project a particular argument or an idea onto it; the image is seen as illustration of the idea.

For example, this happens when Jessica wanted to develop an argument on the bias of involving the connection between evidence and knowledge (basically, data interpretation) using the image she remembered or when Patrick projected his idea of "hands-on activities in the classroom" onto the image he selected.

• *Analytical: image for concept idea inference*: this happens when the participant develops concept inferences using image content either referring to the meaning of the whole picture or its details (any depicted element).

For example, this happens when Shaun infers concept meaning from the depiction of the box's wooden boundary or when Oscar thinks of a microscope depicted in the picture as the tool which imposes a particular scientific reading on the viewer since there is an agreed understanding of what a cell looks like ("knowledge consumerism") or when Jessica infers the idea of historical change in concept meaning from the depiction of theatre setting.

Participants can treat one image in both ways—actually, this is a desired reaction. It is desirable since when this happens, the image has the greatest potential for conceptual thinking as it is being used both as an illustration of the point and as a trigger of creative inferences through its depicted details and the entire content. Other forms of articulation are presented in the following three sub-sections.

## Intentioned Image Effect

It is important to mention participants' definition of what kind of effect an image would have on the viewer—the results echo Reed's (2010) views on *social, cognitive* and *emotional* impact of images on learners-viewers. It can be said that all the participants were aware that the images would have some social impact, since they were intended to be shared and discussed in a group. Hence this overarching social image value would have more of a cognitive focus or an emotional focus—for example, Christian's image of test tubes shows an intention of a "cognitive" image effect—learning some "facts" about core concept properties whereas his image of the measured cranium was meant to have an emotional effect since it is more provocative and controversial. Other examples of emotional effects considered were reported by James and Elisabeth (funny, provoking), Shaun (controversial), Brian (shocking).

## Image Content and Genre Affordances

In terms of image genre, diagrams did not prove to generate notable creative or substantial concept reflection (other than stating what the diagram "says"); whereas cartoons were treated in two ways, as:

- "re-telling" the captions with interpreting and sometimes elaborating the content (James) and
- "re-wording" (changing the words) the captions relating to personal interpretation of the content (Oscar, Elisabeth).

The challenge with cartoons in creating independent and elaborated concept ideas might be if the students stay only at the level of "re-wording" and do not elaborate on the content. The challenge could be overcome if a student creates a cartoon or a panel representation herself, or add speech or thought bubbles to a chosen image or drawing.

In terms of image content in general including photographs and illustrations, *the more details the image showed, the more opportunities there were to infer concept meanings*, as noted by Christian. Christian rightly emphasized that not all images would bring equally rich ground for reflection. Hence a picture lacking in diverse elements and details might not generate much interpretative creativity. However, it is hard to define exactly what is meant by the "lack of detail," since every depiction has more than one quality (there is color, shape, position and other qualities of an individual elements shown that can be inquired—size, material, a historical development of the shown artifact, and so on). It also depends on creative inspiration and inclination by the viewer (to interpret the elements by creating a link to the concept (inferring concept meanings), as well as whether the viewer is an introvert or extrovert communicator if the interpretation is to be voiced (shy or enthusiastic about expressing opinions). An extrovert communicator who is having a creative moment or who has engaged with picture analysis before, could infer rich meaning from even a very simple picture. However, in general, pictures rich in detail should have stronger affordances relating to idea inference and exploration of meanings.

Furthermore, pictures of faces—key people's portraits for instance—seemed not to offer much potential for concept exploration. There is a potential, though, if the viewer knows some details about the person shown, although some inference could be made, for example in terms of presumed gender, age and emotion of the portrayed person.

## Image Familiarity

It seemed that if the participant was familiar with the image, he/ she was able to talk at length about it and develop connections to the concept (James talking about the Dr. Horrible image and Jessica about the Vesalius image). Hence, familiar images—either created by students or related to their prior knowledge (first remembered and then found) could generate elaborated concept reflection. It could be that being familiar with the picture inspired Jessica more to project (impose) her ideas and intentions onto the image than to look for new meanings inferences directly from the image. This might not necessarily happen: image familiarity is mainly good for concept reflection, especially an elaborated reflection.

## Language of Expression

Finally, it should be noted that, contrary to some suggestions that pictures in education are useful to "simplify" the content and support non-native speakers, the application of IG requires a wide-ranging vocabulary and a proficient level of English language, as narratives might otherwise be limited by the limitations posed by the scope of English language vocabulary and related proficiency. Although the doctoral students in this study were proficient users of English language, this proved to be something of a challenge for some non-native English speakers in the second empirical study with MA students, most of whom were international students.

## How Does this Inform a Pedagogic Design?

It can be said that images acted successfully as a point of reference for an argument and for inferring substantial, creative, novel and critical concept ideas. The participants "used" images to project their concept thinking onto them and/or to infer concept meanings from what they saw in image content. When they infer concept meanings, the image is tackled at the level of its overall meaning in terms of what the configuration shows as a whole, or in terms of particular details which got lifted for inferences (e.g. box boundary, dials, TV in the head, uniform outfit). Therefore, the project proved that images can serve to support diverse, rich and creative concept thinking. It showed how one abstract concept can be connected to its "material" manifestations via images, which triggered the reflections about the concept, which might not have been triggered otherwise. Of course, there are always gains and losses, as the image does direct thinking in a particular way, attached to its representational qualities. This case suggests how the students in the following empirical study could be expected to "use" the images they select, and then view in some form of a display—there is an expectation for the way they might treat an image—to *project* or *infer* a concept, idea or both. The researcher will need to see how the student's thinking and performance develops.

One important thing in relation to participant image choices is the mere *variety of images* resulting from their individual choices, hence generating rich opportunities for tackling different perspectives on concepts. Basically, all participants started from the same point, the same concept (empiricism) and the same purpose (an exploratory and animated discussion on the concept), but they developed their search and thinking in quite different directions (the spider diagram on images search words (Fig. 7.11) for example shows the direction in which their searching developed sequentially). A notable value of this type of thinking in relation to edusemiotics and discussed theoretical perspectives on concepts and heterogeneous and open-ended, is in a potential for sharing concept images in a learning community so that the multiplicity of concept meanings come to the foreground, for example via a display of diverse set of images.

Ten participants selected 41 images, of which only two were repeated, although the six participants who inserted the concept word viewed roughly the same set of images "on offer" as I would always give them my own laptop to do the search—all the participants did their study participation searches with me within a month and the image display on Google Images for all of them to view with the same word inserted in the search engine either did not change or changed insignificantly. This points to the prediction that although individuals might share similar starting views on the concept and themes they want to explore, even if they view the same or similar set of images, their image selections will be *personalized and particular* (geared to personal and educational interests, histories, prior knowledge, socio-cultural and identity factors, image genre and aesthetic preference, for instance for black and white photographs or cartoons).

If we imagine that one student might be asked to select one depictive image, this one image will reflect the unique choosing process and thinking of that person. Therefore, the planned activity design in the next chapter, which presents a follow-up study to this one, invites the students to share their representations and discuss a multiple representation display in order to provide a wealth of concept perspectives to unpack and critique.

4. *Do participants elaborate and develop critical and multiple perspectives during the search?*

To what extent do participants elaborate on the concept and develop critical and multiple perspectives on the concept during the search? (RQ 2.3)

The participants provided a multitude of concept ideas ("materialized concept aspects") during the search, which is the best marker of how rich a concept exploration with images can be. There were 46 instances in ten data items where participants provided a concept idea, either a participant mentioned a concept idea (without elaborating on it), 19 times, or a participant would elaborate on an idea 27 times. These numbers do not show the variety of ideas but how many times during the search a concept idea was articulated. In terms of variety, there were altogether 36 distinctly different concept ideas (see RQ 2.4. commentaries after each map), which is a considerable variety of aspects connected to one abstract concept, that of "empiricism." Those ideas might be part of a bigger concept idea or theme, such as "data interpretation," but they do represent particular angles (micro level) of looking at wider concepts (meso level) such as "doing an experiment" within the big overarching concept— "empiricism" here (meta level).

## How Does this Inform a Pedagogic Design?

The richness of concept ideas at the micro level supports the design intention to group students to share multiple representations which directly provide a context for multiple perspectives development and awareness.

One important thing in relation to RQ 2.1, 2.2 and 2.3 that needs to be taken into consideration for all cases is that the researcher's presence and encouragement might have acted as significant support and motivation for the participants to reflect on the pictures and continue their search.

This must be borne in mind once the IBCI activity is implemented. If the students start displaying behaviors which show "easy solution" type of behavior and concept thinking, the researcher will need to work out what kind of scaffolding or instructional support could encourage students to engage more substantially with the search and concept thinking.

5. *Pedagogical Potential of Thinking With Images as Identified by the Participants and the Guidelines.*

Drawing on participants' responses, the guidelines need to be carefully introduced, in a non-suggestive way, stressing that they are created to support, not as an imperative for search or set in stone instructions suggesting a limited scope of image aspects of the concept in question (in the case of guidelines this was "constructivism"). This needs to be emphasized to the students. Student creativity and personalized solutions will need to be encouraged. Yet, the guidelines were seen as necessary for the students who would do this activity for the first time and who would otherwise struggle with the search (e.g. as noted by Mathew). The balanced strategy will be to provide guidelines with a set of worked examples/ image instances linked to what the students learn in week 1 after the session, or ask the students to think of a familiar abstract concept (e.g. "education") as a warm-up activity and then, once they send their images, the researcher or teacher can introduce the guidelines in relation to the students' images and exemplify a range of possibilities about what concept aspects can be shown via images.

It is encouraging and positive that all the participants endorsed pedagogic quality and potential of this activity, as well as the guidelines, with only one seeing the guidelines as unnecessary. All the reflections were unanimously positive. Some participants had suggestions or thoughts on particular activity aspects, all showing positive side of the activity. Therefore, participants' activity evaluation confirms the pedagogical potential of an IG activity, which requires reflective engagement with images.

# Brief Summary of the "Thinking with Images" Study

This chapter offered a detailed and rich micro-level empirical findings as descriptive accounts and examples of the characteristics of thinking with images that constitutes an IG engagement/pedagogy/practice. This was to understand how external pictorial representations of a certain sort (usually photographs, but other types included such as illustrations and cartoons) enter the participants' (doctoral students in education) constructive process of creative, pluralistic and varied reflection and critical thinking. The study findings showed how thinking with images is a concept-expanding activity, that couples external and internal images with concept ideas as a new way of understanding concept and knowledge development. The chapter also concluded some challenges and weaknesses, and expectations for a learning/ pedagogic design and anticipations of student engagement within the design, which will be explored in the next chapter. Project 1 presented here shows a variety and complexity of concept thinking via images and ways of bringing together an image and a concept to form an *inquiry graphics* holistic sign exploration, a versatile image-concept, concrete-abstract way of thinking. It also exemplifies an activity which is edusemiotic in its character, foregrounding student agency, open interpretation, sharing and acknowledgement of continual concept expansion and growth. The study confirms the potential of thinking with images as reported by doctoral students, and informs the design of a teaching scenario, to link a mental world with the external world and artifacts (via images). When images are integrated into thinking and reflection processes, this can yield surprising and stimulating concept development, stereotype/subconscious bias exposure, concept boundary moving, and knowledge probing.

# References

Apple, M. W. (2004). *Ideology and curriculum* (3rd ed.). London: Routledge.
Attride-Stirling, J. (2001). Thematic networks: An analytic tool for qualitative research. *Qualitative Research, 1*, 385–405.
BERA (British Educational Research Association). (2004). Revised guidelines. Retrieved from: http://www.bera.ac.uk/guidelines.html
Braun, V., & Clarke, V. (2006). Using thematic analysis in psychology. *Qualitative Research in Psychology, 3*, 77–101.
Bryman, A. (2008). Why do researchers integrate/combine/mesh/blend/mix/merge/fuse quantitative and qualitative research. *Advances in mixed methods research,* 87–100.
Creswell, J. W., & Clark, V. L. P. (2007). *Designing and conducting mixed methods research*. Wiley Online Library.
Danos X., & Norman E. (2011). Continuity and progression in graphicacy. In *Graphicacy and modelling IDATER 2010*. Design Education Research Group, Loughborough Design School, 103–120.
Dybvig, D. D., & Dybvig, M. (2003). *Det tenkende mennesket*. Oslo: Tapir akademisk forlag. ISBN 8251918642.

Nisbett, R. E., & Wilson, T. D. (1977). Telling more than we can know: Verbal reports on mental processes. *Psychological Review, 84*, 231–259.

Reed, S. K. (2010). *Thinking visually*. Psychology Press.

Taylor, G. W., & Ussher, J. M. (2001). Making sense of S&M: A discourse analytic account. *Sexualities, 4*, 293–314.

Van Someren, M. W., Barnard, Y. F., & Sandberg, J. A. (1994). *The think aloud method: A practical guide to modelling cognitive processes*. London: Academic Press.

# 8

# Exploring Multimodal Designs in Higher Education Practice

This chapter presents a design based research via two empirical case studies applying inquiry graphics (IG) as key artifacts of multimodal higher education teaching–learning and communication mediator. The study design was trialed with MA students taking a module in educational psychology within a larger program in technology mediated learning. This empirical chapter includes examples of IG design-based research and fine-grain analysis to understand the educational potential and formation of IG at a detailed micro level analyzing of how IG is applied for learning purposes. It provides a methodology overview of the design that engaged students to think about some of the key concepts in educational psychology (e.g., constructivism or cognitive load), by choosing digital image examples of aspects of disciplinary concepts and the narrative that links the image to the concept.

The key aim of this empirical work is *an in-depth understanding of IG character* and learners' image–concept application and acts, with regard to:

- whether and how the chosen image is referenced in student IG narratives, and what those references are like;
- whether an image reference is linked to the concept, and how this multimodal anchorage happens—what it is like;

© The Author(s) 2020
N. Lacković, *Inquiry Graphics in Higher Education*,
https://doi.org/10.1007/978-3-030-39387-8_8

- what this relationship between image and concept suggests about the role of the image in the IG (image–concept) narrative;
- whether and what kind of concept themes, ideas and critical thinking are articulated in the narratives.

The findings are fine-grain micro detail descriptions of IG character. The investigation is focused on students' work, namely the created IG artifacts (IGA), consisting of an image and accompanying image–concept narrative. It must be noted that students' dialogue and their closing plenary discussions with me and the module professor are not included in the present analysis and findings. This was done in order to have one focal point, since a rich and detail- heavy IGA analysis is already provided, and adding more equally rich data would over-saturate the chapter and the book.

# Inquiry Graphics Potential in Teaching–Learning Practice: Project 2

Theoretical and empirical pillars for IG pedagogical design were built in previous chapters, and the potential and practice of thinking with images were shown in Chap. 7. The "Thinking with Images" Project 1 study endorsed the pedagogical potential of the activity in two ways. It showed how image-based thinking, and the cross-model or transduction processes it involves, supported participants to explore and theorize an assigned concept. Importantly, it showed how an abstract concept and an image merge and become an IG that brings together the concrete materiality of the world (even if the image shows an abstract painting, the colors used are concrete) with abstract scientific conceptualization. In that way, an IG is a learning artifact that challenges the separation of the abstracted and theoretical concept and knowledge from its link to the "world" and experiences/ senses that are strongly tied to materiality and sociocultural conditions and histories. Moreover, it provides an opportunity to exercise and develop reflective, multiple and critical perspectives, especially when it comes to normative "images" embedded in our subconscious that surface when participants are asked to respond with the first image that comes to mind. These "first images" tend to be stereotypically imbued with sociocultural meaning, not because the participant endorses this meaning or stereotype about a particular concept, but because these meanings have been readily endorsed and visual information viewers or consumers have seen them so many times that they have become "naturalized" in the viewers' schemata as dominant representations of a particular concept. This is one strong reason why images need to be tackled, analyzed, talked about. Finally, the previous study showed participants' positive evaluation of the activity and its pedagogical potential.

In this study, the mentioned potential is applied in an MA seminar-type learning environment mediated by technological artifacts such as a blog, VLE or whiteboard. The purpose of this design-based research project is to understand how IG and the proposed IG learning scenario works in practice.

## Study Design: DBR (Design-Based Research)

The DBR research framework aims to explore developmental trajectories of educational practice, methodologies, and tools (artifacts), as they unfold in authentic learning environments, in real time, and with real students and teachers (Cobb, Confrey, Lehrer, & Schauble, 2003). Such an environment is contrasted to a synthetic lab environment, as in Brown's (1992) pioneering work: she compared her experience in the lab with experience in the classroom and concluded that the lab environment simply cannot address the dynamic nature of classroom social interactions. DBR is usually longitudinal and it requires the researcher's active engagement for a certain (sometimes long) period. This engagement involves planning, intervention, monitoring, participation, observation and data analysis. In short, "design-based research is a collection of innovative methodological approaches that involve the building of theoretically-inspired designs to systematically generate and test theory in naturalistic settings" (Jackson, Arici, & Barab, 2005, p. 15). In this case, what was theoretically "tested" were the underpinnings of relational and multiple voicing characteristics embedded in IG creation and learning engagements. Importantly, in relation to the present project's ambitions, Bell (2004, p. 6) suggests that DBR generates better understanding of "how to orchestrate innovative learning experiences and develop new theoretical insights about the nature of learning."

A DBR approach can be adopted when it comes to understanding the effects of classroom-based practice, especially in supporting and examining pedagogical designs and innovation (Jackson et al., 2005), as sought in this present study. The proposed IG cycle represents an innovative pedagogical design which needs to be examined, refined and implemented in a naturalistic learning environment, in order to provide new insights on learning development and experience when learning with depictive images (or graphics in general). In contrast, many lab-based experimental studies which try to measure and understand the effect of new methods in education typically do not easily account for the changes occurring in time or in authentic everyday learning contexts (Amiel & Reeves, 2008).

However, as this book focuses on the analysis of narratives and not the analysis of discussions, although the research I conducted also analyzed dialogic interactions, the DBR element reported here is partial. This was purely a practical decision with regards to the book length. The reporting and discussion of dialogues would take as much space as the provided in-depth artifact analyses, findings and reflections. The iterative nature of DBR (Cobb, Confrey et al., 2003) provides a good methodological framework for the research aim of identifying various educational trajectories, mechanisms and impediments that may be related to the design and then devising practical recommendations for further theory development and application. DBR resonates with the learning theories addressed in the theoretical and conceptual Part I, in particular, perspectives on learning as adaptation and teaching as student-oriented, resonating with the edusemiotic principles, image–concept "knowledge building" over a period of time, rather than learning as indexed by immediate test results. Therefore, choosing DBR as an umbrella approach for this study is in harmony with theoretical approaches tackled earlier and is in the spirit of an edusemiotic learning design.

DBR can take different forms—for example, an educational researcher might want to develop and test new software or a professional teaching practice. The DBR aim here is to identify the development and character of learning when an IG learning design is implemented. To a certain extent it also tests and develops the potential and applications of a new pedagogical design and approach to knowledge and learning. To emphasize, the "testing" here does not imply the testing of learning outcomes, but rather the understanding of processes, learning acts, the characteristics of the created artifacts and designs, the ways in which students learning trajectories develop via student IG narratives, how they are articulated and the enriching or otherwise of conceptual development. The specific pedagogical goal in this study was student enculturation into semiotic engagement and consciousness of the relational and multiple perspectival character of a domain's body of knowledge, fostering transdisciplinary approaches to knowledge and learning. The aim was to support learners' multiple perspectives, critical and analytical thinking externalization as well as sensitivity and criticality toward visually represented information and the value and shortcomings of images. Ultimately, it aimed to initiate learners' creative growth, criticality and adaptability via such approaches, challenging neoliberal efficiency and non-relational being.

The current research adapts core features of all design-based approaches, as identified by Cobb, et al. (2003). It:

- helps to develop theories of learning and teaching (an edusemiotic theory; and a metatheory model proposed in the end);
- is interventionist (includes some sort of design that is implemented);
- takes place in a naturalistic context;

is iterative (includes introduction of small or bigger changes in order to reach an optimum design solution).

The first claim, for the generation of learning and teaching theory, is an ambitious one. Such a contribution may be of varying scale and impact, but it should always add to the domain of theory. The method is interventionist, since the author conceived a pedagogical method which is implemented as an intervention in a naturalistic context. It is also iterative, since the author was successively and thoughtfully introducing changes in the method's design. Note that those changes were not frequent and large, but gradual and carefully decided. This was so because frequent introduction of changes does not allow for the activity to take its naturalistic course inside the learning environment—with too many changes, it would be hard to claim that an effect is more than a reaction to a change's introduction rather than the change itself.

It is important to state the weaknesses of DBR approaches. DBR research is time-consuming and analytically labor-intensive, as it commonly takes place over a few years across pilot studies (e.g., Project 1) and iterations (Projects 2 and 3). In the case of the studies reported here, development took more than three years. Of course, this can be its strength, but as the resources for research tend to be limited and follow pre-defined agendas in today's research funding environment, one might struggle to maintain focus, dedication, resources and stamina exploring (only) pedagogy and teaching–learning that is not high up on research agendas. Cole and Packer (2016) point to another issue: the contingency and artificiality of the classroom environment in which DBR research is conducted, as these environments are the products of institutional practice designs themselves, and hence might make the learning focus too design-controlled. That is, although DBR has escaped the lab, it "has not escaped so far" (Cole & Packer, 2016). This means that it should be acknowledged that learning environments, whether online or face-to-face classroom-based interactions, are not "natural" settings, but "artificial, designed" environments for learning. Via this logic, any DBR or even AR that explored a learning design within an institution is a study of institutionally bound designs to identify environmentally and design-structured thinking. None the less, these settings are certainly more "natural" than lab experimental ones.

It should be acknowledged that learning happens in heterogeneous learning ecologies, and that these ecologies inevitably affect DBR, or for that matter any learning environment-situated studies. However, by stating in Part I that my approach to learning is relational, contingent, evolutionary and pluralist, I may have gone against the grain of the classical idea and implementation of DBR studies. The DBR findings reported are offered as learning design opportunities and insights that can inform practice, for teachers, researchers and managers, increasing their awareness of these opportunities for creative and reflective engagement, and enabling them to adapt their own practices, acknowledging environmental contingency.

## Contribution to DBR Studies (and to UK DBR Studies in Particular)

In a recent overview of the decade in DBR research - reviewing its history, value and impact - Anderson and Shattuck (p. 17) claim a number of learning benefits as noted in a selection of the top and most cited DBR journals between 2002 and 2012. The present research focuses on the design's potential for an improved student learning experience (where learning is understood as *"idea development"* and the ideas are examined in relation to particular thinking processes), also seeking to provide new understandings about learning with and from pictorial representations in the social sciences. Most DBR studies in the reviews occurred in the USA, but there is a growth of DBR work internationally. The present research adds to the UK DBR corpus (which according to Anderson and Shattuck (2012) was only 4% of all DBR research papers, according to the nationality of the papers' first author). US-originated papers are a massive 73% of the total. Anderson and Shattuck (2012) provide statistics which show that the number of scholarly articles published on DBR steadily increasing, from below 50 in 2002 to more than 350 articles published in 2010, many years after Brown (1992) and Collins (1992) pioneered the approach. This is a relatively new method with a promising future and a perceptible tendency to grow. Of all the DBR research papers in that period, only 13% covered higher education and only 14% investigated a technology-mediated pedagogical activity (Anderson & Shattuck, 2012) such as is the case with this research. This book, therefore, adds significantly to the growing, though still small, body of DBR projects in the UK dealing with technology-mediated pedagogical activity in the context of higher education.

Looking into the DBR research more recently, there is still a low level of DBR studies in the higher education context and in the context of studies in higher education. I highlight Bakker's (2018, p. 3) five key characteristics of design research that inspired my studies:

> The first characteristic is that its purpose is to develop theories about learning and the means that are designed to support that learning. The second characteristic is its interventionist nature. The third characteristic is that design research has prospective and reflective components that need not be separated by a trial or so-called teaching experiment. The fourth characteristic is the cyclic nature of design research: Invention and revision form an iterative process. The fifth characteristic is that the theory under development has to do real work.

## Action Research (AR) and its Relevance to this Study

The DBR approach applied in this study incorporates the perspectives of action research, a method that can be adopted by academic disciplines as a research approach. Both DBR and action research provide frameworks under which more fine-grained research methods are applied—interviewing, observation, reflective diaries, focus groups and so on. The goal of action research, like DBR, is to improve educational practice starting from theory, creating practical interventions and building new theory which emerges from that practice. Brydon-Miller, Greenwood and Maguire (2003, p. 15) acknowledge the practical value of good theory, but they emphasize that:

> theory can and should be generated through practice, and, (it) is really only useful insofar as it is put in the service of a practice focused on achieving positive social change.

What makes action research a distinctive approach is that is involves the researcher's close and intimate connection with the learning environment where the research is conducted. In AR terms, that means that a researcher commonly acts either as an "insider" working with participants (teachers/ tutors and students) or is already a practitioner (teacher/ tutor) wanting to improve and understand better their own practice. The following words of Noffke and Somekh (2009, p. 89) reflect the main character of action research: "Instead of being research on a social setting and the people within it, it is research *from inside* that setting carried out either by the participants themselves or researchers working in collaboration with them." Sometimes, action research is reduced to and criticized as "teachers doing research," implying that the teacher is not well-trained to do research. This is a selective and biased view. In the work described and analysed in this book, I am the researcher and a teacher as well, taking my dual roles seriously, assigning the same value to both roles.

The pioneering action research work in the US was conducted mainly with the aim of *bringing about social change* (e.g., the work of Lewin, 1946). In Britain, the action research tradition has been focused on researching and improving education by examining both theory and practice. However, if we think about education as a platform for civil society and social justice, then we can also see action research in education as contributing to social change or at least providing some insights or arguments for social and educational change; a contribution which might not work as an immediate and visible product but might have an impact and become visible over time.

Action research, just like design-based research, commonly involves: processes of iteration, particular activity cycles (such as problem diagnosis), decisions on action intervention which stem from practice, and reflective learning (Avison et al., 1999, p. 94). Baskerville and Myers (2004, p. 331) refer to Lewin's original iterative model of action research in six phases, which all can be subject to change and adaptation: (1) analysis, (2) fact finding, (3) conceptualization, (4) planning, (5) implementation of action, and (6) evaluation. The phases before action implementation refer to the theoretical examination of resources, literature (which then produces conceptualization of the action) and planning. The implementation of action itself may consist of many cycles of action and appropriate intervention informed by data and practice. The researcher constantly evaluates the action, analyzing the collected data.

Baskerville and Myers (2004, p. 331) argue that the underlying philosophy in most forms of action research is *pragmatism*, which aligns well with the edusemiotics position and Peirce's philosophy and his triadic sign. According to Baskerville and Myers, the four main pragmatist premises that inform action research are:

- C. S. Pierce's view on human concepts being defined by the consequences of human action.
- William James's view that (scientific) truth is embedded in practical outcome.
- Dewey's view on logic of guided inquiry, and
- G. H. Mead's view on inquiry as inseparable from social actors and context

Therefore, action research relates to the pragmatist views on concept definition as inseparable from human action and the idea of validity found in practical outcomes. For Peirce, inquiry can basically take two forms: conceptual and practical (Baskerville & Myers, 2004). Conceptual inquiry means "ideation of possible ways and ends of resolution that instigate new observations," and practical inquiry means "observational activities that include experimental operations that change existing conditions" (Baskerville & Myers, 2004, p. 332). In the case of the IG learning design, the inquiry performed within the design by the students is conceptual—ideation of possible ways and ends of resolution that instigate new observations. In the case of the DBR/AR research itself where the design is embedded, the researcher (myself) adopts both conceptual and practical inquiry.

Finally, Noffke (1997) distinguishes three approaches to action research: personal, professional and political, nearly replicating Grundy's (1982) division of practical, technical and critical. Noffke's first type introduces the personal motivation of gaining deeper knowledge of one's own practice or particular interest and usually is contained within the two other approaches. The second starts with the goal of improving what is offered in professional settings, sometimes as an improvement of a product or service, and the third has the goal of initiating social action against oppression or social injustice.

This research here is driven by both a professional and personal motive to understand teaching and learning practice as related to depictive images. Since I observe education as inherently political, I would say that the research is also political, especially if considered as a reactive activity situated in the neoliberal university. Professional motives are hardly ever separable from personal views, and a political motive is present to the extent it argues pedagogical action and the change of practice for an edu-cation of relationality, unity and multiplicity. They can all contribute to changes related to social justice awareness and practices, realized via criti-cal semiotic consciousness/ awareness.

## My Role: A Researcher–Practitioner

Action research is seen as research which is carried out by practitioners (e.g., teachers) to understand better and improve their practice. (Noffke & Somekh, 2009, p. 90). These practitioners ("insiders") usually conduct their research supported by an expert, a so-called "facilitator," who may help, develop, advise and monitor the process. There are also cases when researchers act as "outsiders" and, for example, come to a school to work with teachers under a set of mutually negotiated parameters, ethics and other agreements.

In the case of this research, I acted both as a researcher and a practitio-ner (MA course Teaching Assistant). The program professor acted both as a research facilitator (author's research advisor) and a practitioner (MA course leader). This raises an issue of blurred roles and subjectivity: one role potentially interfering with the other, bringing into question the authority and objectivity of the process. This is a fair concern, and the roles must be carefully considered and explained. Both actors approached matters with personal and professional interest but different educational background and experience. This helped with challenging each other's subjective views. It was agreed that during the activity implementation I should focus on acting as a practitioner and complete what was planned as a practitioner, whereas while dealing with the collected data, I should mainly adopt the eye of a researcher, although allowing the teaching experience to inform decision-making. The word "mainly" reflects my position that it is hard not to be subjective in any type of educational action research involving contact with humans (students), especially if this is a continuous contact with familiar students and this concerns one's own research. It simply reflects the messy and non-linear nature of edu-cational practice, which is fluid and includes tacit knowledge, on-the-spot  decision-making,  adaptation,  and  multiple  roles  for  the teacher–researcher. For example, a teacher is always a moral role model, yet the responsibilities of teacher as knowledge-building supporter and moral role model are never clearly separable.

I pragmatically aimed to employ as suitable and objective method and analysis coding as I could, in order to generate a strong and rich set of findings, although all research, analyses and findings are subjective, by embedding a researcher's stance, prior knowledge, point of view, way of seeing and interpreting. Following Peirce's quest for empirical and scientific method, I applied pragmatist lenses and devised mixed-method approaches in Projects 1, 2, and 3, with elements of quantitative counting and qualitative interpretation, scripted interviewing and multimodal designs and analyses.

At the very beginning of this research project, it was decided to devise a strategy for managing my dual role. This meant identifying and documenting responsibilities for each role, although the two were seen to inform each other. The dual role, although being challenging and impinging on objectivity, provided to me a beneficial interaction between theory and practice, that foregrounds research-informed teaching. This means that the researcher examines and understands theory by giving the action theoretical purpose and provides research-informed data handling. On the other hand, the researcher also participates in the theory's practical implementation and gains experience of the project's practical nature. This view is in accordance with the argument that higher education academics need to bring theory into practice and practice into theory, thus pursuing a research-informed practice and practice-informed research (Brydon-Miller, Greenwood, & Maguire, 2003).

Importantly, I made sure to explain to the students where I was coming from (in my views and background). I used my role as teacher as well as researcher to openly contest teacher–student power relations in learning environments, and obstacles that students faced, such as their non-native English speaking identity (ethnicity or race), providing activities and interactions that encouraged students to go beyond them. I also noticed that students felt they could relate more to the activity and defuse the power relations inherent in learning environments (Vakil, McKinney de Royston, Suad Nasir, & Kirshner, 2016), once my observations and experiences were shared. This was especially so since I am a non-native

English speaker myself, of marginal(ized) ethnicity, who was at the time a doctoral researcher and an early-career woman. I shared my own awareness with students that often, although not always, my own identity played some role, however minor, on how others make social judgments about me, that is, how they perceive me, my academic work and its quality, and in general, my ideas, mistakes, credibility, style and suggestions.

# Methodology

## Study Design Intervention and its Aims

This study explores how postgraduate MA students perform IG pedagogic activity in an authentic course context, the extent to which they integrate images and their potential for concept exploration and how, and to what extent, they develop elaborated, critical, and multiple-perspective approaches to concepts. It needs to be emphasized that the majority of students in the study are non-native English speakers, since this is the reality of the UK postgraduate system, and probably what will continue to be a rising trend globally, in light of global university internationalization efforts. In short, it will provide insight regarding how students' concept exploration is manifested in their privately generated image-narrative artifacts.

The IG learning design applied in the entire study consists of five consecutive steps, listed below; this chapter focuses only on the first three steps to understand IG created in depth (numbers 1, 2 and 3 in the list). These IG artifacts were discussed in seminar in a procedure of peer-to-peer collective and pluralistic sharing, showing the full scope of an IG design.

1) *Assigning a concept*: Tutor assigns a disciplinary key concept for students that is regarded by the tutor/ teacher as a key, potentially a threshold, concept to explore and understand better; an alternative design could be to ask students to vote and suggest a concept themselves.

2) *Private exploration*: Students engage with the concept-related material and resources, for instance, uploading onto the VLE platform of their program/ course, and selecting an image to represent one concept aspect of their choice. They are encouraged to create an image themselves, for instance by taking a photograph.

3) *Private concept grounding—a multimodal ensemble*: students write a narrative on how the image represents something about the concept and upload that onto their VLE "image blog" or discussion thread, in this case visible to the tutor/ teacher only. An alternative is simply to share images in a forum.

4) *Peer-to-peer discussion*: Students come to the classroom and, in this case of a small group of MA students, form two small groups to discuss concept ideas with peers in relation to a screen display of their images that had been prepared by the teacher/ teacher assistant; groups change group leaders each time when reporting on their discussion.

5) *Plenary session and tutor feedback*: Tutor/ teacher joins the groups for discussion summary and to provide personal interpretations of students' images and also give feedback to the students' narratives, where appropriate, provide extra feedback via students' blogs and/or e-mails (Fig. 8.1).

## Overarching Aims and Main Research Questions

The IG study explores how MA students who are also teachers develop their understanding of concepts by introducing pictures into their private and social thinking, thereby exploiting and challenging concept definitional pronouncement and boundaries by engaging in an inquiry graphics design.

Aim 1 is investigating students' artifacts (steps 1, 2, 3). This involves investigation of the variations, character and richness (or the lack thereof) in concept articulation within student-generated artifacts, relating to steps 1, 2 and 3 (note that this chapter does not cover steps 4 and 5). The aim is defined here in terms of how an image may mediate concept-related reflection, criticality and multiple-perspective attitudes as part of an integrated IG artifact. The act of selecting an image to represent a

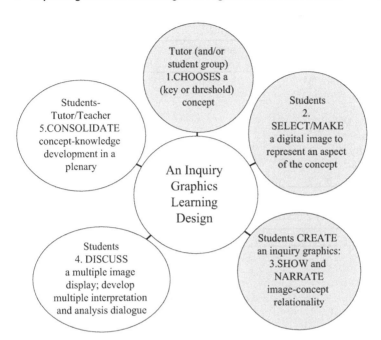

**Fig. 8.1** An IG learning design activity steps/ acts. (Only the findings for steps 1, 2 and 3 are presented here.)

concept and constructing a personal concept interpretation ("narrative reflection") through it is seen as creative—however, the level of creativity achieved is expected to vary, as will the level of criticality. The central research question associated with this aim is:

RQ: What roles and characteristics of inquiry graphics' image–concept relationality can be concluded in the students' image–concept (IG) narratives?

## Participants

Participants were MA students in the University of Nottingham School of Education. The activity was identified as part of the course's novel pedagogy. Table 8.1 summarizes participants' gender, age and status as home or international student. Names are fictional. Most participants had teaching experience.

Table 8.1  IG Project 2 participants

| ID | MA participant pseudonym and reported gender | UK/ International | Teaching level |
|----|-----------------------------------------------|-------------------|----------------|
| P1 | Lewis, Male (M) | UK | College |
| P2 | Becky, Female (F) | International | Primary |
| P3 | Sylvia, F | International | Primary |
| P4 | Alex, M | International | Tertiary |
| P5 | Nick, M | International | Primary |
| P6 | Penny, F | UK | No teaching |
| P7 | Marjan, F | International | Primary |
| P8 | Lily, F | International | Primary |

Table 8.2  Project 2 list of concepts for the seminar session scheduled

| Order (of seminars) | Key concepts and their abbreviations |
|---------------------|--------------------------------------|
| 1. | Constructivism (Con) |
| 2. | Remembering (Rem) |
| 3. | Metacognition (Met) |
| 4. | Classroom (Cla) |
| 5. | Scaffolding (Sca) |
| 6. | Reusable learning objects (RLO) |
| 7. | Cultural tools (CulT) |
| 8. | Cognitive load (CogL) |

International students commonly outnumber UK students on this course. This signals the relevance of English as a second language in the activity's communication dynamic, which will be only briefly reflected on later in the discussion section of this book. The constituency defined in Table 8.1 is representative of UK postgraduate courses, and all students had passed English language requirements for admission.

## Ethical Considerations

Introduction of the activity was in accordance with institutional ethical requirements. Students were provided with a "project information sheet" in order to explain the project and to respect both the (approved) ethical research procedure and compliance with BERA's "Revised Ethical guidelines for Educational Research" (BERA, 2004). As stated in Sect. 4.5, participants were informed as to the reasons and nature of the project and the extent of engagement that was expected. The information explained that students would be performing a task related to a broadly defined research area. The task did not compromise students and they were free to opt out at any stage.

My dual role of both researcher and TA (Teaching Assistant) on the module could also be seen as problematic. However, it was managed by setting up clear responsibilities and focus for each role (researcher and teacher). It is not possible to separate the two totally, but this is in the spirit of action research—an example which promotes research-informed practice and practice-informed research as a core principle in the academic profession. It is acknowledged, though, that it was difficult for the participants to opt out of the pedagogical intervention itself, but they did have the freedom not to participate in the research. However, opting out was certainly made less likely due to the pedagogical character of the research. These tensions and power relations are acknowledged, but without them, there would be no action research, as there are already rare opportunities to do it in any in-depth and longitudinal way. The activity was embedded in the module as it was recognized as a part of the program and module development.

## Instructional Support Resources

Instructional support was provided in a number of ways:

- Introductory seminar (1 hour). This introduced the activity, explaining its educational potential and various indirect links to the course objectives. The resource was a PowerPoint presentation.
- Activity instruction e-mail. An e-mail was sent to the whole group after the introductory seminar with the introductory PowerPoint presentation and a step-by-step activity guide.
- Technical instruction e-mails. Further e-mails provided step-by-step explanations on setting up VLE image blogs and how to blog.

## Introduction to the Activity and Preparation

At the end of their first session (on "behaviorism"), students were introduced to the activity. The rationale of the image-based activity for student learning was explained as a planned pedagogical model, as well as its connection to this research and the character of the intervention. The power relations between the design creators (the researcher as module assistant and the professor of the program) and students was honestly acknowledged, as the activity was an integral part of the module design and pedagogy. The students were advised to treat it as any other activity and to engage as much or as little as they wanted. Indeed, not all the students were not present each time. Not to put pressure on students to do the image activity each week, groups of four were convened in accordance with random allocation to engage with the images each week, making sure that everyone was included fairly. The rest of the students would engage with the content via traditional verbal text and discussions.

Research information sheets and consent forms were distributed. Students were left alone to sign (or not sign) the sheets or take the form home if they wanted to reflect on it. It was explained that they would be selecting images to represent tutor-assigned concepts each week and that after this session they would be sent a worked example for the first concept, "Association" and the guidelines (introduced in Chap. 7 in the guidelines descriptions provided before Tables 7.2 and 7.3). Therefore, after the session, the guidelines, with possible examples of versatile concept approaches and selections regarding images and image–concept relations, were sent to the students, in order to provide their own ideas for the concept "association."

As noted earlier, students' discussion and the plenary session results are not reported, but I stress that they did play an important part of the whole learning design. The discussions were structured around a display of student-chosen images. The students would discuss them first on their own, then they would summarize their discussions in a tutor–student plenary session. The tutors provided feedback to the chosen images, narratives and student summaries. This created a holistic sense of shared knowledge, acknowledgment of students' interpretation and tutors' feedback on the current concept knowledge. These results are not reported here, mainly due to the limits in the scope of the book, but the dialogic engagements were an important part of the activity design.

# Inquiry Graphics Artifacts (IGAs): Analytic Methods

Due to the large and rich scope of data, this chapter tackles in-depth only Inquiry Graphics Artifacts (student provided images and image narratives), and not peer or plenary discussions.

**RQ 1 method:** Collection of 29 IGAs for eight seminar sessions

This section first presents the theoretical model that shapes specific IGA research questions, subsequent IGA coding and analysis, followed by results.

## Peirce-Inspired Concept-Image IG Model for Analysis: Informing RQs and IGA Analyses

Peirce's semiotic image(picture)–concept model presented in Chap. 3 directs the definition of specific IGA RQs and the subsequent analyses. It presents what there is in an image that could possibly be "exploited" for concept inference. It was explained in Chap. 3 that "Representation" (equivalent to Pierce's "Representamen"), within an image meaning-making model, refers to what is depicted in a picture, the particular meaning of the represented elements. This ingredient helps defining the type of image reference. It is the first level of interpretation which names what is depicted (Representamen, or Representation aspect). As a matter of reminder and reference, the model from Chap. 3 is shown again below in Fig. 8.2.

To evoke the discussion and model of the IG sign diagrams in Chap. 3, Fig. 8.10 represents a simple model of how an image can be interrogated with regard to its meaning-making structure within the IG design, by considering how an image and the concepts it is related to are brought together. The main feature of that model is that interpretation and object are twofold: they refer both to the image depiction and existence and the meaning and existence of the concept. The generation of concept ideas and creativity stem from creating links between representation

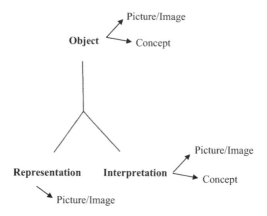

Fig. 8.2   A simple version of an Edusemiotic IG sign model (of meaning-making)

(embodied Representamen's materiality, the depicted), an interpretation of the depicted composition (interpretation) and the concept it refers to (object). It could be considered that the Representamen is twofold as well as the name (in the form of a word) of the concept is superimposed over representation. These characteristics represent opportunities for analysis and inquiry. This is important to understand since it helps define to what extent and how image semiotic characteristics and interpretative opportunities were applied and served the concept narrative.

The two ingredients of image triadic structural characteristics, adapted in the analytical figure as representation and interpretation, can be further theoretically strengthened by Barthes' (1977) views on image denotation and connotation. They inform the development of research questions for IGAs and the creation of relevant analytical codes. It is important to say that every structural ingredient is connected to another and cannot "work" on its own: semiosis happens always at an intersection of representation–interpretation–object. Individual ingredients are singled out for scrutiny and to lead analysis. It must be noted that Representation involves interpretation. Therefore, in order to differentiate those two sides of the model, Representation is related to naming individual elements within picture composition and their meanings, and the meaning of the picture composition as a whole. Interpretation here is a step beyond that where the depicted is referred to in relation to some contexts, task, circumstances, intention and audience. For exploratory educational purposes, the context is shaped by the demand for the picture to represent something about the concept. Representation, Interpretation and Object have been chosen as more classical words than Peirce's (embodied) Representamen and Interpretant for analytical purposes and wider terminology accessibility, discussed in further detail in the following sub-sections.

## Representation (Representamen-denotation)

In the analysis I performed I defend Representation as linked to Representamen pictorial content and the denotation linked to this content. I focused on identifying pictorial image representation as the level of what can be understood as the most basic meaning of the depicted by identifying its elements/ features. It has a strongly descriptive character (describing and naming what is depicted or naming the activity depicted).

*Element* = anything observable in the picture, the meaning of the individual picture element: the presumed identity characteristic, objects, it can include spatial positioning (how are elements positioned, not what that position means), gaze (direction of human gaze). To put it simply, those are the details we see in the picture (adapted from Kress & van Leeuwen, 1996, pp. 74, 75):

• Depicted participants (active) and non-participants (passive): the participant(s) of a depicted action process (humans, animals), either active or passive participants (Kress & van Leeuwen (1996, p. 74), define these participants as "actor" and "goal"). Non-participants are not necessarily participants of an action observed.
• Depicted objects: any object together with or without a viewer-perceived (interpreted) role, a part of an action or not.
• Depicted abstractions: any abstract depiction which does not depict identifiable humans, animals or objects.
• Depicted setting: the setting shown in the picture, with or without any action
• Depicted action: the action happening (a moment of an activity depicted), if the picture depicts an action (*image denotation* as description of action, *image connotation* as the meaning of depicted action), which can also contain:

- Gaze: where the depicted human or animal is looking at (Kress & van Leeuwen, 1996, p. 154); label the gaze which looks at the viewer as "demand" (Martinec & Salway, 2005).
- Proximity: spatial relations between and among the depicted ingredients (e.g., sitting close to each other, in the background, in the foreground, standing–sitting and so on).

Certainly, there are more possibilities. The examples extracted here are seen as the most comprehensive and sufficient for the purpose of this activity and to understand image role in developing a concept narrative.

*Configuration* = the assemblage of the features, the meaning of the picture's composition (what picture means as a whole)—there are two steps distinguished here in image configural meaning. If the elements depicted are boy, girl, a black pentagon and white hexagon ball and the action is running, then configural meaning is both: "a boy and a girl are running after a black pentagon and white hexagon ball" and "a boy and a girl are playing soccer." Both are image configural meanings at different levels of sociocultural interpretation (the more descriptive and the more socio-cultural one).

## Interpretation Anchorage: Concept–Image Connotation

In this activity, the focus of the analysis is on connotation in terms of *how an image is anchored* (linked) to the concept as mentioned earlier. That happens when concept meaning is attributed to the image, here called "anchorage," adapted from Barthes (1977), also "multimodal anchorage," as it is about how a concept and image come together.

According to Barthes (1977), "anchorage" explains how an image is used to lead and direct the viewer toward a certain intended meaning (concept). Usually, captions and labels anchor image meanings in advertisements or newspapers. However, in this analysis, anchorage represents a link between the picture and the assigned concept in a student's narrative. The quality of concept narrative is defined on the basis of what is said about the concept (developed later in this section)—this is expected to happen with an anchorage (link to the image), but it may not be the case.

When the image element or the meaning of configuration is only mentioned in the students' narrative at a descriptive level (naming the action or elements), without linking it to the concept, such image treatment in narratives is termed *(image) "reference."* Whenever this reference is anchored to the concept (meaning that some commentary about the concept follows from precedes that reference), this is termed *"anchorage."* Finally, there is a need to look at the narrative content and how an anchorage is used to provide concept insights. Fig. 8.11 refers to how these structural semiotic entities of image reference and concept anchorage are embedded in the triangulation of image semiosis (Representation (an aspect of Representamen)–Interpretation/ Interpretant–Object).

## Concept/ Conceptual Object

This is the assigned (connected) concept object superimposed over the pictorial object in the analysis. It represents a special case of conceptual object cross-fertilized with image denotation–connotation, in one work anchorage (concept–image connotation, when conceptual object is brought into relationship with the pictorial sign) (Fig. 8.3).

The model serves to *focus attention* on one aspect/ node of it, that is: pictorial representation/ image, interpretation and concept, *not to*

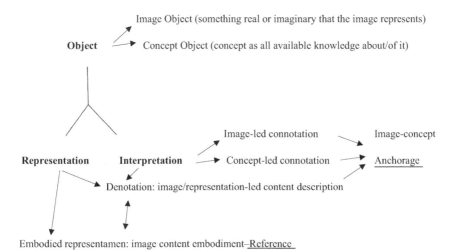

**Fig. 8.3** A detailed IG analytical picture–concept model for IGA analyses

*separate them.* The key analytical elements are underlined—reference and anchorage. Humans assign concepts to images. For example, an image showing a rose is an image of something in the world (its object) that in this case we collectively call a plant, a plant species, a rose. "Rose" is its image-based *reference* (at the level of embodied representation *naming*); we can and do assign descriptions (image-led Interpretation) to rose. e.g., at the denotative level of interpretative descriptions, e.g., its petals are white, fresh and succulent with dew drops (image-led denotation). This could, for example, connote the concept of beauty, innocence and health, and other symbolisms assigned to rose and other characteristics (image-led connotations). If the assigned concept for exploration is, say, "persuasion," then this concept will be explored via these image-led descriptions and connotations. It must be noted that image-led connotations are symbols directly linked to the depictive qualities, and concept-led connotations infuse a new concept, that would not be directly linked to the depictive quality or the rose itself, thus opening up an entirely new way of thinking. Due to the complexity of the model, the analysis focuses on: *anchorage* as the act of bringing together an aspect or aspects of image and concept in one holistic IG sign, and it focuses on reference, to understand how anchorage relates to image referencing (or the lack thereof), varied forms of reference and anchorage, and the way that the concept and images are actually narrated in IGA (inquiry graphics artifacts).

Considering the semiotic characteristics explained above, RQ1 was developed to define analytical focus with three sub-questions to RQ1:

*Focusing research question (RQ) 1:*
How are IGAs defined in relation to (1) image reference, (2) anchorage and (3) the quality of the IG narrative?
*Sub-questions*
On (Image) Reference
RQ 1.1: Whether the image is referenced in the narrative, and if so, how?
On (Multimodal/ Image–Concept) AnchorageRQ 1.2: Whether an image reference is applied: is it anchored to the concept and if so, how? (What does it suggest about the role of the image in the concept narrative?)
On Multimodal Narrative Quality (Criticality, Insight)
RQ 1.3: What is the quality of an IGA narrative? In particular, whether and what kind of concept themes and critical thinking are articulated in the narratives?

# IGA (Concept–Image Narrative) Analysis and Coding Strategy

IGA analytical strategy codes were devised both inductively from an in-depth engagement with the narrative and deductively from the Peirce's diagrammatic sign in Chap. 3 meaning that the formation of the codes was first influenced by the established theoretical base of structural meaning-making model, but engaging with the narrative helped in shaping particular coding types.

There are three main coding foci, to answer three main RQs, that build the portrait of the created IGAs, which were devised having familiarized myself with the IGAs provided:

1. image reference (IG image focus);
2. anchorage (IG image–concept focus and narration);
3. concept narration (IG concept focus).

### Reference: Image Element/ Configuration

Reference (Image Reference) = the point where the text refers to the picture: this reference to the picture happens by either referring to the picture as its compositional meaning or to one or more of its elements (constituents of that composition). An image reference can be explicit (configural and element reference) and implicit (metaphor reference):

* Configural
* Element
* Metaphorical

When we consider Representation and its structural properties, there are two different types of *explicit* reference, where the student either mentions the picture's holistic meaning or any of its compositional features—an element:

1. Configural/ Holistic Image Reference = the meaning of the picture/ quotation configuration (what it means as a whole): the narrative

mentions a picture's configural meaning and simply describes the depicted matter, for example, "a boy and a girl are doing a chemistry experiment"; there is a sentence that explicitly points at the meaning of the picture as composition/ configuration.

2. Element/Feature Image Reference = referring to one or more picture features in an explanation. Feature/ element accounts for anything that can be extracted to have individual meaning: in a picture of a classroom, for example, some elements might be: chairs, books, desks, children's clothes, pencils, a boy, a girl, a teacher, walls.

There is another possibility for *implicit* reference when there is no direct mentioning of the picture or quotation in the narrative but an element or meaning is presented metaphorically. This case is also some sort of reference, here called "metaphorical reference."

3. Metaphorical Image Reference = implicit reference to the image or picture in the narrative: there is no explicit reference, but metaphorical meaning is assumed (some element is referred to metaphorically; for instance, a depiction of a "brain" is referred to as "mind," as a brain can be symbolically referred to as mind, or stacked microchip codes may symbolically be referred to as a "brain").

## (Multimodal) Anchorage: Linking Image and Concept, Image–Concept Connotation

This considers how the narrative is realized focusing on an interpretation of the concept connected to a particular anchorage to the image.

1. Configural Anchorage: stems from configural reference: the artifact is responded to in terms of its apparent holistic/ compositional meaning which then creates the base for concept commentary. This commentary is the manner of narrating the configural reference, that is, narrating the link between the picture configural meaning and the concept meaning.

2. Elements anchorage: stems from element reference: a particular image element is highlighted as the base of some concept commentary (e.g., in a picture showing a person with a book, the book is taken to be

commented on, or the profession/ feelings of the person is commented on, as relating to the concept (the concept does not have to be explicitly mentioned, but, if it is, the anchorage is made clearer and stronger).
3. Metaphor anchorage: observed to:

* stem from element/ configural metaphor reference—a comment on a metaphor reference; and/or
* there is no literal, direct and documented reference to the image in the narrative; the image is taken to be a metaphor for the narrative without any explicit image mention or explanations.

## Concept Idea: Generation of Ideas in Concept-Image Narratives

This analytical angle looked at how the narrative is realized focusing on an interpretation of the concept connected to a particular anchorage to the image.

* *Main concept idea* (main CI) is to mark the key idea; it is the theme/ idea that links the image and the concept most explicitly; it leads the narrative; it is a dominant idea, usually accompanied by its sub-ideas or additional concept ideas. It usually contains a "configural reference" (e.g., constructivism as happening by allowing children to freely explore an experiment, linked to the picture showing children interacting around artifacts).
* *Sub-ideas* (sub-CI): when the narrative develop ideas related to the main idea, this is a sub-idea (sub-CI) of main idea (e.g.in relation to the main idea above of free experimentation in constructivism, a new related idea is introduced, considering this activity as giving "ownership" to children)
* *(New) concept idea* (CI) = a distinctive idea or insight related to the concept, but a novel and/or different insight adding to the main idea; a distinctive point made about the concept. For example, constructivism as happening by allowing children to freely explore an experiment was used as one main concept idea, but then a new idea introduced an interest in what this means for formative assessment and another one questioned the entire system of evaluation.

If the narrative contains one or two concept ideas that could be, this is also coded as CI. Sub-CI and CI when accompanying MCI are treated as concept elaborations since they add to the main idea.

- Concept declaration (CD) = something is said about the concept that can stand on its own without the picture or any anchorage made, as there is no clear or logical connection to picture or the anchoring of the picture to the concept statement; statements about the concept are definition-based and formulaic (as if copy–pasted from textbook). Concept statements stand like entities independent from the reference made, as there is no logical linking between them (for example, first describing the picture and then providing a definition of constructivism, without making a link between the two).
- Concept Critical Inference (CCI) = critical commentary about the concept. It involves identifying issues and tensions about the concept anchored to the picture. There is a critical insight and/or conclusion, or something is remarked and/or asked thanks to a tension, ambiguity and inspiration found in the image–concept link. Sometimes if the image is taken metaphorically, its elements are explicit in CCI.
- Evaluation = something qualitative about the concept is evaluated via adjectives, it is expected to be connected to picture description; e.g., something is good, bad, desirable, true, problematic.

Two more features were noted in relation to concept content and anchorage action:

- Comparison: two images are compared in order to make a concept point if a student provides more than one image, for example as a collaged image.
- Example/ Exemplification = providing an example as a way of linking image and concept, invoking a concrete instance that illustrates a concept idea mentioned in the narrative, can be contained in a concept idea. It is an illustrative example when real life situations are described, usually as a first-person example from personal life, but also a third person example from someone else's life.

## IGA Data Visualizations: IGA Maps

IGAs were first coded on the basis of respective coding grid and then that coded table was used to extract key instances for the defined codes and to present them visually in what I have termed "visual coding maps." I used a digital mind-mapping software to create the coding maps. This was a lengthy but rewarding process, since it required double checking all the coded material and provided a further opportunity for in-depth consideration and reflection on analytical codes and their meanings and relationships.

Figure 8.12 presents a color coding legend for all the maps on individual concepts and the artifacts sent by students for those concepts. It replicates the codes of the coding grid strategy and codes introduced above. It serves as an introduction to the visual coding maps. Those maps show a display of students' images, usually four of them in one map, grouped under eight different concepts and the coded characteristics of image accompanied narratives, with examples of key points and summaries of concept ideas (CI, main CI, sub-CI). The maps show coding decisions. It is acknowledged that the map font size might be difficult to read due to the intention to show a full map per page. The mapping software (spiderscribe) allows zooming and clear viewing of the content, whereas the affordances of the page are different, and some images that I exported from the platform were less readable than others. Therefore, the visual coding maps serve the purpose of showing how the data were systematically transformed and coded in the mode of visual maps. These are included as they can be informative and interesting for readers; the findings will also be provided in tables and in the text (Figs. 8.4, 8.5, 8.6, 8.7, 8.8, 8.9, 8.10, 8.11 and 8.12).

# The Findings: Characterizing Inquiry Graphics as Applied by Students

Summary findings tables were created from the eight analytical maps presented in Figs. 8.5, 8.6, 8.7, 8.8, 8.9, 8.10, 8.11 and 8.12, focusing on relevant IGA research questions:

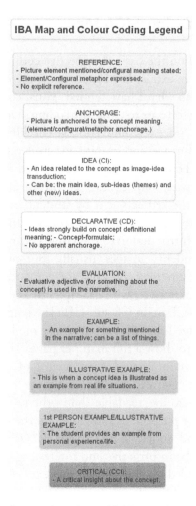

Fig. 8.4   Map color coding to show how thinking pathways map were created

- On image reference and anchorage:
  - *RQ 1.1*: RQ 1.1: Whether the image is referenced in the narrative, and if so, how?
  - *RQ 1.2*: Whether an image reference is applied: is it anchored to the concept and if so, how? (What does it suggest about the role of the image in the concept narrative?)

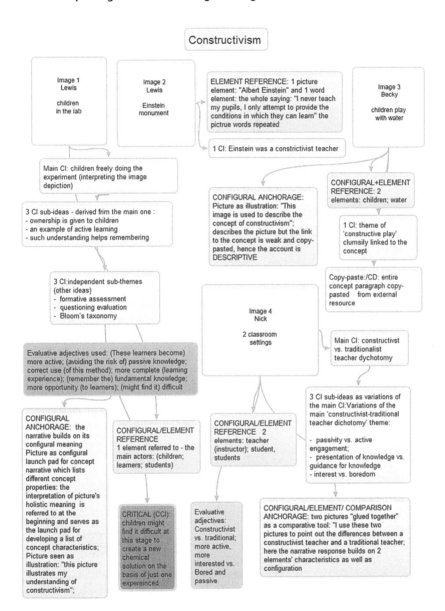

**Fig. 8.5** "Constructivism" IGA map

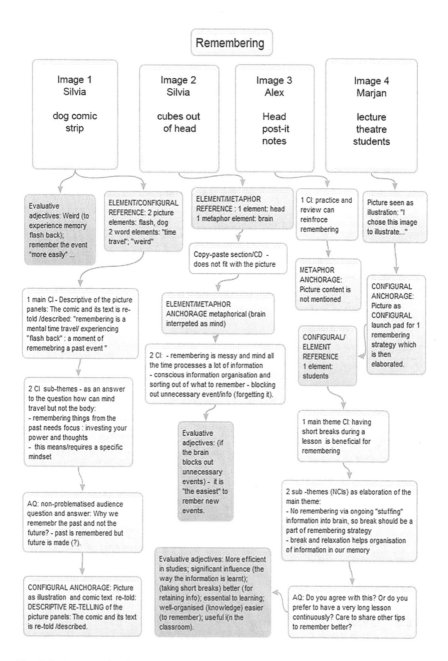

**Fig. 8.6** "Remembering" IGA map

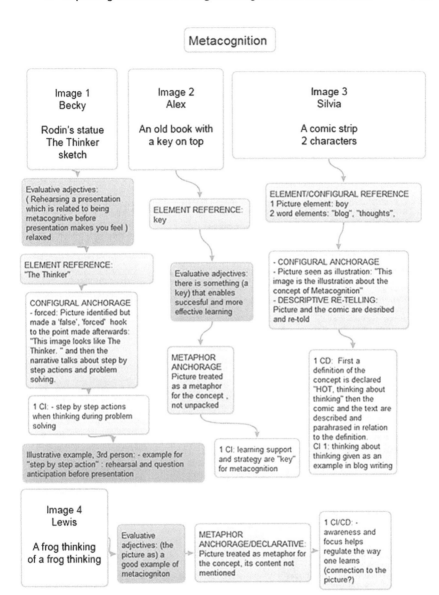

Fig. 8.7   "Metacognition" IGA map

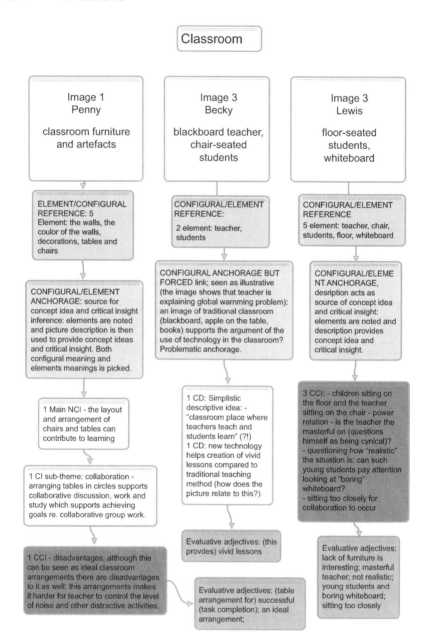

**Fig. 8.8** "Classroom" IGA map

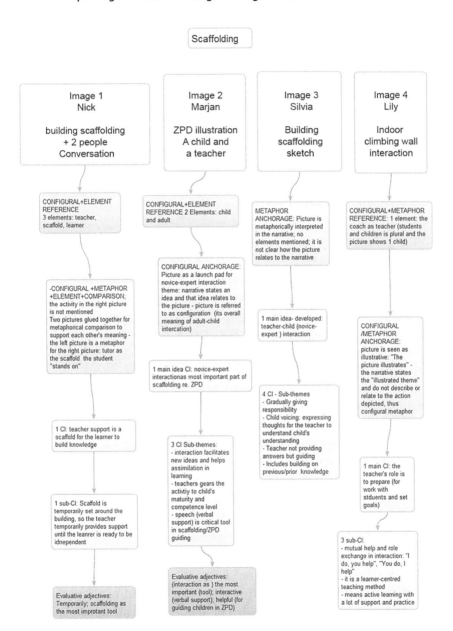

**Fig. 8.9** "Scaffolding" IGA map

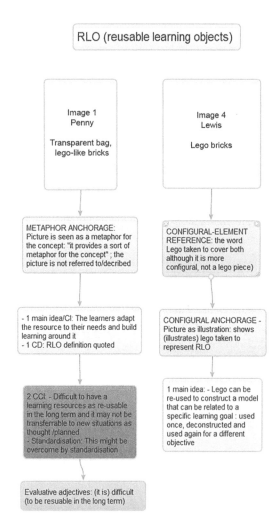

**Fig. 8.10** "RLO" IGA map

- **On image narrative conceptual quality:**
    - *RQ 1.3*: What is the quality of the IGA narrative in relation to pedagogical aims? That is, what kind of concept themes and critical thinking are articulated?

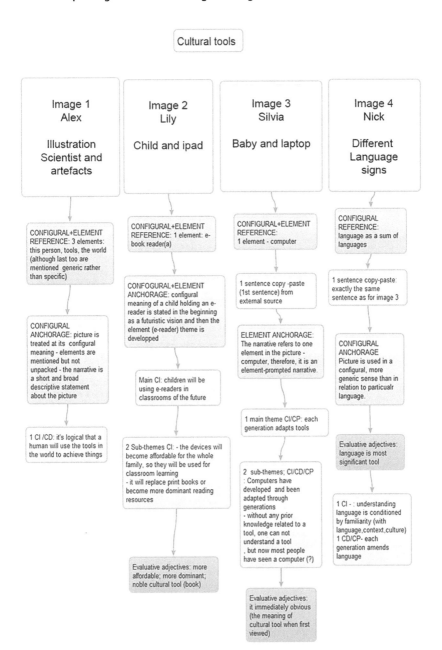

**Fig. 8.11** "Cultural tools" IGA map

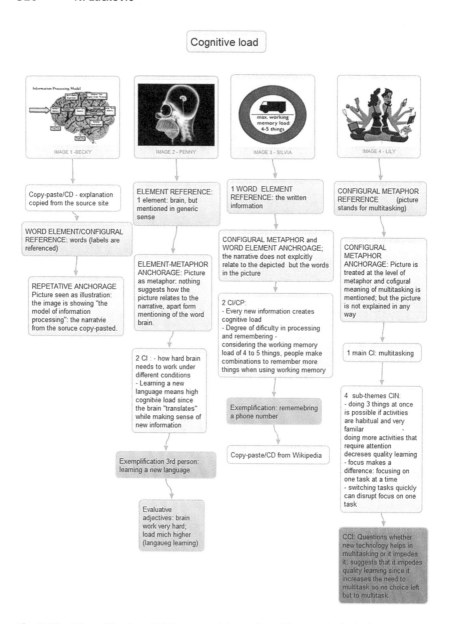

**Fig. 8.12**   "Cognitive Load" IGA map with students' images included

Table 8.3 shows that in 29 narratives reference was made most often to an element in the picture, mainly in combination with configural picture reference. I looked at how many times they occurred in the total of 29 narratives—one narrative might have several reference types. Altogether, a picture element (including a represented word in one case) was mentioned in 24 narratives, as 15 narratives with configural metaphor also had an element metaphor. Four narratives did not mention any image reference. The mentioning of the word in the picture only or with other references was noted as a specific "word element."

Configural picture meaning was mentioned in 15 cases (on its own only once and the rest of the time in combination with other reference types). No reference to the picture was found in four cases. That means that, in most cases, picture content is noted in the narrative and commonly both configural and element reference was made. However, configural and element referencing is different from inferring concept relevance, that is, whether and how any reference was anchored to the concept; this will be presented in Table 8.5 on anchorage–reference relationship.

Table 8.3 A range of image references types and occurrence frequency in IGA narratives

| Image reference types across all 29 narratives | Frequency of image type reference occurrence |
| --- | --- |
| No image reference | 4 of 29 |
| Element reference (total for all narratives) | 24 of 29 |
| Picture element reference only | 6 |
| Word element reference only | 1 |
| Picture element reference + picture element metaphor | 2 |
| Picture element metaphor | 1 |
| Configural references (total for all narratives) | 15 of 29 |
| Configural + picture element | 9 |
| Configural + word element | 1 |
| Configural metaphor | 1 |
| Configural–element (for pictures showing a group of elements that are of the same kind: Lego pieces stack, language names all representing a language) | 2 |
| Configural + word element + picture element | 2 |

Reference to an element on its own was also categorized in terms of content being animate (human or animal) or inanimate (object) in order to understand what kind of picture element is referenced most: humans, animals or objects (non-animate entities). Table 8.4 shows the distribution of element type across narratives.

The sum of *39 referenced picture elements* (19 humans; 19 objects and 1 animal) in 29 narratives suggest that image animate and inanimate material elements are referenced, albeit partially, since every picture contains at least two easily noticeable elements (except RLO2, which strictly points at Lego pieces), which accounts for *at least 57 easily noticeable picture elements that could be unpacked. No plants as animate beings were referenced* and only one plant occurred in one image. As an example of an easily noticeable element in the picture Con 1 (from Table 8.4), one can easily identify goggles that children are wearing and that they are holding some dishes (chemical dishes). Objects are less referenced than humans which suggests an anthropocentric relationship to images as students focus on stating the image actors (humans) first and foremost; attention is not given to picture details and things as much as could potentially be the case. The "easily noticeable elements" do not include any nuanced semiotic element identification, like elements within elements (such as eye gaze, hands, proximity, positioning and gender; recall that the Con 1 picture of "children doing an experiment" was dealt with extensively in Chap. 3 as an example of how elements can mediate a rich concept exploration).

Although most pictures were quite simplistic in their element content (Met 2; Rem 3; RLO2), there were also pictures rich in elements, for example CulT 1 and Cog L4: there are six elements clearly visible in CulT1 (after all, the theme was cultural tools) and eight elements in CogL 4, offering a possible fertile ground for concept-element reference and creative elaboration, but none of those 14 elements were mentioned in the accompanying narratives. Although the photographs were referenced in the narratives, both at configural and element level, a finer consideration of and reflection on picture elements and their characteristics that could inform concept reflection were not developed in student narratives.

Table 8.4 Image material element types referenced across narratives: human, object, animal

| Image no. | Concepts | | | | | | | |
|---|---|---|---|---|---|---|---|---|
| | Con | Rem | Met | Cla | Sca | RLO | CulT | CogL |
| 1 | 1 hu | 1 ani + ob | 1 hu | 5 ob | 2 hu + ob | 1 ob | hu + ob | — |
| 2 | 1 hu | 1 ob | 1 ob | 2 hu | 2 hu | — | 2ob + hu | 1 ob |
| 3 | 1 hu +1 ob | — | 1 hu | 2hu + 3o b | — | | 1 ob | — |
| 4 | 2hu | 1 hu | — | | 1 hu | | | |
| Sum (39) | 65 hu+1 ob | 4 hu+ani+2 ob | 32 hu+ 1 ob | 128 ob + 4 hu | 65 hu +1 ob | 11 ob | 64 ob+2 hu | 11 ob |

hu = human; ob = object; ani = animal; concept abbreviations (see Table 8.2): Constructivism (Con); Remembering (Rem); Metacognition (Met); Classroom (Cla); Scaffolding (Sca); Reusable learning objects (RLO); Cultural tools (CulT); Cognitive load (CogL)

**Table 8.5** Types of IG references and anchorage across students concept narratives

| Image no. | Reference (Ref) Anchorage (Anc) | Con | Rem | Met | Cla | Sca | RLO | CulT | CogL |
|---|---|---|---|---|---|---|---|---|---|
| | | | | | | Concepts | | | |
| 1 | Ref | C + E | C + E | E | C + E | E + EM | None | C + E | C + E |
| | Anc | C | C csr | CM fo | C + E | C + EM + Co | M | C | C + E/ cp |
| 2 | Ref | E | E + EM | E | C + E | C + E | C-E | E | E |
| | Anc | E | E + EM | EM + CM | C fo | C | C | C + E | EM |
| 3 | Ref | C + E | None | E + C | C + E | None | — | E | E |
| | Anc | C/cp | M | C csr | C + E | M | | E/cp | CM + E/cp |
| 4 | Ref | C + E | C + E | None | — | EM | | C-E | CM |
| | Anc | C + E + Co | C | M | | CM | | C/cp | CM |

Ref = Reference; Anc = Anchorage; C = configural; E = element; EM = element metaphor; CM = configural metaphor; C-E = configural-element; csr = comic strip re-telling; Co = Comparison; fo = forced; cp = copy-paste; Con = Constructivism (and other abbreviations as introduced earlier); different shade applied for distinguishing Ref–Anc pairs

To answer RQ1.2, all the anchorage types in the visual maps were considered. Table 8.5 shows all the anchorage types realized in narratives in relation to its reference type.

Table 8.5 shows that most of the time picture anchorage is configural, often realized in combination with an element and/or metaphor anchorage. This points at the role of metaphors in making image–concept anchorage as metaphorical analogy. Configural reference, whenever it occurred (alone or in combination with another reference) was developed into configural anchorage in all cases (it is whenever "C" occurs in both Ref and Anc in an individual IGA 1-4 across eight concepts).

Out of 24 element reference combinations, only half were further "used" as the base for creating a concept inference (point/ idea) based on that reference (when a C+E reference has only a C anchorage rather than a C+E anchorage). This finding suggests that although picture elements were widely noted, they were not unpacked or tackled in many of the referenced cases to make a concept point/ idea, whereas configural reference was in most cases developed into a point/idea about the concept or was a concept idea alone (configural reference can be a part of the concept idea, e.g., free experimentation for constructivism and students having a break as a remembering strategy for remembering). This means that the picture was mostly treated at its configural meaning as the support for a concept point—for example, in case of Rem 4, the meaning of the picture as "students having a break" is then taken as the basis for pointing out that having a break is good for students' memory and hence coming to "remembering strategies."

There were two cases of picture comparisons—this is innovative and independent engagement since the student took the initiative himself to compare two pictures. The so-called forced anchorage occurred where it seems that the pictures served as an imposed, forced anchorage to the narrative (the narrative does not relate explicitly to the picture, although it is claimed to do so in the text—for instance Cla 2 and Met 1 in visualization maps). There were also cases of metaphor anchorage—it happened in the cases of no reference to the picture and when there was also a configural or element metaphor. Therefore, when a picture is not referenced in the narrative at all, this is not something bad per se. However, it was surprising, considering that the task asked the students to explain in their narratives how the picture related to the concept, even if it served as the concept meaning's metaphorical illustration (e.g., Rem 3, RLO1). This signals the commonplace importance placed on the concept rather than the picture, as the concept is treated as important to report on, and the picture as an embellishment.

In the cases of narratives that contained the main concept idea, and sub-ideas and other ideas, it was common to make a reference to the picture (usually configural reference) and then spin off the concept "story" from there. This kind of use of the picture here for launching the concept narrative has been termed a "launch pad," evoking the "projective" role of the image. There appears to be two different types of projective, launch pad strategies:

- Launch pad into concept ideas (image Con 1)
- Launch pad into idea elaboration (images: Rem 4; Cla 1; Sca 4; CulT 2; CulT 3; CogL 4)

The variation when the picture is referenced and then the same reference is developed into an idea elaboration (sub-ideas) was much more common than an introduction of new concept ideas.

## How Was the Image Role in an IG Defined in the Narratives by Students?

I also considered how the students themselves referred to the image in their narratives; pictures were mostly seen as "illustrations" and "visual metaphors," having an illustrative role to support the narrative (text) rather than being the resource for concept inquiry. Their illustrative role was taken as "given" and that is why the picture was mostly treated at configural anchorage level. The students' language to define the image role in 11 narratives was as follows (students' words in quotation marks):

- Illustrative role:

  - The image *"illustrates"* a point—this view was expressed in five narratives: Lewis (Con1), Marjan (Sca), Lily (Sca, Penny (CogL), Silvia (Met).
  - The *image is "showing"* (= illustrates): Becky (CogL).
  - This image is *"used to describe"* the concept: (= illustrates): (Becky, Con).

- Metaphor role: The image *"is a metaphor"* for the concept: Penny (RLO1)

However. there were few cases (three) when some other role than illustrative or metaphor was mentioned, as linked to image affective and persuasive character:

- Emotional role: The image *makes me feel*: Alex (Met).
- Suggestive role: The image *suggests*: Silvia (Rem).
- Comparative role: I use these two pictures to *point out the difference*— Nick (Con).

The students did not use words that would overtly relate to thinking and reflection, such as "it can be concluded or inferred from the image," the image "supports," "mediates," "helps," "reflecting," or similar.

## The Quality of IGA Concept Narratives in Terms of Creative Insights

The type of reference and relevant anchorage informs how the picture was treated in students' narratives and how it was related to the concept but it does not tell us about the quality of that concept narrative. There was a hope, if not an expectation, that the narratives would show a fair amount of critical and reflective thinking about the concept. Critical thinking was marked in the case of IGA coding via the code CCI (=critical concept insight). The cases of CMI (concept main idea) and sub-ideas and additional/other ideas developed in one narrative were taken to be the sign of reflective thinking, as well as a case of picture comparison. Table 8.6 shows qualitative IGA content profiles, that is: unique formula for each IG narrative consisting of concept content codes (Table 8.6). A novel code was added (AQ = audience questioning) to signify when a rhetorical question is asked to an imaginary audience, but no answer is offered.

**Table 8.6** Number and variety of qualitative concept content in IG narratives

| | |
|---|---|
| CI (concept idea) | 16 |
| CD (concept definitional idea; formulaic) | 5 |
| CP (copy-paste text) | 5 |
| MCI (main concept idea) | 1 |
| MCI+CP | 12 |
| Sub-CI (sub idea to the MCI) | 26 |
| CCI (critical concept insight) | 8 |
| E (example/list) | 3 |
| AQ (audience questioning) | 2 |

What can be concluded is that IGA narratives did not feature many critical insights: only eight critical concept insights altogether were present only in five narratives out of 29. However, they did generate many creative concept ideas: 36 concept ideas (MCI, CI, E, including CCI) and 26 elaborative commentaries on the main concept idea (sub-CI), which is a sum of 62 varied concept perspectives altogether that were not definitional or copy-pasted. Eleven concept ideas were merely definitional and some also included copy-pasted content. If we consider that the students are concept novices, this is still an excellent result, although the occurrence of copy-pasted material was worrying as the source was not reported, and was easy to detect (I would run sentences in the Google search engine, but even before finding exact wording on a website, I was able to spot the odd one out).

# Design Iteration Reflection

## Creative Thinking

One of the pedagogical aims of IG is to support students' creative thinking. IGAs did generate creative narratives with insights that might not have occurred without images. To recap: creativity in this book is seen in terms of *how novel the assemblage of the available resources is and how an image–concept coupling energize new ways of thinking*. Therefore, the transmodal nature of image–language IGA assemblage required re-invention of the picture's meaning by creating an image–concept anchorage. The very nature of inferring concept ideas from images that might not have been meant to refer to the concept by the author(s) who uploaded them on the internet is a greater challenge to creative thinking and reflection than merely inferring ideas from the text that *is* in fact about the concept. These acts are tightly connected to transmodality and multimodal transduction, where meanings are interrelated, also in some way "translated," and shift across modes. What distinguishes an IG is that it encourages the view of concepts as transmodal.

However, it might be that the student image narrative paraphrased the textual resource where the image was found on the internet, if there was one, and if it "talked" about the concept (presumably after typing the concept in Google image engine, this could have happened). An attempt to detect such cases was related to identifying any "copy–paste" cases from the internet, made by inserting the narratives into Google search to see whether anything in the narratives was copy-pasted. Such cases were indeed noted.

## Multiplicity: Multiple Perspectives on Concepts and Community Sharing

Supporting the development of multiple perspectives and communally shared understanding on concepts was one of the pedagogical aims to enhance students' concept understanding. This was achieved through the opportunity provided to the students to discuss their images and quotations on the basis of a multiple-representation display. There was a variety of four images to discuss each week and that was a fertile platform for forming multiple perspectives on concepts.

However, the students could benefit even more from the image display if that display showed more images and if two student groups discussed them separately and then they all convened in one big plenary session. This would also allow more equal support in plenaries, since this time the students received support from either the course leader or TA. All in all, there were opportunities for multiple sharing of perspectives. However, in spite of the opportunities to first engage with the concept in private, create their own narratives and then share their artifacts with their peers, students struggled to be resource-analytical, concept–image imaginative and critical, except in few cases. This signals, perhaps, that the exercise is understood in a particular way (a compulsory activity or a chore), the image is not being adopted in a deeper way. Specific analytical support might be needed to support students' reflection, and that they might not engage with the concept material sufficiently and therefore fail to assemble enough initial concept understanding or idea before choosing an image. This will inform the activity design and its instructional guidance.

## Picture Content Selection: Stereotypical vs. Alternative

If we look at the image selection, there seemed to be a common pattern of choosing a picture that would attempt to support some core meaning of the concept in most cases (see scaffolding pictures). The students tried to find a more alternative depiction in much fewer cases, commonly treating the picture as a metaphor for the concept (Met 2). This poses a question as to whether the students should be encouraged to think about their picture selection in both ways: as in iconic, commonly recognizable depiction related to the concept but also as a challenge and alternative to an iconic depiction. This would encourage students to think about the concept more. Arguably, it is hard to be critical and challenge the concept if there is not enough confidence about what the concept core meaning is.

The question suggests an instructional change toward the selection of two images—an iconic and an alternative one (possibly related to the guidelines varieties). This resonates with Christian's idea from Project 1 to encourage students to find different image contents relating to the guidelines. This would support the need to understand the core meaning but also go beyond that boundary. The risk with this method is that the students might resist "seeing" any concept meaning if the depicted happens to be perhaps too personalized or alternative (this resonates with Natalie's comment in Project 1). Nevertheless, this challenge might be solved by tutor selection of images to be displayed in the discussion, where there should be a balance of more common and more challenging depictions. Hence further design recommendation is:

- Ask students to select two pictures: an iconic one and an alternative one (informed by the guidelines but not prescribed).

## Support to See: Images Acting as Illustrations Rather than Analytic Source

Images were mostly treated as illustrative resources rather than the source of analysis for concept inference. Arguably, this is not an easy task for concept novices. The students were not provided with any picture semiotic training. This was in order to understand to what extent they would actually infer meanings from the pictures (their configuration and elements) and develop critical insights from those meanings, without any excessive training, but with sufficient guidelines provided. In most of the cases picture configural meaning or its elements were mentioned (the picture was referenced in the narrative) but only in five cases was this taken further to serve concept problematization. Most of the time, the picture would serve the purpose of being related to some concept idea and reflection All in all, the images in IGAs mainly had the role of:

- visual metaphor for the narrative;
- narrative illustration (see below).

## Narrative Illustration Via Images as a "Launch Pad"

A pattern of "launch pad" occurred when the configural and/or element picture reference and meaning was provided in the beginning and linked to the concept, and then this meaning was the basis for an elaboration on that concept meaning (in most cases within this pattern) or a list of concept characteristics, without referring back to the image. It was as if the narratives did so to tick the box of referencing the image and then continued with the "real" stuff of discussing the concept. An important finding is that in most cases, the picture did not represent to the students a source to be analyzed itself in order to infer concept insights across levels of semiosis (image denotation–connotation). Picture elements were not readily unpacked to lead to concept ideas and insights. Therefore, it can be concluded that it is hard for students to infer concept meaning from a picture element, unless they are provided with more explicit training and instructional support (e.g., different task design). This support needs to be based on the principles of image meaning-making theories in combination with critical thinking principles, perhaps avoiding semiotic terminology in practice, as it might be too specialist so use alternative terms (indeed, I acknowledge the opacity of Peirce's terminology). In particular, students did not scrutinize the picture: the picture was in most cases glanced at to recall Sless's (1981) words, rather than scrutinized to support creative concept exploration and critique.

In order to get the most out of the picture as a narrative support, the suggestion is to treat it both at its configuration and element-meaning level. Students need to be prompted to notice picture elements as a resource, they need worked examples and more support in understanding how this can be done prior to the activity. The following recommendation for design improvement stems from the findings:

• provide more support in understanding the analytical potential and semiotic picture structure, without being too specialist and obscure in semiotic terminology.

# Support to Go Deeper in Conceptualization: Hard to Infer and Hard to Be Critical

This section tackles the issue of the lack of concept problematization in relation to a picture. All the narratives contained concept ideas. If we consider the benefit of rehearsing the core concept meaning, which is certainly necessary when concept understanding is at an underdeveloped level, every idea expressed was beneficial for the strengthening of concept understanding. Therefore, every artifact the students made and discussed helped them strengthen their threshold concepts and move from the periphery of being a student novice toward being a professional who can be called an "educational technologist" (a possible profile and expertise promoted by the course).

Sometimes, those ideas were rather similar for one concept and disappointingly repetitive. For example, it seems that one published text was the basis for all ideas expressed in both IGA and QBA for the "cultural tools" concept. It was rephrased and copied across all narratives. Although the pictures in IGAs provided a rich variety of opportunities to infer different concept ideas (which happened in few cases), in a fair number of cases the narratives provided a basic, definitional concept meaning and the picture was not used to support an elaboration of that meaning. Those were characterized as weak narratives, and in many cases, "weak to average" lies barely above "weak," and "average" goes only a small step further. So, narrative weakness or strength were defined in terms of concept inference and ideas' quality and richness. In essence, it was hard for students to go beyond concept statements; they had difficulties in problematizing the concept and providing critical insights on them.

The following recommendations for design improvement stem from such findings:

- provide more support in showing the steps of concept inference and adapt instructional requirements to explicitly point at different levels of concept inference and actively encourage problematization and critique;
- in order to encourage more engagement with concept literature before exploring the concept creatively, students need to report on their thinking prior to selection and report how they selected an image.

These changes will be explained in Project 3.

## Identifying Tutor Support

Faced with the constructivist dilemma of whether and to what extent to provide explicit and stronger guidance and support, the answer is: do a lot of preparation and induction. Students were sent guidance e-mails, they had a presentation on different concept aspects, they were provided with the guidelines, they were provided with many examples of how to do a more substantial inquiry during the plenaries by the tutors. Yet, the extent to which the guidelines were used is questionable.

Drawing on the results, the following recommendation for design improvement is offered:

- Provide regular reminders and support to students on how they can improve their engagement and narrative quality; praise good work in e-mails and write e-mails to individual students if they are struggling with any aspect of the activity.
- Ask students to devise an activity design iteration or activity themselves, ask for student suggestions, invite student design solutions.

# Overarching Lessons for Activity Design Improvement

The following insights have been generated to further inform IG activity design:

- *Transduction complexity*: Turning abstract concepts into visual representations and screen hypertext is not as straightforward and easy as might be thought; more guidance and student-relevant, engaging worked examples are needed.
- *Bypassing*: Students found ways to bypass serious engagement with the task *in private*. This was manifest in the lack of concept generalization and critique stemming from the picture. The design and task requirements can and needs to be shaped to encourage students to invest the necessary familiarization and creative effort in the task.
- *Learners' action visibility*: there is a need to make learning actions more visible (such as making learners' image search 'visible' by reporting on how the search was performed in this case and report on distinctive thinking cycles, such as first ideas, image and concept interpretation and link, concept generalization and critique). This might trigger more effort to perform more serious engagement. If we compare Project 1 with Project 2, it seems that my presence in Project 1 (as well as the student doctoral researcher status) could be one of the drivers of the activity to unravel and gain critical impetus—a similar kind of scaffolding "presence" could be "simulated" via carefully worded task requirements for narrative writing.

The design recommendations will be implemented in a final empirical passage in an attempt to devise an improved design. Chapter 9 will be an overall conceptual–theoretical commentary on Part I and the empirical studies in Part II. It will point to discussion patterns and success achieved with improved quality of image-based narratives which in some cases surpassed activity requirements and my expectations as a teacher-researcher of this DBR/AR longitudinal study.

# Project 3: An Overview of the Next Design Iteration

After Project 2, a new cohort of MA students arrived. I revised the activity design with the same aims as in Project 2.

## Participants

Participants were, again, MA students, a new cohort. Table 8.7 classifies participants as home or international, and records their teaching experience status. Names are fictional. Most participants had teaching.

**Ethical considerations:** Ethical considerations remain as explained in Section 8.2.4.

## Guidance Resource

Instructional support built on the recommendations identified. However, it was much strengthened, although it retained the same structure. The following recommendations were implemented in this project iteration:

*Introductory Seminar Featuring Students' Image Contributions*

The seminar introduced the activity, explaining its educational potential and the links to course objectives. The change introduced here was students' own contribution to presentation. Therefore, one week before the seminar, students did a "warm-up" image exercise, returning any

**Table 8.7** Project 3 participants

|   | Name/ Gender | UK/ International | Teaching |
|---|---|---|---|
| A | Jarvis, M | UK | Adults |
| B | Mary, F | International–EU | All ages |
| C | Victoria, F | UK | Primary |
| D | Jack, M | International | Primary |
| E | Sophie, F | International | No |
| F | Justin, M | International | Primary |
| G | Amy, F | International–EU | Primary |
| H | Elliot, M | International | Primary |
| I | Jay, M | International | Primary |

image representing the concept "education." They were encouraged to think about the concept from different perspectives. It was specified that the image should not contain any words. Their images were incorporated into the introductory seminar PowerPoint slides as worked examples of different approaches to the concept. One was picked for analysis to show how images' holistic meaning and particular details (elements) can serve concept inferences and insights.

*Guiding e-mails*

An e-mail was sent to the whole group after the introductory seminar with the introductory presentation and a step-by-step activity guide. There was no quotation group but, rather, author/ non-author groups. It was explained that they would swap groups to discuss either their own images or the ones of the other group in order to gain more varied experience from the activity. The course leader provided step-by-step explanations on setting up VLE image blogs and how to blog.

*Major CHANGE in Multimodal IG Narrative Activity Instruction*

Chapter 6 stated that the students were failing to engage deeply with the concept and needed to be more reflective, analytical and critical of both image and concept. More explicit structuring of the narrative was provided, compatible with structural semiotic principles. Students were first advised to structure their narratives in the following way:

1) *First thoughts*: define concept idea focus after exploration/reading.
2) *Finding an image*: report on how you selected/created/searched for an image.
3) *Interpretation*: interpret the image and how it relates to the concept reflectively and critically.

It became clear after two sessions that they were still struggling to go beyond inferring general concept meaning (concept generalization) to provide a critical insight, therefore the levels of inference were explained as illustrated below and given to the students as a reminder (Fig. 8.13).

In accordance with the diagram, the narrative structuring scaffolding was further improved with requests for reporting/reflecting on:

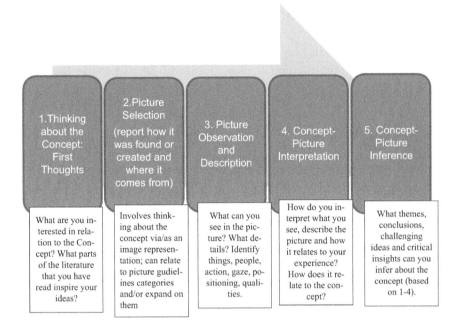

**Fig. 8.13**  Concept–image IG activity design steps: activity improvement iteration

1. First thought;
2. route to the image (report on how the image was selected/ created/ searched for);
3. interpretation (image observation and image–concept interpretation);
4. generalization and critique (concept inference).

*Group and Individual Blog, e-mail Feedback and Meetings*

Students uploaded images and accompanying explanatory and reflective narratives on their blog—the tutor and researcher would comment on those. The researcher would also write individual e-mails when necessary to clarify or to send appraisal and encouragement. But now students were asked to meet the researcher/ teacher to discuss possible difficulties.

# Target Concepts and Their Assignments

As in Project 2, the tutor assigned a concept for each upcoming week that built upon the last teaching session. Table 8.8 identifies the concepts discussed.

## Activity Introduction

Students were introduced to the activity during their first session. The rationale of the image-based activity for student learning was explained, this time in a more explicit manner, as well as its connection to this research project and the character of the intervention as an innovative design. Research information sheets and consent forms were distributed. It was explained that they would be selecting images to support their thinking about the concepts they were learning each week. An hour seminar as an introduction to the activity was agreed in the following session, which I built around students' images. I asked the students to send me images which would depict "education" in some way. The guidelines concerning versatile concept and image approaches and selections were also introduced and discussed in that session. The guidelines were distributed after the session. The students were particularly encouraged to invent their own guideline categories and reassured that one image usually fell into a few categories.

**Table 8.8** A list of Project 3 concepts explored in seminars with abbreviations

| Order of seminars | Key concepts and their abbreviations |
|---|---|
| 1. | Reinforcement (Rei) |
| 2. | Instruction (Ins) |
| 3. | Constructivism (Con) |
| 4. | Classroom (Cla) |
| 5. | Orchestrating learning (OrcL) |
| 6. | Metacognition (Met) |
| 7. | Cultural tools (CulT) |
| 8. | Cognitive load (CogL) |

# Results Overview from the Follow-Up Project 3

Students had various approaches to the concepts and selected images that represented a range of topics related to them. There was an explicit demand for two images from each student: an iconic one and an "alternative" one. Students were advised to consult the guidelines for alternative image ideas or invent approaches of their own. This required thinking about the concept from two different angles and prevented the "bypassing" of a more serious engagement with the concept in private, as was symptomatic in the previous study.

Students talked about the concept and the picture more in relation to their own experience. There were five cases of students' personal photos. Once, a student took a photo about the concept while going to the supermarket, realizing that one situation was an interesting concept example. This indicates that the concept and activity thinking occupied the students mind into everyday actions.

Furthermore, narrative structure requirements to report on the route to the image and first thoughts were also seen as supportive of deeper engagement. Encouraging students to report how they thought about the concept and how they reached the image created a "window" into their private work. In fact, there is a correlation between not reporting on first thoughts or image routes and the absence of critical insight and concept generalization: when a student did not provide this "report," the narrative was weak (lacking in quality, reflective and critical insight). This is indicative of the importance of such reporting and narrative structuring to stimulate deeper engagement.

Out of all the reported strategies to select an image, only three were exactly repeating the concept: typing "instruction, constructivism, classroom" into Google images search engine—all other cases were either combinations of the concept and other words or other words altogether and quite particular words at times (e.g., "Underbank," "female Afghani pilots," "pamper pole," "national proverb"). This is suggestive of the students' efforts to find an image by first thinking about the concept and, eventually, making their image selection more autonomous.

This "autonomy" represents a certain level of "autonomy" from the image offered by Google images' algorithm (the images previously tagged to relate to the concept). Therefore, having been advised to report their image route, the students also gained awareness that reporting on "just" inserted the concept would perhaps suggest the "easy way round" this task. Hence, they took more control of the search engine. This means that user autonomy is weaker when typing the concept since the decision on which image to represent the concept is more shaped by the engine algorithm. However, user autonomy is higher in the case of more personal suggestions of the kind of image the algorithm should search for. The more particular and personalized the words, the more engine-autonomous the search. This is not to say that by "just" typing the concept, the user would not be able to explore the concept usefully and infer creative and deep thoughts.

Section 8.11 comments further on the findings, adding examples and extracts from students' narratives to illustrate the points made.

# Reflective Insights and Criticality

Reflectivity and criticality were strong in the narratives. The following list shows my paraphrasing of reflective anchorage made by students, as well as critical points for each concept to illustrate cases of subtly nuanced reflective and critical thinking:

## Reinforcement: Examples of Reflective and Critical Thought in Students' Narratives

*Example 1 (Picture of a Man in a Blue Shirt)*
*Reflective:* The example of a "blue collar worker" as "roboticized" and the hard position of working classes having to "do whatever ordered" as such. The description taken to infer the meaning of "automaticity" in behavior: factory production and workers turned into "robots."
*Critical:*

- Reinforcement strategy can be given priority to the behavior and its meaning (expectations or reward, praise).
- Reinforcement strategies in education may be problematic and condition instrumental behaviors in adulthood.
- Reinforcement strategy can cause addictive behaviors.
- Reinforcement strategies can be used to "enslave" people.

*Example 2 (Picture of Potty Training)*
*Reflective*: The example of potty training and the feelings of happiness the picture emits due to the successful training; Non-material reinforcement; not a material reward—a smile—is taken as an example of positive reinforcement in potty training strategy alongside the colorful stickers play (material "reward" strategy)

*Example 3 (Skinner box illustration)*
*Critical*: Critical insight about teaching reinforcement and the difference in interpretation and seeing: reinforcement image and its interpretation by differently "trained" eyes: how differently trained people (e.g., engineers (experts) vs. children (novices)) will be looking for different properties of pictures.

*Example 4 (RAF Parade)*
*Reflective*:

- Effectiveness of didactic reinforcement by didactic training: repetition drill and practice in the army (RAF); aggressive instructional attitude toward failure to comply with instructions/commands
- Reinforcement strategy is directly connected to feelings and conditioning by feeling: if the drill is connected to negative emotions, the memory of the drill is connected to negative emotions as well (compared to the Little Albert experiment)

*Critical*: Reinforcement strategies are used to generate uniform behaviors which do not account for people's individual personalities.

*Example 5 (Skinner Box Photograph)*
*Reflective*: Whiteness of the box suggestive of clinical feel of the experiment which is contrasted to reinforcement in education which cannot be cold and clinical.

*Critical*: Reinforcement cannot be generalized across humans, and Skinner's experiment with rats cannot be merely transported in the classroom: individuals (children) need adaptations of strategies.

## Instruction: Selected Examples of Reflective and Critical Thought

*Example 1 (The Poster "Your Country Needs You")*
*Reflective*: The message on the poster is a type of an order which actually works as an instruction to men to go and fight for their country; linking order and instruction; media message and instruction.
*Critical*: propaganda is implicitly "instructive" using a statement as both an order and instruction
*Example 2 (Snapshot of Black and White Illustration)*
*Reflective*: Instruction in the classroom needs a variety of media tools to mediate it.
*Critical*: the current technology and media climate dictates that, no excuse not to turn to multimedia instruction—are paradigms really changing from the teacher as holder of knowledge into the teacher as guide/scaffolder?
*Example 3 (Photo: Teacher in Front of Students, Whiteboard)*
*Critical*: Rare to have the full, undivided attention of all pupils at once; the classroom is never as spotless as this one; questioning whether the image shows a genuine classroom event or whether it is a staged representation of instruction
*Example 5 (Horizontal Photo: Four Students and the Teacher's Hand)*
*Critical*: Instruction to the whole class is contrasted to the instruction to individual students, the latter as a more personalized one but due to the limited lesson time less practiced; a challenge of a mixed-type instruction to fluctuate between the class as a whole and individual students
*Example 6 (The Driving Lesson Photo)*
*Critical*: Instruction can be stressful and not enjoyable which questions the "image" of instruction promoted in the media, like in the case of driving or educational promo images—they commonly do not show the "bad" side of instruction (unpleasantness, frustration, tiredness,

nervousness and so on); this then generalized into a reflection about general beautifications of social media images, and also image control and management.

## Constructivism: Selected Examples of Reflective and Critical Thought

*Example 1 (The Baby and the Cobra Video Snapshot)*
*Reflective*: The link between the baby's fearlessness and the lack of prior experience and understanding that cobras bite with deadly poison; hence, prior experience—which affects learning in new situations - is an important point in constructivism
*Example 2 (Three Children Using Shovels)*
*Reflective*: The link between the difference in how the children are using shovels and their schema of the same activity; hence participating in apparently the same kind of "constructivist" activity, different people can have different ideas and experiences of that activity.
*Example 3 (The Illustration with the Pear Tree, the Person Lying Down and Eating a Pear)*
*Reflective*: The proverb "Waiting for a ripe pear to fall into your mouth" is linked to the idea of passivity and instrumentalism, of learners interested in "one truth," which poses challenges to the realization of constructivist learning.
*Critical*:

- Students' instrumental orientation toward learning prevails but you can't just blame the students: their resistance and reluctance to be constructivist learners (it's easier to be told what to do and what to learn) is reinforced by the system—and also the discrepancy between teachers' and students' expectations and attitudes
- The education system needs to reinforce different views on education and not act as the rope in the picture limiting (killing) students' creativity and awareness of the existence of truth that comes through their own selves, rather than the prescribed truth. Such orientation, reinforced by the educational system's drive toward prescribed answers, kills creativity.

*Example 4 (The Learner Showing Hands Covered in Blue Paint)*
*Critical:* too much playing, not enough learning?—but this is challenged on the basis that prescribed goals of pre-school curriculum can and need to be reached through the kind of constructive play as depicted in the picture.
*Example 5 (Children in a Sand Pit)*
*Critical:* Is playing learning? The student argues that learning can be and, especially for nursery learners, should be, discovery and play-based and experiential: it is particularly good as a transitional link between informal domestic learning and formal structured learning in primary school.
*Example 6 (Stacked Lego Brick)*
*Critical:* The question of how are experiences stacked and the existence of dominant experiences of higher importance (the top brick?); the stacked bricks are neatly layered but experiences do not neatly fir into one category (schema), hence every new situation provides experiences and learning of different areas of understanding which are blended rather than stacked.
*Example 7 (Pamper Pole with Two Tiny People AND Trees)*
*Critical:*

- Experiential learning as adventure training is not just construction of personal knowledge but getting to know yourself and another being (team)
- Putting teams of co-workers together to solve problems on adventure training introduces disequilibrium of power – this challenge of power relations is needed: for example, "bosses" can learn to appreciate the capabilities of employees more and vice versa (so the assimilative, everyday recognition that the cook cooks well is subject to accommodative recognition that the cook can also have other valuable attributes).
- However, experiential learning is not panacea for education—some studies point at destructive effect of experiential learning when a learner is put in a position which is regarded as uncomfortable and creates panic, negative emotions (embarrassment) and fear rather than positive learning experience (here it is fear of height, falling, failing)

## Classroom: Selected Examples of Reflective and Critical Thought

*Example 1 (Pupils with Helmets and Bicycles Crossing the Road)*
  *Critical*: Hands-on learning outside the classroom is challenging for the teacher in terms of securing pupils' safety: the outside world is an environment for improvised classrooms in order to "match" classroom learning and real-life situations; however, it also puts a great responsibility on teachers in terms of health and safety.
  *Example 2 (Second Life Virtual Classroom)*
  *Critical*: Challenge with virtual classrooms – such as Second Life virtual classrooms): one does not see the unravelling of the participants' meaning-making processes: not seeing the real person and their facial expressions, it is easy to misinterpret the communication/ comments.
  *Example 3 ("Underbank" Adventure Park Collage Pictures)*
  *Critical*: No adult seen in the image gives an illusion of the lack of adult presence and that children are having fun running wild; but some adult must be there, as adults act as supervisors for children at that age, so the invisible person is important for the visible activity to take place.
  *Example 4 (One-To-One Computer Screens and Students)*
  *Critical*: Futuristic classroom marked by the absence of the teacher and too many computers—the image suggests the question of an "over-use" of technologies (screens everywhere, what kind of learning it actually mediates/ generates?)
  *Example 5 (Afghani Female Pilots)*
  *Critical*: how difficult it is has been for the student to get to the point at which we the educator meet them in the classroom? What baggage do they bring? What threats have they faced? How much pressure is placed on the student by the family, life condition, work or the institution in terms of achievement/ success or, in some cases, the pressure of not failing?
  All the examples above illustrate how the picture was the trigger for reflective concept thinking or a critical insight that went beyond the pictorial Representamen and denotation and provided deep conceptual reflection. The following section tackles further the act of "critical seeing."

## Critical Visual Edusemiotics in Action

Students were not only approaching the image conceptual meaning from a critical perspective but also practicing critical visual pedagogy, raising a number of critical insights and questioning the authority and claim to the truth of photographs. Goldstein (2007) claims that "all photos lie" and offers a compelling set of reasons why they need to be interrogated. Although a photo does not lie as a print record of what is captured in a photo frame, there is a "lie" at the intersection of intention of the photographer, viewer's interpretation, context of showing, and context of making. It is dangerous to take images at face value since they may promote and reinforce particular and intended beliefs and the idea of the lived reality, the same concern expressed by a critical pedagogue Michael Apple (2005). The activity generated critical image awareness among students. In a few cases students exercised this "critical eye" and their comments contained critical acumen related to the represented "truth" and/or creators' intentions as well as viewer's role and, importantly, the viewer's emotional response to an image. The following excerpts from narratives illustrate those points (reference to the image is provided at the end of each quotation):

> I also wonder if, as an engineer, I was drawn to the image as the tags described the component parts of the image, perhaps engineers need to know how things are put together and operate. I also hoped that it would appeal to children via the use of various colors; further I was drawn to the way the rat looked and wondered if the image had been toned down for a children's textbook? (Image: The mouse and a lever Skinner's box illustration).

> The image made the hairs on the back of my neck stand up when I saw it, for the trained eye it includes a mass of detail and shows some of the ceremonial duties the RAF undertake. Some may see this as an arrogant strut around by the military, some of the older generation will reminisce over the training they had and how cruel the drill instructor was to them or their friends. (Image: RAF parade photo).

The classroom in this image is very neat and orderly and all of the children are paying attention—which could just be down to very good teaching and a well-organized teacher, but it could also be that this image is used for promotional material of some kind. From my own experience of teaching, it is rare to have the full, undivided attention of all pupils at once, and the classroom is never as spotless as this one—it wouldn't be a primary school classroom if it was. To me this image looks a little too good to be true. (Image: teacher in front of a whiteboard and students dressed in white).

I feel that this is a constructed image insofar as it is not a naturally occurring event and to some extent the babies may have had to do this some number of times to create this seemingly perfect image for the photographer and the customer (mum & dad)? (Image: two babies swimming).

# Meeting and Surpassing Expectations

In this cohort of students, Jarvis's narratives are models of what this exercise aimed to achieve. His first few narratives were not as academically well-rounded and critical as his later narratives. His last four artifacts surpassed expectation. His two narratives for the concept "Cognitive load" (refer to Appendix 4 for reading the image narratives provided by the student—an elaborated reflection, built mainly around configural picture meaning and anchorage). The images that Jarvis provided as narrated in Appendix 4, are illustrations of Mexico City metro icons and an image of a 2006 Virgin Digital quiz marketing campaign poster inviting audience to find famous music industry individuals and bands. Virgin Digital service was discontinued in 2006 (US) and 2007 (UK): a range of uploaded images can be found on the internet, but I could not trace it back to Virgin Digital platform. The image is an interesting visual metaphor guessing game and can be viewed on the internet by searching with words "virgin digital bands quiz," leading to the image posted on various websites such as mollusions.com and Flickr.

The empirical projects showed how images generated varied concept ideas (to a notable extent) in students' inquiry graphics narratives. Such an activity foregrounded the multiplicity of meanings and open-endedness of concepts. Although the empirical part does not report on students' discussion of images, the plenary proved a potent space for negotiating and sharing meanings and highlighted the plurality of Interpretants (different learners' interpretations), the plurality and learning as a collective dialectic–dialogic meaning-making exploration, growth and development. These discussions constitute another exploration altogether, which I did carry out, but have not dealt with here, having resolved to keep the scope focused in light of an already long and encompassing book. The first pedagogical study made a case for sustained support and the difficulty of thinking with images, as this is not, after all, an easy, illustrative task to be accomplished at a deeper level. They showed how they were under-used for generating critical concept insights and concept reflections during the first iteration when learners are doing the activity independently of the teacher/ tutor.

Therefore, it was shown that learning design matters, and it can significantly change how students relate to the task, thus challenging some of the long-held beliefs about student orientation (deep or surface) and student learning types and styles (visual, verbal or otherwise). Project 3's diverse group of students all provided IGA that offered deep and creative insights. The task requirements guided the engagement. When the tutors entered the conversation about images, they added another layer of complexity and shared insights based on their experience and knowledge of the concept, in various ways of concept realizations, which illuminated how complex the concept were and how many nuances thinking with images can generate.

In light of all these considerations, it could be said that the IG activity succeeded being the platform for supporting multiple perspectives and subsequent pluralistic development of concept understanding and illustrated the scope of the various pictorial manifestations and scenarios within which a concept could be realized. The learners needed support to develop depth of concept elaboration and critical insights, which was provided in the second iteration of the activity, based on the findings in Project 2, and proved to trigger stronger engagement, richer concept ideas, and some exemplary reflection cases. Throughout Project 2 and Project 3, there was a feeling of meeting, failing to meet, and exceeding pedagogical/learning expectations (of creative and deep concept expansion). An overall evaluation is the one of valuable insights, appreciation of multiple interpretants (interpretations), and recognition of concept's multiple characteristics and their many possible manifestations (from stereotypical to quite alternative yet possible), which contributed to collective knowledge building, and transformative learning experiences for both the teacher-researcher and the students.

# References

Amiel, T., & Reeves, T. C. (2008). Design-based research and educational technology: Rethinking technology and the research agenda. *Educational Technology & Society, 11*, 29–40.

Anderson, T., & Shattuck, J. (2012). Design-based research A decade of Progress in education research? *Educational Researcher, 41*, 16–25.

Baskerville, R., & Myers, M. D. (2004). Special issue on action research in information systems: Making is research relevant to practice–foreword. *MIS Quarterly, 28*, 329–335.

Bell, P. (2004). On the theoretical breadth of design-based research in education. *Educational Psychologist, 39*, 243–253.

BERA (British Educational Research Association). (2004). Revised guidelines. Retrieved from: http://www.bera.ac.uk/guidelines.html

Brydon-Miller, M., Greenwood, D., & Maguire, P. (2003). Why action research? *Action Research, 1*, 9–28.

Cobb, P., Confrey, J., Lehrer, R., & Schauble, L. (2003). Design experiments in educational research. *Educational Researcher, 32*, 9–13.

Cole, M., & Packer, M. (2016). Design-based intervention research as the science of the doubly artificial. *Journal of the Learning Sciences, 25*(4), 503–530.

Goldstein, B. M. (2007). All photos lie: Images as data. In G. S. Stanczak (Ed.), *Visual research methods: Image, society, and representation* (pp. 61–81). Los Angeles: Sage.

Grundy, S. (1982). Three modes of action research. *Curriculum Perspectives, 2*, 23–34.

Jackson, C., Arici, A., & Barab, S. (2005). Eat your vegetables and do your homework: A design-based investigation of enjoyment and meaning in learning. *Educational technology: The magazine for managers of change in education* 15–20.

Kress, G., & van Leeuwen, T. (1996). *Reading images: The grammar of visual design*. Routledge.

Lewin, K. (1946). Action research and minority problems. *Journal of Social Issues, 2*, 34–46.

Martinec, R., & Salway, A. (2005). A system for image–text relations in new (and old) media. *Visual Communication, 4*, 337–371.

Noffke, S. E. (1997). Professional, personal, and political dimensions of action research. *Review of Research in Education, 22*, 305–343.

Noffke, S. E., & Somekh, B. (2009). *The Sage handbook of educational action research*. Los Angeles: Sage.

Sless, D. (1981). *Learning and visual communication*. Halsted Press.

Vakil, S., McKinney de Royston, M., Suad Nasir, N. I., & Kirshner, B. (2016). Rethinking race and power in design-based research: Reflections from the field. *Cognition and Instruction, 34*(3), 194–209.

# 9

# Edusemiotic Relationality: Implications for Educational Futures

This chapter reflects on the empirical findings in Part II, linking them to the conceptual and theoretical contributions and developments in Part I. It considers the implications and inspiration for global educational futures and further developments, theorizations and expansion of inquiry graphics (IG) and related approaches.

## Empirical Studies Recap: The Potential and Challenge of Learning via Relational IGs

It was shown in the first empirical study, Project 1 in Chap. 7, how complex the explored task of thinking with images was. To remind the reader, Chap. 7 reported how a group of doctoral students in education thought about an abstract concept (empiricism) by selecting images that they thought could be related to the concept, using the Google images search engine and reporting their thinking while doing so. The study was carefully designed to understand first associative thoughts about a pictorial representation (dominant image schemas about a concept), then how the digital image search was conducted, how the images seen by the students

© The Author(s) 2020
N. Lacković, *Inquiry Graphics in Higher Education*,
https://doi.org/10.1007/978-3-030-39387-8_9

triggered thinking, how their thinking and their prior knowledge and conceptions informed their interpretations of the images. The teaching–learning (pedagogic) potential of the activity was evaluated by the participants, as was the role of the image–concept guidance provided to them. The guidance was meant to provide non-exhaustive guidelines on the diversity of concept aspects materialized in image content (ranging from more iconic *meaning*, defined as "stereotypical," to more alternative meanings, including specific foci, such as photographs to represent a different time in history, or a focus on particular place or artifact). The study showed how such an edusemiotic activity with images can bring to learners' attention and awareness of the plurality of meanings associated with an image–concept (an inquiry graphics, abbreviated to IG) and proved a strong pedagogical potential of the activity, as performed and evaluated by the participants.

The first iteration of the pedagogical activity in the subsequent Project 2, embedded in an MA module in educational psychology, showed that students needed more guidance to be helped to cross the boundary of subject concepts (such as constructivism or cognitive load) for deeper engagement. However, this was not surprising, considering the difficulty of connecting everyday and abstract sides of a concept in a way that was new to all participating students. I personally believe that all students have the capacity to achieve deep engagement. Although engagement can happen across the continuum of deep or surface, I am skeptical about deep and surface learning to lable individual students' manner of learning as well as students' "learning styles" as indicative of their exclusive preferance or ability, such as the label of visual or verbal learner; rather, I see them as behaviors shaped by both the character of the situated educational context and practice (led by a learning design) and prior educational and personal (social) experience of all participants, including the teacher. Teachers' design and pedagogic efforts need to be encouraged and acknowledged at organizational and professional level for teachers to invest time and efforts in them, to move forward and develop further. This links to Chap. 2, which identified scarcity of institutional mechanisms and policies of praise and recognition, for instance as linked to promotion for higher education practitioners who champion innovative and creative pedagogy. If the support mechanism of innovation recognition is not in place from departmental to institutional level, championing innovation in teaching–learning practices will continue to be the province of the enthusiasts, who might get caught up and suffer in between individual passion for innovation/experimentation/change and structural obstacles.

Project 2 in Chap. 8 showed that IG could generate a fantastic range of conceptual and critical insights (also evidenced in Project 1 in Chap. 7) in the spirit of multimodal edusemiotic engagement, but that there were obstacles to deeper engagement that needed to be considered. These included: the novelty of the activity, the linguistic proficiency demands placed upon non-native English speakers in master's degree programs in the English-speaking world, the level of student's private engagement with the concept/ the activity design, students' prior experiences and other con-textual factors. Whereas language proficiency could not be swiftly devel-oped, the activity design could. This led to the second iteration of the learning design. The second iteration, with a different MA cohort, showed how an improved and empirically evaluated design could indeed result in the thinking as a *journey from definitional concept to beyond-the-concept-boundaries realm of rhizomatic shared conceptual development and exemplary creative engagements*. Admittedly, a new cohort could have been a deter-mining factor of success, although the profiles of learners were similar in terms of diversity, even coming from the same countries and cultures, including the UK, though in both cases predominantly international. The two cohorts acted as two cases within the overarching design-based study. Although the book does not tackle the dialogic classroom engagement of the students (which was also researched and analyzed but not reported here), the holistic IG design in Project 3 was designed to connect students' private reflection and creation of IG artifacts with the dialogic exploration of them with colleagues and tutors (which also was not without challenges that needed to be addressed). As a teacher–researcher, I can confirm that the dialogue triggered by multiple images among students and tutors was and is important for holistic IG exploration, especially the tutor's role in providing feedback and interpretation of all the artifacts provided during those dialogues. I decided to focus on the multimodal IG artifacts, as much is known about the benefits (and challenges) of dialogic communi-cation between peers, and between tutors and learners, but in-depth insights into conceptual development and thinking with images in higher education studies are rare. A complete design necessitates a dialogic component, in real physical places or online.

The first iteration of the pedagogical Project 2 pointed to the students' use of images more as illustrations of the concept than a platform or source for critical inquiry and exploration of the image content (also see Hallewell & Lackovic, 2017). The potential to develop creative insight stemming from individual image elements was scarcely unpacked. The images served more as "*launch pads*" for concept ideas where concept meaning was "instilled" into the picture. Students rarely "distilled" meanings from a picture to connect it to the concept. The link between image and concept (MA = multimodal anchorage) was established mainly in relation to the holistic (configural) meaning of the picture rather than the meaning of individual picture details (its elements) as vehicles for creative insight. Photographic details were mentioned in most narratives, but those were descriptive details that rarely served as sources of creative and imaginative concept inference. It can be said that the potential of the image was not really built upon in this first pedagogic study, Project 2, and one of the reasons for that was the difficulty to think differently and see images in a different way other than simple illustration as the students were asked to interact the images in such level of critical and serious analysis for the first time in their educational trajectory. Therefore, the thinking and IG character, diagrams and figures explained in Chap. 3 do not mediate an easy way of thinking; on the contrary, the process is demanding, complex and unusual; the material and procedures promotes the view of images beyond just "pretty pictures". In UK and international primary and secondary education, it is presumed that images are not readily used as vehicles for deep, multifaceted and critical *thinking and learning to push and explore concept boundaries*, but as illustrations. Therefore, students' focusing on the concept, rather than equally on the concept and the image, is unsurprising. This only proves that these types of thinking and understanding of knowledge are new and unfamiliar to university learners as well as most teachers, as they indeed confirmed in our interactions. Drawing inferences from individual image elements proved to be a great challenge for students as well as generating critical insights about the concept itself (although this did happened). That is why the second study introduced changes in instructional and activity design and offered a more comprehensive model for image–concept exploration that made the exploratory thinking pathways and image-searching process more visible, thus supporting more creative, in-depth and critical engagement.

Further explanation for the struggle to think deeply about new concepts in disciplines is offered by the threshold concept challenge as commonly reported by teachers (Meyer & Land, 2003). I have already suggested that the activity of thinking with images and other forms of graphics to grapple with threshold concepts is called a *Threshold Graphics* activity, (see Chap. 4). The dialogic plenary with the tutors was crucial for building students' knowledge from their own representations, a consequence of the tutors commenting on students' IG contributions and sharing their own interpretations as trained and experienced scholars in the field. Students were, and are generally expected to be, less confident in using particular specialist semiotic and new conceptual ideas and terminology and models at the beginning of the activity; confidence can develop over time. It takes time for an inquiry graphics novice to start exploring photographs and their "constituents" (object, embodied representamen's elements, metaphors, analogy) in light of the concept, even when these technical terms are translated into more commonplace terms such as image elements or details, pictorial representation, or merging image and concept interpretation. Arguably, all students still did an excellent job given the short period of time they had to engage with such a new and demanding design.

The iteration in Project 3 went on to refine the IG activity design, implementing it with a subsequent cohort of MA students of the same program, focusing on tutor-provided guidance and students' independent task structuring. The results showed a solid number of concept ideas and critical insights and examples of students exercising "critical visual culture" (Sturken, Cartwright, & Sturken, 2001). What this means is that the students expressed a critical attitude not only toward the concept meanings "behind" and developed from an image but also toward the depiction itself and its claim to "truth" (Lackovic, 2020), as there were cases of referring to the "staged," stock photograph platforms and non-genuine status of images in students' multimodal artifact narratives. The activity strengthened students' visual and media literacy and critical graphicacy, supporting a deeper, more informed, critical view of the world and all media-promoted imagery. It also enhanced students' understanding of relationality and plurality of conceptual meanings and its material embeddedness. Such plurality and focusing on the meaning-making processes is essentially edusemiotic. The narratives in iteration 2 (Project 3) were much more elaborated than in iteration 1 (Project 2). All concept meanings were anchored in selected pictures, still more as configural (whole-picture) meaning rather than teasing out the meanings of elements, but the engagements did show a notable move forward in terms of a particular multimodal element anchorage (linking an element to a concept idea), concept reflection and critical inference from that anchorage.

The design activity in iteration 2 of Project 3 (see Fig. 8.12 in Chap. 8) can be taken as the one which can stand as an example of an IG activity design for practitioners, still flexible enough to adapt to changes and improvements as practitioners implement it to suit their teaching needs and/or other modes of expression. It is not to say that it is optimal and ideal, as teaching is always tacit, fluid, varied and contextualized, with different cohorts and other factors influencing it. It is a flexible and adaptable learning design. I find any aim to provide some "optimal" or "ideal" learning design problematic. What teachers can achieve with an IG activity is what Stables (2010) emphasizes when he talks about *teaching as disruptive* and *teaching as student-oriented engagement*: an IG activity challenges the prevailing view of pictures as "entertainment" and puts students at the center of meaning-making activities where they provide their own creation or selection, their opinions and world views in a creative manner. The teacher was there in the plenary session to provide a point of view and interpretation as a trained and experienced professional, not to undermine learners' interpretations but start from them, from learners' points of view, from their expressed interpretants. The activity can be a useful platform for development of shared-concept knowledge. It has the potential to result in a creative and transformative experience with disciplinary and interdisciplinary concepts. It helps students to understand that disciplinary concepts have an interdisciplinary nature, via holistic image–concept signs epitomized in an inquiry graphic.

IG can be embedded in pedagogic designs in higher education for students to exercise new approaches to concepts and therefore knowledge, learning and methods, by embracing and exploring "everyday–scientific" concept relationality and multiplicity as rhizomatic or multimodal concepts. The explored IG activity design supports the uncovering of a wide scope of possible concept realizations and manifestations by coupling everyday life (everyday concepts) with reflective and critical concept verbalization (scientific concepts). This bridges mediational and dialogic approaches to learning (e.g., the views of Vygotsky, 1978, and Bakhtin, 1981), with Peircean inquiry graphics, bringing them together. As Stables (2010, p. 21) puts it, educational theory has had particular tendencies over time: it has tended to valorize broadly cognitivist tradition over crude behaviorism, then challenged it "through social conceptions of mind (Vygotsky, 1978, and his interpreters) but have not challenged its narrow anthropocentrism or taken full account of the uniqueness of individual response." *The uniqueness of individual response* is exactly what an IG activity emphasizes in order to bring to the fore students' unique individual interpretations and experiences that constitute collective knowledge development. In addition, the encouragement in an IG sign model to focus on material things in pictures (via its material elements) introduced the needed non-anthropocentrism and awareness of the mediative and influential role material artifacts have in our lives. The demand to provide individual interpretations for sharing informs the building and negotiating of shared meanings in disciplines in order to develop a true knowledge community of equal interpreters. However, equal interpreters via equality of choice and voicing opportunity still might not mean equal access to and participation in the activity, and this has to be taken into consideration when designing the activity. I was fully aware that many international students would have expressed themselves more proficiently and elaborately if English had been their native language (you, dear reader, may well notice that I am a non-native English speaker myself). I am also talking about blind and visually impaired students who would need support and/ or specific tasking, for example to choose an object in their environment and photograph it or to choose a song or newspaper article. These options need to be prepared and discussed with those students needing support. Text explanations or verbal commentary about the images have to be provided. This is where Peirce's triadic schematic model for interpreting photographs can help by emphasizing the importance of providing denotative descriptions of photographs (an Interpretant-led description) with the purpose of helping visually impaired students to access the IG activity. In fact, such a scenario would enhance everyone's sensitivity to denotative descriptions and other people's needs as well as showing both the overlapping and variations of individual denotative and connotative image descriptions.

An edusemiotic approach to education and teaching–learning suggested in this work foregrounds the need of externalization, and the *voicing, exploration* and merging of learners' and teachers' experiences, practices, thinking habits and beliefs, acknowledging and accounting for the existence of things (matter) and other beings within larger relational dynamics. In such a climate, individual knowledge is accounted for, yet its social and relational character is exposed and never undermined; knowledge grows in a web of experiential and interpretative exchanges between the two (individual and social knowledge), as they are always present and always interdependent (Burkitt, 2008, 2014). Humans are, building on Burkitt (2016, p. 322), "dependents," that is, beings dependent on their complex environments, physical or digital, other things and beings, and sociocultural norms that mediate their identity (Öztok, 2016). This is in contradiction to the prevailing Western moral and political view of agents as autonomous, independent and reflexive individuals who only need an equality of opportunity; instead, human agency is always located in manifold social relations intersected with manifold interpretations conditioned by the environment and social structures.

It is acknowledged that this kind of learning and inquiry merging the image and the concept might be faced with students' or teachers' resistance, perhaps more so in the beginning when it might be perceived as an "unconventional" and artistic activity for the "creative" students and might prompt confusing and conflicting interpretations. However, this struggle is indeed evidence of conceptual complexity, and provides the impetus for transformative experiences. All students are creative. The teacher would need to balance interpretations: it poses a demand upon a teacher to encourage students to provide their interpretations freely and confidently, while gently pointing to what agreement the scientific community has reached about the concept so far, in case the two diverge. Yet, the teacher should always remind students that a scientific interpretation is still human knowledge and interpretation, aligned with Peirce's fallibalism, representing some dominant community's agreement, and the teacher's point of view. This approach allows for and encourages any and all scientific agreements, theories, rules or laws and their provenance to be cracked open and challenged, a prerequisite for any scientific progress, as advancement is the product of such creativity and creative work. We need to acknowledge that transformative learning designs, and discussions therein, might cause discomfort by shaking strongly held habits and beliefs (of both learners and tutors).

IG activity steps in Project 3 that made the learning scenario succeed in helping students cross the everyday–scientific and concrete–abstract dichotomy provide these learning design recommendations that teachers and programme designers can tweak:

1. An introductory seminar about the activity must include student image contributions as worked examples in order to explain the task through students' images from the very beginning, thus making it relevant to students' own interpretations from the start. It should also ask questions that will engage them in an extensive debate on the role of the image in thinking about concepts.
2. Students' development in this activity can be practically connected to their end-of-module assignment and to the educational goals of the program or module to clearly acknowledge the importance of such thinking and exploration.
3. One-to-one tutoring can solve misunderstanding or struggles, and inspire students.
4. The activity's requirements can stimulate deeper engagement with the structuring of the task in particular ways (e.g. the improvement of narrative task instruction, as shown in Project 3), in particular the requirement *to provide one iconic and one "alternative" image.*

# Beyond Conceptual Dualism and Determinism: IG as Transmodal, Concept-Rhizome Sign

Inquiry graphics involve transductive transformation between interacting and changing modes, hence representing a *multimodal effort for knowledge development, teasing and stretching the boundaries of concepts.* I propose that concepts, when understood as such multiple and multi-modal objects, can be called *multimodal (or transmodal) concepts,* to emphasise their image-concept character, perhaps *concept-rhizomes (or rhizomatic concepts)*, as they are imbued with a variety of modal meaning potentials and many pathways for creative insight, depending on varied contexts, interpreters and environments. Although everyday communication is seen as creative, since we create new meanings all the time by interpreting events and the world around us (Kress, 2004), the IG studies presented in Chaps. 7 and 8 shed light on a *particular manifestation of creativity.* This manifestation is defined by the occurrence of transmodality and transmediation, a creative transformation from one mode to another, referring both to the mode of thinking (concept–image sign description, imagination and (inter)disciplinary exploration) and the mode form (linguistic–pictorial, an embodied sign). In that way IG engagements facilitate creative transmodal reasoning as a type of diagrammatic and iconic reasoning. IGs act as semiotic scaffolds for the development not only of conceptual knowledge but also creative and imaginative thinking.

An IG practice is built on integrative principles of concrete–abstract, image–concept relationship explorations, where external artifacts (here photographs) are crucial rather than peripheral for knowledge-building. Alongside Peirce's tripartite sign model and discussed edusemiotic approaches, it incorporates Vygotskian idea on *everyday–scientific* concepts as a holistic, metaconceptual learning sign, the sign that mediates learning as a mediating artifact, having an integral role in thinking processes. This dash is purposeful in epitomizing *everyday–scientific* interdependence. Put simply, scientific concepts exist in everyday circumstances and scenarios (here embodied in image material and physically represented aspects or instances), and everyday concepts and objects (e.g. elements in images) can be abstracted and generalized as containing scientific knowledge and discourse. These two are complementary, they contain one another. In addition, this is also aligned with an extended-mind hypothesis and material engagement theory, where external artifacts are a part of mind function (Malafoursi, 2013). Therefore, IG supports an inquiry where students explore the relationship between abstract concept (or a concrete one) and its concrete manifestations (possibly real or imaginary) with an aim of understanding it at an elaborated, creative and pluralist level of reflection and criticality. Students explore how the world's materiality and its environment relates to theoretical and conceptual knowledge in a higher education discipline, thus moving toward an interdisciplinary view of knowledge and ways of knowing. Such elaboration can initiate an insight which marks that the threshold of understanding has been crossed. Fig. 9.1 shows how an inquiry graphics (IG) process works by inviting thinking that is multimodal/ transmodal and multidirectional, involving abstract concepts, concrete images and related elaborations on the multimodal anchorage (A).

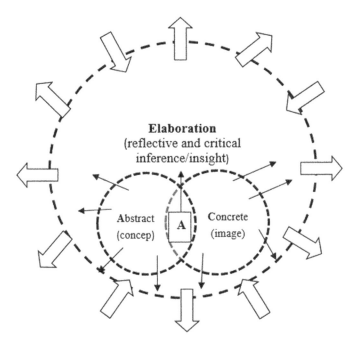

**Fig. 9.1** "ACE" (abstract–concrete elaboration) thinking processes of an IG rhizome. Black arrows = possibilities for interpretation; A = (concept–image; abstract–concrete; multimodal) Anchorage; White arrows = further interpretation possibilities, all diagram relations and arrows acknowledge the dynamic relationship with the immediate sociocultural context, environment, actors, historicity, materiality

The overlapping point between Abstract and Concrete circles in Fig. 9.1 is a multimodal anchorage (A for anchorage), or MA, when the concept and image are linked in some way. The "Abstract" circle represents concept ideas and definitions. The "Concrete" circle represents depiction and meanings inferred from the picture as a whole, or its details (Elements). One needs to "elaborate" on this link (A) in a manner of concept generalization and critical consideration in order to realize the concept inquiry more fully (What does this anchorage mean and what it brings in light of the explored concept?) The concrete representation of a photograph (picture) helps insofar as it represents something in the real or imaginary world, an entity on its own without the assigned concept. The photograph can be interpreted in many ways (different interpretation directions are represented by black arrows coming out of the Concrete image circle). This is the key character of an IG that creates a space for surprise and creativity. Both image depiction and concept itself could have manifold interpretations and aspects (the black arrows from both circles). The point is in exploring those opportunities of meaning-making and connecting them, which is by no means an easy task for a student. Naïve interpretations and explanations can surface. But the naïve here is not "bad" or "wrong"; it is simply contained in a scientific concept, as it says something about it from someone's point of view, which needs to be voiced and discussed, without the prejudice against this possible "naïvety." This is connected to the case of the discrepancies between "authorized" and "alternative" concept understandings when learning threshold concepts (Land et al., 2005). "Authorized" in the present case means as defined in the discipline; "alternative" means as believed (by the learner) to be manifested in real life (ibid.). The IG exploration embraces both types of understanding as legitimate parts of *learning exploration*. While acknowledging "authorized" knowledge, because educational institutions are built on and depend on such expert-knowledge pillars, teachers are encouraged always to leave the doors open to challenge this authority. These doors are the way into an alternative view, an invitation and an offer of respect which might lead students to great discoveries if something really captures their curiosity and sparks their enthusiasm to continue exploring theoretically or empirically.

Creativity, and digital creativity in learning, can be defined as making new connections from available resources that contribute to the development of concept understanding and demand an effort of re-invention of the existing resources for the creation of new ones. In addition, it is connected to the effort of modal transduction and a similar concept of transmodality. What I propose is that the empirical IG practices exemplify technosemiotic creativity via transmodal moments (Newfield, 2009). There are many views on "creativity," and defining it was not a purpose of the book. However, the book does propose a specific and novel perspective on creativity as useful for learning, as: (1) semiotic inter- or cross-modal "transduction" (Newfield, 2009) manifest in thinking through more than one mode, and as (2) "the transmodal moment" (Newfield, 2009). Transmodal moment is defined in the multimodality glossary of the MODE center (edited by Diane Mavers) as follows, building on the work by Denise Newfield:

"The transmodal moment" (Newfield, 2009) focuses attention on the multiple transformations that occur in processes of transduction—in materiality, genre, meaning, subjectivity and learning—as well as revealing the situatedness of transmodal semiotic action.

"Transmodal redesign" (Mavers, 2011) refers to how form and meaning are remade in response to the framing of the social environment.

This "framing of the social environment" is the educational framing of the task and the framing of an image created in the society in a type of social environment (an actual classroom, but also possible in online learning spaces). Therefore, a holistic and dynamic inquiry graphics practice is a practice of technosemiotic creativity via transmodal moments and redesign. Thinking with images, as exemplified in the maps in Chaps. 7 and 8, integrates transmodal moments. I would add to "transmodal redesign" that it is not only the framing of the social environment, but the effect and framing of the *sociomaterial* environment. Referring to this view of creativity, one might look at a creative effort and relationship between modes within such transmodal redesign. The creative effort invested is greater if more than one mode is involved in artifact production meaning-making. Looking at how different modes in image-based (but also in other multimodal) ensembles connect, and exploring the origins and background of the produced connection, can shed more light on creativity and creative efforts invested by students.

# Understanding the Potential and Use of Technology: Developing (Post) Digital Semiotics

Another contribution of inquiry graphics to pedagogy is the critical evaluation of modern technology visuality that furnishes an orientation of digital semiotics (O'Halloran, Tan, Smith, & Podlasov, 2009) or an (edu) semiotic analysis and treatment of technology. If digital communication is at the core of present-day communication and education, the key unit of digital communication is a *digital sign. Digital semiotics* therefore tackles studying, analyzing, conceptualizing, theorizing, producing and using digital signs across domains of digital media, educational and everyday life (Lackovic, 2020). Simply put, a digital sign is anything used in digital communication that makes meaning. Digital sign is here explored as a relational, tripartite entity of a sign's embodied form subjected to interpretation and description (a version of Peirce's representamen), what the sign form refers to (its object) and its interpretation (interpretant). A post-digital sign (Lackovic, 2020) is introduced as a sign that can and does appear both in virtual and physical world environments, acting as communication and meaning-making mediator in both, blurring the boundaries between them. The study of post-digital signs can be called *post-digital semiotics, characterized by studying the meanings and effects of signs in online and offline environments, and their relationships with sociocultural and ecological change (e.g., changes in structure, being, action)* (Lackovic, 2020). The term digital semiotics is related to the word *technosemiotic,* defined by Allard-Huver and Gilewicz (2015) in their key terminology list that can be adapted here as "(a) way to understand and analyze media and communication phenomenon as being at the crossroad between a construction and a circulation of knowledge and signification, and information and communication technologies." In that way inquiry graphics practices that apply digital images, as it was the case of the empirical studies in the book, provide a case of (post-)digital or tech-nosemiotic practices. Websites, digital photographs, hybrid signs such as memes, linguistic text and narratives, numbers, gestures, digital devices' portability and functions, gaze or environmental, architectural, material and industrial design particularities can all act as post-digital signs, and they can be subjected to inquiry.

Few studies provide insights into the use of digital search engine Google images within a higher education pedagogical model. The findings in Chaps. 7 and 8 offer an understanding of three main user approaches and three main search strategies and possible student orientation in that task, during the thinking aloud and search via the search engine for an image to represent a concept:

Strategies employed at the beginning of the Google images search engine activity in Project 1:

- **Concept repetition** (learner as image search task simplifier/ econo-mizer) When starting the image search by typing the concept
- **Concept idea-led** (learner as image search task conceptualizer) When starting the image search by typing an abstract idea related to the concept
- **Image idea-led** (learner as image search task visualizer) When starting the image search by typing the words which can be related to the description of the imagined image content (the particular image content they expect to find).

This can be subverted by an open discussion of these search strategies in a learning community, yielding further activity ideas. As students worked with digital images found on the internet or made themselves, the inquiry graphics practice applied is a type of techno-semiotic or post-digital practice, as technologically mediated, originated and supported artifacts are subjected to semiotic inquiry.

There is a substantial potential of developing creative digital and tech-nosemiotic (or postdigtial semiotic) practices with inquiry graphics. The technologies that supported IG were: the VLE system where students created their image blogs, Google images search engine and interactive whiteboard for presenting images in discussions (the discussion part of the research was not reported here, but I could mention that the interactive whiteboard was not used to its potential—the students could have "annotated" and "labeled" the images using the whiteboard or any annotation platform such as ThingLink). Hence, thinking about technologies which could mediate creative IG technosemiosis is truly an open field, one with many opportunities and possibilities. For example, apps and platforms with "annotation" properties could help with highlighting picture elements, technologies and apps which allow recording a voice over the picture would bring a different dimension to IG (where voice would take role of the narrative), using mobile phones for taking pictures and as a repository could support IG activities as well, and so on. In the teaching practice that followed this DBR set of studies I used various digital platforms such as Thinglink, Voice Thread and Padlet. Many possibilities for further implementation, development, and adjustment of inquiry graphics applications exist. An inquiry can be organized around any graphics or any artifact, not exclusively images: 3-D objects created by students, a found object, a multimedia production, social media artifacts, video, dance, performance, any scenario as a multimodal event. There is a vast array of artifacts that can be inquired, not just images, and inquiry of the graphics around Peirce's triadic sign can be developed and adapted into various directions.

## A Selection of Key IG Messages and Contributions

The findings across the empirical chapters in Part II and the conceptual–theoretical chapter in Part I are suggestive of the following insights which comprise the contribution to knowledge of this book.

- IG Practice can be a Transformative Interdisciplinary Practice/Learning Design Model in Higher Education

Inquiry graphics pedagogy has shown that using images for serious academic inquiry is possible but challenging; it has illustrated the initially superficial approach to images by students—something that needs to be challenged through cultivating critical visual inquiry, critical graphicacy, multimodality and edusemiotics. It offers a comprehensive and detailed design for image-based concept inquiry in higher education for social sciences and more broadly, fostering interdisciplinary exploration. There might be some discomfort in the apparent rivalry and tensions between psychology and semiotics, but in reality, they complement each other well, such that many psychological concepts have their partners in the semiotic world (e.g., "mediational tools" as central to sociocultural constructivism are actually "signs" with their "structure" in semiotics). Relating disciplines and approaches is a challenging but rewarding and mind-expanding endeavor, because it permits going beyond the discipline into new transdisciplinary realms of inquiry.

- IG can Support Creative Exploration of Threshold Concepts as *Threshold Graphics* (TG)

Inquiry graphics offers a pedagogical inquiry framework for the creative connection of abstract definitions of critical disciplinary concepts for transformative learning to help a student move from the periphery toward belonging to a disciplinary community—threshold concepts—to their concrete life-examples, as instantiated in images. Inquiry graphics explicitly applied in relation to and for tackling threshold concepts are termed *threshold graphics*.

- IG Practice is a Form of *Edusemiotic and Transmodal Practice*

"Intermodal transduction" and transmediation are suggested here as the basis for understanding and exploring creative effort and creativity within concept knowledge development. It provides insights on how people reason when they are asked to perform transductive thinking bridging abstract ideas and concrete image representations, also a type of transmodal and iconic thinking.

- IG Practices Bring to the Surface and Challenge "Stereotypical"/ "Iconic" Images Embedded in Our Mind Schemata

The studies uncovered the embeddedness of "stereotypical" images in our cognitive schemata which are here called "iconic images," that is, stereotypical and formulaic images that have been repeated so many times in the society and culture that they become embedded is psychological schemata. These need to be exposed and challenged, and such exposure and challenging practice is termed *iconic surfacing*.

- IG Practices Expose the Approach to Images as Embellishment, thus Encouraging a Move from "Illustration" to "Inquiry"

The empirical Part II of the book adds to an understanding that students are inclined to view and use images as illustrations rather than rich semiotic inquiry resources. It is hard for novice students to infer or refer to abstract meanings and models from an image. This has been already problematized within the theory of threshold concepts (Land, Cousin, Meyer, & Davies, 2005). However, the IG scenario in Part II offers an image-based pedagogical scenario underpinned by semiotic image investigation as a possible avenue for supporting students to link conceptual *abstract–concrete* identity toward its generalization, critique and integration.

- IG Practices can Utilize Various Technologies and Further Develop Techno-, Digital- or Post-Digital Semiotics

Google images used with different search autonomies is exemplified when starting and performing the image search; IG can be applied with many other digital platforms such as Thinglink or Voice Thread. There are insights on how people use and could use the ubiquitous Google images search engine for concept reflection. A wide range of digital visual platforms and apps can mediate IG activities, for instance, students can use a mobile phone to capture photographs and notes.

- IG Artifacts and Practice Mediate *Semiotic Scaffolding*.

The IG studies described and analyzed in this book offer to educational practitioners scaffolding strategies and teaching scenarios (scripts, worked examples) that are more likely to "work." The study also estimates challenges pertaining to the implementation of IG practices in a wide range of disciplines.

- IG Suggests a View on Concepts as *Transmodal or Rhizome Concepts*

Aligned with the anti-dualist and exemplified image–concept unity and multiplicity, the view on concepts proposed is that of a transmodal concept, or, as suggested earlier, it could be *concept-rhizome* (inspired by Deleuze, 1987, 1995) that refers to an open-ended, heterogenous and evolving inquiry and becoming, with many possibilities of concept-image branching, or *rhizome-concept*. Any concept is to be understood as a multiple perspectival and branching entity, consisting of both verbal and visual/spatial entities.

- IG can Underpin Introduction of New Approaches into HE Training and Professional Development

Via both theory and empirical explorations based on the theory, this book can provide an inspiration for the introduction of and related training or professional higher education development that would incorporate:

- critical visual literacy/graphicacy into higher education courses;
- relational (visual) edusemiotics as a reflective and encompassing teaching-learning approach in practices across disciplines;
- and, overall, inquiry graphics practice in higher education, to practice the two above.
- organizational or institutional practice (courses and programs), policy development and change toward incorporating various modalities of being and thinking and their relationships, perhaps under a broader vision of "Relational Education Futures," a new different type of REF abbreviation (different from the Research Excellence Framework), toward the development of centers, institutes, or labs to explore relational research, methods, theories and practices.

# Inquiry Graphics Limitations

Like any approach, IG approaches have limitations. These could be first related to the lack of time and preparedness, at human, institutional and programmatic level, to develop innovative and detailed practices, connected to the issues of contemporary higher education governance, policy demands and pressures (Chap. 2). However, expenditure of this time and effort can be worthwhile, as it can provide memorable engagement for learners and teachers and open up transformative experiences. IG is one possible approach of many and does not offer any panacea to educational or social problems, but it can inform the much-needed creative and transformative development of interdisciplinary programs and online education with digital semiotic practices. IG activities can be mixed with a range of other activities in higher education programs and modules, but it requires at least some level of sustained engagement (due to all its characteristics and novelty explained earlier). It foregrounds the role and value of semiotics and edusemiotics in education and higher education. It can be said that the field of higher education studies and educational research has been "unsemiotic" or semiotic-dry. The simplified and unfavorable view on semiotics might be summarized as some people doing some fancy, untheoretical, self-indulgent interpretations of some stuff, with no field research, more interpreters, and empirical explorations. I personally see merits in individual semiotic interpretations and after all, what is an interview analysis other than an interpetation, but I also recognized the lack of empirical semiotic studies and multiple interpretations in higher education settings. That is why I developed Projects 1, 2 and 3, and this book.

Another challenge is in a possible view that IG is merely a methodological and analytical tool and that developing edusemiotic and semiotic approaches does not necessarily contribute to educational or higher education theory or theoretical development, but only to methods and teaching practice. It is acknowledged that Part II of the book is focused on methods and the narration of findings. However, edusemiotics and a semiotic theory of learning are theoretical and philosophical positions that the book contributes to by developing their theoretical grounds in relation to the application of graphics in education and educational designs. The semiotics stemming from Peirce's philosophy, logic and pragmatism is a theoretical field, a theory of mind, aligned with an international group of authors who have been developing a semiotic theory of learning quoted throughout the book (in particular, see Chap. 3). Here, I have provided rare examples of action and design-based research, and situated higher education practice that incorporated inquiry graphics as a species of *learning as dynamic relationality, and as a part of edusemiotics*, via fine-grain empirical data, cross-fertilizing Peirce's triadic diagram and edusemiotics with selected theoretical and conceptual perspectives in learning sciences and visual approaches.

The choice of presenting just one side of the holistic activity design in Projects 2 and 3 (and not the dialogic engagement with images) is the weakness linked to the scope of the book. I fully acknowledge it. Student and tutor dialogues were indispensable elements of the holistic activity design. Student–student and student–tutor dialogues significantly developed IG concept–image exploration, with tutors playing a decisive part in providing further layers of critical and multifaceted interpretation of images and concepts.

Another weakness is that students' feedback on the activity in Projects 2 and 3 was not obtained. I did not collect students' opinions or experiences of the activity, which would have provided an important dimension of how they related to the whole experience. As I was their teacher, I talked about the activity with the students all the time, and kept notes to inform the design. I focused on participants' feedback in Project 1, although this project was of a different design and setting, but helped evaluate the reflective and idea generating potential of the designed activity. If I had provided an anonymous qualitative survey link to MA students, they might have openly reported their opinion, as I felt that interviews would yield mostly positive feedback because I was their teacher and activity designer. I did undertake another study, however, in which I interviewed doctoral students about an IG activity (Lackovic, 2016). One thing that can be reported from my experience with Projects 2 and 3 participants and my doctoral students (Lackovic, 2016) is that for most students the IG activity was new, intriguing and surprising, and that over time, even if they were resistant and skeptical about it, they came to realize its transformational value (as a student told me, it opened their eyes, and the way they saw and engaged with the world would never be the same). Of course, I cannot claim that this was the case for every student.

What might be a factor for the generation of lower-quality narratives in terms of IG generalization, reflection and criticality is the level of concept knowledge that students bring to the activity. It is presumed that when the students did not invest enough effort and time in familiarizing themselves with the concept, which could take time, they turned to the core, definitional concept meaning as the only "safe" and "confident" option. They might have simply *Google-imaged* the concept (i.e., written the concept in the Google image engine), quickly picked an image that appealed to them and written something to complete the task quickly. The occurrence of copy-pasted narrative sections in Project 2 was particularly indicative of this strategy of bypassing deep engagement. However, the mere search for an image and the narrative writing did help student understanding of a concept, at least by providing a regular semiotic scaffold for thinking about concepts. Hence, even a definitional concept rehearsal is beneficial for developing student understanding when subsequently shared and commented on by peers and tutors. It contributes to the growth of knowledge in a learning community, starting from the definition (definitional concept), and progressively moving forward to a complex concept branching with diverse pictures and student–tutor's interpretations (as transmodal, rhizomatic concept). The uncovering of students' "bypassing" strategies usefully informed the following iteration of the activity and instructional guidance. With the development and improvement of instructional design in Project 3, the students provided narratives and showed an engagement at a deeper level, with some exceptionally reflective and notable IG narratives.

Last, but not least, the focus on pictorial/ depictive images such as photographs raises questions of accessibility and the slow progress of automated image screen readers for visually impaired and blind people. In relation to the empirical study designs, we could provide an alternative activity that included finding interesting quotes or songs about the concepts and then provide image content descriptions to visually impaired or blind users. Although visually saturated social media such as Facebook and Instagram have introduced automated image alt text, more work needs to be invested in developing nuanced descriptive functions for screen readers. The difficulty in doing so only proves the complexity of human interpretation. This is where naming pictures' representamen elements and interpretant's descriptive denotation and connotation could help further development of image screen readers and artificial intelligence.

## Arguments in Favor of Edusemiotics with Inquiry Graphics in Higher Education

The empirical studies relate to edusemiotics as they exemplify an interdisciplinary exploration of open-ended concepts as signs in a learning community and critical approaches to visual information, relatable to the main premises of edusemiotics grounded in Chap. 3. The first part of the book provided a rationale behind an IG design in higher education, with reference to the ever-increasing image of everyday media and post-digital culture, affecting the understanding of what meanings, truth, knowledge, learning and living as semiotic engagement are. Essentially it called upon the embedding of critical edusemiotic pedagogy of the visual in HE practice, in the spirit of the statement eloquently put by Sebastien Pesce that 'instead of concept acquisition, the aim of education needs to be concept inquiry, probing, challenge and expansion, even if concept negation' (Pesce, 2010, p. 103).

Inquiry graphics encourages students to inquire and expand rather than merely acquire concepts in a manner of a definition written in a book, or found or heard in any available resource. Arguably, some, if not most, of the concepts taught in higher education had to be first introduced at a basic definition level with related examples, as part of a learning trajectory. Inquiry graphics requires that this basic definition gets expanded and related directly to learners' prior experiences and the world's materiality. It reinforces triadic rather than binary sign meanings. To illustrate this point, I refer to Pesce (2010) who observes the innovative and creative conceptualization of Peirce's interpretant, juxtaposing it with the "binarist" teaching of signifier–signified (in a manner of "this thing means that") rather than a more open-ended heterogenous

Interpretant that encourages innovation and creativity, as human cannot ever know the exact Object of the sign (if it is what we mean it is), we only know and develop sign Interpretants, our interpretations of signs. That is why our knowledge and science always develops, it is evolutionary in such semiotic sense.

Concepts are practiced along the spectrum from scientific-definitional to alternative, pluralistic and ever-evolving, and anything in between (branching in various directions as concept-rhizomes). Therefore, IG promotes the practicing of creative and so-called "alternative" education by teachers and institutions, before it is accepted and integrated more widely. IG practices can help us to rethink certain social issues that go far beyond the mere matter of "learning" concepts: interpreting the world, developing one's critical abilities, becoming a world citizen, building one's own and a social relation to knowledge and concept development.

As Pesce (2010, p.104) notes with regard to Peirce's semiotics and education, commonly the work done in educational research offers either "1) theoretical and foundational research, considering Peirce but ignoring the call for fieldwork" or "2) research including fieldwork but ignoring Peirce's semiotics and concepts." This book has done a pioneering work in bringing together (1)Peirce's theorization and philosophy (albeit focused and limited to the aspects adopted in the book, such as the tripartite diagrammatic sign related to edusemiotics) and (2) relational approaches to images, learning, concepts, knowledge and inquiry through fieldwork/empirical lenses.

Edusemiotics supports a non-dualist way of thinking and learning (to argue interconnectedness of body and mind, material and non-material), such as the one epitomized in an IG sign. It stimulates a search for connections rather than separations (without imposing some general similarity, but recognising diversity in similarity), connections between micro practices and macro level system functioning, conceptualizing and theorizing. Going back to some arguments in the first part of the book, Smith-Shank (2010, p. 4) reminds us that everything that has meaning is a sign, hence:

> Reasoning from sign to sign is semiosis, and semiosis is the subject matter of semiotics. Semiotic pedagogy is purposeful nurturing of semiosis…

within an unlimited arena of signs... and unlimited semiosis is the process of lifelong learning, and is built upon intellectual guidance.

Building on Peircean pragmatism, the author suggests three main tenets of semiotic education that IG activities embrace:

1. "collateral experience" makes learning possible;
2. historically determined disciplinary boundaries constrain learning; and
3. the consequences of learning and teaching change when the notion of "environment" is understood broadly as evolving and interconnected to creatures which share space, rather than as simple surroundings for human beings (Smith-Shank, 2010, p. 4).

"Collateral experience" is "previous experience, which makes a novel situation accessible" (ibid.). In that way, learning builds on students' prior experience and memory—compatible with the learning theories reviewed in this book that state the importance of prior experience in creating concept understanding. In relation to point 2), "when learning is understood as inquiry or semiosis, it is a process and not a product. It becomes a lifelong process that cannot be defined by the limits of subject matter parameters" (Smith-Shank, 2010, p. 4). Hence there are no limits in finding examples and cases which can illustrate a "disciplinary" point, and they often go outside the boundary of a discipline. Although having particular disciplines is seen as useful, "learning and inquiry are inherently interdisciplinary and there is no non-artificial way to isolate one subject from another" (Smith-Shank, 2010, p. 4). Finally, the last point 3) is closely connected to multiple perspectives aim of inquiry graphics, mindfulness, non-anthropocentrism, and knowledge, as developing with a community of inquiry for seeing an environment (or a picture) in pluralistic, *Umweltian* ways:

> Content and pedagogical practice change when education is situated within a community of enquiry, when the sites of learning shift from environment (which is outside an individual) to *Umwelt* (which is part and parcel with an individual), and when the content of our overloaded curriculum is used to help students know and develop new ideas unrestrained by disciplinary boundaries. When these shifts occur, pedagogy becomes a

process of nurturing and directing ongoing processes of semiosis. Education changes from an activity of transmission of knowledge to students, to an activity in which teachers actively help students become aware of ways in which cultures code knowledge. Teachers can help students develop the confidence and power to explore and deconstruct these codes as they become aware of them. (Smith-Shank, 2010, p. 6)

This view is resonant with the earlier introduced view of distributed cognition and extended mind (see also the work by Malafouris, e.g., Malafouris, 2013) and the view on developing (and crossing) threshold concepts when previously unconsidered aspects of a concept or an experience have now been considered and the seeing and understanding of it has been changed. Furthermore, as mentioned earlier "*Umwelt*" (Uexküll, 1982) refers to the environment as existing in relation to other organisms and objects, not just humans. For example, a tree is a different entity and "environment" for a baby, an older child, crop production or cattle industry, a bug, a bird, a Greenpeace activist or a lumberjack (Smith-Shank, 2010, p. 6). Such an approach to education celebrates multiple perspectives to concepts, and the "shifting" of concepts across environments and settings (which students in the second iteration of the pedagogic study managed to achieve to a fairly satisfying deep engagement extent, albeit novice-like, but how else would it be? The exact concepts they were learning were new to them.) Students would not have the same level of confidence and concept schemata to generate concept meanings as an experienced expert would. That is why the teacher is present. However, IG pedagogical activities and tasks are meant to be a space for meaning exchange, where no knowledge is most powerful and no meaning is set in stone, but, rather, meanings are shared and the teacher-expert steps in as the assigned subject authority to share the latest development in the field, the concept in constant evolution. Students are encouraged to provide a considerable scope of concept manifestations as chosen and developed by themselves and hence enrich their own developing notion of the concept, offering possibilities for metacognition and criticality, ultimately leading toward transformative, multimodal and integrative learning. This is the educational vision that this book supports and promotes.

The activity took the students by surprise, resembling Peirce's *learning by surprise*, highlighted by Nöth (2010, p. 3):

It is by surprise that experience teaches us all she deigns to teach us (EP 2, p. 154)… only surprise and new experience can change old beliefs. We believe until some surprise breaks up the habit. The breaking of a belief can only be due to some novel experience. (CP 5.524, 1905)

Once IG designs and ways of thinking become integrated in higher education practices and possibly stifle the element of surprise and novelty, new forms of designs and surprises will be needed. This book has comprehensively argued for a move toward an edusemiotic type of teaching—learning in which variations of IG and other practices are embedded.

Graphics can be both material objects and representations of material objects in the physical world. Via inquiry graphics, an integrative approach is achieved, just as Cunningham (1985, p. 432; 1987, p. 196, quoted in Nöth, 2010) "sensitizes us to the notion that cognition always involves an interaction between the physical world and the cognizing organism," and as he "questions the possibility of absolute knowledge, which stresses the provisional nature of questions and which emphasizes the knowledge generating process itself."

IG acts can support transformative education in today's world of hyper fast ephemeral instant messaging, a plethora of images, and vigorous life on and of social media. One role for education may be to moderate the pace of this information exchange (as mentioned earlier in Chap. 1 with the reference to dromology (Kellner, 1999), slow it down, and help students be critical and well-informed, as consumers, producers and citizens. The role of education on a wider plane, then, is to support pausing and reflecting on our everyday communication and concerns, balancing out the constant pressures of fast living, productivity, and ever-speedier technology immersion, mobile phone attachments and entertainment media binge-watching. Technology is formidable but we need not become too dependent on it, or uncritical of its help and wonders.

The IG approach supports the role of mindful and pluralist education-of-possibilities, and education for social justice, as outlined by Maxine Greene (1995, p. 182):

As we ponder educational purposes, we might take into account the possibility that the main point of education… is to enable a human being to become increasingly mindful with regard to his or her lived situation-and its untapped possibilities. The languages and symbol systems we make available ought to provide possibilities for thematizing very diverse human experiences and, not incidentally, for diverse introductions to the conversations among people that carries the culture on in time.

This idea is wonderfully developed by Nick Sousanis (see excerpts from Nick's work in Appendix 1) in his work on bridging the dualism of word and image in education via graphic novel and comics format. His book, *Unflattening* (Sousanis, 2015), contains images that integrate a reference to Marcuse's (2013) *One-dimensional Man*, criticizing the world that abounds with "a flatness of possibilities," where inhabitants conform to what Marcuse called "a pattern of one-dimensional thought and behavior." Inquiry graphics analyses and methods place to the fore a search for and an inquiry into possibilities, "an infinite progress of becoming by which signs and meanings are connected by the human mind" (Sebeok et al., 1988, pp. 24–25). In short, life happens by constantly blurring and moving disciplinary and interdisciplinary boundaries. Perhaps the way forward in education, as exemplified earlier with reference to some ongoing postgraduate interdisciplinary programs, might be to organize teaching around "themes, global challenges, and scenarios" that will cross disciplinary boundaries, but still preserve the disciplines. Perhaps the future will continue seeing the developments of professional expertise built around multidisciplinary approaches.

# Inquiry Graphics in a "Production–Signification–Consumption" Critical Media Literacy Method

I have been developing IG activities over a number of years. One such development has been to incorporate an IG sign as a Peircean sign informed activity in a Production–Signification–Consumption (PSC) visual analysis method to support critical media literacy (Lackovic, 2020). The method builds on the triadic sign cross-fertilized with the premise of the three sites of image meaning-making in the context of digital media: (1) production (that encompasses reproduction or circulation), (2) consumption, and (3) the image itself (Rose, 2006).

## Production–Consumption Site Questions

When tackling pictorial meaning, Rose (2006) talks about three sites of image meaning-making that are important when considering picture interpretation and its effects in the society: image production, the image itself (e.g., its materiality and composition), and the site of the audience who consume images. The PSC method builds on this aspect of visual research methods (Rose, 2006). In terms of digital image production and reuse, human intent is important in defining the meaning and intentions "behind" image uses. Some key questions aligned with image production and consumption inquiry as well as affect are exemplified here, with the focus on photographs:

*Photo-production Critical Questions*

- Where does the photograph come from? Who is the source of information?
- Can its origin be defined (could possibly be traced via Google's "Search by image" function (the photo camera icon))?
- Who created it, why that author/ organization/ group?
- Where was the photograph taken?
- When was the photograph taken (an era/ decade/ year)?
- Why was it created, with what purpose?
- Does it look staged, is it a stock photo?

*Photo-production Affect Question*

- Is there an affective intention behind its production, what could it be (what are the intended desires and values of the consumers/audiences that are targeted by the producer(s))?

*Photo-consumption and Reproduction Critical Questions*

- Who consumes the photograph? Who are the photograph's intended consumers/ audiences (this links to production)?
- Is the site of photograph consumption the site of primary author and creator of the photograph? How can we know this ("Search by image" function)?

- What is the photograph's digital life? How is it repurposed and reused on the web, to serve what purposes? Does it appear everywhere in the same form or it is modified, (e.g. into a hybrid sign such as meme)? Where (what digital platforms and media) has it been uploaded on? ("Search by image" function)?
- What words are used with it, what labels and descriptions?

*Photo-consumption Affect Questions*

- What are (can be) the affective reactions to the photograph consumption by various audiences? Why? Was this reaction intended by the person creating and/or the person uploading the photograph?
- Could a dominant reaction be identified in particular groups and across groups and why? Is there any evidence of how viewers react to the photograph?
- What are/could be the differences in reactions by different viewers, and why?

In today's post-digital landscape of photographic upload frenzy, it can be hard to trace the digital life, birth and re-authoring of photographs, as they are readily appropriated, repurposed, modified, collaged, and/or labeled with new texts. Even if some questions above are hard to answer, or cannot be answered, considering them supports critical reflection and acknowledges that complex factors contribute to visual media meaning-making, although they are not transparent or readily available to the public. In the frantic digital production and dissemination medley, the visual has become a part of a power game and media wars, where careful orchestrations of film, television and advertisement production goes around in global circles (Mirzeoff, 2002).

## Signification Site of the Image Itself via Focused Inquiry Graphics Analysis and Questions

The signification aspect of Production–Signification–Consumption embeds an IG analysis as it is aligned with Peirce's tripartite sign. Each of the triadic nodes (representamen–object–interpretant) focuses the analysis and inquiry on the sign as follows: the embodied representamen focuses the analysis on researcher's, learners' or participants' observing, naming (as singular nouns) and listing the content of the photograph; the interpretant-led analytical step focuses analytical attention on researcher's, learners' or participants' interpretations; and the object of inquiry (conceptual object; research object) step focuses attention on the symbolic meanings linked to theory, research questions or pedagogic goal. Such an inquiry of the relations between graphic embodied representamen, its symbolic object, and interpretations concerning a theory or concept is a central tenet of turning any graphics, such as digital photographs, into *inquiry graphics*. For example, an inquiry graphic activity would encourage learners or research participants to find or make photographs that can represent an aspect of an abstract concept, such as the broad concepts of democracy or social (in)justice or more specific concepts of constructivist learning in educational psychology. The steps of inquiry graphics are thoroughly explained below as: 1. digital materiality and photo content naming (embodied representamen), 2. descriptive interpretation (interpretant), and 3. object of inquiry (conceptual/ research/ thematic object, what the photograph refers to in conceptual and theoretical inquiry terms).

1. Digital Materiality and Photo Content Naming (Embodied Representamen)

Imagine a photograph showing a person, let us say someone who looks like a man (could be a different gender) being physically assaulted by some hands pulling this man from the back. His face and facial expression are visible. An analysis of the photograph itself would start with identifying and listing all individual elements shown in the photographic content as singular nouns (this is $R$ = embodied representamen-led interpretation). Elements are listed as nouns (a man, a jumper, a hand, a pavement, and so on). Nouns as elements are used to state that something is present in the photograph. Considering details in photographs focuses the attention on how pictorial materiality and the individual elements shown all contribute equally to overall meaning-making and can serve as springboards for creative and critical insights. Elements can be listed with regards to their positioning and to the space occupied, from larger to smaller spatial characteristics (e.g., a man, a body, a face, an eye, a pupil, and so on). Element-naming can involve interpretative category variations (e.g., shoes or a shoe type such as sneakers or sandals). Element naming is also interpretative, as all sides of the triadic relation are interpretative. If the researcher is interested in even more sense-nuanced aspects of representamen such as color and shapes, this can also be the starting point. The point is to first focus on the art of perceiving (Arnheim, 1997) and naming. Example questions for this step in the analysis would be:

- Can you name, list and number everything you see, from bigger to smaller individual items (things or elements) represented (to the extent that can serve your analysis goals)? For a fine-grain analysis, note the smaller things that are a part of larger things (e.g., eyes–head–body; graphite pencil; handle of mug, and so on).
- Do you think that this photograph has been modified in any way? If so, what might have been modified?

2. Descriptive Interpretation of Interpretant: Denotation and Connotation

Interpretant (*I*) analytical focus proceeds to describe the photograph in two distinct steps. These distinct steps build on Barthes' (1988) semiotic distinction of denotation and connotation. A denotation level description of the photograph adapted from Barthes (1988) would go on to describe these elements; what they look like, what is happening to them (e.g., for the element "eye": "the eyes look (seem) wide open"). This means describing human action or things (e.g. the man is wearing shoes; the shoes are worn-out or brown). These descriptions would take a form of "simple" descriptions, with the speculative verbs such as "seems," "looks like," or "is possibly" together with descriptive adjectives or adverbs. The use of speculative verbs as an open-ended description is important, in order to stress that something one person sees and describes might not be the same as what someone else sees or might not be what it seems to the interpreter, hence the heterogeneity of meanings is practiced. The denotative descriptions can be compared to see what occurs in all learners (or research participants') interpretations, if anything, and where the main differences arise or what is omitted.

Some of the key question for this step would be:

- Can you describe what is happening in the photograph, by using words and constructs that signal individual interpretation such as: "it looks like," "it seems to me," "it is possibly"? This description is a simple-level description that involves speculative verbs (seems, looks appears), descriptive adjectives of states (open, closed, red, muddy, dry, small, etc.) and adverbs to denote what things or phenomena represented look like to individual interpreters at a basic level of interpretation.
- What is not shown in the photograph, but it could have been? Do you feel that something is omitted/ missing from the photograph, but it could be there?

The interpretation would then move on to connotation adapted from Barthes (1996), which is where the interpretative diversity starts to become more distinct. Further sociocultural meaning of the description is assigned by interpreters, for instance when the denotatively described expression in the man's wide-open eyes is interpreted as "victim's discomfort and fear (the man in the photo becomes a victim as the roles of victims and perpetrators, powerful and powerless are socioculturally assigned meanings to the described acts)." At this stage it is important to stress that various interpreters would have different interpretation of what sociocultural meaning is shown, determined by their background, prior knowledge, upbringing and experiences. The exploration of these connotative meanings can include these questions:

- What do you think the sociocultural meaning(s) of the descriptions is?
- How do you know its cultural/ social/ national context?
- What could the gazes (e.g., direct, away, upwards, downwards), body positioning and interaction of the people be suggesting, and what effects these can have on viewers?

- What about the roles of the observed people and what function would material things have? (e.g., an observed woman could adopt a role of a student, teacher, manager, mother, housewife, scientist, prisoner; a heavy book can be a learning, art or assault object, and so on).
- Why? Why do you interpret the look of this image or its element(s) to mean what you assign to it? What informs you? How have your social and cultural experiences informed the meanings assigned to this image?
- How can we estimate the era/ decade/ year when it was taken?
- What could have happened before and after the photograph was taken?
- What are the possible alternative interpretations of the sociocultural meanings that were possibly intended and interpreted by you?
- How would meanings change dependent on different viewers/ context/ place/ time of consumption? (e.g., if the photograph relates to your sociocultural context, would a similar photograph exist in your context, in what ways and what informs your claims? If it does relate to your context, how would it exist or be presented in other contexts?)
- How have the represented things and their meanings changed historically, over time?

These discussions would illuminate human embeddedness in the society and socially constructed meanings, as well as human vulnerability to accepting or seeking a truth in media information that most appeal to their prior knowledge, experiences and desires (Arnheim, 1997), including human need for certainty and stability in life, defined by class, economic, educational and demographic background. A digital photographic image is powerful in shaping the value attached to the external world, which can be used to enhance the packaging of the truths promoted in the public media. Photographic and pictorial interpretants in the media (connotations) in general have become so symbolically commercialized, status- and success-driven that they act as ideological signs, a Barthesian myth (Barthes, 2009). This also signals the political meaning of visual signs, for example, via the politics of pictures selected to be promoted in the news media, in education and international curricula (Lackovic, 2010).

It is important to be careful when making claims in an image description, as suggestions need to be derived from a careful act of perceiving and reflecting on what the image shows and what it does not show. For example, no image shows fear via its representational quality (embodied representamen here) but humans *interpret it* as such. That is why it is advisable to use probabilistic verbs, or at least signal this when interpreting. A photograph shows a material form, such as a facial expression and action that we interpret as "fear" or related to fear. This means that in a learning community, a teacher can ask students to search and choose or create images that represent one and the same concept to them, in order to share and discuss those, to explore nuances of meanings and sociocultural practices at the intersection of meaning and materiality. In the post-truth times, learners could, for example, find and analyze images on the same concepts and topics on various websites or social media accounts that offer contradictory interpretations and images of that concept.

3. Object of Inquiry: What the Photograph Refers to in Conceptual and Theoretical Inquiry Terms

In the final analytical stage of inquiry graphics, signification, the inquiry would tease out possible links between the image and the focal concept, theme or question in the inquiry. This educational concept is analytical (conceptual and research) object or the superimposed object of inquiry. It can be a concept assigned to an image (but not necessarily), a theme, its claim to truth and a label given to the image or any statements in the media attached to it (perhaps in the news), by posing questions such as:

- How are individual image elements of embodied representamen and interpretant linked to the concept/ theme/ the chosen theory of inquiry or any truth claimed or statements about the photograph made?
- What theoretical or conceptual knowledge can help illuminate the meanings and effects of the sign?
- How can the characteristics of the listed individual elements and interpretant descriptions bring in new ideas and insights about the concept explored or the claims that the image is supposed to offer (e.g. via caption or text)?
- Can I probe this concept further, stretch it, challenge it?

Teachers rarely encounter such approaches when preparing to teach. Inquiry graphics can help teachers go beyond assimilating visual media at the level of an illustrative role toward integrating those at a deeper learning level into subjects' inquiry (Lackovic, Crook, Cobb, Shalloe, & Cruz, 2015). The power and uniqueness of an IG analysis is in creating this exploratory space in-between a picture and idea, a possibility and actuality (Bruner, 2009), for tackling sociocultural interpretation seriously. It is a space for considering possibilities for meanings at the intersection of the conceptual and the material, including previously unimaginable or unconsidered possibilities and solutions.

## Toward a Relational Theory of Education: An Edusemiotic Relationality metamodel

Finally, I begin to close this book by providing a larger ecological and edusemiotic map (Lackovic, 2020) that I introduced and promised at the beginning of this book. Edusemiotic relationality is an idea of a metamodel for an exploration of educational and disciplinary concepts and ideas as interconnected/relational. This involves graphics such as photographs in education and digital education, in relation to theories and concepts that can be positioned along the diverse and relational spectrum of the sociomaterial world (Fig. 9.2). I have earlier proposed relational approaches to graduate employability (GE), arguing against a dominant individualist anthropocentric employability paradigm, proposing a paradigm shift in how graduate employability is conceptualized in higher education (Lackovic, 2019). It positions individual students as relational to their closest community as well as global social communities, emotions, technology and ecology (ibid.). In a similar vein, photographs and what individuals and groups do with them are always relational to a larger sociomaterial landscape. I note that the distinction between animate and inanimate nature/matter is fluid, especially if observed from the perspectives of recent posthumanist approaches such as "vibrant matter" and "vital materiality" (Bennett, 2009) that argues distinct influences of various matter in human life, as ad hoc configurations of human and nonhuman forces; how to interpret this distinction depends on a point of view.

It has been stated several times that photographs, due to their representational quality and embeddedness in materiality (digital screens or the matter of the print) are objects of both visual and sociomaterial cultures, but are also scholarly objects. This aligns with the growing field of sociomateriality in relation to education (Silva, 2019; Fenwick, Edwards, & Sawchuk, 2015), which argues that materiality cannot be separated from social inquiry. The PSC IG method adopts this sociomaterial view of the world, as the book so far has emphasized how the materiality of

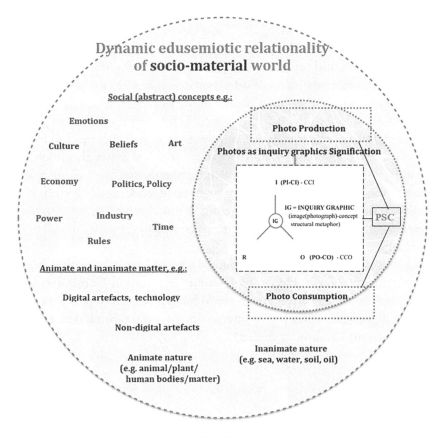

**Fig. 9.2**  Dynamic Edusemiotic Relationality (ER) metamodel

pictures and photographs are deeply embedded in and relational to sociocultural meanings. This relationality is shown in the metamodel/framework of Edusemiotic Relationality in Fig. 9.2.

The assemblages of pictures and abstract thinking with all their historicity, context, culture, emotions, prior knowledge and other sociomaterial aspects of world signification are emergent and evolving, just as Peirce's *synechism* proposes the evolutionary character of all signs. However, we can "freeze" this emergence, and pause accelerated hypervisuality, not to worship it, but to think, explore and unpack the image–concept, a multimodal concept-rhizome, a rhizomatic concept. Teachers and researchers can explore what it consists of and what relations exist, how they are made and why it is so, as much as this is possible, as it is hard to catch constantly flying, fluid and developing worldly sign emergence and assemblages. This model (Fig. 9.2) can be the basis for a sociomaterial method and analysis, with photographs as the starting unit of analysis, that expands into considerations of sociocultural production and consumption of the things shown in the photograph and the graph itself, linking those to the worldly concepts and theories, linked to politics, economy, policy, time, space, or power via related theories and concepts. This includes considerations of various forms of materiality, such as technology matter or minerals and oil as inanimate matter. It signifies an edusemiotic turn beyond the Anthropocene in education, to embrace relational inquiry that integrate questions around human action with the questions of ecology, materiality, artifacts, technology, media, and all living things.

Fig. 9.2. shows a dynamic multimodal edusemiotic relationality map of photo/ graphics PSC (Production-Signification-Consumption) embeddedness in the sociomaterial world for exploration of photographs as IG in higher education (at the intersection of social (abstract) concepts and animate and inanimate matter).

# IG Data Collection and Analysis in Higher Education Research

In terms of how IG artefacts and approach can be applied in educational research, any method can be enriched with visual media; visual or multi-modal data can be collected for an IG analysis, for example, by following Signification IG questions or PSC method (Lackovic, 2020) to set tasks or embed into an interview or focus group schedule that would include images for particants' reflection. Participants can keep multimodal diaries, using either photographs or videos (for a related video analysis example in educational research, see Lackovic, 2018). Researchers can photograph or video-record spaces dedicated to private or collective study, such as libraries and various facilities that library spaces provide, including learning, collaborative work and snack zones. However, it is acknowledged that recording in large spaces can be particularly challenging. While planning these and any other image-related action, it is essential to devise the best strategy to assure an ethically sound project. Obtaining relevant information from ethical committees and external specialist organizations is important in the planning stage. A growing body of research that has utilized videos in various contexts outside of education can provide insights about approaches and solutions applied in those different contexts and lessons learnt. *An Introduction to Using Video for Research* (Jewitt, 2012), an NCRM (National Centre for Research Methods) working paper, offers an overview of video approaches such as videography or video elicitation. Today's advances in technology include portable mobile cameras as well as portable devices like GoPro. Such cameras provide opportunities to create "video trails," for example of students'/ participants'/ researcher's movements (e.g., around campus, when commuting, when doing an activity, and so on). Again, this must be handled carefully in terms of impinging on people's privacy and anonymity, and aligned with ethical practice and informed of other questions surrounding visual methods (e.g., Simco & Warin, 1997, discuss visual methods' validity). Today's technology software has advanced so that it can offer possibilities to protect the anonymity of video-recorded people, such as face or body blurring technique and photo modification.

An IG analysis offers a novel approach to educational research and research methods designs, as it offers the model and structures around which research can be developed. IG questions (such as the PSC questions in the section above) can be used for an IG elicitation (IGE) interview, as a species of multimodal and visual research method such as photo elicitation (PE) or its sub-method "photo-voice." An IGE, as reflected in Chap. 4, like photo-voice (also spelled photovoice), would be realized by asking research participants or learners to provide images that they make or find, which are also fit for research, to relate to an issue, a problem, an experience, and/or to represent a concept or a research key interest or theme. Participants can be asked to take photographs of objects, people, events and places and find photographs online. The IG triadic structure provides opportunities for task-setting and interpretation analysis. Embedding an IG Signification analysis (Lackovic, 2020) within a photo-voice interview provides focus and gives greater value to the photo itself and its propreties, as otherwise, applications of photo-voice might observe photos as mainly being triggers for participants' creative work or reflection, without involving the image per se more in reflectvie and analytical considerations. Again, this has to be done in an ethically acceptable manner. This mens that the researcher may devise questions for participants that follow the IG analysis step (e.g., participants could first name elements, then describe them, then think of their sociocultural meanings and finally reflect on how all those elements individually and compositionally link to the "big" umbrella research concept, question or issue). One possible way of exploring the life of photographs is to try to devise photo trails, as was mentioned in Chap. 2, and understand how digital photographs get circulated – how and where they appear and reappear, for example by using the reverse photo search provided by Google images search engine (the little photo camera icon allows for uploading an image to search the internet for web places where it has been uploaded). Trails, maps or "lifelines" can be created with photographs. Clusters of pictures can be explored, for example ones that are labeled in similar way or occur in clusters on the media, such as institutional websites or news media.

The IG triadic sign and related coding (Lackovic, 2020; 2018) can be applied to analyze visual artifacts beyond educational research. Educational research and studies in higher education are cross-disciplinary fields. Researchers in any discipline can apply the IG approach to analyze the observed data led by the research object and pertinent to their area of interest, either disciplinary or cross-disciplinary. For example, sociologists can find IG useful for considering and unpacking renewed sociological relationships between artifacts, actors, action and their social context, meaning and uses. Psychologist can unpack further the extended cognition of human action and its link to material environment via images or other graphics and modes. Researchers interested in the use of digital technologies and the umbrella research communities such as TEL (technology enhanced learning) and digital education and pedagogy research) can observe and understand the complex interpretative signification of how humans use and relate to any type of technologies by considering visual, material and symbolic technology affordances (the design and functionality) and characteristics in relation to interpretation, production, dialogue afforder by specific technological features, which are highly visual. Researchers working in the area of language learning can observe how language learning is entwined with contextualized signification of environments, and signification in and through action and artifact mediation, linguist articulation and the entire interpretative repertoire of the tangible, material world that language learners carry around. Historians might want to apply IG approach to analyze and understand the meanings of historical places or objects. Researchers working in prominently tactile and visual fields such as medicine, design or engineering can explore various situations and engagement which require constant interpretation in conjunction between actors and material surroundings, and so on. To understand how environments and actions in those environments make meaning at various levels (micro, meso, macro) is one of the goals of international research across disciplines, not only educational research.

# Future Work on Developing Inquiry Graphics with Other Perspectives

This book has tackled the approaches related to inquiry graphics based on their relevance to education and learning as a specific type of learning and knowledge development, that of rhizomatic image–concept signs. The empirical part of the book mainly focused on understanding thinking processes that integrate images as edusemiotic inquiry graphics, their relevance to knowledge-building and an open-ended conceptual development. Much more attention could be dedicated to the unpacking of the findings via further theorizing as well as conceptual perspectives. Although the book deals with digital photographs as the main IG examples in the book, the image mode can be replaced or complemented with any other mode, such as sound, objects, movement, graphic art or video, potentially forming other compound signs such as *inquiry sounding, inquiry dancing, inquiry drawing*, perhaps in one word, *multimodal inquiry*.

As the foundations of the approach have been established, further analyses and theorization around applications of inquiry graphics can provide other insights about the meanings and environmental context that surrounds IGs as part of a relational educational and edusemiotic practice. Further elaborations can be done on concepts introduced here, such as (post)digital semiotics, (digital) semiotic creativity, edusemiotic relationality, threshold graphics or iconic surfacing. The following list offers possible relevant theoretical and conceptual perspectives that can be creatively cross-fertilized with an inquiry graphics and edusemiotics, including other semiotic approaches and concepts, such as ecosemiotics (Nöth, 1998; Maran & Kull, 2014) and semioethics (Petrilli & Ponzio, 2007). I am providing this list to invite further collaborations and developments across borders and boundaries that I think are possible and flexible. The list is not exhaustive, and no term excludes any other. The world of opportunities is wide open.

- Actor–Network Theory
- Affective theories
- Assemblage theory
- CHAT; The Change Laboratory

- Conceptual change
- Critical media studies
- Critical theory (e.g., race/ gender/ curriculum)
- Identity theories
- Interactionist approaches
- Material engagement theory
- Multiple representations
- Other semiotic approaches (other than edusemiotics)
- Post-humanism, and ecological development
- Problem based learning (PBL)
- Relational theories (sociology)
- Social practice theory
- Sociomateriality and new materiality
- Threshold concepts
- Visual and material culture

## Looking Ahead

Having reached the final page of this book, I can pause, as the foundations of an Inquiry Graphics (IGs) practice are set, a relational theory of learning is seeded, and my modest contributions to edusemiotics and semiotics with/of images in higher education provided, with hope and plans for developing them further. I sincerely hope for an adoption of IG approaches and the concepts developed in the book, to inform education futures at universities and beyond (e.g. arts, environment and health organisations, third sector). IG studies presented in this book provide abundant examples of how graphics, and digital photographs as types of graphics can be integrated into teaching in education programs and courses as well as into educational research methods and analysis. In a nutshell, this book has introduced Inquiry Graphics practice and eclectic theoretical underpinnings as new approaches to knowledge (development), thinking, learning and methods with images. It argues for an acknowledgment of learning and concept as an abstract-concrete, image-concept, icon-index-symbol engagement, adaptation and growth (via dialogue,    externalisation    of    interpretation    and    creation    of artefacts). Inquiry Graphics can bring into higher education a new, boundary moving notion of creativity and meaning-making as transmodal, relational (non-dualist) thinking, being and culture. I hope that the presented new approaches to knowledge, learning and methods will mediate interdisciplinarity, support and inspire international practitioners, scholars and students in higher education studies, teaching and learning, TEL and digital education research, semiotics, teacher training, and anyone interested in how to use digital images and other visual media, art forms and objects, modes and graphics. Finally, I hope that you, dear reader, will embrace Inquiry Graphics and Edusemiotic Relationality in your own practice, adding sparks, tweaks, criticality and value of your own experience, goals, imagination and creativity, wherever you are in this ever-evolving, colorful world.

# References

Allard-Huver, F., & Gilewicz, N. (2015). Digital Parrhesia 2.0: Moving beyond deceptive communications strategies in the digital world. In D. Harrison (Ed.), *Handbook of research on digital media and creative technologies* (pp. 404–416). Hershey PA: IGI Global.

Bakhtin, M. M. (1981). *The dialogic imagination: Four essays* (Michael Holquist, Ed. and Caryl Emerson & Michael Holquist, Trans.). Austin, TX: University of Texas Press. *84*(8), 80–82.

Bruner, J. S. (2009). *Actual minds, possible worlds*. Cambridge, MA: Harvard University Press.

Burkitt, I. (2008). *Social selves: Theories of self and society*. London: Sage.

Burkitt, I. (2014). *Emotions and social relations*. London: Sage.

Burkitt, I. (2016). Relational agency: Relational sociology, agency and interaction. *European Journal of Social Theory, 19*(3), 322–339.

Cunningham, D. J. (1985). Semiosis and learning. In J. Deely (Ed.), *Semiotics* 1984 (pp. 427–434). Lanham: University Press of America.

Deleuze, G. (1987) *Dialogues* (with Claire Parnet) (H. Tomlinson & G. Burchell, Trans.). New York: Columbia University Press.

Deleuze, G. (1995). *Negotiations 1972–1990* (M. Joughin, Trans.). New York: Columbia University Press.

Greene, M. (1995). *Releasing the imagination: Essays on education, the arts, and social change*. San Francisco: Jossey-Bass Publishers.

Hallewell, M. J., & Lackovic, N. (2017). Do pictures 'tell' a thousand words in lectures? How lecturers vocalise photographs in their presentations. *Higher Education Research & Development, 36*(6), 1166–1180.

Jewitt, C. (2012). An Introduction to Using Video for Research. In *NCRM Working Paper*, National Centre for Research Methods: Southampton, UK.

Kellner, D. (1999). Virilio, war and technology: Some critical reflections. *Theory, Culture & Society, 16*(5–6), 103–125.

Kress, G. (2004). *Literacy in the new media age.* London: Routledge.

Lackovic, N. (2010). Creating and reading images: Towards a communication framework for higher education learning. In *Seminar. Net: Media, technology & life-long learning* (pp. 121–135).

Lackovic, N. (2016). MultiMAP: Exploring multimodal artefact pedagogy in digital higher education. *Proceedings, 148–162.*

Lackovic, N. (2018). Analysing videos in educational research: An "Inquiry Graphics" approach for multimodal, Peircean semiotic coding of video data. *Video Journal of Education and Pedagogy, 3*(1), 1–23.

Lackovic, N. (2019). Graduate employability (GE) paradigm shift: Towards greater socio-emotional and eco-technological relationalities of graduates' futures. In M. Peters, P. Jandrić, & A. Means (Eds.), *Education and technological unemployment* (pp. 193–212). Singapore: Springer.

Lackovic, N. (2020). Thinking with digital images in the post-truth era: A method in critical media literacy. In *Postdigtial science and education.* Springer.

Lackovic, N., Crook, C., Cobb, S., Shalloe, S., & D'Cruz, M. (2015). Imagining technology-enhanced learning with heritage artefacts: Teacher-perceived potential of 2D and 3D heritage site visualisations. *Educational Research, 57*(3), 331–351.

Land, R., Cousin, G., Meyer, J. H., & Davies, P. (2005). Threshold concepts and troublesome knowledge (3): Implications for course design and evaluation. In *Improving student learning–equality and diversity.* Oxford, UK: OCSLD.

Malafouris, L. (2013). *How things shape the mind.* Cambridge, MA: MIT Press.

Maran, T., & Kull, K. (2014). Ecosemiotics: Main principles and current developments. *Geografiska Annaler: Series B, Human Geography, 96*(1), 41–50.

Marcuse, H. (2013). *One-dimensional man: Studies in the ideology of advanced industrial society.* New York: Routledge.

Mavers, D. (2011). *Children's drawing and writing: The remarkable in the unremarkable.* New York: Routledge.

Meyer, J., & Land, R. (2003). *Threshold concepts and troublesome knowledge: Linkages to ways of thinking and practising within the disciplines.* Edinburgh, UK: University of Edinburgh.

Mirzoeff, N. (Ed.). (2002). *The visual culture reader.* Psychology Press.

Newfield, D. R. (2009). Transmodal semiosis in classrooms: Case studies from South Africa (Doctoral dissertation, Institute of Education, University of London).

Nöth, W. (1998). Ecosemiotics. Σημειωτκή-*Sign Systems Studies,* 26(1), 332–343.

Nöth, W. (2010). The semiotics of teaching and the teaching of semiotics. In I. Semetsky (Ed.), *Semiotics education experience* (pp. 1–19). Brill/Sense.

O'Halloran, K., Tan, S., Smith, B., & Podlasov, A. (2009, September). Digital semiotics. In *Proceedings 10th IASS-AIS world congress of semiotics, A Coruña Spain* (pp. 22–26).

Öztok, M. (2016). Cultural ways of constructing knowledge: The role of identities in online group discussions. *International Journal of Computer-Supported Collaborative Learning, 11*(2), 157–186.

Pesce, S. (2010). From semiotics of teaching to educational semiotics: The case of French-speaking research in education. In I. Semetsky (Ed.), *Semiotics education experience* (pp. 99–113). Brill/Sense.

Petrilli, S., & Ponzio, A. (2007). Semiotics today. From global semiotics to semio-ethics, a dialogic response. *Signs, 1,* 29–127.

Rose, G. (2006, 2nd edition). *Visual methodologies: An introduction to researching with visual materials.* London: Sage.

Sebeok, T. A., Umiker-Sebeok, D. J., & Young, E. P. (Eds.). (1988). *The semiotic web 1987.* Mouton de Gruyter.

Silva, P. (2019, March). Sociomateriality and the agency of objects/things in education. In *Conference proceedings EDUNOVATIC 2018: 3rd virtual international conference on education, innovation and ICT* (p. 85).

Simco, N., & Warin, J. (1997). Validity in image-based research: An elaborated illustration of the issues. *British Educational Research Journal, 23*(5), 661–672.

Smith-Shank, D. L. (2010). Semiotic pedagogy and visual culture curriculum. In Inna Semetsky (Ed.), *Semiotics education experience* (pp. 247–258). Brill Sense Publishers.

Sousanis, N. (2015). *Unflattening.* Harvard University Press.

Stables, A. (2010). Semiosis and the collapse of mind-body dualism: Implications for education. In Inna Semestky (Ed.), *Semiotics education experience* (pp. 21–36). Brill/Sense.

Sturken, M., Cartwright, L., & Sturken, M. (2001). *Practices of looking: An introduction to visual culture.* Oxford University Press.

von Uexkull, J. (1982). The theory of meaning. *Semiotica, 42,* 25–82.

# Appendices

## Appendix 1: Graphic Narratives that Can Be a Part of an Inquiry Graphics Activity

Illustrations by Nick Sousanis and Andi Setiawan, courtesy of Nick Sosuanis and Andi Setiawan

© The Author(s) 2020
N. Lacković, *Inquiry Graphics in Higher Education*,
https://doi.org/10.1007/978-3-030-39387-8

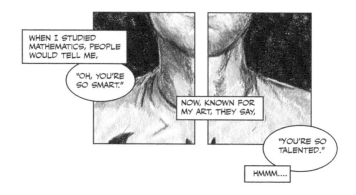

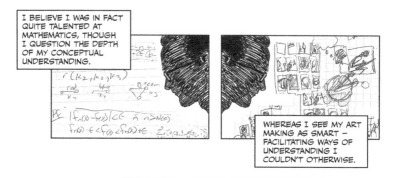

See the whole Frames of Thought paper at: https://humanitiesfutures. org/papers/frames-of-thought/

---

# Unflattening

**v. tr., gerund**

1. An action of opening eyes, seeing through multiple perspectives simultaneously.

2. Attitude and orientation for seeing depths within depths.

3. Process of continual asking.

4. Looking from multiple vantage points simultaneously.

5. Something not reducible to purely verbal description.

---

Adapted from Nick Sousanis' www.spinweaveandcut.com entry on 30/11/2010 © nick sousanis 2010/2020, all rights reserved

Illustrations by Andi Setiawan
Credit: Andi Setiawan @2020, all rights reserved

Permission for the use of images provided by the author/images modified from colour to black and white/.

## Farmer Against Cement Plant

**Image 1**

### Description
Farmers protested in front of the presidential palace because their rice fields were evicted by a cement plant. The protest was carried out by cementing their feet into the wooden box. The President responded by saying that the issue related to establishing the cement plant was a policy of the local government, not to be brought to the central government.
Jakarta, March 2017
### Translation
Balloon text: …do not bring that local issue to my office…
Box text: One day in front of the presidential palace…

## New Airport Development Protest

### Image 2

### Description

Farmers protest the eviction of their rice fields, homes and villages for the purpose of building a new airport. They fight when bulldozers begin to destroy their land. They refused the compensation offered and insisted on remaining as farmers and refused to be evicted.

Yogyakarta, November 2017

### Translation

Balloon box: ... we remain standing for our self and determined to maintain our living space

## Image 2

### Description

Mrs Wagirah, a farmer, fought against the eviction of her land and rice fields. She stopped the bulldozer by sitting on its shovel.

Yogyakarta, June 2018

### Translation

Balloon box: …what's wrong with my plantation? …can you just stop….

Box text: Mrs. Wagirah, a farmer from Kulon Progo, fights for her land and plantation

# Appendix 2: Project 1 Doctoral Students Quotes that Support the Thematic Evaluation of the IG "Thinking with Images" Activity -The Saved Screengrab Format

- <u>Challenging stereotypes</u> Patrick:

    "The idea that you confront the stereotypes that you have about thing by looking at visual representations of them and then thinking what is going on behind your choice, even of photos that represent something. I think that's the main point. Get your ideas, preconceived notions out there; then, they are open to be challenged by other people with their different ideas. The idea that in teaching, from my own point of view, you get their background knowledge and that would be that you are trying to build on top of that."

- <u>Deconstruction of historical artefacts; multiple perspectives (history subject)</u>

Jessica:

    "This is exactly the sort of process I would try and scaffold the students through if you know what I mean - there is an artefact from a time. I think what is quite powerful about this is as an artefact of the scientific world (...) this is as close to a photograph of the time, it has that immediacy as an image. I think it is quite useful for achieving that multi perspective notion of epistemology which is very useful to actually understanding empiricism"

- <u>Discussion and presentation scaffolding</u>

Shaun:

    "I think it could be an interesting way to either scaffold a discussion or for them to do a sort of presentation work. In fact it might be good for presentation because the students tend to put too much text and if you gave them something like this it may be a way of helping them express meaning through image rather than just of PowerPoint slides with text. I think the image to set the tone and the expectation and the text to provide examples."

James:

> "It's rare that you as a student have to find an image to represent things but teachers do it fairly often, with their slides and might have a clip from a film that they think exemplifies what they're talking about. Certainly in a presentation based led or initiated discussion where someone has to do a presentation bit and everyone has to have a debate, that really encourages and works really well when you've got pictures that represent concepts or different ideas or viewpoints. If someone had all these things that they had them pre-prepared and then presented them and was then: "ah, what do you think?""

Christian:

> "It's useful to find images to initiate a discussion on some topics. I could see myself doing it in a teaching situation. I could definitely see myself having PowerPoint with an image and then asking students what you get from this image. What do you think? I have done something like that previously. I told them for instance talk about a topic and then bring five PowerPoint slides. And then I might do the same with the images. Just tell them that you just need to talk about this topic and discuss it and then you need to find, for instance, three images or just one image and then I would help them a little bit, like you have helped me. I can see that the task of finding the images is a very good task for actually thinking about a topic yourself. So I think that learning is two step learning. You learn something yourself and you find the image and then you learn something else when you bring the image to somebody; to the classroom and you discuss it. So it's a two step learning process."

- Less suitable for some disciplines

Shaun thought that the activity was hard to be implemented for computer sciences students, especially for teaching programming, which is his subject area. Christian also thought that it might be more suitable for particular disciplines:

I think that some disciplines would benefit more but yes I can definitely see the value.

- Visual literacy

Mathew:

> "I have never been asked to think through images in my education except when I was doing my MA (digital photography). (…) Do people understand images? An image is only worth a thousand words if it's used within the right context. There is a need for a real appreciation of images… To know when to use them… I think it's enormously important. As soon as we've got this era of desktop publishing and easy access to images we've gone absolutely mental. I've seen academic posters that have to be the worst offenders ever, where they put 50 images…."

- Comparing images

Mathew also envisaged the value of the images for discussion in terms of developing a comparative narrative between Popper and Skinner and discussing the meaning of "measurement" in empiricism: *"Do we really know what measurement is? I think no one really knows"*

- Picture selection as personalised learning

Elisabeth:

> "I definitely think it's useful and I thought about doing it occasionally, trying to get the students to think about their own examples of things so I guess taking that further is to look for their own examples of things, or even create it by drawing it. Because you're kind of playing around with your own understanding of it rather than me just standing here and telling you stuff, you see if you understand it (…) even if you take it simply and say well find a picture that represents Freud say, psychoanalysis, and then you could find an illustrative picture. But even that you have to justify: why you've chosen the picture and then you start thinking a bit more about it. Even if it's a simple picture, it's useful."

- Memory prompt

Elisabeth thought of picture usefulness as a memory prompt for an exam.

- The value of picture selection over picture drawing

Natalie made an interesting point that selecting pictures was better than drawing, since the students would "find" an image which is not originally made by them. Such cases, according to Elisabeth, would create fewer issues with authorship and fear of criticising someone's work or your own work being criticised:

> "For critiquing each others because it's easier to critique something like this where you've got a picture and you've found it and it's not yours. Whereas if they've done a presentation or a piece of writing or something that they've created they feel a bit more intimidated about people critiquing it and discussing why it's not relevant."

- Novel way of seeing things

Oscar:

> "I see it as a useful activity in trying to engage the students at a different level, in a different way. So, it could be useful... Because you want to explore.... And this could work for some students: let me think outside the box. I would definitely like to try it out with my students."

Andrew:

> So an image of a historical mathematician might prompt some ....what is he doing in that picture? And it might just prompt some different way of thinking into .... But you can't really pin it down. You couldn't really put it into words, but it might spark off a different way of seeing things. It reminds me of that book somebody lent me. They lent me a John Berger, written in the sixties, "Ways of seeing".

- Developing concept understanding

Natalie:

It's interesting because it makes you think of the concept more. Because this (empiricism) is a concept you hear about it a lot but it's made me think: do I actually really understand it? Because I just relate it to research and you don't really think about it in depth but when you've got to think of images and images that can provoke a discussion, it makes you think in more depths in terms of what you take for granted, or you know the term but you don't really think about what it means. If you have a conversation with somebody who's your friends or family members and doesn't know anything about research; when you try to explain it to them, it's quite hard.

- Suitable for dyslexic students

Natalie also noted the possible advantage of the image method for the students who have difficulties with language, such as dyslexic students.

- Exercises students' creativity

Natalie:

"I know when I was at secondary school it was just a bit boring, the teacher at the front telling you what to do. Having to do a task like this brings out people's creative side and normally in the educational setting in this country, well when I was in school we didn't really have much chance to do that. With the Google Images, if you were learning a concept you could type in what the concept was and you could see what came up on it, and it could give you different ideas and it could reinforce the learning. I think possibly with doing this kind of activity it makes you think more."

- Interesting and thought-provoking

Andrew:

Exploration of empiricism in terms of images... I find this interesting, provocative for a number of reasons. I don't know how to label it. I just think I could label that empiricism and let ideas flow from that because there's enough in the image and the name empiricism to say well actually where's that going with that? That's provoking, isn't it?

# Appendix 3 : Project 1 Doctoral Students' Feedback Quotes on the Guidelines – The Saved Screengrab Format

1) Guidelines were useful for supporting multiple perspectives

Patrick:

"really good "that was easy for me to go and look for certain ideas that I had in mind but maybe if I thought I had to fulfil a few different criteria, that might be more difficult".

Jessica:

"It is quite a useful way in… scaffolding someone into the image, asking questions that bring somebody to the image and force them to engage with it… there is a certain amount of shock element in this image which is quite useful … an emotional pull".

Shaun:

"I am looking at most of the titles (in the guidelines) and think if you have these and said: "Select an image that would fit each category and then maybe said select one that fits two categories… it would be important not to just have one per thing but to get mixing going on, but yes I think it could be a useful checklist."

The guidelines were seen as useful by James:

"If only because they show you all the different aspects that any one concept can have. So empiricism has lots of different focuses, this thing and cultural things and you might not necessarily think about that. So there's a list of things you should think about a concept. It's quite useful."

Christian:

"I think that they're pretty useful when you're searching for an image because you can give me a task to search for iconic and I would find an image and then you would ask me to search for a contrast and a metaphor and so on. That would be useful because I think that a lot of the time you would tend to find iconic images so you would find the test tubes and that would be it. And to be honest they are not that thought provoking. You can talk a lot about empiricism but you don't get a lot from the picture because it's just 6 test tubes with coloured liquid. So it's okay to pick any of these others for discussion but you don't get a lot from the picture. The categories seem good because if you can actually find an image to fit a lot of the categories then I think it would be a very good image for discussion because you could discuss a lot of different things."

Natalie:

"Yes I think if you'd seen those before having been asked to look for pictures it could help you think more about …because you've got the before and after and timeline. Those are the things I wouldn't have thought about."

"It's quite difficult to show in an image (…) They can mean so many things so that's quite interesting…"

Brian:

"I can think lots of things would be very useful I can see this working as a suite of images, a grade of images, as a continuum."

2) Necessary vs. unnecessary

Unnecessary: Oscar and Andrew:

Andrew:

> I say it's just ... it all seems a bit alien still. It's very difficult for me. There seems to be a block there. I just don't seem to be seeing these images in that sort of way."|

Oscar:

> "I can see why you created them, yes. I would prefer a more deductive approach. I would totally have a blank sheet and they would come up with those assumptions and from that we can make meaning from that. So to come up with a list like that I think predisposes that their thinking, as you said familiarity and it's within quite a bounded frame. And for me I would come up with a blank sheet and from there, yes, come with that at the end. It puts everyone in a straight jacket in that we have to fit. We have understanding, we have environment and if you are coming to understand that, not just telling you what it is."

Necessary: Mathew:

> "I think that's really, really helpful. If I had that beforehand there would be a very different set of images. You'd have more images. They'd have made more sense. They'd have something to do with the narrative perhaps. And I would have still liked what I have chosen; because we have a nice contrast here; but there is far more... It would be a lot clearer. "

3) Prior vs. after the search

Furthermore, Natalie thought that the guidelines should be given to the students prior to the search whereas David suggested to let students to do the activity first on their own without any guidelines and then to map their images to the guidelines images.

4) Supporting image interpretation

Jessica had an idea of using the guidelines not just as support for thinking about the concept and image depictions but as a support for interpreting images during the discussion.

# Appendix 4: Extracts from Jarvis's Mexico Metro and the Virgin Bands Poster Narrative in Project 3 – The Saved Screengrab Format

### Cognitive load Image 1 – Mexico City metro

**First thoughts:** What is cognitive workload? How does it affect us? I liked the idea of culture and how it can steer learning. I was thinking of how people from different cultures get on with ours? As a diverse group of people from different countries, continents and religions how do we as a group come together and interact, obviously we have some common ground as students of education. I have travelled widely myself and I do struggle to get to grips with different cultures. How do we understand cognitive load? Perhaps Induction day at University, meeting all these different people, places, new accounts library computer etc... or moving to a new country to live and learn another language? What happens when we encounter new or different technology, when we don't understand what we need to do? That feeling of helplessness or the use of substantial cognitive loading, in to try and overcome the barrier and deduce meaning from a different language?

I remember standing in the central transport terminal in Mexico City 15 years ago trying to figure out which train & bus I should be getting on to travel out 25 miles from the city to the ancient city of Teotihuacan, having tried to understand the system or use similarity e.g. the London Underground as a starting point and failed, I sat down dejectedly, however someone took pity on me and explained in English that the hub had trains, trams, tubes & buses and that each station is identified by a minimalist logo related to the name of the station or the area around it. This is because, at the time of the first line's opening, the illiteracy rate was extremely high, so people found it easier to guide themselves, with a system based on colors and visual signs. The design of the icons and the typography are a creation of Lance Wyman, who also designed the logotype for the 1968 Summer Olympic Games at Mexico City, the logos are not assigned at random. However to the outsider the logos and colour meant nothing. Using my newly found knowledge I ranged far and wide in Mexico City for three days visiting many ancient sites.

**Finding an Image:** Google search using phrase Mexico City Metro.

**Interpretation:** Cognitive load and overload the evolution of communication using images rather than words, and the old adage that "a picture paints a 1000 words". Prenksy talks about digital natives and digital immigrants, I remain for the most part a digital immigrant, given the choice I will print documents to read, assignments are always proofed in print as I can feel my way along the text. The amount of information conveyed in an image can be a boon and a burden, a picture is a picture and cannot be the same 1000 words to two different people, so which person is right?

**Conclusions/challenges/critique:** The map, symbols and logo's show that without understanding the context and how to decipher cultural (local) knowledge it is harder to go about ones daily business. That some people take for granted that because you are this or that person that you know x, y, or z they assume you are part of their culture or exclude you perhaps because they think you are not part of it? What I found in Mexico City was that to start with I encountered cognitive overload, being in a strange city and a somewhat dangerous city, I was overwhelmed by the quantity of information I had to try and decipher and the lack of options or help available. I could have tried trial and error or given up or paid for a taxi to take me closer to my destination but since it was a backpacking holiday I wanted to face the challenge and after a few days I was comfortable with the cognitive load and I could function adequately within the Metro system.

The same can be said for learning something totally new or learning something that is way above your current level of understanding eg swimming I thought I was a competent swimmer ( previously a swimming teacher and life-guard) when I started to compete in triathlons my wife bought me a Christmas present of swimming sessions with a coach, at the time I scoffed at what I could possibly learn... after the first session I was totally dazed about how little I actually knew about swimming and the advances in technique. I never managed to learn the stroke the coach was showing me, such as body rotation kick timing and stroke/ hand entry, can you teach an old dog new tricks? Seemingly not this one as the main impediment to improvement in swimming is muscle memory.

Returning to learning the teacher must be careful not to apply a cognitive overload to the student otherwise the student will switch off as the amount and or complexity overruns their ability to process it in a meaningful way. I have suffered cognitive overload on a course about 3yrs ago, my progress test scores where low and at times bordered failure as the course was delivered using a learn and test method, sometimes the testing was the same day as the learning, with no final exam the course was "learn and dump" with a final practical consolidation. The course runs in this way today and will continue to run this way even though feedback is given about its methodology on most course debriefs. The instructors are aware of the issues, however they are either unwilling or unable to change the way the course is delivered.

### Cognitive Load Image 2 – Virgin media poster

**First thoughts:** how can you express cognitive load? What do you see and why do you see it? We talked previously about how the mind makes up for the gaps like this word teaser:

"Aoccdrnig to rscheearch at Cmabrigde Uinervtisy, it deosn't mttaer in waht oredr the ltteers in a wrod are, the olny ipmroetnt tihng is taht the frist and lsat ltteer be at the rghit pclae. The rset can be a toatl mses and you can sitll raed it wouthit a porbelm. Tihs is bcuseae the huamn mnid deos not raed ervey lteter by istlef, but the wrod as a wlohe."

Easy enough to read, but what have you figured out about the image? Did you even stop to consider it carefully? Have you seen it before? This pop quiz teaser gripped the nation for a few days in 2005. In reality I could have used a fighter pilot multi-tasking and interacting with an array of computer generated symbology at Mach 1, but how about looking at the picture above and having 10 minutes to name as many bands/artists as possible? You are looking for 70 in total. It is quite a challenge my wife and I got around 40 each, I lost so had to wash up after tea... can you better my total?

**Finding an Image:** Google images and pop band quiz, I used this image years ago as a communications exercise with two groups of 18 – 25yr olds at about the time it came out in the press late 2005 I think.

**Interpretation:** Seventy artists/bands represented in the picture. Can you name them? If you did not know the context for the image how long would you have dwelled on it for, how much effort would it have taken to draw meaning from the image and make the connections that I think so much of this image work has been about? What draws us to images on a bus, poster, billboard, TV etc... did your mind make the link? How does a picture support the advertisers desire to sell you something, what does it imply, understate or suggest to you? The old adage was sex sells... the more you think about images the more you can understand advertising and the suggestive power of the image.

**Conclusions/challenges/critique:** If you were an avid listener to music or follower of the music scene this quiz could have bugged you to the point of distracting you from anything else. Reports in the paper say that people were so caught up in trying to solve it or be the first to solve it that some people did not sleep for 48hrs trying to solve it. The picture can be used as discovery learning or problem solving learning in so much as the picture challenges your mental agility. Part of cognitive load theory is the development of flexible mental strategies to handle the Cognitive Load. Three types of load exist:

**Intrinsic Cognitive Load:** The Intrinsic Cognitive Load is the inherent complexity of the task in hand. Drawing a square is a lot easier than drawing a portrait. There is little we can do about the intrinsic cognitive load, some things are simply harder than others. However, we can manage it by chunking the information into smaller problems so that each can be dealt with in turn before re-integrating the information back into the whole.

**Extraneous cognitive load:** Extraneous Cognitive Load is the result of the way that the interface or information is presented and structured. As designers this is where we have the greatest impact. For any given task, a well designed and clear interface will have a lower extraneous cognitive load than a badly designed one. Obviously, we should not add to the complexity of the underlying problem by producing complicated interfaces! Intrinsic and Extraneous load are additive – they combine to form the load of the task. A simple problem presented badly can have the same total cognitive load as a complex problem presented well.

**Germane Cognitive Load:** This is the "good load" and we want to maximize it. It's the spare capacity to deal with the underlying information (the intrinsic load) – the capacity available to perform the mental work that leads to understanding. If a task has a high intrinsic load but a low extraneous load, then the Germane load will be high as the user is able to focus their available resources on understanding the problem. If the same task has a higher extraneous load then the Germane load decreases because the user is having to expend resources on dealing with the extraneous elements.

**How to lower cognitive load:** Minimise the "noise" in your interface by remove unnecessary visual elements. These increase the cognitive load as they need to be processed in order to determine their relevance. Chunking – reduce number of things that a user has to worry about at once by breaking the task down in to chunks. Ensure the information relevant to the task in hand is available (so the user doesn't have to remember it) people are much better at recognizing the thing they want than they are at remembering it! The time it takes to make a decision increases with the number of choices available.

How does the picture achieve a cognitive load? If you look again it is an extremely busy image with a mass of information available and that information has to be deduced. I gave you no instructions at the start to help, no reason to look at it no numbers to aim for. The image leaves choices take a look again you have a postman policemen and a cowboy, each represent a band but put together you could come up with "men at work" this is not a correct answer but it can be an answer so with the number of choices available the decisions as to what is right can take longer, under pressure as well... remember 10 mins 40 groups plus ... on a final serious note if you did this task in the 10 mins, how did you feel at the end of it? tried, frustrated, sore eyes or a headache? This was a bit of fun but what about the digital objects we provide to our learners: do they feel the same way after a period of e-learning? how many times have we stopped to ask our learners for feedback?

# Glossary

**Concepts**  Concepts are not viewed here as some mental entities in the head that can be concluded or tested in experimental laboratory conditions; they are also not viewed as finite, neatly categorizable entities in/of sciences or disciplines; concepts are here viewed as *open-ended, expansive, evolutionary up-to-now concept and theory agreements and descriptions in scientific or disciplinary fields*; they bridge cognition with the external environment, its materiality, and sociocultural contexts and histories. Concepts are *multimodal, plural, and embed a continuum of world developments*. I suggest a new compound term to signify these characteristics: a transmodal or rhizomatic concept. This term challenges conceptual determinism and emphasizes conceptual mode complexity and multiplicity concerning its form, history, effect and being.

**Creativity**  This term has many interpretations, but here is specifically observed as creative coupling of image and concept; forming new relations; not a distinct characteristic only of the "artsy" and the "creatives."

**Edusemiotic Relationality (ER)**  This is a metamodel for the future development of a relational educational theory that incorporates a dynamic exploration of the world's sociomateriality via edusemiotic practices, such as an inquiry graphics (IG) practice; relational as it challenges dualist, compartmentalized, individualist views of knowledge, education and identity; edusemiotic as it takes Peirce's triadic signification as its key principle; dynamic as knowledge, education and concepts change, fluctuate, interact at various levels across various factors in an evolutionary process of growth; multimodal as it entails various modes of communication beyond language. Critical ER would be an approach to focus on the issues of power, inequality and oppression relation to learning in the socio-material world.

**Edusemiotics** An emerging approach (theory; project) for connecting semiotics and education; adopts Peirce's semiotics and related views to develop a transdisciplinary domain of educational theory, philosophy and practice.

**Graphics** anything that leaves a trace on a surface such as a paper or screen surface; here mainly referring to *digital photographs*; graphics could be static/still (e.g. a non-animated drawing, photographs, written words, collage, murals) and animated (a video, an animation, any graphics in motion).

**Higher Education (HE)** Tertiary education; here concerning teaching–learning, research, policy, governance and culture of contemporary universities.

**Human Learning** an *adaptation* towards a change as a person; a development of *semiotic consciousness*; hard to assess with any immediate testing. Andrew Stables (2010, p. 27) suggests that "learning" is "a term used to validate certain kinds and examples of personal, social and institutional change: generally speaking, those of which we approve (teachers and/or educational institutions, curriculum developers and policy). At times when we speak of learning, we mean social reproduction; at its most exciting it refers to something that at least feels new for the individual… learning is part of being a person, and being a person is subject to social judgments."

**Iconic Surfacing** What happens when any held stereotypical icon (image) surfaces to one's mind; iconic stereotypical image exposure (from the subconscious, the mind schemata) and subsequent critical reflection on it; an IG pedagogy and analysis expose stereotypical images of our mind schemata (examples in the empirical studies, Part II)

**Iconicity** A sign functioning by "similarity"; not necessarily an external iconic sign; also linked to iconic reasoning and creativity, foregrounds the noticing of similarity in thinking process.

**Images** Here used to refer to external iconic image signs with pictorial quality such as pictures, photographs, drawings; they are similar via their depicted form to something that they show/depict.

**Inquiry Graphics (IG)** Singular: an inquiry graphic. A graphic or graphics that act (are applied) as integrated vehicles of thinking and learning in educational practice or research; they spark semiotic inquiry thinking at the intersection of image-concept knowledge building and sharing; they support the externalization, sharing and building of learning and research communities. Inquiry graphics are compound, multimodal image-concept signs. They manifest a move in higher education towards new practices in teaching-learning theorization, methods and conceptual development that are embodied, non-dualist, multimodal, dynamic and semiotic.

**Inquiry** A key term in Peirce's and Dewey's approach to education; central to Peirce's views on the importance of *scientific inquiry*. It means an in-depth, and often empirical study and analysis of any given educational theme/ topic/ phenomenon or concept.

**Interdisciplinarity** Something that education and higher education needs, at least at a postgraduate level, towards more holistic knowledge progress and the tackling of global challenges; a key ingredient of educational futures in research and postgraduate programs, course and teaching-learning.

**Meaning-making (semiosis/ semeosis)** A key aspect of semiotic theory of mind and meaning, the sign-action addressed via Peirce's diagrammatic sign meaning-making triad of *Representamen–Object–Interpretant* relations; in the case of photographs, here the interrelated adapted semiosis involves: the picture/ photograph embodied material form (a part of photographic embodied representamen), what the photographs relates to (photographic or pictorial object), and the interpretation of it (photographic interpretant). This interpretation is contingent upon immediate environmental context, prior knowledge, cognition, and sociocultural and historical factors.

**Multimodal Anchorage Elaboration** When any image-concept linkage made is reflected upon in further depth.

**Multimodal Anchorage** The image–concept linkage made in a multimodal inquiry graphics narrative or reflection; it means to link an aspect of the embodied pictorial sign description with a theoretical perspective or abstract concept statements and ideas.

**Multimodal** Consisting of more than one mode, material or not; the view expressed here is that all thinking and expression is multimodal.

**Multiplicity** Heterogeneity and plurality of meanings dependent on contextual factors and interpreters' prior knowledge and positionality; strongly linked to interpretation another key principle of the ER metamodel.

**Relationality** A key principle of the ER metamodel, a relational theory of education and IG that emphasizes the inherent relationality of all diverse things that enter processes of meaning-making; individual and collective human interpretation, emotions and action, animate and inanimate environmental matter, including technology. It supports a non-dualistic view of learning, knowledge and concepts, challenging mind–body, nature–nurture, concept–image, internal–external and similar dualistic views, without descending into relativism, but seeking truth while recognising connectedness in diversity. It promotes a relational ontology and interdisciplinarity, also supporting relational academic culture and being by promoting genuine collegiality and care; cherish connectedness across various levels of activities or interests; cherish relational practices. Further work is needed to develop a relational theory of education as edusemiotic relationality (ER) or a relational theory of learning.

**Sign** The main unit of communication; the core unit and term in semiotics; anything that communicates information. In Peircean terms, a sign is a tripartite entity of anything that stands for something else (its Object) in some respect to some mind that interprets it (interpretation; interpretant, not to be confused with interpreter).

**Teaching** "a fully semiotic approach to teaching might best be thought of as activity-centered and learner-aware… a *person-oriented engagement*; teaching is a disruptive activity (…) what is key to its success is how students respond to this disruption" (Andrew Stables, 2010, pp. 28–30); eliciting meanings through signs, supporting the externalization and creative acts of sign creation and interpretations.

**Threshold Graphics** The term used for inquiry graphics applied to address threshold concepts.

**Unity** a holistic interpretation of knowledge and concepts that observes action and interpretation as *whole units* at the intersection of cognitive, social, cultural, historical, natural and material aspects of it. It contains relationality and does not support uniformity, in some globalist manner, emphasizing relationality of unique entities in a holistic system unity; in favor of such unity perspective in education.

**Writing approach and style** This is not a typical glossary term but is included here to state clearly that the book content and writing style is the one of a series of *relevant scientific or theoretical approaches and examples in the literature and popular culture (vignettes) that are all related to the central focus, that of inquiry graphics and image–concept relationality. They all help in understanding what inquiry graphics are and what they are related to*; this means that the key arguments are developed by putting together an eclectic variety of ideas and approaches around the main focus in Part I, proceeding to explore empirical studies with IG in Part II. I use both the first person and the third person in the book, as I view my relationship to the empirical data and the book content as a subjective–objective perspective. The whole book is envisaged as an opening pathway for the development of a relational theory of education and learning, contributing to the development of edusemiotic empirical studies, and sociomaterial theorizations of higher education, as well as engaging other theories that can be cross-fertilized with inquiry graphics practices and concepts in the future.

# References

Abbas, A., & McLean, M. (2003). Communicative competence and the improvement of university teaching: Insights from the field. *British Journal of Sociology of Education, 24*, 69–82.

ACRL. (2013). Visual literacy competency standards for higher education [WWW document]. Retrieved from: http://www.ala.org/acrl/standards/visualliteracy

Adelman, R. A. (2012). Tangled complicities: Extracting knowledge from images of Abu Ghraib. In *Knowledge and pain* (pp. 353–379). New York: Brill/Rodopi.

Agbenyega, J., Deppeler, J., & Moss, J. (2011). Knowing schooling, identity and pedagogy visually. In *AARE 2008: Changing climates: Education for sustainable futures. Proceedings of the 2008 Australian Association for research in education conference*, 1–12.

Agbenyega, J. S. (2008). Developing the understanding of the influence of school place on students' identity, pedagogy and learning, visually. *International Journal of Whole Schooling, 4*, 52–66.

Ainsworth, S. (1999). The functions of multiple representations. *Computers & Education, 33*, 131–152.

Ainsworth, S. (2006). DeFT: A conceptual framework for learning with multiple representations. *Learning and Instruction, 16*(3), 183–198.

© The Author(s) 2020
N. Lacković, *Inquiry Graphics in Higher Education*,
https://doi.org/10.1007/978-3-030-39387-8

Ainsworth, S. (2008). The educational value of multiple-representations when learning complex scientific concepts. In J. K. Gilbert, M. Reiner, & M. Nakhleh (Eds.), *Visualization: Theory and practice in science education* (pp. 191–208). Dordrecht, Netherlands: Springer.

Aldrich, F., & Sheppard, L. (2000). Graphicacy: The fourth R? *Primary Science Review, 64*, 8–11.

Almeder, R. (1980). *The philosophy of Charles S. Peirce: A critical introduction.* Oxford, UK: Blackwell Publishing.

Amiel, T., & Reeves, T. C. (2008). Design-based research and educational technology: Rethinking technology and the research agenda. *Educational Technology & Society, 11*, 29–40.

Amit-Danhi, E. R., & Shifman, L. (2018). Digital political infographics: A rhetorical palette of an emergent genre. *New Media & Society, 20*(10), 3540–3559.

Amouzadeh, M., & Tavangar, M. (2004). Decoding pictorial metaphor: Ideologies in Persian commercial advertising. *International Journal of Cultural Studies, 7*(2), 147–174.

Anderson, T., & Shattuck, J. (2012). Design-based research A decade of Progress in education research? *Educational Researcher, 41*, 16–25.

Anderson, V., Rabello, R., Wass, R., Golding, C., Rangi, A., Eteuati, E., Bristowe, Z., & Waller, A. (2019). Good teaching as care in higher education. *Higher Education, 79*, 1–19.

Andrienko, N., Andrienko, G., & Gatalsky, P. (2003). Exploratory spatio-temporal visualization: An analytical review. *Journal of Visual Languages & Computing, 14*(6), 503–541.

Angeli, C., & Valanides, N. (2009). Epistemological and methodological issues for the conceptualization, development, and assessment of ICT–TPCK: Advances in technological pedagogical content knowledge (TPCK). *Computers & Education, 52*, 154–168.

Apple, M. W. (2004). *Ideology and curriculum* (3rd ed.). London: Routledge.

Archer, A. (2006). A multimodal approach to academic 'literacies': Problematising the visual/verbal divide. *Language and Education, 20*(6), 449–462.

Archer, A. (2010). Multimodal texts in Higher Education and the implications for writing pedagogy. *English in Education, 44*, 201–213.

Arias-Hernandez, R., Green, T. M., & Fisher, B. (2012). From cognitive amplifiers to cognitive prostheses: Understandings of the material basis of cognition in visual analytics. *Interdisciplinary Science Reviews, 37*, 4–18.

Arnheim, R. (1969). *Visual thinking.* Berkeley, CA: University of California Press.

Arslan, R., & Nalinci, G. Z. (2014). Development of visual literacy levels scale in higher education. *Turkish Online Journal of Educational Technology-TOJET, 13*(2), 61–70.

Ashwin, P., Abbas, A., & McLean, M. (2014). How do students' accounts of sociology change over the course of their undergraduate degrees? *Higher Education, 67*(2), 219–234.

Attride-Stirling, J. (2001). Thematic networks: An analytic tool for qualitative research. *Qualitative Research, 1*, 385–405.

Attwood, R. (2009). Pedagogy a poor second in promotion. *Times Higher Education*, online version published on 10/12/2009. Retrieved from: https://www.timeshighereducation.com/news/pedagogy-a-poor-second-in-promotions/409511.article

Avgerinou, M., & Ericson, J. (1997). A review of the concept of visual literacy. *British Journal of Educational Technology, 28*, 280–291.

Avison, D., Baskerville, R., & Myers, M. (2001). Controlling action research projects. *Information Technology & People, 14*, 28–45.

Aydede, M., & Robbins, P. (2009). *The Cambridge handbook of situated cognition*. Cambridge, UK: Cambridge University Press.

Bacevic, J. (2019). With or without U? Assemblage theory and (de) territorialising the university. *Globalisation, Societies and Education, 17*(1), 78–91.

Bakhtin, M. M. (1981). *The dialogic imagination: Four essays* (Michael Holquist, Ed. and Caryl Emerson & Michael Holquist, Trans.). Austin, TX: University of Texas Press. *84*(8), 80–82.

Barab, S. (2006). *Design-based research: A methodological toolkit for the learning scientist*. Cambridge, UK: Cambridge University Press.

Barab, S., & Squire, K. (2004). Design-based research: Putting a stake in the ground. *The Journal of the Learning Sciences, 13*, 1–14.

Barad, K. (2003). Posthumanist performativity: Toward an understanding of how matter comes to matter. *Signs: Journal of Women in Culture and Society, 28*(3), 801–831.

Barad, K. (2007). *Meeting the universe halfway: Quantum physics and the entanglement of matter and meaning*. Durham, NC: Duke University Press.

Barad, K. (2011). Erasers and erasures: Pinch's unfortunate 'uncertainty principle'. *Social Studies of Science, 41*(3), 443–454.

Barlex, D., & Carré, C. (1985). *Visual communication in science: Learning through sharing images*. Cambridge, UK: Cambridge University Press.

Barnett, Roland. (1990). *The idea of higher education*. Bristol, PA: Open University Press.

Barthes, R. (1977). *Image music text*. London: HarperCollins.

Barthes, R. (2000/1972). *Mythologies* (Annette Lavers, Trans.). Vintage Classics.

Barthes, Roland ([1964] 1967). *Elements of semiology* (Annette Lavers & Colin Smith, Trans.). London: Jonathan Cape.

Bartram, R. (2004). Visuality, dromology and time compression: Paul Virilio's new ocularcentrism. *Time & Society, 13*(2–3), 285–300.

Baskerville, R., & Myers, M. D. (2004). Special issue on action research in information systems: Making is research relevant to practice–foreword. *MIS Quarterly, 28*, 329–335.

Bayne, S. (2008). Higher education as a visual practice: Seeing through the virtual learning environment. *Teaching in Higher Education, 13*, 395–410.

Bell, P. (2004). On the theoretical breadth of design-based research in education. *Educational Psychologist, 39*, 243–253.

Bell, T., Urhahne, D., Schanze, S., & Ploetzner, R. (2010). Collaborative inquiry learning: Models, tools, and challenges. *International Journal of Science Education, 32*, 349–377.

Belluigi, D. Z. (2009). Exploring the discourses around "creativity" and "critical thinking" in a South African creative arts curriculum. *Studies in Higher Education, 34*, 699–717.

Benedict, G. A. (1985). What are representamens? *Transactions of the Charles S. Peirce Society, 21(2),* 241–270. Retrieved from: https://www.jstor.org/stable/40320088?seq=1

Bennett, J. (2010). *Vibrant matter: A political ecology of things*. Durham & London: Duke University Press.

Bense, M. (1977). Die semiotische Konzeption der Ästhetik. *Zeitschrift für Literaturwissenschaft und Linguistik, 7*(27), 188.

BERA (British Educational Research Association). (2004). Revised guidelines. Retrieved from: http://www.bera.ac.uk/guidelines.html

Bereiter, C. (2002). Design research for sustained innovation. *Cognitive Studies: Bulletin of the Japanese Cognitive Science Society, 9*, 321–327.

Bereiter, C., & Scardamalia, M. (2008). *Toward research-based innovation. Innovating to learn, learning to innovate* (pp. 67–87). Paris: OECD.

Berger, J., Blomberg, S., Fox, C., Dibb, M., & Hollis, R. (1972). *Ways of seeing*. London: British Broadcasting Corporation & Penguin.

Bernhard, J., & Sanit, N. (2007). Thinking and learning through technology-mediating tools and insights from philosophy of technology applied to science and engineering education. In *The Pantaneto*. https://www.researchgate.net/profile/Jonte_Bernhard/publication/280620600_Thinking_and_learning_through_technology__Mediating_tools_and_insights_from_philosophy_of_technology_applied_to_science_and_engineering_education/

links/55bf2feb08ae9289a099e8e3/Thinking-and-learning-through-technology-Mediating-tools-and-insights-from-philosophy-of-technology-applied-to-science-and-engineering-education.pdf

Bernstein, B. (2006). Vertical and horizontal discourse: An essay. In *Education and society* (pp. 53–73). London: Routledge.

Bielaczyc, K. (2006). Designing social infrastructure: Critical issues in creating learning environments with technology. *The Journal of the Learning Sciences, 15*, 301–329.

BIS. (2009). The Digital Britain report, DCMS (Department for culture, media and sport). https://www.gov.uk/government/publications/digital-britain-final-report

Bleed, R. (2005). Visual literacy in higher education, Maricopa Community Colleges, *ELI explorations*, August 2005, Educause Learning Initiative.

Blin, F., & Munro, M. (2008). Why hasn't technology disrupted academics' teaching practices? Understanding resistance to change through the lens of activity theory. *Computers & Education, 50*, 475–490.

Blunden, A. (2012). *Concepts: A critical approach* (Vol. 44). Leiden, Netherlands: Brill.

Boehm, G., & Mitchell, W. J. T. (2009). Pictorial versus iconic turn: Two letters. *Culture, Theory and Critique, 50*(2–3), 103–121.

Boisvert, R. D. (1998). *John Dewey: Rethinking our time*. New York: SUNY Press.

Bone, J. (2009). Writing research: Narrative, bricolage and everyday spirituality. *New Zealand Research in Early Childhood Education, 12*, 143.

Braden, R. A. (1996). Visual literacy. In J. M. Spector, M. D. Merrill, J. Elen, & M. J. Bishop (Eds.), *Handbook of research for educational communications and technology* (pp. 491–520). Cham, Switzerland: Springer Nature.

Bransford, J., Vye, N., Stevens, R., Kuhl, P., Schwartz, D., Bell, P., Meltzoff, A., Barron, B., Pea, R. D., & Reeves, B. (2005). Learning theories and education: Toward a decade of synergy. In P. Alexander & P. Winne (Eds.), *Handbook of educational psychology* (2nd ed.). Mahwah, NJ: Erlbaum.

Bransford, J. D., & Schwartz, D. L. (1999). Rethinking transfer: A simple proposal with multiple implications. *Review of Research in Education, 24*, 61–100.

Braun, V., & Clarke, V. (2006). Using thematic analysis in psychology. *Qualitative Research in Psychology, 3*, 77–101.

Breuer, E., & Archer, A. (Eds.). (2016). Multimodality in higher education. Brill, Boston.

Brockbank, A., & McGill, I. (2007). *Facilitating reflective learning in higher education*. London: McGraw-Hill International.

Bronfenbrenner, U. (1979). *The ecology of human development*. Cambridge, MA: Harvard University Press.

Brooks, M. (2005). Drawing as a unique mental development tool for young children: Interpersonal and intrapersonal dialogues. *Contemporary Issues in Early Childhood, 6*, 80–91.

Brown, J. S. (2000). Growing up: Digital: How the web changes work, education, and the ways people learn. *Change: The Magazine of Higher Learning, 32*, 11–20.

Bruner, J. S. (1957). *Going beyond the information given*. New York: Norton.

Bruner, J. S. (1960). *The process of education*. Cambridge, MA: Harvard University Press.

Bruner, J. S. (1966). *Toward a theory of instruction*. Cambridge, MA: Belknap.

Bruner, J. S. (2009). *Actual minds, possible worlds*. Cambridge, MA: Harvard University Press.

Bruno, S., & Munoz, G. (2010). Education and interactivism: Levels of interaction influencing learning processes. *New Ideas in Psychology, 28*, 365–379.

Brydon-Miller, M., Greenwood, D., & Maguire, P. (2003). Why action research? *Action Research, 1*, 9–28.

Brydon-Miller, M., & Maguire, P. (2009). Participatory action research: Contributions to the development of practitioner inquiry in education. *Educational Action Research, 17*, 79–93.

Bryman, A. (2008). Why do researchers integrate/combine/mesh/blend/mix/merge/fuse quantitative and qualitative research. *Advances in mixed methods research*, 87–100.

Buckingham, D. (2010). Defining digital literacy. In *Medienbildung in Neuen Kulturräumen* (pp. 59–71). Springer.

Budd, R. (2019/accepted/in press). Looking for love in the student experience. In N. Hogson, J. Vlieghe, & P. Zamojski (Eds.), *Post-critical perspectives on higher education: Retrieving the educational in the university* (Debating Higher Education). Springer.

Burkitt, I. (2008). *Social selves: Theories of self and society*. London: Sage.

Burkitt, I. (2014). *Emotions and social relations*. London: Sage.

Burkitt, I. (2016). Relational agency: Relational sociology, agency and interaction. *European Journal of Social Theory, 19*(3), 322–339.

Canning, J. (2007). Pedagogy as a discipline: Emergence, sustainability and professionalisation. *Teaching in Higher Education, 12*, 393–403.

Card, S. K., Mackinlay, J. D., & Schneiderman, B. (1999). *Readings in information visualization: Using vision to think*. San Francisco: Morgan Kaufmann.

Carney, R. N., & Levin, J. R. (2002). Pictorial illustrations still improve students' learning from text. *Educational Psychology Review, 14*, 5–26.

Carpenter, P. A., & Shah, P. (1998). A model of the perceptual and conceptual processes in graph comprehension. *Journal of Experimental Psychology: Applied, 4*, 75–100.

Cartney, P. (2013). Researching pedagogy in a contested space. *British Journal of Social Work, 45*(4), 1–18.

Cassidy, M. F., & Knowlton, J. Q. (1983). Visual literacy: A failed metaphor? *ECTJ, 31*, 67–90.

Castells, M. (1996). *The rise of the network society, Volume I of The information age: Economy, society and culture.* Reading, MA: Blackwell Publishing.

Cazden, C., Cope, B., Fairclough, N., Gee, J., Kalantzis, M., Kress, G., Luke, A., Luke, C., Michaels, S., & Nakata, M. (1996). A pedagogy of multiliteracies: Designing social futures. *Harvard Educational Review, 66*, 60–92.

Chai, C. L. (2019). Enhancing visual literacy of students through photo elicitation. *Journal of Visual Literacy, 38*(1–2), 120–129. https://doi.org/10.108 0/1051144X.2019.1567071.

Chandler, D. (1994). *Semiotics for beginners.* Retrieved from: http://www.aber.ac.uk/media/Documents/S4B/

Chandler, D. (2002). *The basics: Semiotics.* London: Routledge.

Chandler, D. (2007). *Semiotics: The basics.* New York: Taylor & Francis.

Cin, F. M., & Doğan, N. (2020). Navigating university spaces as refugees: Syrian students' pathways of access to and through higher education in Turkey. *International Journal of Inclusive Education*, 1–15.

Clark, A., & Chalmers, D. (1998). The extended mind. *Analysis, 58*, 7–19.

Clark, C. D. (1999). The autodriven interview: A photographic viewfinder into children's experience. *Visual Studies, 14*, 39–50.

Clarke, J., Dede, C., Ketelhut, D. J., Nelson, B., & Bowman, C. (2006). A design-based research strategy to promote scalability for educational innovations. *Educational Technology, 46*, 27–36.

Cobb, P., Confrey, J., Lehrer, R., & Schauble, L. (2003). Design experiments in educational research. *Educational Researcher, 32*, 9–13.

Cobb, P., Yackel, E. & Wood, T. (1992). A constructivist alternative to the representational view of mind in mathematics education. *Journal for Research in Mathematics Education, 23*(1), 2–33.

Cobley, P. (2016). *Cultural implications of biosemiotics.* Dordrecht, Netherlands: Springer.

Cobley, P. (2017). What the humanities are for – A semiotic perspective. In B. Kristian & P. Cobley (Eds.), *Semiotics and its masters* (pp. 3–23). Berlin, Germany: de Gruyter Mouton.

Cobley, P., & Stjernfelt, F. (2015). Scaffolding development and the human condition. *Biosemiotics, 8*(2), 219–304.

Cole, M., & Packer, M. (2016). Design-based intervention research as the science of the doubly artificial. *Journal of the Learning Sciences, 25*(4), 503–530.

Collier, J. J. (1967). *Visual anthropology: Photography as a research method.* New York: Holt, Rinehart and Winston.

Conole, G., & Dyke, M. (2004). What are the affordances of information and communication technologies? *Association for Learning Technology Journal, 12*, 113–124.

Cooke, N. A. (2019). Impolite hostilities and vague sympathies: Academia as a site of cyclical abuse. *Journal of Education for Library and Information Science, 60*(3), 223–230.

Cope, B., & Kalantzis, M. (2009). Multiliteracies: New literacies, new learning. *Pedagogies: An International Journal, 4*, 164–195.

Cranmer, S. (2019, April). How teachers' inclusionary and exclusionary pedagogical practices manifest in disabled children's uses of technologies in schools. In *Sustainable ICT, education and learning conference.*

Creswell, J. W., & Clark, V. L. P. (2007). *Designing and conducting mixed methods research.* Wiley Online Library.

Crook, C. (2010). Versions of computer-supported collaborating in higher education. In *Learning across sites: New tools, infrastructures and practices* (pp. 156–171). London: Routledge.

Crook, C., & Lackovic, N. (2017). Images of educational practice: How school websites represent digital learning. In *Handbook on digital learning for K-12 schools* (pp. 75–90). Cham, Switzerland: Springer.

Crow, D. (2003). *Visible signs: An introduction to semiotics* (AVA Academia). London: AVA publishing.

Cunningham, D. J. (1987a). Semiotics and education–strands in the web. In *The semiotic web* (pp. 367–378). Berlin, Germany: Mouton de Gryuter.

Cunningham, D. J. (1987b). Outline of an education semiotic. *American Journal of Semiotics, 5*, 201–216.

Cunningham, D. J. (1987c). Semiotics and education: An instance of the 'new' paradigm. *American Journal of Semiotics, 5*, 195–199.

Curtis, N. (2009). *The pictorial turn.* London: Routledge.

Cyphert, D. (2007). Presentation technology in the age of electronic eloquence: From visual aid to visual rhetoric. *Communication Education, 56*, 168–192.

Dahlin, B. (2001). The primacy of cognition–or of perception? A phenomenological critique of the theoretical bases of science education. *Science & Education, 10*, 453–475.

Danesi, M. (2002). *Semiotics in education.* Dresden, Germany: Thelem.

Danesi, M. (2010). *Foreword: Edusemiotics. Semiotics education experience* (pp. vii–vxi). Sense/Brill.

Danesi, M. (2017). Semiotics as a metalanguage for the sciences. In B. Kristian & Paul C. (Eds.), *Semiotics and its masters, 1* (pp. 61–83). Berlin: Walter de Gruyter Inc.

Daniels, H., Cole, M., & Wertsch, J. V. (2007). *The Cambridge companion to Vygotsky.* Cambridge, UK: Cambridge University Press.

Danos X., & Norman E. (2011). Continuity and progression in graphicacy. In *Graphicacy and modelling IDATER 2010.* Design Education Research Group, Loughborough Design School, 103–120.

De Haan, R. L. (2009). Teaching creativity and inventive problem solving in science. *CBE-Life Sciences Education, 8*, 172–181.

De Jong, T. (2006). Technological advances in inquiry learning. *The Educational Forum*, 532–533.

De Saussure, F. (2011). *Course in general linguistics.* New York: Columbia University Press.

Dearden, R. F., Hirst, P., & Peters, R. S. (Eds.). (1972). *Education and the development of reason.* London: Routledge & Kegan Paul.

Debes, J. L. (1969). *The loom of visual literacy – An overview.* Audiovisual Instr.

Debord, G. (1994). *The society of the spectacle* (Donald Nicholson Smith, Trans.). Brooklyn/New York: Zone Books.

Dede, C. (2005). Why design-based research is both important and difficult. *Educational Technology, 45*, 5–8.

Dede, C. (2007). Reinventing the role of information and communications technologies in education. *Yearbook of the National Society for the Study of Education, 106*, 11–38.

Deely, J. (2009). Semiotics and the academe. In J. Deely (Ed.), *Semiotics 2008* (pp. 476–493). Toronto, ON: Legas.

Deleuze, G. (1987) *Dialogues* (with Claire Parnet) (H. Tomlinson & G. Burchell, Trans.). New York: Columbia University Press.

Deleuze, G. (1995). *Negotiations 1972–1990* (M. Joughin, Trans.). New York: Columbia University Press.

Demick, J. (2000). Toward a mindful psychological science: Theory and application. *Journal of Social Issues, 56,* 141–159.

Derrick, G. (2018). *The evaluators' eye: Impact assessment and academic peer review.* Cham: Springer.

Derrida, J. (1978) [1967]. *Writing and difference* (Alan Bass, Trans.). London: Routledge.

Devereux, L. (2010). From Congo: Newspaper photographs, public images and personal memories. *Visual Studies, 25*(2), 124–134.

Dewey, J. (1997/1910). *How we think.* Mineola, New York: Dover Publications, Inc.

Dewey, J., & Bentley, A. F. (1960). *Knowing and the known* (No. 111). Boston: Beacon Press.

Dillenbourg, P., & Jermann, P. (2007). Designing integrative scripts. In *Scripting computer-supported collaborative learning* (pp. 275–301). New York: Springer.

Dirkx, J. M., Mezirow, J., & Cranton, P. (2006). Musings and reflections on the meaning, context, and process of transformative learning a dialogue between John M. Dirkx and Jack Mezirow. *Journal of Transformative Education, 4,* 123–139.

Donald, M. (1991). *Origins of the modern mind: Three stages in the evolution of culture and cognition.* Cambridge, MA: Harvard University Press.

Duchastel, P., & Waller, R. (1979). Pictorial illustration in instructional texts. *Educational Technology, 19,* 20–25.

Duchastel, P. C. (1978). Illustrating instructional texts. *Educational Technology, 18,* 36–39.

Earl, C. (2018). *Spaces of political pedagogy: Occupy! And other radical experiments in adult learning.* London: Routledge.

Eason, K. D. (1989). *Information technology and organisational change.* Hoboken, NJ: CRC Press.

Eisenberg, M. B., Lowe, C. A., & Spitzer, K. L. (2004). *Information literacy: Essential skills for the information age* (2nd ed.). Westport, CT: Libraries Unlimited.

Elkonin, D. B. (1989). Ob istochnikakh neklassicheskoi psikhologii (On the sources of non-classical psychology). In D. B. Elkonin (Ed.), *Izbrannye psikhologicheskie trudy* (Selected psychological writings) (pp. 475–478). Moscow: Pedagogika.

Elleström, L. (2014). Material and mental representation: Peirce adapted to the study of media and arts. *The American Journal of Semiotics, 30*(1/2), 83–138. https://doi.org/10.5840/ajs2014301/24.

Ellis, G., & Dix, A. (2007). A taxonomy of clutter reduction for information visualisation. *Visualization and Computer Graphics, IEEE Transactions on 13,* 1216–1223.

Ellsworth, E. (1989). Why doesn't this feel empowering? Working through the repressive myths of critical pedagogy. *Harvard Educational Review, 59*(3), 297–325.

Elmborg, J. (2006). Critical information literacy: Implications for instructional practice. *The Journal of Academic Librarianship, 32*(2), 192–199.

Engeström, Y., et al. (1999). Activity theory and individual and social transformation. *Perspectives on Activity Theory,* 19–38.

Epstein, I., Stevens, B., McKeever, P., & Baruchel, S. (2008). Photo elicitation interview (PEI): Using photos to elicit children's perspectives. *International Journal of Qualitative Methods, 5,* 1–11.

Ericsson, K. A., & Simon, H. A. (1980). Verbal reports as data. *Psychological Review, 87,* 215–251.

Evans, G. S. (2005). *This could be a pipe: Foucault, irrealism and Ceci n'est pas use pipe.* The CafeIrreal: International Imagination. Retrieved from: http://cafeirreal.alicewhittenburg.com/review5.htm

Ewen, S., & Ewen, E. (1992). *Channels of desire: Mass images and the shaping of American consciousness.* Minneapolis, London: University of Minnesota Press.

Ewen, S., & Ewen, E. (2011). *Typecasting: On the arts and sciences of human inequality.* New York: Seven Stories Press.

Fairclough, N., Jessop, B., & Sayer, A. (2002). Critical realism and semiosis. *Journal of Critical Realism, 5,* 2–10.

Fauconnier, G., & Turner, M. (2002). *The way we think: Conceptual blending and the mind's hidden complexities.* New York: Basic Books.

Fenwick, T. (2010). Re-thinking the "thing" sociomaterial approaches to understanding and researching learning in work. *Journal of Workplace Learning, 22*(1/2), 104–116.

Fenwick, T., & Edwards, R. (2013). Performative ontologies. Sociomaterial approaches to researching adult education and lifelong learning. *European journal for Research on the Education and Learning of Adults, 4*(1), 49–63.

Ferraro, J. M. (2000). Reflective practice and professional development. In *ERIC Digest.* Washington, DC: ERIC Clearinghouse on Teaching and Teacher Education, American Association of Colleges for Teacher Education.

Fishman, B., Marx, R. W., Blumenfeld, P., Krajcik, J., & Soloway, E. (2004). Creating a framework for research on systemic technology innovations. *The Journal of the Learning Sciences, 13,* 43–76.

Fosnot, C. T., & Perry, R. S. (2005). Constructivism: A psychological theory of learning. In C. Fosnot (Ed.), *Constructivism: Theory, Perspectives and Practice* (2nd ed., pp. 276–291). New York: Teachers College Press.

Freadman, A. (2001). *The classifications of signs (II): 1903. Digital encyclopedia of CS Peirce.* Retrieved from: http://www.digitalpeirce.fee.unicamp. br/190fre.htm

Freire, P. (1970/1993). *Pedagogy of the oppressed* (Rev. ed.). New York: Continuum International Publishing Group.

Friedman, M. (2005). Martin Buber and Mikhail Bakhtin. In B. Banathy & P. M. Jenlink (Eds.), *Dialogue as a means of collective communication* (pp. 29–39). New York: Springer.

Fuchs, C. (2008). *Internet and society: Social theory in the information age.* New York: Psychology Press.

Fulkova, M., & Tipton, T. (2008). A (con)text for new discourse as semiotic praxis. *The International Journal of Art and Design Education, 27*(1), 27–42.

Gabriel, M., Campbell, B., Wiebe, S., MacDonald, R. J., & McAuley, A. (2012). The role of digital technologies in learning: Expectations of first year university students/Le rôle des technologies numériques dans l'apprentissage: Les attentes des étudiants de première année universitaire. *Canadian Journal of Learning and Technology/La revue canadienne de l'apprentissage et de la technologie 38.*

Gagne, R. M., & Briggs, L. J. (1974). *Principles of instructional design.* Oxford, England: Holt, Rinehart & Winston.

Gao, Y. (2015). Constructing internationalisation in flagship universities from the policy-maker's perspective. *Higher Education, 70*(3), 359–373.

Gardner, H. (1993). *Creating minds: An anatomy of creativity seen through the lives of Freud, Einstein, Pieasso, Stravinskv, Eliot, Graham, and Gandhi.* New York: Basic Books.

Gillespie, A., & Zittoun, T. (2010). Using resources: Conceptualizing the mediation and reflective use of tools and signs. *Culture & Psychology, 16*, 37–62.

Gilloch, G. (2013). *Walter Benjamin: Critical constellations.* New York: Wiley.

Giroux, H. A. (1994). *Disturbing pleasures: Learning popular culture.* New York: Routledge.

Goldman, S. R. (2003). Learning in complex domains: When and why do multiple representations help? *Learning and Instruction, 13*, 239–244.

Goldstein, B. M. (2007). All photos lie: Images as data. In G. S. Stanczak (Ed.), *Visual research methods: Image, society, and representation* (pp. 61–81). Los Angeles: Sage.

Gornall, L., & Salisbury, J. (2012). Compulsive working, 'hyperprofessionality' and the unseen pleasures of academic work. *Higher Education Quarterly, 66*(2), 135–154.

Gough, S., & Stables, A. (2012). Interpretation as adaptation: Education for survival in uncertain times. *Curriculum Inquiry, 42*(3), 368–385.

Greene, M. (1995). *Releasing the imagination: Essays on education, the arts, and social change.* San Francisco: Jossey-Bass Publishers.

Greer, C., & Jewkes, Y. (2005). Towards "them", the people that are not like "us". Extremes of otherness: Media images of social exclusion. *Social Justice, 32*(1(99)), 20–31.

Grey, S. J. (2013). Activist academics: What future? *Policy Futures in Education, 11*(6), 700–711.

Grundy, S. (1982). Three modes of action research. *Curriculum Perspectives, 2*, 23–34.

Guri-Rosenblit, S., Sebková, H., & Teichler, U. (2007). Massification and diversity of higher education systems: Interplay of complex dimensions. *Higher Education Policy, 20*, 373–389.

Guthrie, S., Lichten, C. A., Van Belle, J., Ball, S., Knack, A., & Hofman, J. (2017). Understanding mental health in the research environment: A rapid evidence assessment. Cambridge: RAND.

Haertel, G. D., & Means, B. (2003). *Evaluating educational technology: Effective research designs for improving learning.* New York: Teachers College Press.

Hall, S. (1973). *Encoding and decoding in the television discourse.* Retrieved from: http://epapers.bham.ac.uk/2962/1/Hall,_1973,_Encoding_and_Decoding_in_the_Television_Discourse.pdf

Hall, S. (1997). *Representation: Cultural representations and signifying practices.* London: Sage.

Hall, S. (2001). Encoding/decoding. In M. G. Durham & D. M. Kellner (Eds.), *Media and cultural studies: Keyworks* (Vol. 2, pp. 163–174). Oxford: Blackwell Publishing.

Hallewell, M. J., & Lackovic, N. (2017). Do pictures 'tell' a thousand words in lectures? How lecturers vocalise photographs in their presentations. *Higher Education Research & Development, 36*(6), 1166–1180.

Hammerness, K., Darling-Hammond, L., Bransford, J., Berliner, D., Cochran-Smith, M., McDonald, M., & Zeichner, K. (2005). How teachers learn and develop. Preparing teachers for a changing world: What teachers should learn and be able to do, 358–389.

Hammett, R. F. (2018). Intermediality, hypermedia, and critical media literacy. In *Intermediality* (pp. 207–221). London: Routledge.

Hannafin, M. J., & Land, S. M. (1997). The foundations and assumptions of technology-enhanced student-centered learning environments. *Instructional Science, 25*, 167–202.

Harper, D. (2002). Talking about pictures: A case for photo elicitation. *Visual Studies, 17*, 13–26.

Hasted, C., & Bligh, B. (2019). *Theorising practices of relational working across the boundaries of higher education* (6). Emerald Group Publishing Ltd.

Hedberg, J. G., & Brown, I. (2002). Understanding cross-cultural meaning through visual media. *Educational Media International, 39*, 23–30.

Heisley, D. D., & Levy, S. J. (1991). Autodriving: A photoelicitation technique. *Journal of Consumer Research*, 257–272.

Hemsley-Brown, J., & Oplatka, I. (2006). Universities in a competitive global marketplace: A systematic review of the literature on higher education marketing. *International Journal of Public Sector Management, 19*, 316–338.

Hemsley-Brown, J., & Oplatka, I. (2010). Market orientation in universities: A comparative study of two national higher education systems. *International Journal of Educational Management, 24*, 204–220.

Henderson, M., Finger, G., & Selwyn, N. (2016). What's used and what's useful? Exploring digital technology use (s) among taught postgraduate students. *Active Learning in Higher Education, 17*(3), 235–247.

Henderson, M., Selwyn, N., Finger, G., & Aston, R. (2015). Students' everyday engagement with digital technology in university: Exploring patterns of use and 'usefulness'. *Journal of Higher Edu-cation Policy and Management, 37*(3), 308–319.

Hill, J. R., & Hannafin, M. J. (2001). Teaching and learning in digital environments: The resurgence of resource-based learning. *Educational Technology Research and Development, 49*, 37–52.

Hill, Y. (2017). Loneliness as an occupational hazard. Narratives of loneliness. In O. Sagan & E. D. Miller (Eds.), *Narratives of lonileness: Multidisciplinary perspectives from the 21st century*. London: Routledge.

Hmelo-Silver, C. E., Duncan, R. G., & Chinn, C. A. (2007). Scaffolding and achievement in problem-based and inquiry learning: A response to Kirschner, Sweller, and Clark (2006). *Educational Psychologist, 42*, 99–107.

Hodge, B. R. I. V., & Kress, G. R. (1988). *Social semiotics*. Cambridge, UK: Polity Press.

Hodgson, A., & Spours, K. (1997). From the 1991 white paper to the Dearing report: A conceptual and historical framework for the 1990s.

Hoffmeyer, J. (2006). Semiotic scaffolding of living systems. In M. Barbieri (Ed.), *Introduction to biosemiotics: The new biological synthesis* (pp. 149–166). Dordrecht, Netherlands: Springer.

Hoffmeyer, J. (2014). The semiome: From genetic to semiotic scaffolding. *Semiotica, 198,* 11–31.

Hoffmeyer, J. (2015a). Introduction: Semiotic scaffolding. *Biosemiotics, 8*(2), 153–158.

Hoffmeyer, J. (2015b). Semiotic scaffolding of multicellularity. *Biosemiotics, 8*(2), 159–171.

Hoffmeyer, J. (2015c). Semiotic scaffolding: A unitary principle gluing life and culture together. *Green Letters: Studies in Ecocriticism, 19*(3), 243–245.

Hollan, J., Hutchins, E., & Kirsh, D. (2000). Distributed cognition: Toward a new foundation for human-computer interaction research. *ACM Transactions on Computer-Human Interaction (TOCHI), 7,* 174–196.

Hong, H.-Y., & Sullivan, F. R. (2009). Towards an idea-centered, principle-based design approach to support learning as knowledge creation. *Educational Technology Research and Development, 57,* 613–627.

Hooks, B./hooks, b. (2014). *Teaching to transgress.* New York: Routledge.

Howard, R. W. (1987). *Concepts and schemata: An introduction.* Cassell Educational.

Huang, W., & Tan, C. L. (2007). A system for understanding imaged info-graphics and its applications. *Proceedings of the 2007 ACM symposium on document engineering,* 9–18.

Hull, G. A., & Nelson, M. E. (2005). Locating the semiotic power of multimo-dality. *Written Communication, 22,* 224–261.

Hurworth, R. (2003). Photo-interviewing for research. *Social Research Update, 40*(1).

Hutchins, E. (1995). How a cockpit remembers its speeds. *Cognitive Science, 19,* 265–288.

Iedema, R. (2003). Multimodality, resemiotization: Extending the analysis of discourse as multi-semiotic practice. *Visual Communication, 2,* 29–57.

Jackson, C. (2018). Affective dimensions of learning. In K. Illeris (Ed.), *Contemporary theories of learning* (pp. 139–152). London: Routledge.

Jackson, C., Arici, A., & Barab, S. (2005). Eat your vegetables and do your homework: A design-based investigation of enjoyment and meaning in learn-ing. *Educational technology: The magazine for managers of change in educa-tion* 15–20.

Jamieson, G. H. (2007). *Visual communication: More than meets the eye*. Bristol, UK: Intellect Ltd.

Jandrić, P. (2017). *Learning in the age of digital reason*. New York: Springer.

Jandrić, P., Ryberg, T., Knox, J., Lacković, N., Hayes, S., Suoranta, J., et al. (2019). Postdigital dialogue. *Postdigital Science and Education, 1*(1), 163–189.

Jay, M. (2002). That visual turn. *Journal of Visual Culture, 1*, 87–92.

Jay, P. (2014). *The humanities "crisis" and the future of literary studies*. New York: Palgrave Macmillan.

Jenkins, A., Breen, R., Lindsay, R., & Brew, A. (2002). *Linking teaching and research: A guide for academics and policy makers*. London: Kogan Page.

Jenkins, A., Healey, M., & Zetter, R. (2007). *Linking teaching and research in disciplines and departments*. Higher Education Academy York.

Jewitt, C. (2002). The move from page to screen: The multimodal reshaping of school English. *Visual Communication, 1*, 171–195.

Jewitt, C. (2005). Multimodality, "reading", and "writing" for the 21st century. *Discourse: Studies in the Cultural Politics of Education, 26*, 315–331.

Jewitt, C. (2006). *Technology, literacy and learning: A multimodal approach*. London and New York: Routledge/Psychology Press.

Jewitt, C. (2008). *The visual in learning and creativity: A review of the literature*. https://www.creativitycultureeducation.org/wp-content/uploads/2018/10/the-visual-in-learning-and-creativity-92.pdf. London: Arts Council England.

Jewitt, C. (2011). *The Routledge handbook of multimodal analysis*. London & New York: Routledge.

Jewitt, C., Bezemer, J., & O'Halloran, K. (2016). *Introducing multimodality*. London: Routledge.

Jewitt, C., & Kress, G. R. (2003). *Multimodal literacy*. New York: Lang.

JISC. (2009). Higher education in a web 2.0 world [WWW document]. http://www.jisc.ac.uk/publications/generalpublications/2009/heweb2.aspx#downloads

Johnson, L., Adams, S., Cummins, M., Estrada, V., Freeman, A., & Ludgate, H. (2013). *The NMC horizon report: 2012 higher education edition*. Austin, TX: New Media Consortium.

Johnson, R. B., & Onwuegbuzie, A. J. (2004). Mixed methods research: A research paradigm whose time has come. *Educational Researcher, 33*, 14–26.

Jolley, R., & Zhang, Z. (2012). How drawing is taught in Chinese infant schools. *International Journal of Art & Design Education, 31*, 30–43.

Jolley, R. P., Fenn, K., & Jones, L. (2004). The development of children's expressive drawing. *British Journal of Developmental Psychology, 22*, 545–567.

Kafai, Y. B. (2005). The classroom as "living laboratory": Design-based research for understanding, comparing, and evaluating learning science through design. *Educational Technology: The Magazine for Managers of Change in Education*, 28–33.

Kavanagh, D. (2004). Ocularcentrism and its others: A framework for metatheoretical analysis. *Organization Studies, 25*(3), 445–464.

Kędra, J. (2018). What does it mean to be visually literate? Examination of visual literacy definitions in a context of higher education. *Journal of Visual Literacy, 37*(2), 67–84. https://doi.org/10.1080/1051144X.2018.1492234.

Kędra, J., & Žakevičiūtė, R. (2019). Visual literacy practices in higher education: What, why and how? *Journal of Visual Literacy, 38*(1–2), 1–7. https://doi.org/10.1080/1051144X.2019.1580438.

Kellner, D. (1999). Virilio, war and technology: Some critical reflections. *Theory, Culture & Society, 16*(5–6), 103–125.

Kellner, D., & Share, J. (2007). Critical media literacy, democracy, and the reconstruction of education. *Media Literacy: A Reader*, 3–23.

Kirschner, P. A., Sweller, J., & Clark, R. E. (2006). Why minimal guidance during instruction does not work: An analysis of the failure of constructivist, discovery, problem-based, experiential, and inquiry-based teaching. *Educational Psychologist, 41*, 75–86.

Kirsh, D. (1995). The intelligent use of space. *Artificial Intelligence, 72*, 1–52.

Kirsh, D. (2010). Thinking with external representations. *AI & SOCIETY, 25*, 441–454.

Kirsh, D. (2013). Thinking with external representations. In S. J. Cowley & F. Valle-Tourangeau (Eds.), *Cognition beyond the brain: Computation, Interactivity and Human artifice* (pp. 171–194). Cham: Springer.

Knight, P. T., & Trowler, P. R. (1999). It takes a village to raise a child: Mentoring and the socialisation of new entrants to the academic professions. *Mentoring & Tutoring, 7*(1), 23–34.

Knorr-Cetina, K., & Amann, K. (1990). Image dissection in natural scientific inquiry. *Science, Technology & Human Values, 15*, 259–283.

Knowles, C. (2014). *Flip-flop: A journey through globalisation's backroads*. London: Pluto.

Knox, J. (2019). What does the 'postdigital' mean for education? Three critical perspectives on the digital, with implications for educational research and practice. *Postdigital Science and Education, 1*, 357–370.

Komljenovic, J. (2019). Linkedin, platforming labour, and the new employability mandate for universities. *Globalisation, Societies and Education, 17*(1), 28–43.

Kozulin, A. (2003). Psychological tools and mediated learning. In *Vygotsky's educational theory in cultural context* (pp. 15–38). Cambridge, UK: Cambridge University Press.

Krajcik, J. S., & Blumenfeld, P. C. (2007). Project-based learning. In R. K. Sawyer (Ed.), *The Cambridge handbook of the learning sciences.* Cambridge, UK: Cambridge University Press.

Krane, H., & Dyson, L. (1981). *Graphics communication.* Victoria: Education Department Victoria.

Kress, G. (2004). *Literacy in the new media age.* London: Routledge.

Kress, G. (2009). Assessment in the perspective of a social semiotic theory of multimodal teaching and learning. In *Educational assessment in the 21st century* (pp. 19–41). New York: Springer.

Kress, G., & van Leeuwen, T. (1996). *Reading images: The grammar of visual design.* London: Routledge.

Kress, G. R. (2010). *Multimodality: A social semiotic approach to contemporary communication.* New Yorks: Routledge.

Kruk, S. (2008). Semiotics of visual iconicity in Leninist 'monumental' propaganda. *Visual Communication, 7*(1), 27–57.

Kuhn, D. (2009). Do students need to be taught how to reason? *Educational Research Review, 4,* 1–6.

Kull, K. (2008). The importance of semiotics to University: Semiosis makes the world locally plural. *Semiotics,* 494–514.

Kuo, H. M. (2009). Understanding relationships between academic staff and administrators: An organisational culture perspective. *Journal of Higher Education Policy and Management, 31*(1), 43–54.

Lackovic, N. (2010a). Creating and reading images: Towards a communication framework for higher education learning. In *Seminar. Net: Media, technology & life-long learning* (pp. 121–135).

Lackovic, N. (2010b). Beyond the surface: Image affordances in language textbooks that affect National Identity Formation (NIF). In M. Raesch (Ed.), *Mapping minds* (pp. 53–65, 13 p.) Inter-disciplinary Press.

Lackovic, N. (2016). MultiMAP: Exploring multimodal artefact pedagogy in digital higher education. *Proceedings,* 148–162.

Lackovic, N. (2017). Book review: Collective knowledge arises from multimodal, dialogic intertextuality: Learning in the age of digital reason (2017) by Petar Jandrić. *Knowledge Cultures, 5*(05), 131–135.

Lacković, N. (2018). Analysing videos in educational research: An "Inquiry Graphics" approach for multimodal, Peircean semiotic coding of video data. *Video Journal of Education and Pedagogy, 3*(1), 1–23.

Lacković, N. (2019). Graduate employability (GE) paradigm shift: Towards greater socio-emotional and eco-technological relationalities of graduates' futures. In M. Peters, P. Jandrić, & A. Means (Eds.), *Education and technological unemployment* (pp. 193–212). Singapore: Springer.

Lackovic, N. (2020). Thinking with digital images in the post-truth era: A method in critical media literacy. *Postdigit Sci Educ, 2*, 442–462.

Lackovic, N., Crook, C., Cobb, S., Shalloe, S., & D'Cruz, M. (2015). Imagining technology-enhanced learning with heritage artefacts: Teacher-perceived potential of 2D and 3D heritage site visualisations. *Educational Research, 57*(3), 331–351.

Lackovic, N., & Olteanu, A. (under review). New approach to educational theory and method in the postdigital world: Bridging the separation between the concept and the image. *Educational Theory and Philosophy.*

Lakkala, M., Lallimo, J., & Hakkarainen, K. (2005). Teachers' pedagogical designs for technology-supported collective inquiry: A national case study. *Computers & Education, 45*, 337–356.

Land, R., & Bayne, S. (1999). Computer-mediated learning, synchronicity and the metaphysics of presence. In *World Conference on Educational Multimedia, Hypermedia and Telecommunications*, 736–741.

Land, R., Cousin, G., Meyer, J. H., & Davies, P. (2005). Threshold concepts and troublesome knowledge (3): Implications for course design and evaluation. In *Improving student learning–equality and diversity*. Oxford, UK: OCSLD.

Langer, E. J. (1989). *Mindfulness.* Boston: Addison Wesley Longman.

Langer, E. J. (1997). *The power of mindful learning.* Boston: Addison Wesley Longman.

Langer, E. J., & Moldoveanu, M. (2000). The construct of mindfulness. *Journal of Social Issues, 56*, 1–9.

Lankow, J., Ritchie, J., & Crooks, R. (2012). *Infographics: The power of visual storytelling.* Hoboken, New Jersey: John Wiley & Sons.

Laurillard, D. (2002). *Rethinking university education: A conversational framework for the effective use of learning technologies.* London: Routledge Falmer.

Lave, J. (1991). Situating learning in communities of practice. *Perspectives on socially shared cognition, 2*, 63–82.

Lawless, B., & Chen, Y. W. (2017). Multicultural neoliberalism and academic labor: Experiences of female immigrant faculty in the US academy. *Cultural Studies↔ Critical Methodologies, 17*(3), 236–243.

Lea, M. R. (2004). Academic literacies: A pedagogy for course design. *Studies in Higher Education, 29*(6), 739–756.

Lee, K. (2020). Openness and innovation in online higher education: A historical review of the two discourses. *Open Learning: The Journal of Open, Distance and e-Learning, 24*, 1–21.

Lehrer, R., & Schauble, L. (2006). Cultivating model-based reasoning in science education. In *Cambridge handbook of the learning sciences* (pp. 371–388).

Lehrer, R., Schauble, L., & Lucas, D. (2008). Supporting development of the epistemology of inquiry. *Cognitive Development, 23*, 512–529.

Leonardi, P. M. (2010). Digital materiality? How artifacts without matter, matter. *First Monday, 15*(6).

Lester, P. M. (2006). *yntactic theory of visual communication*. Fullerton, CA: California State University. http://paulmartinlester.info/writings/viscomtheory.html

Lewin, K. (1946). Action research and minority problems. *Journal of Social Issues, 2*, 34–46.

Lipman, M. (2003). *Thinking in education*. Cambridge, UK: Cambridge University Press.

Loader, B. D., Vromen, A., & Xenos, M. A. (2014). The networked young citizen: Social media, political participation and civic engagement. *Information, Communication & Society, 17*, 143–150.

Loveless, A. (2007). *Creativity, technology and learning – A review of recent literature*. Report 4 update, Futurelab. Retrieved from: http://www2.futurelab.org.uk/resources/documents/lit_reviews/Creativity_Review_update.pdf

Loveless, A. (2011). Didactic analysis as a creative process: Pedagogy for creativity with digital tools. In *Beyond fragmentation: Didactics, learning and teaching in Europe* (pp. 239–251). Verlag Barbara Budrich.

Loveless, A. M. (2002). *Literature review in creativity, new technologies and learning*. Bristol, UK: Futurelab.

Lynch, K. (2006). Neo-liberalism and marketisation: The implications for higher education. *European Educational Research Journal, 5*, 1–17.

Lyotard, J. F. (1984). *The postmodern condition: A report on knowledge* (G. Bennington & B. Massumi, Trans.). Minneapolis, MN: University of Minnesota Press.

MacLaren, I. (2012). The contradictions of policy and practice: Creativity in higher education. *London Review of Education, 10*, 159–172.

Malafouris, L. (2013). *How things shape the mind.* Cambridge, MA: MIT Press.

Maran, T., & Kull, K. (2014). Ecosemiotics: Main principles and current developments. *Geografiska Annaler: Series B, Human Geography, 96*(1), 41–50.

Marcuse, H. (2013). *One-dimensional man: Studies in the ideology of advanced industrial society.* New York: Routledge.

Maringe, F., Molesworth, M., Scullion, R., & Nixon, E. (2011). The student as consumer: Affordances and constraints in a transforming higher education environment. In Scullion, R., M. Molesworth, and E. Nixon (Eds.). *The marketisation of higher education and the student as consumer* (pp. 142–154). Routledge: New York.

Martinec, R. (2000). Construction of identity in Michael Jackson's Jam. *Social Semiotics, 10*(3), 313–329.

Martinec, R., & Salway, A. (2005). A system for image–text relations in new (and old) media. *Visual Communication, 4*, 337–371.

Martinelli, D. (2016). *Arts and humanities in progress: A manifesto of numanities.* Cham, Switzerland: Springer.

Martinet, A. (1962). *A functional view of language.* Oxford, UK: Oxford University Press.

Marton, F., Dall'alba, G., & Beaty, E. (1993). Conceptions of learning. *International Journal of Educational Research, 19*, 277–300.

Marton, F., & Säaljö, R. (1976). On qualitative difference in learning – Outcome as a function of the learner's conception of the task. *British Journal of Educational Psychology, 46*, 115–127.

Mascolo, M. F. (2009). Beyond student-centered and teacher-centered pedagogy: Teaching and learning as guided participation. *Pedagogy and the Human Sciences, 1*, 3–27.

Mason, M. (2008). *Critical thinking and learning.* New York: Wiley.

Mavers, D. (2011). *Children's drawing and writing: The remarkable in the unremarkable.* New York: Routledge.

Mayer, R. E. (2009). *Multimedia learning* (2nd ed.). Cambridge, UK: Cambridge University Press.

Mayer, R. E., & Gallini, J. K. (1990). When is an illustration worth ten thousand words? *Journal of Educational Psychology, 82*, 715.

Mayer, R. E., & Moreno, R. (2002). Animation as an aid to multimedia learning. *Educational Psychology Review, 14*, 87–99.

McArthur, J. (2010). Time to look anew: Critical pedagogy and disciplines within higher education. *Studies in Higher Education, 35*, 301–315.

McArthur, J. (2011). Reconsidering the social and economic purposes of higher education. *Higher Education Research & Development, 30*, 737–749.

McCarthy, C. L. (2005). Knowing truth: Peirce's epistemology in an educational context. *Educational Philosophy and Theory, 37*(2), 157–176.

McCloud, S. (1994). *Understanding comics.* New York: HarperCollins.

McKay, J., & Marshall, P. (2001). The dual imperatives of action research. *Information Technology & People, 14*, 46–59.

McLean, M. (2006). *Pedagogy and the university: Critical theory and practice.* New York: Continuum International Publishing Group.

McLean, M., & Blackwell, R. (1997). Opportunity knocks? Professionalism and excellence in university teaching. *Teachers and Teaching: Theory and Practice, 3*, 85–99.

Merrill, M. D., Tennyson, R. D., & Posey, L. O. (1992). *Teaching concepts: An instructional design guide.* Englewood Cliffs, NJ: Educational Technology Publications.

Messaris, P. (1994). *Visual "literacy": Image, mind, and reality.* Englewood Cliffs, NJ: Westview Press.

Messick, D. M., & Schell, T. (1992). Evidence for an equality heuristic in social decision making. *Acta Psychologica, 80*, 311–323.

Meyer, J., & Land, R. (2003). *Threshold concepts and troublesome knowledge: Linkages to ways of thinking and practising within the disciplines.* Edinburgh, UK: University of Edinburgh.

Mezirow, J. (1990). *Fostering critical reflection in adulthood.* San Francisco: Jossey-Bass.

Midtgarden, T. (2005). Toward a semiotic theory of learning. In I. Semestky (Ed.), *Semiotics, education, experience* (pp. 71–82). Rotterdam, The Netherlands: Sense Publishers.

Midtgarden, T. (2013). On the prospects of a semiotic theory of learning. *Educational Philosophy and Theory 37*(2): 239–252.

Mihailidis, P. (2018). Civic media literacies: Re-imagining engagement for civic intentionality. *Learning, Media and Technology*, 1–13.

Mills, K. A. (2010). A review of the "digital turn" in the new literacy studies. *Review of Educational Research, 80*, 246–271.

Mirzoeff, N. (Ed.). (2002). *The visual culture reader.* London & New York: Routledge/Psychology Press.

Mitchell, C. (2008). Getting the picture and changing the picture: Visual methodologies and educational research in South Africa. *South African Journal of Education, 28*, 365–383.

Mitchell, M. (2003). *IMEJ article – Constructing multimedia: Benefits of student-generated multimedia on learning*. Retrieved from: http://imej.wfu.edu/articles/2003/1/03/

Mitchell, W. J. (2002). Showing seeing: A critique of visual culture. *Journal of Visual Culture, 1*, 165–181.

Mitchell, W. J. T. (1995). Interdisciplinarity and visual culture. *Art Bulletin, 77*, 540–544.

Molesworth, M., Nixon, E., & Scullion, R. (2009). Having, being and higher education: The marketisation of the university and the transformation of the student into consumer. *Teaching in Higher Education, 14*, 277–287.

Moore, D. M., & Dwyer, F. M. (1994). *Visual literacy: A spectrum of visual learning*. Englewood Cliffs, NJ: Educational Technology Publications.

Moseley, D., Baumfield, V., Elliott, J., Higgins, S., Miller, J., & Newton, D. P. (2005). *Frameworks for thinking: A handbook for teachers and learning*. Cambridge, UK: Cambridge University Press.

Müller, M. G. (2008). Visual competence: A new paradigm for studying visuals in the social sciences? *Visual Studies, 23*, 101–112.

Naidoo, R., & Jamieson, I. (2005). Empowering participants or corroding learning? Towards a research agenda on the impact of student consumerism in higher education. *Journal of Education Policy, 20*, 267–281.

Neary, M. (2010). Student as producer: Bringing critical theory to life through the life of students. *Roundhouse: Journal of Critical Social Theory*, 36–45.

Nellhaus, T. (1998). Signs, social ontology, and critical realism. *Journal for the Theory of Social Behaviour, 28*, 1–24.

Nelson, B., Ketelhut, D. J., Clarke, J., Bowman, C., & Dede, C. (2005). Design-based research strategies for developing a scientific inquiry curriculum in a multi-user virtual environment. *Educational Technology, 45*, 21–27.

Nelson, M. E., Hull, G. A., & Roche-Smith, J. (2008). Challenges of multimedia self-presentation taking, and mistaking, the show on the road. *Written Communication, 25*, 415–440.

New London Group. (1996). A pedagogy of multiliteracies: Designing social futures. *Harvard Educational Review, 66*, 60–92.

Newfield, D. (2013). Transduction, transformation and the transmodal moment. In C. Jewitt (Ed.), *The Routledge handbook of multimodal analysis* (2nd ed.). Routledge, London.

Newman, D., Griffin, P., & Cole, M. (1989). *The construction zone: Working for cognitive change in school*. Cambridge, UK: Cambridge University Press.

Newman, S., & Jahdi, K. (2009). Marketisation of education: Marketing, rhetoric and reality. *Journal of Further and Higher Education, 33*, 1–11.

Nisbett, R. E., & Wilson, T. D. (1977). Telling more than we can know: Verbal reports on mental processes. *Psychological Review, 84*, 231–259.

Noffke, S. E. (1997). Professional, personal, and political dimensions of action research. *Review of Research in Education, 22*, 305–343.

Noffke, S. E., & Somekh, B. (2009). *The Sage handbook of educational action research*. Los Angeles: Sage.

Norman, D. A. (1993). *Things that make us smart: Defending human attributes in the age of the machine*. Boston: Addison-Wesley Longman.

Nöth, W. (1994). Semiotic foundations of the cognitive paradigm. *Semiosis, 73*(1994), 5–16.

Nöth, W. (2002). Can pictures lie. In *Semiotics of the media. State of the art, projects, and perspectives* (pp. 133–146). New York: Mouton de Gruyter.

Nöth, W. (2010). The semiotics of teaching and the teaching of semiotics. In I. Semetsky (Ed.), *Semiotics education experience* (pp. 1–19). Rotterdam, The Netherlands: Sense Publishers.

Nöth, W. (2011). From representation to thirdness and representamen to medium: Evolution of Peircean key terms and topics. *Transactions of the Charles S. Peirce Society: A Quarterly Journal in American Philosophy, 47*(4), 445–481. https://doi.org/10.2979/trancharpeirsoc.47.4.445.

Nöth, W. (2014). The semiotics of learning new words. *Journal of Philosophy of Education, 48*(3), 446–456.

Nussbaum, M. C. (2010). *Not for profit – Why democracy needs the humanities*. Princeton, NJ: Princeton University Press.

O'Donnell, A. M., & Dansereau, D. F. (1992). Scripted cooperation in student dyads: A method for analyzing and enhancing academic learning and performance. In *Interaction in cooperative groups: The theoretical anatomy of group learning* (pp. 120–141).

O'Halloran, K., Tan, S., Smith, B., & Podlasov, A. (2009, September). Digital semiotics. In *Proceedings 10th IASS-AIS world congress of semiotics, A Coruña Spain* (pp. 22–26).

Oancea, A. (2019). Research governance and the future(s) of research assessment. *Palgrave Communications*. Palgrave Macmillan (part of Springer Nature). doi:https://doi.org/10.1057/s41599-018-0213-6

Ofsted. (2009). *Drawing together: Art, craft and design in schools*. London: OFSTED.

Oliffe, J. L., & Bottorff, J. L. (2007). Further than the eye can see? Photo elicitation and research with men. *Qualitative Health Research, 17*, 850–858.

Olteanu, A. (2015). *Philosophy of education in the semiotics of Charles Peirce: A cosmology of learning and loving.* Oxford, UK: Peter Lang.

Olteanu, A. (2017). Reading history: Education, semiotics, and edusemiotics. In *Edusemiotics – A handbook* (pp. 193–205). Singapore: Springer.

Olteanu, A. (2019). *Multiculturalism as multimodal communication.* Cham, Switzerland: Springer.

Olteanu, A., & Campbell, C. (2018). A short introduction to edusemiotics. *Chinese Semiotic Studies, 14*(2), 245–260.

Ormond, B. (2011). Pedagogy and pictorial evidence: Interpreting post-reformation English prints in context. *Curriculum Journal, 22*, 3–27.

Orton, D. J. (2007). *The use of visual imagery and reflective writing as a measure of social work students' capstone experience.* PhD dissertation submitted to the University of Stellenbosch, Australia.

Öztok, M. (2016). Cultural ways of constructing knowledge: The role of identities in online group discussions. *International Journal of Computer-Supported Collaborative Learning, 11*(2), 157–186.

Paavola, S., & Hakkarainen, K. (2005). The knowledge creation metaphor–An emergent epistemological approach to learning. *Science & Education, 14*, 535–557.

Palmer, M., Simmons, G., & Hall, M. (2013). Textbook (non-) adoption motives, legitimizing strategies and academic field configuration. *Studies in Higher Education, 38*(4), 485–505.

Pangrazio, L. (2016). Reconceptualising critical digital literacy. *Discourse: Studies in the Cultural Politics of Education, 37*(2), 163–174.

Parker, J. (2002). A new disciplinarity: Communities of knowledge, learning and practice. *Teaching in Higher Education, 7*, 373–386.

Parker, K. A. (1998). *The continuity of Peirce's thought.* Nashville, TN: Vanderbilt University Press.

Parker, L. (2011). University corporatisation: Driving redefinition. *Critical Perspectives on Accounting, 22*, 434–450.

Passey, D., Shonfeld, M., Appleby, L., Judge, M., Saito, T., & Smits, A. (2018). Digital agency: Empowering equity in and through education. *Technology, Knowledge and Learning, 23*(3), 425–439.

Peirce, C. P. (1900/1940). Logic as semiotic: The theory of signs. In J. Buchel (Ed.), *The Philosophy of Peirce: Selected writings by C.S Peirce* (pp. 98–119). London: Routledge & Kegan Paul.

Peirce, C. S. (2017 (1998/1923)). *Chance, love, and logic: Philosophical essays.* Routledge.

[CP =] Peirce, C. S. (1931–1935, 1958). *The collected papers of Charles Sanders Peirce.* Cambridge, MA: Belknap. [In-text references are to CP, followed by paragraph number].

[EP =] Peirce, C. S. (1893–1913). *The essential Peirce* (Vol. 2). Bloomington, IN: Indiana University Press. [In-text references are to EP2, followed by page].

[MS =] Peirce, C. S. (1967, 1971). *Manuscripts in the Houghton Library of Harvard University, as identified by Richard Robin, "Annotated catalogue of the papers of Charles S. Peirce".* Amherst, MA: University of Massachusetts Press (1967), and in The Peirce Papers: A supplementary catalogue. *Transactions of the C. S. Peirce Society, 7*(1971), 37–57. [In-text references are to MS number, followed, when available, by page number].

Pesce, S. (2010). From semiotics of teaching to educational semiotics: The case of French-speaking research in education. In I. Semetsky (Ed.), *Semiotics education experience* (pp. 99–113). Brill/Sense.

Pesce, S. (2011). Institutional pedagogy and semiosis: Investigating the link between Peirce's semiotics and effective semiotics. *Educational Philosophy and Theory, 43*(10), 1145–1160.

Pesce, S. (2013). Teachers' educational gestures and habits of practical action: Edusemiotics as a framework for Teachers's education. *Journal of Philosophy of Education, 48*(3), 474–489.

Pesce, S. (2014). From Peirce's speculative rhetoric to educational rhetoric. *Educational Philosophy and Theory, 45*(7), 755–780.

Peters, M. A., Besley, T., Jandrić, P., & Bajic, M. (2016, January). Educational research and visual cultures: The case of video publishing. In *American Educational Research Association Annual Meeting.*

Peters, M. A., Jandrić, P., & Means, A. (2019). *Education and technological unemployment.* Singapore: Springer.

Petrilli, S., & Ponzio, A. (2007). Semiotics today. From global semiotics to semioethics, a dialogic response. *Signs, 1,* 29–127.

Phipps, A. M., & Guilherme, M. (2004). *Critical pedagogy: Political approaches to language and intercultural communication.* Buffalo, NY: Multilingual Matters.

Piaget, J., Brown, T., & Thampy, K. J. (1985). *The equilibration of cognitive structures: The central problem of intellectual development.* Chicago: University of Chicago Press.

Pietarinen, A.-V. (2006). *Signs of logic: Peircean themes on the philosophy of language, games, and communication.* Dordrecht, Netherlands: Springer.

Pietarinen, A. V., & Bellucci, F. (2016). The iconic moment. Towards a Peircean theory of diagrammatic imagination. In *Epistemology, knowledge and the impact of interaction* (pp. 463–481). Cham, Switzerland: Springer.

Pikkarainen, E. (2011). The semiotics of education: A new vision in an old landscape. *Educational Philosophy and Theory, 43*(10), 1135–1144.

Pikkarainen, E. (2018). Adaptation, learning, Bildung: Discussion with edu- and biosemiotics. *Sign Systems Studies, 46*(4), 435–451.

Pines, A. L., & West, L. H. (1986). Conceptual understanding and science learning: An interpretation of research within a sources-of-knowledge framework. *Science Education, 70*, 583–604.

Potter, W. J. (2004). *Theory of media literacy: A cognitive approach.* Thousand Oaks, CA: Sage.

Preston, B. (1998). Cognition and tool use. *Mind & Language, 13*, 513–547.

Prosser, J. (1998). *Image-based research: A sourcebook for qualitative researchers.* London: Routledge/Psychology Press.

Prosser, J., & Loxley, A. (2008). *Introducing visual methods.* ESRC National Center for Research Methods (NCRM) Review Paper. Retrieved from: http://eprints.ncrm.ac.uk/420

Quay, J. (2017). Education and reasoning: Advancing a Peircean semiotic. In I. Simietsky (Ed.), *Semiotics – A handbook* (pp. 79–91). Berlin, Germany: Springer Nature.

Reed, I. (2008). Justifying sociological knowledge: From realism to interpretation. *Sociological Theory, 26*, 101–129.

Reed, S. K. (2010). *Thinking visually.* New York: Psychology Press, Taylor & Francis.

Reiser, R. A. (2001). A history of instructional design and technology: Part I: A history of instructional media. *Educational Technology Research and Development, 49*, 53–64.

Robbins, D. (2003). *Vygotsky's and AA Leontiev's semiotics and psycholinguistics: Applications for education, second language acquisition, and theories of language.* Westport, CO: Praeger Publishers.

Robbins, D. (2005). Generalized holographic visions of language in Vygotsky, Luria, Pribram, Eisenstein, and Volosinov. *Intercultural Pragmatics, 2*, 25–39.

Robbins, D. (2007, June). Vygotsky's and Leontiev's non-classical psychology related to second language acquisition. In *International Nordic-Baltic region conference of FIPLV innovations in language teaching and learning in the multicultural context* (Vol. 47057).

Robbins, P., & Aydede, M. (2009). A short primer on situated cognition. In *The Cambridge handbook of situated cognition* (pp. 3–10).

Robertson, S., & Komljenovic, J. (2016). 13 Unbundling the university and making higher education markets. *World Yearbook of Education 2016: The Global Education Industry*, 211–239.

Rose, G. (2011/2006). *Visual methodologies: An introduction to researching with visual materials*. London: Sage Publications.

Roth, W. M., & Lee, Y. (2007). 'Vygotsky's neglected legacy': Cultural-historical activity theory. *Review of Educational Research, 77*, 186–232.

Roth, W. M., Pozzer-Ardenghi, L., & Han, J. Y. (2005). *Critical graphicacy: Understanding visual representation practices in school science*. Dordrecht, Netherlands: Springer.

Ryan, J. (2011). Teaching and learning for international students: Towards a transcultural approach. *Teachers and Teaching, 17*, 631–648.

Ryan, J. (2012). Internationalisation of doctoral education: Possibilities for new knowledge and understandings. *Australian Universities' Review, 54*, 55–63.

Säljö, R. (2010). Digital tools and challenges to institutional traditions of learning: Technologies, social memory and the performative nature of learning. *Journal of Computer Assisted Learning, 26*, 53–64.

Samuels, J. (2004). Breaking the ethnographer's frames reflections on the use of photo elicitation in understanding Sri Lankan Monastic Culture. *American Behavioral Scientist, 47*, 1528–1550.

Scaife, M., & Rogers, Y. (1996). External cognition: How do graphical representations work? *International Journal of Human-Computer Studies, 45*, 185–213.

Scaife, M., & Rogers, Y. (2005). External cognition, innovative technologies and effective learning. In *Cognition, education and communication technology* (pp. 181–202).

Scardamalia, M., & Bereiter, C. (1993). Technologies for knowledge-building discourse. *Communications of the ACM, 36*, 37–41.

Scardamalia, M., & Bereiter, C. (1994). Computer support for knowledge-building communities. *The Journal of the Learning Sciences, 3*, 265–283.

Scardamalia, M., & Bereiter, C. (2006). Knowledge building: Theory, pedagogy, and technology. In *The Cambridge handbook of the learning sciences* (pp. 97–115).

Schlichte, J., Yssel, N., & Merbler, J. (2005). Pathways to burnout: Case studies in teacher isolation and alienation. *Preventing School Failure: Alternative Education for Children and Youth, 50*(1), 35–40.

Schmit, K. M. (2013). Making the connection: Transmediation and Children's literature in library settings. *New Review of Children's Literature and Librarianship, 19*, 33–46.

Schnotz, W. (2002). Commentary: Towards an integrated view of learning from text and visual displays. *Educational Psychology Review, 14*, 101–120.

Schnotz, W., & Bannert, M. (2003). Construction and interference in learning from multiple representation. *Learning and Instruction, 13*, 141–156.

Sebeok, T. A. (1991). *Semiotics in the United States*. Indianapolis: Indiana University Press.

Sebeok, T. A., Umiker-Sebeok, D. J., & Young, E. P. (Eds.). (1988). *The semiotic web 1987*. Mouton de Gruyter.

Sefton-Green, J. (2005). Timelines, timeframes and special effects: Software and creative media production. *Education, Communication & Information, 5*, 99–110.

Sefton-Green, J., & Sinker, R. (1999). *Evaluating creativity: Making and learning by young people*. London: Routledge.

Selwyn, N. (2011). *Education and technology: Key issues and debates*. New York: Continuum International Publication Group.

Selwyn, N. (2014). *Digital technology and the contemporary university*. London: Routledge.

Semetsky, I. (2007). Introduction: Semiotics, education, philosophy. *Studies in Philosophy and Education, 26*, 179–183.

Semetsky, I. (Ed.). (2010). *Semiotics education experience*. Sense/Brill.

Semetsky, I., & Stables, A. (Eds.). (2014). *Pedagogy and edusemiotics: Theoretical challenges/practical opportunities* (Vol. 62). Rotterdam: Sense Publisher/Springer.

Sfard, A. (1998). On two metaphors for learning and the dangers of choosing just one. *Educational Researcher, 27*, 4–13.

Sharples, M., Taylor, J., & Vavoula, G. (2007). A theory of learning for the mobile age. In R. Andrews & C. Haythornthwaite (Eds.), *The Sage handbook of E-learning research* (pp. 221–247). Los Angeles: Sage.

Shephard, K. (2008). Higher education for sustainability: Seeking affective learning outcomes. *International Journal of Sustainability in Higher Education, 9*, 87–98.

Shore, C. (2008). Audit culture and illiberal governance: Universities and the politics of accountability. *Anthropological Theory, 8*, 278–298.

Short, K. G., & Kauffman, G. (2000). *Exploring sign systems within an inquiry system in what counts as literacy: Challenging the school standard*. Teachers College Press (pp. 42–61).

Simco, N., & Warin, J. (1997). Validity in image-based research: An elaborated illustration of the issues. *British Educational Research Journal, 23*(5), 661–672.

Sinatra, R., Beaudry, J. S., Stahl-Gemake, J., & Guastello, E. F. (1990). Combining visual literacy, text understanding, and writing for culturally diverse students. *Journal of Reading, 33*, 612–617.

Sless, D. (1981). *Learning and visual communication*. New York: Halsted Press/ John Wiley & Sons.

Sless, D. (1984). Visual literacy: A failed opportunity. *Educational Technology Research and Development, 32*, 224–228.

Smagorinsky, P. (2001). If meaning is constructed, what is it made from? Toward a cultural theory of reading. *Review of Educational Research, 71*, 133–169.

Smallwood, P. (2002). "More creative than creation" on the idea of criticism and the student critic. *Arts and Humanities in Higher Education, 1*, 59–71.

Smiciklas, M. (2012). *The power of infographics: Using pictures to communicate and connect with your audiences*. Que Publishing.

Smith, H. A. (2010). Peircean theory, psychosemiotics, and education. In Inna Semetsky (ed.) *Semiotics education experience* (pp. 37–52). Brill/Sense.

Smith, J. (2005). From flowers to palms: 40 years of policy for online learning. *Research in Learning Technology, 13*, 93–108.

Smith-Shank, D. L. (2004). *Semiotics and visual culture: Sights, signs, and significance*. National Art Education Association, 1916 Association Drive, Reston, VA 20191.

Smith-Shank, D. L. (2010). Semiotic pedagogy and visual culture curriculum. In Inna Semetsky (Ed.), *Semiotics education experience* (pp. 247–258). Sense Publishers.

Songer, N. B., Lee, H.-S., & McDonald, S. (2003). Research towards an expanded understanding of inquiry science beyond one idealized standard. *Science Education, 87*, 490–516.

Sousanis, N. (2015). *Unflattening*. Cambridge, Massachusetts: Harvard University Press.

Spalter, A. M., & Van Dam, A. (2008). Digital visual literacy. *Theory Into Practice, 47*, 93–101.

Speight, S., Lackovic, N., & Cooker, L. (2013). The contested curriculum: Academic learning and employability in higher education. *Tertiary Education and Management, 19*, 112–126.

Srnicek, N. (2017). *Platform capitalism*. Cambridge: Polity Press, John Wiley & Sons.

Stables, A. (2005). *Living and learning as semiotic engagement: A new theory of education*. Lewiston, NY: Edwin Mellen Press.

Stables, A. (2006). Sign(al)s: Living and learning as semiotic engagement. *Journal of Curriculum Studies, 38*(4), 373–387.

Stables, A. (2010). Semiosis and the collapse of mind-body dualism: Implications for education. In Inna Semestky (Ed.), *Semiotics education experience* (pp. 21–36). Brill/Sense.

Stables, A. (2012). *Be(com)ing human: Semiosis and the myth of reason.* Rotterdam, Netherlands: Sense Publishers.

Stables, A., Nöth, W., Olteanu, A., Pesce, S., & Pikkarainen, E. (2018). *Semiotic theory of learning: New perspectives in the philosophy of education.* London: Routledge.

Stables, A., & Semetsky, I. (2014). *Edusemiotics: Semiotic philosophy as educational foundation.* London: Routledge.

Stanczak, G. C. (2004). Introduction: Visual representation. *American Behavioral Scientist, 47*(12), 1471–1476.

Starr R. G. Jr., & Fernandez, K. V. (2007). *A pluralistic examination of mall store patronage.* Retrieved from: https://anzmac.org/conference_archive/2007/papers/R%20Starr_1a.pdf

Sterelny, K. (2004). Externalism, epistemic artefacts and the extended mind. In R. Schantz (Ed.). *The externalist challenge* (pp. 239–254). Berlin & New York: Walter de Gruyter & Co.

Stjernfelt, F. (2007). *Diagrammatology. An investigation on the borderlines of phenomenology, ontology and semiotics.* Dordrecht, Netherlands: Springer.

Stjernfelt, F. (2011). On operational and optimal iconicity in Peirce's diagrammatology. *Semiotica, 2011*(186), 395–419.

Stjernfelt, F. (2014). *Natural propositions: The actuality of Peirce's doctrine of Dicisigns.* Boston: Docent Press.

Strand, T. (2013). Peirce's rhetorical turn: Conceptualizing education as semiosis. *Educational Philosophy and Theory, 45*(7), 789–803.

Sturken, M., Cartwright, L., & Sturken, M. (2001). *Practices of looking: An introduction to visual culture.* New York: Oxford University Press.

Suhor, C. (1984). Towards a semiotics-based curriculum. *Journal of Curriculum Studies, 16,* 247–257.

Tan, S. (2002). *Picture books: Who are they for?* Retrieved from: http://www.shauntan.net/images/whypicbooks.pdf

Tan, S., Nolan, J., Hughes, L., Parker, K., Rawiri, J., Graham, C., & Theatre, R. L. (2007). *The arrival.* New York: Arthur A. Levine Books.

Tateo, L. (2018). Affective semiosis and affective logic. *New Ideas in Psychology, 48,* 1–11.

Tavin, K. M. (2003). Wrestling with angels, searching for ghosts: Toward a critical pedagogy of visual culture. *Studies in Art Education, 44,* 197–213.

Taylor, E. W. (2007). An update of transformative learning theory: A critical review of the empirical research (1999–2005). *International Journal of Lifelong Education, 26,* 173–191.

Taylor, G. W., & Ussher, J. M. (2001). Making sense of S&M: A discourse analytic account. *Sexualities, 4,* 293–314.

Teichler, U. (2004). The changing debate on internationalisation of higher education. *Higher Education, 48,* 5–26.

Tett, L., & Hamilton, M. (2019). Introduction: Resisting neoliberalism in education. In L. Tett, & M. Hamilton (Eds.), *Resisting neoliberalism in education: Local, national and transnational perspectives* (pp. 1–13). Policy Press.

Themelis, C., & Sime, J. A. (2020). From video-conferencing to holoportation and haptics: How emerging technologies can enhance presence in online education? In *Emerging technologies and pedagogies in the curriculum* (pp. 261–276). Singapore: Springer.

Thomas, D. W. (1987). Semiotics: The pattern which connects. *American Journal of Semiotics, 5,* 291–302.

Thomas, E. F., McGarty, C., & Mavor, K. I. (2009). Transforming "apathy into movement": The role of prosocial emotions in motivating action for social change. *Personality and Social Psychology Review, 13*(4), 310–333.

Thompson, D. S. (2019). Teaching students to critically read digital images: A visual literacy approach using the DIG method. *Journal of Visual Literacy, 38*(1–2), 110–119. https://doi.org/10.1080/1051144X.2018.1564604.

Thompson, P. (2012). Both dialogic and dialectic: Translation at the crossroads. *Learning, Culture and Social Interaction, 1,* 90–101.

Tight, M. (2012). Higher education research 2000–2010: Changing journal publication patterns. *Higher Education Research & Development, 31*(5), 723–740.

Tight, M. (2013). Discipline and methodology in higher education research. *Higher Education Research and Development, 32*(1), 136–151.

Trowler, P., Saunders, M., & Bamber, V. (Eds.). (2012). *Tribes and territories in the 21st century: Rethinking the significance of disciplines in higher education.* New York: Routledge.

Tufte, E. R. (1983). *The visual display of quantitative information.* Cheshire, Connecticut: Graphics Press.

Tufte, E. R. (1991). Envisioning information. *Optometry & Vision Science, 68,* 322–324.

Tufte, E. R. (2001). *The visual display of quantitative information* (2nd ed.). Cheshire, CO: Graphics Press.

Unsworth, L. (Ed.). (2008). *Multimodal semiotics: Functional analysis in contexts of education.* London: Bloomsbury Publishing.

Vakil, S., McKinney de Royston, M., Suad Nasir, N. I., & Kirshner, B. (2016). Rethinking race and power in design-based research: Reflections from the field. *Cognition and Instruction, 34*(3), 194–209.

Van der Veer, R., & Valsiner, J. (1994). *The Vygotsky reader.* Oxford, UK: Blackwell Publishing.

Van Leeuwen, T. (1999). *Speech, music, sound.* London: Macmillan International Higher Education.

Van Someren, M. W., Barnard, Y. F., & Sandberg, J. A. (1994). *The think aloud method: A practical guide to modelling cognitive processes.* London: Academic Press.

von Uexkull, J. (1982). The theory of meaning. *Semiotica, 42,* 25–82.

Vygotsky, L. S. (Rieber, R. W., Carton, A. S.). (1987). *The collected works of LS Vygotsky: Volume 1: Problems of general psychology, including the volume thinking and speech.* Springer.

Walker, M. (2011). A capital or capabilities education narrative in a world of staggering inequalities? *International Journal of Educational Development, 32,* 384–393.

Wang, C., & Burris, M. (1994). Empowerment through photo-novella: Portraits of participation. *Health Education Quarterly, 21,* 171–186.

Wellington, J. (2000). *Educational research: Contemporary issues and practical approaches.* London: Continuum International Publishing Group.

Wenger, E. (1998). Communities of practice: Learning as a social system. *Systems Thinker, 9,* 2–3.

Wertsch, J. V. (1985). *Vygotsky and the social formation of mind.* Cambridge, Massachusetts: Harvard University Press.

Wertsch, J. V. (1991). A sociocultural approach to socially shared cognition. In *Perspectives on socially shared cognition. American Psychological Association* (pp. 85–100).

Wertsch, J. V. (1998). *Mind as action.* New York: Oxford University Press.

White, E. J. (2014). Bakhtinian dialogic and Vygotskian dialectic: Compatabilities and contradictions in the classroom? *Educational Philosophy and Theory, 46*(3), 220–236.

Williamson, J. (1978). *Decoding advertisements: Ideology and meaning in advertising.* New York: Marion Boyars.

Winters, K. L. (2010). Quilts of authorship: A literature review of multimodal assemblage in the field of literacy education. *Canadian Journal for New*

*Scholars in Education/Revue canadienne des jeunes chercheures et chercheurs en éducation, 3*(1), 1–12.

Wood, D., Bruner, J. S., & Ross, G. (1976). The role of tutoring in problem solving. *Journal of Child Psychology and Psychiatry, 17*, 89–100.

Woolner, P., Clark, J., Hall, E., Tiplady, L., Thomas, U., & Wall, K. (2010). Pictures are necessary but not sufficient: Using a range of visual methods to engage users about school design. *Learning Environments Research, 13*, 1–22.

Worth, S., & Gross, L. (1974). Symbolic strategies. *Journal of Communication, 24*, 27–39.

Wyndhamn, J., & Säljö, R. (1997). Word problems and mathematical reasoning – A study of children's mastery of reference and meaning in textual realities. *Learning and Instruction, 7*, 361–382.

Zimmerman, C. (2007). The development of scientific thinking skills in elementary and middle school. *Developmental Review, 27*, 172–122.

# Index[1]

---

[1] Note: Page numbers followed by 'n' refer to notes.

© The Author(s) 2020
N. Lacković, *Inquiry Graphics in Higher Education*,
https://doi.org/10.1007/978-3-030-39387-8